Music School
in Europe

Musikschule
in Europa

L'Ecole de Musique
en Europe

T0078738

Music Schools
in Europe

**Handbook of the European
Union of Music Schools**

Musikschule
in Europa

**Handbuch der Europäischen
Musikschul-Union**

L'Ecole de Musique
en Europe

**Guide de l'Union Européenne
des Ecoles de Musique**

Summary

Inhalt

Table des matières

Editorial

The member states of Europe are developing a closer alliance, and the process of integration brings with it an additional need for information. The European ideal of «unity within diversity» can only be realised if these countries learn more about one another and thus come to recognize and value each other's individual characteristics.

Since its foundation in 1973 the European Union of Music Schools has made it one of its chief tasks to collect and pass on information relating to its member states, currently 21 in number. This provides the opportunity not only for music schools and their national associations, but also for the national authorities responsible for musical education in every country to make comparisons, to study the laws and regulations of other countries, to consult statistics for the whole of Europe and, where necessary, to obtain additional information relevant to specific problems.

The book in hand, «Music Schools in Europe», on the one hand shows the major contribution made by music schools to the general and social education of our young people; it also gives an impressive picture of the diversity and cultural significance of these important educational establishments. The specialist articles focus on particular aspects of educational theory and methodology, while the national reports add to our knowledge of the position and status of music schools in the member states.

It is hoped that this book will have some political impact, for it is the first time that such a comprehensive review has been presented. The facts and figures will surely be used as providing a sound basis for political debate.

It is my hope that this book will arouse interest all over Europe and influence both education policy and political decisions in favour of supporting the work of music schools.

I would like to thank the authors, my colleagues on the editorial team and the publishers Schott Musik International, Mainz, for their valuable contribution.

Josef Frommelt
President of the EMU

Die Länder Europas rücken näher zusammen. Der Integrationsprozeß bringt einen zusätzlichen Bedarf an Information mit sich. Die europäische «Einheit in der Vielfalt» kann nur zum Tragen kommen, wenn die Länder mehr voneinander wissen und damit die jeweiligen Eigenheiten anerkennen und schätzen lernen.

Die Europäische Musikschul-Union hat seit ihrer Gründung im Jahre 1973 das Sammeln und Weitervermitteln von Informationen aus den derzeit 21 Mitgliedsländern zu einer ihrer Hauptaufgaben gemacht. Dadurch haben nicht nur die Musikschulen und ihre nationalen Verbände, sondern auch die für die Musikerziehung zuständigen Stellen aller Staaten die Möglichkeit, Vergleiche anzustellen, Gesetze und Erlasse anderer Länder zu studieren, europäische Statistiken zu Rate zu ziehen und gezielt zusätzliche Informationen über besonders interessante Lösungen einzuholen.

Das vorliegende Buch «Musikschule in Europa» zeigt einerseits den bedeutenden Beitrag auf, den die Musikschulen zur Allgemein- und Humanbildung unserer Jugend leisten, und gibt andererseits ein beeindruckendes Bild von der Vielfalt und der kulturellen Wirksamkeit dieser wichtigen Bildungseinrichtungen. Die Sachartikel zeigen besondere Aspekte der Pädagogik und Didaktik des Musikschulunterrichts auf, während die Länderberichte das Wissen um die Bedingungen und die Stellung der Musikschule in den Mitgliedsländern bereichern.

Wir erhoffen uns von diesem Buch auch eine politische Wirksamkeit, denn es ist das erste Mal, daß eine solch umfassende Zusammenschau vorgelegt wird. Die Zahlen und Fakten werden sicherlich als gesicherte Basis politischer Argumentationen genutzt werden.

Ich wünsche unserem Buch, daß es in ganz Europa auf Interesse stößt und sowohl die pädagogischen wie auch die politischen Entscheide positiv im Sinne der Musikschularbeit beeinflussen wird.

Den Autorinnen und Autoren, den Mitarbeitern im Redaktionsteam sowie dem Verlag Schott Musik International, Mainz, danke ich herzlich für ihre wertvolle Arbeit.

Josef Frommelt
Präsident der EMU

Les pays européens se rapprochent l'un de l'autre. Ce processus d'intégration entraîne un besoin d'information supplémentaire. L'«unité» européenne «dans la variété» ne peut être réalisée que si les pays se connaissent mieux et apprennent ainsi à connaître et à estimer leurs particularités respectives.

L'un des objectifs principaux de l'Union Européenne des Ecoles de Musique, depuis sa fondation en 1973, est de réunir et de transmettre des informations provenant des 21 Etats actuellement membres. Ainsi, les écoles de musique et leurs associations nationales, mais aussi les organismes responsables de l'éducation musicale dans l'ensemble de ces pays, ont la possibilité de faire des comparaisons, d'étudier les lois et décrets d'autres pays, de consulter des statistiques européennes et de rechercher de manière ponctuelle des informations supplémentaires concernant des solutions particulièrement intéressantes.

Le présent livre, «L'Ecole de musique en Europe», montre, d'une part, l'importance de la contribution apportée par les écoles de musique sur le plan de la culture générale et humaine de la jeunesse, et offre, d'autre part, un tableau impressionnant de la variété et de l'influence culturelle de ces institutions ô combien importantes. Les articles spécialisés exposent des aspects particuliers de la pédagogie de l'enseignement musical, tandis que les rapports des divers pays enrichissent les connaissances dans le domaine des conditions d'enseignement et de la position des écoles de musique dans les Etats membres. Nous espérons que ce livre aura également un effet politique, car c'est la première fois qu'un aperçu aussi complet de l'enseignement musical est présenté au public. Les chiffres et les faits seront sans nul doute utilisés à titre de base solide dans le cadre d'argumentations politiques.

Je souhaite à notre livre qu'il éveille un grand intérêt en Europe, et qu'il influence de manière positive les décisions tant pédagogiques que politiques dans le sens du travail des écoles de musique.

Merci aux auteurs, aux collaborateurs de l'équipe de rédaction et aux Editions Schott Musik International de Mayence pour leur précieux travail.

Josef Frommelt
Président de l'EMU

Parliamentary Assembly of the Council of Europe

Thirty Third Ordinary Session

Recommendation 929 (1981)[1]
on music education for all

The Assembly,

1. Having noted the report of its Committee on Culture and Education on music education for all (Doc. 4760);

2. Believing music, in all its forms, to be an important means of human expression and also an accepted part of the cultural heritage of Europe;

3. Wishing to encourage the continuing development of this heritage through aids to contemporary music creativity, but also concerned that every individual should be enabled to develop a critical appreciation of music and, where possible, the ability of musical self-expression whether in singing or playing an instrument or in its interpretation in related cultural activity such as dancing;

4. Convinced that music education, in addition to the provision of special training for particularly gifted children, should be recognized as forming a continuous part of general education in all countries;

5. Stressing the importance of music education and the discipline of music training for the development of the individual's total personality and cultural behaviour;

6. Pointing out also the contribution music can make in remedial education, and underlining its positive social value as a leisure pursuit;

7. Noting with interest that the results of research have shown that music education can make a direct contribution to performance in other subjects taught in school;

8. Noting the omnipresence of music in modern society in particular through the mass media, and stressing the need for young people to be able to discriminate within this constant acoustic bombardment;

9. Welcoming, however, the opportunities offered by the present availability of music in all forms, and the increasing interest shown in music over the last two decades by young people and adults, many of whom are seeking training in singing or instrumental playing;

10. Recalling its Resolution 624 (1976) on the democratic renewal of the performing arts, and Recommendation 781 (1976) on Council of Europe action for the future of the performing arts;

11. Welcoming the recognition of the importance of music education as part of government policy, shown by the European Ministers with responsibility for Cultural Affairs in Resolution No. 1 of their 3rd Conference (Luxembourg, 1981);

12. Regretting, however, the low priority placed on music education in many member countries, and particularly concerned lest present provi-

sion for music education in primary and secondary schools be cut back in the interests of reducing government spending;

13.   Drawing attention to the vast turnover in the music industry, and hoping that some of the profits made might be redistributed to support the training of musicians and to improve public appreciation of music;

14.   Believing that the number of music schools in member countries is inadequate to meet the need for specialized vocal and instrumental training alongside primary and secondary education;

15.   Regretting the lack of sufficient general or specialized teachers competent to teach music, as a result of inadequate teacher-training, outmoded techniques and the lack of incentives for potential music teachers in view of their poor employment prospects,

16.   Recommends that the Committee of Ministers:

a.   prepare a recommendation on music education for all, calling on member governments to ensure:

i.   that parents are aware of the importance of the musical interpretation of sounds for children from birth, and that they are given guidelines on their role in developing such perception;

ii.   that music education is provided on a continuous basis in all schools from pre-school to the end of secondary education;

iii.   that sufficient special schools be maintained with an even distribution throughout each country to cater for children with a special interest in, or talent for music, and which can prepare them for a school-leaving examination in music;

iv.   that the teachers and facilities in such specialized schools are also made available to assist music education in general schools;

v.   that provision is made for adult education, either through distance teaching courses, evening classes, or adult education institutions;

vi.   that attention is paid to the training of teachers of music, and in particular:

– that the training of pre-school and primary teachers includes music;

– that provision is made for the training of suffi-

cient specialized music teachers for secondary schools and adult education;

– that in-service training in music is provided for established teachers with stress on the relevance of music to other disciplines;

– that effective contact is maintained between teachers (both general and specialized), universities or research institutions, and training courses for teachers, so that music education constantly reflects both the experience of teaching music and new musical developments;

vii.   that the status of music school teachers and the conditions of their employment is recognized as equivalent to those of music teachers in general schools;

viii.   that agreement be reached on the recognition of equivalences of music degrees and diplomas throughout Europe;

ix.   that greater use is made of the mass media (radio, television, records, tapes or cassettes) in music education, and of other technological developments;

x.   that encouragement is given to the composition of contemporary music that does not require too high a standard either for appreciation or performance and can be used by those learning music;

xi.   that support be provided for amateur performances (in particular by youth orchestras, pupils at music schools, choirs, etc.) and also for performances of touring professional groups in classrooms or to young people throughout all countries;

xii.   that innovations and pilot projects in music be introduced and encouraged at all levels;

b.   ask the Council for Cultural Co-operation to give consideration, in the context of its future work on the culture industries, to the possibility of redistributing for educational ends some of the profits made by the music industry;

c.   report to the Assembly in the course of European Music Year 1985 on the progress made towards the implementation of this recommendation.

_____

1. *Assembly debate on 8 October 1981 (19th Sitting) (see Doc. 4760. report of the Committee on Culture and Education).*

Text adopted by the Assembly on 8 October 1981 (19th Sitting).

Assemblée Parlementaire du Conseil de l'Europe

Trente-troisième Session ordinaire

Recommandation 929 (1981)[1]
relative à l'éducation musicale pour tous

L'Assemblée,

1.   Ayant pris note du rapport de sa commission de la culture et de l'éducation sur l'éducation musicale pour tous (Doc. 4760);

2.   Convaincue que la musique, sous toutes ses formes, est pour les hommes un important moyen d'expression et une composante naturelle du patrimoine culturel de l'Europe;

3.   Souhaitant encourager la poursuite du développement de ce patrimoine grâce à des aides à la création musicale contemporaine, mais estimant aussi que chaque individu doit pouvoir apprendre à porter un jugement critique sur la musique et, le cas échéant, développer son aptitude à l'expression musicale, qu'il s'agisse du chant, de la pratique d'un instrument ou d'une activité culturelle liée à la musique telle que la danse;

4.   Persuadée que l'éducation musicale, en dehors de la formation spéciale qui doit être donnée aux enfants particulièrement doués, devrait être reconnue comme faisant partie de l'éducation générale dans tous les pays;

5.   Soulignant l'importance de l'éducation musicale et de la formation musicale pour l'épanouissement de la personnalité de l'individu et pour son comportement culturel;

6.   Soulignant également la contribution que la musique peut apporter à l'éducation corrective et son rôle social positif en tant qu'activité de loisir;

7.   Relevant avec intérêt que des recherches ont montré que l'éducation musicale peut directement contribuer à l'amélioration des résultats scolaires dans d'autres disciplines;

8.   Notant l'omniprésence de la musique dans la société moderne, du fait en particulier des mass media, et soulignant la nécessité pour les jeunes de pouvoir faire preuve de discernement au milieu de ce continuel matraquage acoustique;

9.   Se félicitant, toutefois, des perspectives ouvertes par l'actuelle invasion de la musique sous toutes ses formes, et de l'intérêt croissant manifesté pour la musique au cours des vingt dernières années par les jeunes et les adultes, dont beaucoup veulent s'initier au chant ou apprendre à jouer d'un instrument;

10.   Rappelant sa Résolution 624 (1976), relative au renouveau démocratique des arts du spectacle, et sa Recommandation 781 (1976), relative à l'action du Conseil de l'Europe pour l'avenir des arts du spectacle;

11.   Se félicitant de ce que l'éducation musicale ait été reconnue par les ministres européens responsables des Affaires culturelles dans la Résolution n° 1 de leur 3e Conférence (Luxembourg, 1981) comme faisant partie de la politique gouvernementale;

12.   Déplorant, toutefois, la faible priorité accordée à l'éducation musicale dans de nombreux pays membres, et craignant tout spécialement que des coupes ne soient opérées dans les crédits affectés à l'éducation musicale dans les écoles primaires et secondaires afin d'alléger les dépenses publiques;

13.   Appelant l'attention sur l'énorme chiffre d'affaires des industries de la musique, et exprimant l'espoir qu'une partie des bénéfices réalisés pourront être redistribués pour financer la formation de musiciens et aider le public à mieux apprécier la musique;

14. Estimant que le nombre des écoles de musique dans les pays membres est insuffisant et ne permet pas de répondre aux besoins en matière de formation spécialisée, qu'il s'agisse d'art vocal ou d'art instrumental, à côté de l'enseignement primaire et secondaire;

15. Regrettant le manque d'enseignants et de professeurs spécialisés compétents pour enseigner la musique qu'expliquerait l'insuffisance des moyens de formation, le recours à des méthodes dépassées et les perspectives d'emploi fort peu brillantes qui leur sont offertes,

16. Recommande au Comité des Ministres:

a. d'élaborer une recommandation relative à l'éducation musicale pour tous, demandant aux gouvernements membres de faire en sorte:

i. que les parents prennent conscience de l'importance pour les enfants de l'interprétation musicale des sons dès la naissance, et que des indications leur soient données quant à la manière d'éveiller une telle sensibilité;

ii. que l'éducation musicale soit assurée en permanence dans tous les établissements depuis le préscolaire jusqu'à la fin de l'enseignement secondaire;

iii. que des écoles spécialisées soient maintenue en nombre suffisant (et réparties uniformément sur tout le territoire) à l'intention des enfants spécialement doués pour la musique, et qu'elles les préparent à un examen musical de fin d'études;

iv. que les professeurs et les équipements de ces écoles spécialisées soient également mis à la disposition des établissements d'enseignement général;

v. que des mesures soient prises en vue de l'éducation musicale des adultes: télé-enseignement, cours du soir ou centres de formation des adultes;

vi. qu'une attention soit accordée à la formation des professeurs de musique, en particulier:

– en faisant une place à la musique dans la formation des maîtres de l'éducation préscolaire et primaire;

– en prévoyant la formation d'un nombre suffisant de professeurs de musique spécialisés pour les écoles secondaires et l'éducation des adultes;

– en assurant aux enseignants en exercice une formation musicale qui mette l'accent sur les correspondances entre la musique et les autres disciplines,

– en maintenant de solides contacts entre les enseignants (de l'enseignement général et spécialisé), les universités ou les instituts de recherche et les cours de formation pour les enseignants, afin que l'éducation musicale soit le reflet constant de l'expérience acquise dans cette discipline et des innovations dans le domaine musical;

vii. que soit reconnue l'équivalence du statut des professeurs des écoles de musique et de leurs conditions d'emploi avec ceux des professeurs de musique de l'enseignement général;

viii. que soit conclu un accord sur la reconnaissance des équivalences des diplômes de musique dans toute l'Europe;

ix. que les mass media (radio, télévision, disques, bandes d'enregistrement ou cassettes) et autres innovations technologiques soient mieux utilisés dans l'éducation musicale;

x. que soit encouragée une composition de musique contemporaine n'exigeant pas une trop grande finesse d'appréciation ou d'exécution et pouvant servir aux apprentis musiciens;

xi. que soient soutenues les manifestations d'amateurs (en particulier des orchestres de jeunes, des élèves d'écoles de musique, des chorales, etc.), ainsi que les spectacles de groupes professionnels en tournée organisés dans des écoles ou pour des auditoires de jeunes à travers tous les pays;

xii. que soient introduits et encouragés à tous les niveaux des innovations et des projets pilotes dans le domaine musical;

b. d'inviter le Conseil de la coopération culturelle à examiner, dans le cadre de ses travaux futurs sur les industries culturelles, la possibilité qu'une partie des bénéfices de l'industrie de la musique soit réinvestie dans l'enseignement musical;

c. d'informer l'Assemblée, au cours de l'Année européenne de la musique en 1985, des progrès réalisés dans la mise en œuvre de la présente recommandation.

1. Discussion par l'Assemblée le 8 octobre 1981 (19e séance), (voir Doc. 4760. rapport de la commission de la culture et de l'éducation).

Texte adopté par l'Assemblée le 8 octobre 1981 (19e séance).

The EMU preparing the way forward to a united Europe

Die EMU als Wegbereiter einer gesamteuropäischen Idee

L'Union Européenne des Ecoles de Musique, précurseur d'une idée globale de l'Europe

The concept of one Europe, its peoples united across all national borders, rests on the awareness of a common cultural tradition of extraordinary diversity. Here music plays a central role: the Western harmonic and polyphonic tradition and the tradition of written music perhaps define the European cultural identity better than any other art form. «European» music is a tonal language accessible to all, transcending national distinctions and language barriers, and whose influence has spread all over the world. It has always been a medium capable of reflecting a great variety of national idiom, thus exemplifying the openness of European cultural tradition which has always drawn its vitality and diversity from a meeting of cultures: indeed, music itself is a European idea and capable of providing a common ground for the meeting of nations.

Now, more than ever before, it has also become something global, something that can be disposed of by everybody, at all times, in all places, in any style, quality and quantity that may be desired and in every form imaginable. There is little recognition, however, of the real economic importance of musical activity. Admittedly, the predominant place of music in most people's lives is the kind of media oriented listening to which children and adolescents become accustomed at an early age by the popular music market and the mass media. The chief aim of musical education in our society should therefore be to enable young people (and not only the young) to engage in self-determined music-making. Those who commit part of their lives to music consciously and full of awareness experience a sense of security, identification and a quality of

Was Europa über Länder und Grenzen hinweg zu einer die Völker einigenden Idee werden läßt, ist das Bewußtsein für einen gemeinsamen Kulturraum von gleichwohl außerordentlicher Vielfalt. In diesem spielt die Musik eine zentrale Rolle: Die harmonische und mehrstimmige und schriftliche Musik ist ein spezifisch abendländisches Phänomen, das den Kulturraum Europa vielleicht wie keine andere Kunst zu definieren vermag. «Europäische» Musik ist eine über nationale Abgrenzungen und Sprachbarrieren hinweg allen gleichermaßen zugängliche Tonsprache, die sich inzwischen über den gesamten Globus verbreitet hat. Und sie war stets in der Lage, die Idiome der unterschiedlichsten Nationalstile in sich aufzunehmen. Mit dieser Eigenschaft kennzeichnet sie Europa als einen «offenen» Kulturraum, der seine Vitalität und Vielfalt immer aus einer Begegnung der Kulturen gewonnen hat. Die Musik selbst ist also eine europäische Idee und zweifellos eine Ebene der Völkerverständigung.

In der Gegenwart ist sie darüber hinaus mehr als je zuvor zum Allgemeingut der Menschen geworden: Sie ist zu jeder Zeit, an jedem Ort, in jeder gewünschten Stilrichtung, Qualität und Quantität und in jeder vorstellbaren Form verfügbar. Kaum bekannt ist, daß Musik auch einen beträchtlichen «Wirtschaftsfaktor» darstellt. Der vorherrschende Umgang mit Musik ist allerdings das medienorientierte Hören, auf das Kinder und Jugendliche schon früh durch das Angebot des Musikmarktes und der Massenmedien festgelegt werden. Wichtigstes Ziel der Musikerziehung in unserer Gesellschaft ist es daher, (nicht nur) jungen Menschen einen selbständigen Umgang mit Musik zu ermöglichen. Menschen, denen die bewußte, kritische und engagierte Beschäftigung mit Musik zu einem wichtigen Bestandteil ihres Lebens geworden ist, erfahren Geborgenheit, Identifikation und Lebensqualität in einer Weise, wie sie in der modernen Gesellschaft immer seltener zu finden ist. Dabei haben die Musikschulen den Auftrag, Kindern, Jugendlichen und Erwachsenen Wege des aktiven Musizierens aufzuzeigen und sie fachlich dazu auszubilden.

Aktiver Umgang mit Musik ist eine wertvolle Förderung der Entwicklung und Ausbildung des Menschen, eine Förderung, die deshalb schon in frühester Kindheit beginnen sollte. Die musikalische

Ce qui, au-delà des pays et des frontières, fait de l'Europe une idée qui unit les peuples, c'est la conscience d'un espace culturel commun, encore que d'une extraordinaire variété. Dans cet espace, la musique joue un rôle central: la musique écrite harmonique à plusieurs voix est un phénomène spécifiquement occidental, qui, plus que tout autre forme d'art peut-être, permet de définir l'espace culturel de l'Europe. La musique «européenne», au-delà des limites nationales et de la barrière de la langue, est une langue tonale accessible à tous dans la même mesure, et qui, entre-temps, s'est étendue à l'ensemble du globe. Et elle a toujours été capable d'assimiler les idiomes des styles nationaux les plus divers. De par cette caractéristique, elle définit l'Europe comme un espace culturel «ouvert», puisant sa vitalité et sa variété dans la rencontre des cultures. La musique même est donc une idée européenne et, sans aucun doute, l'un des niveaux de l'entente entre les peuples.

Aujourd'hui, elle est en outre, plus que jamais, devenue un bien commun de l'humanité: elle est disponible à tout moment, en tout lieu, dans tous les styles et les qualités et quantités souhaités, et sous toutes les formes imaginables. Fait pratiquement inconnu, la musique est également un «facteur économique» non négligeable. La manière prédominante d'appréhender la musique est, il est vrai, l'écoute orientée vers les médias, sur laquelle enfants et adolescents se fixent très tôt, de par la palette proposée par le marché musical et les massmédias. L'objectif principal de l'éducation musicale dans notre société est donc de permettre à de jeunes gens (et pas seulement aux jeunes) une appréhension autonome de la musique. Les gens pour lesquels le fait de s'occuper de musique de manière consciente, critique et engagée est devenu une partie importante de leur vie, font l'expérience d'un refuge, d'une identification et d'une qualité de la vie d'une manière que l'on trouve de plus en plus rarement dans la société moderne. La tâche des écoles de musique est alors de montrer aux enfants, aux adolescents et aux adultes des possibilités d'exercer une activité musicale et de recevoir à cet effet une formation spécialisée.

La pratique active de la musique constitue une contribution précieuse au développement et à la formation de l'être humain, et elle devrait donc

life which is becoming increasingly rare in modern society. It is the task of music schools to introduce children, adolescents and adults to forms of active music-making and to provide them with expert tuition.

Active involvement with music promotes human development and stimulates learning, which is why it should begin in early childhood. The development of a musical sensibility awakens creativity and enhances intellectual and emotional resources, so as to be of benefit in other areas of life: it influences the general approach to learning and increases the quality of human life and experience. Music making creates a bond between people of differing ages and social backgrounds, even where spoken communication fails. Music has the power to cross national borders and language barriers and to become a positive expression of the spiritual and cultural resources on which the essential unity of Europe is founded.

These beliefs generate the principles of the education which the European Music Schools aim to provide. The functions of a Music School can be described here, as applying to the whole of Europe:

- Promoting interest in music and musical understanding from early childhood
- Providing proper music teaching at a primary level, with instrumental tuition, voice training and dancing lessons
- Bringing up a new generation of amateur musicians
- Creating opportunities for group music-making in a variety of forms and styles
- Discovering and fostering exceptional musical talents
- Preparing young people for training as professional musicians
- Collaborating with general schools and other educational and cultural organizations and institutions
- Educating informed and critical listeners
- Providing musical education for adults

(see also EMU resolution on «The Founding and Extension of Music Schools», St. Pölten 1978)

This list shows the role of music schools not only as valuable providers of leisure courses, but also as

Sensibilisierung weckt schöpferische Kräfte und intellektuelle wie emotionale Fähigkeiten, die dem Menschen auch anderweitig zugute kommen: im allgemeinen Lernverhalten und in der Steigerung der persönlichen Lebens- und Erlebensqualität. Musikmachen verbindet Menschen jeden Alters und überwindet soziale Unterschiede, ist selbst da noch wirksam, wo menschliche Sprache versagt. Musik setzt sich über Sprach- und Ländergrenzen hinweg und wird zum positiven Ausdruck der Mobilisierung unseres geistigen und kulturellen Kräftepotentials, auf dem die innere Einheit Europas gründet.

Diese Überzeugungen sind wesentliche Grundlagen eines Bildungsangebots, für das die Musikschulen Europas heute stehen. Für den gesamten europäischen Raum lassen sich die Aufgaben einer Musikschule klar beschreiben:

- Förderung des Musikinteresses und -verständnisses von frühester Kindheit an
- fachgerechter Musikunterricht in der Grundstufe, am Instrument oder im Fach Gesang sowie im tänzerischen Bereich
- Heranbildung des Nachwuchses für das Laienmusizieren
- Angebote des gemeinsamen Musizierens in vielfältigen Formationen und Stilrichtungen
- Begabtenfindung und Begabtenförderung
- Vorbereitung auf ein Berufsstudium
- Zusammenarbeit mit allgemeinbildenden Schulen und anderen Bildungs- und Kultur-Organisationen und -Institutionen
- Heranbildung zum informierten und kritischen Musikhören
- Musikalische Erwachsenenbildung

(siehe auch EMU-Resolution «Einrichtung und Ausbau der Musikschulen», St. Pölten 1978)

Dieser Aufgabenkatalog zeigt die Musikschule nicht nur als ein sinnvolles Angebot zur Freizeitgestaltung, sondern zugleich als eine Einrichtung mit wichtigen Bildungsfunktionen. Ein so umfangreicher und fachlich qualifizierter Unterricht kann nicht in den allgemeinen Schulen geleistet werden. Die Musikschule hat innerhalb der Bildungssysteme der Staaten einen eigenen Platz mit einem eigenen, klar definierten Bildungsauftrag. Dieses Angebot wird in allen Ländern Europas mit

commencer dès la plus tendre enfance. La sensibilisation musicale éveille des forces créatrices et des facultés intellectuelles et émotionnelles dont l'être humain profite également dans d'autres domaines: dans le comportement général à l'apprentissage et dans l'amélioration de la qualité de la vie et du vécu personnel. Faire de la musique crée un lien entre les individus de tous âges et contribue à vaincre les différences sociales; la musique est encore efficace là où le langage humain échoue. La musique passe outre les frontières de la langue et des pays, elle devient l'expression positive de la mobilisation de notre potentiel de forces intellectuelles et culturelles, potentiel sur lequel repose l'unité interne de l'Europe.

Ces convictions sont les bases essentielles d'une palette de possibilités de formation représentée aujourd'hui par les écoles de musique européennes. Les tâches incombant à l'école de musique pour l'espace européen global sont faciles à décrire:

- encouragement et soutien de l'intérêt pour la musique et de la compréhension musicale dès la plus tendre enfance
- enseignement musical adapté, dès l'école primaire, d'un instrument ou du chant ainsi que dans le domaine de la danse
- formation des générations suivantes pour la musique d'amateur
- possibilités de pratique commune de la musique dans des formations et des styles divers
- sélection, encouragement et soutien des enfants les plus doués
- préparation à des études de formation professionnelle
- collaboration avec les écoles d'enseignement général et autres organismes et institutions relevant du domaine de la formation et de la culture
- formation à une écoute musicale critique et informée
- formation musicale des adultes

(voir également la résolution de l'EMU «Aménagement et développement des Ecoles de Musique», St. Pölten 1978)

«Ohne Liebe kann man keine Musik machen...»

Josef Krips

institutions with an important educational purpose. The breadth and expertise of teaching offered in such schools cannot be provided by the general schools. Music schools have their own place within national education systems and their own clearly defined educational goals. There is great demand all over Europe for the services they offer, as is shown by recent statistics:

- 5,175 music schools
- 3,250,000 students
- 113,000 teachers
- 3 billion DM in funding

Impressive figures – and yet they could be greater: hundreds of thousands of children, young people and adults are on the waiting lists of these music schools because there is not sufficient funding available to take them all: unfortunately, music schools are among those to feel the cuts in public spending which are affecting so many.

When in 1973 the representatives of music schools from 11 member states of the European Community formed the «European Union of Music Schools» (EMU), an important motive behind this initiative was the common conviction that music and music teaching should be accorded a new status, in the context of technological, economic and social change. The EMU accordingly identified these as its chief aims:

- Drawing the attention of policy-makers, the authorities and the general public to questions of musical education and the work of Music Schools in particular;
- Helping to found and develop national Music School associations;
- Promoting musical education and music-making;
- Involvement in all matters concerning music schools;
- Encouraging exchange visits by study delegations, teachers, students, orchestras, choirs and other groups of musicians;
- Organizing European music festivals;
- Holding conferences.

(□ see also the statutes of the EMU)

At its regular general meetings and conferences the EMU has worked out statements of principle in

großem Zuspruch angenommen, wie die aktuelle Statistik zeigt:

- 5 175 Musikschulen
- 3 250 000 Schüler
- 113 000 Lehrer
- 3 Milliarden DM Finanzvolumen

Beeindruckende Zahlen – und doch könnten es noch mehr sein: Hunderttausende von Kindern, Jugendlichen und Erwachsenen stehen auf den Wartelisten der Musikschulen, weil die finanziellen Mittel fehlen, sie alle aufzunehmen – die vielerorts schwierige Lage der öffentlichen Zuschußgeber bekommen leider auch die Musikschulen empfindlich zu spüren.

Als 1973 die Vertreter der Musikschulen aus zunächst 11 europäischen Ländern die «Europäische Musikschul-Union» (EMU) gründeten, war eine entscheidende Grundlage für diese Initiative die gemeinsame Feststellung, daß der Musik und der Musikerziehung angesichts technischer, wirtschaftlicher und sozialer Veränderungen ein neuer Stellenwert zuerkannt werden müsse. Für ihre Arbeit formuliert die EMU daher als vorrangige Ziele:

- Wecken des Interesses der zuständigen Politiker, Behörden und der Öffentlichkeit an Fragen der Musikerziehung und im besonderen der Musikschularbeit
- Mithilfe bei Gründung und Aufbau nationaler Zusammenschlüsse von Musikschulen
- Förderung der Musikerziehung und der musikalischen Praxis
- Zusammenarbeit in allen die Musikschule betreffenden Fragen
- Förderung des Austausches von Studiendelegationen, Lehrern, Schülern, Orchestern, Chören und anderen Musiziergruppen
- Veranstaltung von europäischen Musikfesten
- Durchführung von Kongressen

(□ Formulierungen aus der Satzung der EMU)

Auf ihren regelmäßigen Generalversammlungen und Kongressen hat die EMU in etlichen Resolutionen Grundsatzaussagen erarbeitet und Organisationshilfen für die Musikschularbeit bereitgestellt. In den letzten Jahren wurde mit der Einrichtung von Dauer-Arbeitsgruppen (politische Beziehungen EMU–Europa, pädagogische Forschung und Be-

Ce catalogue de tâches présente l'école de musique non seulement comme une palette de possibilités judicieuses d'organisation des loisirs, mais aussi comme une institution aux fonctions éducatives importantes. Un enseignement de cette ampleur et de ce niveau de qualification et de spécialisation ne peut être assuré dans les écoles d'enseignement général. L'école de musique occupe, au sein des systèmes d'éducation des états, une place propre, avec une mission propre et clairement définie. Cette possibilité est saluée de manière fort positive dans tous les pays d'Europe, comme le montre cette statistique actuelle:

- 5.175 écoles de musique
- 3.250.000 élèves
- 113.000 enseignants
- 3 milliards de DM de volume financier

Des chiffres impressionnants – et pourtant, ils pourraient être bien supérieurs: des centaines de milliers d'enfants, d'adolescents et d'adultes sont sur les listes d'attente des écoles de musique parce que les moyens financiers manquent pour les prendre tous en charge – la situation, souvent difficile, des donneurs de subventions publiques se reporte hélas douloureusement sur les écoles de musique.

Lorsque, en 1973, les représentants des écoles de musique des – tout d'abord – 11 pays européens fondèrent l'EMU, l'une des bases décisives de cette initiative était le constat commun qu'une valeur nouvelle devait être accordée à la musique et à l'éducation musicale eu égard aux changements techniques, économiques et sociaux. L'EMU formule ainsi les objectifs prédominants de son travail:

- éveil de l'intérêt des politiciens et des autorités compétentes et du public en général pour les questions de l'exercice de la musique, et, en particulier du travail des écoles de musique,
- aide à la fondation et au développement d'associations nationales d'écoles de musique,
- encouragement de l'éducation musicale et de la pratique de la musique,
- collaboration dans toutes les questions concernant les écoles de musique,
- encouragement et soutien des échanges de délégations d'études, d'enseignants, d'élèves,

a number of resolutions and strategies for assisting the work of music schools. In recent years, the establishing of working teams (on the political position of the EMU in Europe, educational research and professional training, Music School statutes and the status of Music School teachers) has brought about the development of new modes of operation. Part of the reason for this is a reaction by the EMU to the political changes brought about by the creation of the European Union and the opening up of Eastern Europe.

In 1995, associations of music schools from 21 countries belong to the European Union of Music Schools. The EMU is an associate member of the International Music Council (IMC) and since 1982 it has had advisory status in the Council of Europe – a mark of recognition for its work in promoting music schools in Europe.

With a view to extending its influence in a united Europe the EMU has set itself high goals in terms of educational and cultural policies. The wording of these is based on resolutions previously passed,

rufsausbildung, Statuten der Musikschulen und Status der Musikschullehrer) eine neue Arbeitsform entwickelt. Damit reagiert die EMU auch auf die politischen Veränderungen, die mit der Schaffung der Europäischen Union und der Öffnung Osteuropas eingetreten sind.

Im Jahr 1995 gehören der Europäischen Musikschul-Union die Musikschulverbände aus 21 Ländern an. Die EMU ist assoziiertes Mitglied im Internationalen Musikrat (IMC) und hat seit 1982 beratenden Status beim Europarat – Zeichen und Anerkennung ihrer Arbeit für die Musikschulidee in Europa.

Für ihre weitere Wirksamkeit im vereinten Europa hat sich die EMU hohe bildungs- und kulturpolitische Ziele gesteckt. Ihre Formulierung fußt auf früheren Resolutionen, berücksichtigt inzwischen eingetretene Wandlungen und faßt zukünftige Entwicklungen ins Auge:

1. In allen Ländern Europas ist eine ausreichende Anzahl von Musikschulen einzurichten und eine

d'orchestres, de choeurs et d'autres groupements de musique et similaires

- organisation de Fêtes Européennes de la Musique
- réalisation de congrès.

(□ formulations extraites des statuts de l'EMU)

Lors de ses assemblées générales et des congrès qu'elle tient régulièrement, l'EMU a élaboré, dans de nombreuses résolutions, des affirmations de principe et mis à disposition des auxiliaires d'organisation pour le travail des écoles de musique. Au cours des dernières années, une nouvelle forme de travail a été développée: l'organisation de groupes de travail permanents (relations politiques EMU-Europe, recherche pédagogique et formation professionnelle, statuts des écoles de musique et des enseignants y travaillant). L'EMU réagit ainsi également aux changements politiques survenus lors de la création de l'Union Européenne et l'ouverture de l'Europe de l'Est.

En 1995, les associations d'écoles de musique de 21 pays font partie de l'Union Européenne des Ecoles de Musique. L'EMU est membre associé du Comité International de la Musique (IMC) et a un statut consultatif auprès du Conseil de l'Europe depuis 1982, un signe de reconnaissance de son travail pour l'idée des écoles de musique en Europe.

Pour poursuivre son action dans l'Europe unie, l'EMU s'est fixée des objectifs éducatifs et culturels élevés. Leur formulation est basée sur des résolutions antérieures, tenant compte des changements survenus entre-temps, et elle envisage les évolutions à venir:

1. Un nombre suffisant d'écoles de musique doit être implanté dans l'ensemble des pays d'Europe, et il conviendra d'aspirer à une répartition géographique équitable.
2. L'Etat et les communes assureront une base financière saine des écoles de musique.
3. Pour toutes les matières de l'enseignement musical, des programmes devront être créés; le contrôle de l'enseignement musical et le conseil des professeurs de musique sont d'une nécessité absolue.
4. Une éducation musicale préscolaire doit être proposée par toutes les écoles de musique; il

«*The re-establishing of a true music culture rests with the young generation. And if the current main stream is to be turned the music schools must lead the way.*»

Finn Egeland Hansen

«Die Schüler sind wie Pflanzen – wenn sie einen guten Boden finden und einen guten Gärtner, dann haben Sie gute Pflanzen.»

Yehudi Menuhin

while taking account of changes that have occurred in the meantime and considering likely future developments:

1. A sufficient number of music schools is to be established in all the European member states, with the fairest possible geographical distribution.
2. National and local authorities are to provide adequate funding for these music schools.
3. A curriculum is to be devised for all subjects of teaching in such schools; the quality of music lessons must be monitored and advice made available to music teachers.
4. A programme of preschool musical education should be offered by all music schools; provision should also be made for adult musical education.
5. In training music teachers the needs of music schools are to be borne in mind; teacher training courses must be extended to include new modes of teaching; attention should also be paid to providing continuing in service training for teachers.
6. Teachers at music schools are to have their conditions of employment brought into line with those of teachers at general schools.
7. Close collaboration between general schools and music schools is essential.
8. Music schools are to be developed as important cultural centres in each town and region.

With this statement of objectives the EMU intends to prepare the way forward towards the realization of an ideal involving music schools all over Europe. Through many changing circumstances, the work of the EMU is still driven by the impetus which led to its founding more than 20 years ago and which has informed its work ever since: the wish to provide proper representation for «The Value of Music Schools in our Age» (title of the 1987 EMU Resolution), to assure the future of musical experience for all the people of Europe, as an essential part of our common Western culture.

Heinz Preiss
Vice President of the EMU

geographisch gleichmäßige Verteilung anzustreben.

2. Staat und Kommunen sorgen für eine gesunde finanzielle Basis der Musikschulen.

3. Für alle Teilgebiete des Musikschulunterrichts sind Lehrpläne zu schaffen; die Kontrolle des Musikunterrichts und die Beratung der Musiklehrer sind unerläßlich.

4. Eine vorschulische Musikerziehung soll von allen Musikschulen angeboten werden; ebenso ist für die musikalische Erwachsenenbildung Vorsorge zu treffen.

5. Bei der Ausbildung der Musiklehrer ist den Bedürfnissen der Musikschulen Rechnung zu tragen; eine Ausweitung der pädagogisch-methodisch-didaktischen Ausbildung in Richtung auf neue Unterrichtsformen ist unerläßlich; ebenso ist auf eine ständige Lehrerfortbildung zu achten.

6. Die Lehrer an Musikschulen sind in bezug auf Anstellungsbedingungen und Sozialleistungen den Lehrern an allgemeinbildenden Schulen gleichzustellen.

7. Eine enge Zusammenarbeit zwischen allgemeinbildender Schule und Musikschule ist unumgänglich.

8. Die Musikschule ist als ein wichtiges Kulturzentrum in ihrer Stadt und ihrer Region auszubauen.

Mit diesen Zielsetzungen versteht sich die EMU als Wegbereiter zur Realisierung einer gesamteuropäischen Musikschul-Idee. Unter vielen veränderten Vorzeichen bleibt die Arbeit der EMU von jenem Willen getragen, der vor über 20 Jahren zu ihrer Gründung führte und ihre Arbeit seither geprägt hat: kompetent für den «Stellenwert der Musikschule in unserer Zeit» (Titel der EMU-Resolution 1987) einzutreten, um damit den Menschen in Europa eine intensive Teilhabe an der Musik als einem wesentlichen Bestandteil der gemeinsamen abendländischen Kultur auch in Zukunft zu sichern.

Heinz Preiss
Vizepräsident der EMU

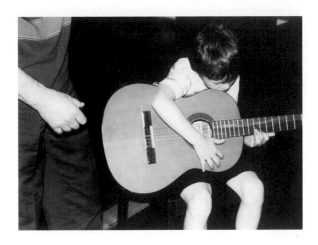

faudra également pourvoir à la formation musicale des adultes.

5. Lors de la formation des professeurs de musique, il faudra tenir compte des besoins des écoles de musique; un élargissement de la formation pédagogique méthodique didactique au sens de formes d'enseignement nouvelles est indispensable; de même, il faudra veiller à une formation continue permanente des enseignants.

6. Les professeurs enseignant dans des écoles de musique doivent être placés sur le même plan que les enseignants des écoles d'enseignement général en ce qui concerne leurs conditions contractuelles et les prestations sociales.

7. Une collaboration étroite entre les écoles d'enseignement général et les écoles de musique est inéluctable.

8. L'école de musique doit être développée en tant que centre culturel important dans sa ville et sa région.

Avec ces objectifs, l'EMU se conçoit comme le précurseur de la réalisation d'une idée européenne globale de l'école de musique. Le travail de l'EMU, sous beaucoup d'auspices modifiés, reste porté par la volonté qui a conduit à sa fondation, voici plus de 20 ans, et qui a empreint son travail depuis: défendre de manière compétente «l'importance de l'école de musique à notre époque» (titre de la résolution de l'EMU de 1987), afin d'assurer également à l'avenir, en Europe, une participation intense des hommes à la musique en tant qu'élément essentiel de la culture occidentale commune.

Heinz Preiss
Vice-Président de l'EMU

The Importance of Music Schools during Economically Difficult Times

Resolution
1993 EMU Congress/General Assembly
in Arvika, Sweden

Der Stellenwert der Musik-schulen in wirtschaftlich schwierigen Zeiten

Resolution des EMU-Kongresses 1993
in Arvika/Schweden

L'importance des écoles de musique dans les périodes économiques difficiles

Assemblée Générale de l'EMU, 1993 à
Arvika/Suède

The General Assembly of the European Union of Music Schools (EMU) notes with concern that, owing to the difficult economic situation, the music schools in Europe are obliged to suffer financial cuts which jeopardize the service they render to society in the field of culture and education.

Attention is drawn to the fact, that a cultural asset of great educational significance has been created through the institution of the music school: music instruction, frequently a privilege in former times, is now available to interested people from all levels of society. In addition to the communication of artistic and technical skills, the music schools of the late twentieth century contribute substantially to a holistic classical education.

Precisely in times when aimlessness, disunity and potential violence are increasing dramatically, even among children and young people, music schools are indispensable. An upbringing with music strengthens the young person, boosts self confidence, the sense of one's own value, one's keenness of perception. It leads the individual towards teamwork and promotes the forces of social harmony. To grapple actively with other or earlier cultures is to forge links with the present, thereby creating equableness and tolerance. Making music togehter, a typical music school activity, whether singing, whether in the chamber music group, the jazz band, the rock group or the orchestra, conveys an experience of success in the community and counteracts the tendency towards disunity. Thus the regular gatherings of ensembles from music schools of the European Union of Music Schools contribute decisively to the mutual understanding and the growing together of Europe's youth.

The politicians in the Europan countries who are responsible for the music schools are therefore called upon to ensure that

■ the number of music schools and the pupils they teach as well as the quality of their work is not decreased,

Die Generalversammlung der Europäischen Musikschul-Union (EMU) stellt mit Besorgnis fest, daß die Musikschulen in Europa aufgrund der schwierigen wirtschaftlichen Lage finanzielle Kürzungen hinnehmen müssen, die ihren gesellschafts- und kulturpolitischen Auftrag in Frage stellen.

Sie weist darauf hin, daß durch die Institution Musikschule ein kulturelles Angebot von hoher bildungspolitischer Bedeutung geschaffen wurde: Musikunterricht, der früher häufig ein Privileg war, steht nun Interessierten aus allen sozialen Gruppen der Bevölkerung offen. Die Musikschulen des ausgehenden 20. Jahrhunderts leisten neben der Vermittlung von künstlerischen und technischen Fertigkeiten einen wesentlichen Beitrag zur ganzheitlichen Humanbildung.

Gerade in Zeiten, wo Orientierungslosigkeit, Vereinzelung und Gewaltbereitschaft auch unter Kindern und Jugendlichen dramatisch zunehmen, sind Musikschulen unverzichtbar. Erziehung durch Musik festigt den jungen Menschen, stärkt sein Selbstvertrauen, sein Selbstwertgefühl und seine Urteilsfähigkeit. Sie führt den Einzelnen zum Gemeinschaftserlebnis und entwickelt Kräfte des sozialen Friedens. Die aktive Auseinandersetzung mit anderen oder früheren Kulturen schlägt Brücken zur Gegenwart, vermittelt Ausgeglichenheit und Toleranz. Das für die Musikschule typische gemeinsame Musizieren – beim Singen, in der Kammermusik, in der Jazzband, in der Rockgruppe oder im Orchester – vermittelt Erfolgserlebnisse in der Gemeinschaft und steuert der Tendenz zur Vereinzelung entgegen. So tragen die regelmäßig durchgeführten Treffen von Ensembles aus Musikschulen der Europäischen Musikschul-Union zum gegenseitigen Verständnis und zum Zusammenwachsen der Jugend Europas entscheidend bei.

Die für die Musikschulen verantwortlichen Politikerinnen und Politiker in den europäischen Staaten werden deshalb aufgerufen, daür zu sorgen, daß

- die Anzahl der Musikschulen und der durch sie betreuten Schülerinnen und Schüler sowie die Qualität ihrer Arbeit nicht vermindert werden,
- die finanzielle Basis der Musikschulen in Zeiten erheblicher jugendpolitischer Probleme vom

L'Assemblée Générale de l'Union Européenne des Ecoles de Musique (EMU) exprime sa préoccupation de voir que les écoles de musique en Europe sont amenées de plus en plus à accepter des restrictions financières dues aux difficultés de la situation économique, ce qui remet en question la bonne réalisation de leur mission sociale et culturelle.

Elle souligne que, grâce à l'institution école de musique, une offre de formation culturelle de haut niveau a pu être proposée, pour la première fois, à toutes les catégories sociales de la population : l'éducation par la musique, qui était autrefois un privilège. Parallèlement à un enseignement artistique et technique, les écoles de musique de cette fin du 20e siècle fournissent une contribution essentielle à la formation totale de l'homme.

C'est notamment à une époque où l'on constate de plus en plus de désorientation, d'isolement et une tendance à la violence parmi les enfants et les adolescents, que les écoles de musique sont devenues indispensables. L'éducation par la musique renforce la personnalité des jeunes, augmente leur confiance en eux, leur assurance et leur jugement propre. Elle crée chez chaque individu le sentiment d'appartenir à une communauté et développe les forces qui mènent vers la paix sociale. La recherche active d'autres formes ou de formes plus anciennes de culture, jette des ponts avec le présent et apporte équilibre et tolérance. Faire de la musique ensemble – activité typique des écoles de musique – principalement en chantant, dans la pratique de la musique de chambre, dans un ensemble de jazz, dans un groupe rock ou dans un orchestre, crée un sentiment de réussite à l'intérieur d'une communauté et permet de lutter contre l'isolement. Enfin, les rencontres régulières d'ensembles d'écoles de musique réunies au sein de l'Union Européenne des Ecoles de Musique contribuent véritablement à une compréhension mutuelle et à un rapprochement de la jeunesse européenne.

Les écoles de musique appellent ainsi les responsables politiques des pays européens à assurer

- la préservation du nombre des écoles de musique et des élèves, ainsi que la qualité du travail de celles-ci, le maintien, dans une période de problèmes graves pour la jeunesse, d'un soutien financier sans limitations aux écoles de mu-

- in times of grave juvenile problems, the financial basis of the music schools is not restricted by the state, the lands and the communes,
- the Music School, as a centre of culture and communication in its town or region, is preserved and further developed,
- the music schools' long-term existence and ability to work is safeguarded by legal regulations in all European countries.

The EMU is open to all Countries

Die EMU ist für alle Länder offen

L'EMU est ouverte à tous les pays

One of the most important fundamental principles of the EMU is that it should be open to all countries. Contact with those European countries which do not (yet) figure among its member states has been an important task for committee members ever since the foundation of the EMU in 1973. In 1991 these activities were reinforced by the creation of a permanent «Working party on International Relations».

In the years following its foundation, members of the EMU committee regularly visited countries that were in the process of establishing music schools, as advisors to local, regional and national authorities. They also offered to help by establishing national associations of music schools who would then be better able to represent the interests of music schools and their teaching staff, even becoming members of the EMU as national associations. This happened most recently in the case of Spain, Greece and Turkey.

Initial contact is usually made when representatives of nonmember states take up the invitation from the EMU to attend one of their conferences. National representatives are always offered the opportunity to give an extensive report on musical education and the status and activities of music schools in their country. At the same time, all are given the opportunity to examine all the various documents of the EMU, such as its statutes and accounts, resolutions, specialist reports, seminar papers, national profiles, statistics etc.

Staat, von den Ländern und Kommunen nicht eingeschränkt wird,

- die Musikschule als ein kulturelles und kommunikatives Zentrum ihrer Stadt oder ihrer Region erhalten bleibt und weiterentwickelt wird,
- die Existenz und die Arbeitsfähigkeit der Musikschulen in allen europäischen Staaten durch gesetzliche Regelungen langfristig abgesichert werden.

Eines der wichtigsten Grundprinzipien der EMU ist ihre Offenheit gegenüber allen Ländern. Die Kontakte zu jenen europäischen Ländern, die (noch) nicht zu ihren Mitgliedern zählen, waren seit der Gründung der EMU im Jahr 1973 eine wichtige Aufgabe der Präsidiumsmitglieder. 1991 wurden diese Aktivitäten durch die Bestellung einer ständigen «Arbeitsgruppe für internationale Beziehungen» verstärkt.

In den Jahren nach der Gründung waren regelmäßig Mitglieder des EMU-Präsidiums in Ländern, die dabei waren, Musikschulsysteme aufzubauen, als Berater städtischer, regionaler und staatlicher Behörden tätig. Sie boten dabei gleichzeitig auch Hilfestellung bei der Gründung von nationalen Musikschulverbänden an, die dann die Interessen der Musikschulen und der Musiklehrer stärker vertreten und als Nationalverband auch Mitglied der EMU werden konnten. In neuester Zeit war dies bei Spanien, Griechenland und der Türkei der Fall.

Die ersten Kontakte werden meistens hergestellt, wenn Vertreter von Nichtmitgliedsländern der Einladung der EMU zum Besuch eines ihrer Kongresse Folge leisten. Jedem Ländervertreter wird jeweils die Möglichkeit gegeben, die Musikerziehung seines Landes und die Stellung und Tätigkeit der Musikschulen in einem ausführlichen Bericht zu beschreiben. Allen werden dabei sämtliche Unterlagen der EMU, wie z.B. Statut und Geschäftsordnung, Resolutionen, Fachberichte, Referate, Länderberichte, Statistiken etc. zugänglich gemacht.

sique, par les Etats, les régions et les communes,

- le développement de l'école de musique en tant que centre de culture et de communication dans sa ville ou sa région et la préservation de celle-ci,
- et enfin, dans les pays qui n'ont pas de législation dans le domaine des écoles de musique, la mise en place progressive, avec l'aide des associations nationales et compétentes d'écoles de musique, d'un cadre juridique approprié.

L'un des principes fondamentaux les plus importants de l'EMU est son ouverture envers tous les pays. Les contacts avec les pays européens ne faisant pas (encore) partie de ses membres furent, depuis la fondation de l'EMU en 1973, une tâche importante des membres du conseil de direction. En 1991, ces activités furent renforcées par la constitution d'un «groupe de travail pour les relations internationales» permanent.

Au cours des années succédant à sa fondation, des membres du conseil de direction de l'EMU ont exercé régulièrement, dans des pays qui étaient en train d'élaborer des systèmes d'écoles musicales, des activités de conseiller des autorités communales, régionales et nationales. Ils proposèrent également leur soutien dans le cadre de la fondation d'associations nationales d'écoles de musique, celles-ci étant plus influentes dans le cadre de la défense des intérêts des écoles et des professeurs de musique et pouvant, en leur qualité d'associations nationales, devenir membres de l'EMU. Récemment, ce fut le cas en Espagne, en Grèce et en Turquie.

Les premiers contacts sont, la plupart du temps, noués lorsque les représentants de pays non membres donnent suite à l'invitation de l'EMU à se rendre à son congrès. Chaque représentant de chaque pays a ainsi la possibilité de décrire, dans un rapport exhaustif, l'éducation musicale et la position et l'activité des écoles de musique dans son pays. Tous ont alors accès à l'ensemble des documenta-

In the past England, Ireland, Croatia, Lithuania, Malta, Romania, Russia, Slovenia, Slovakia, the Czech provinces, Hungary and Poland have taken up this opportunity. Hungary, Slovenia and Croatia have in the meantime become members of the EMU. The president is in regular communication with representatives of music schools in Russia, the Czech provinces, Slovakia, Lithuania, Malta, Poland and Romania and it is hoped that the founding and establishment of Music School Associations will progress rapidly, so that these countries too may soon join the EMU.

In many countries with a long tradition of music teaching within and outside general schools and a highly developed musical culture, these areas of responsibility are not assigned to specialist music schools, with instrumental and vocal tuition forming an integral part of the general schools' curriculum. In such instances there may be no associations of Music Schools. To give these countries also the opportunity to join the EMU, a working team is currently examining the question of associate membership.

The openheartedness of the EMU becomes evident at the «European Youth Music Festivals» which are held every three years. For the 4th Music Festival, which is to take place in Budapest in 1995, applications have already been received from 35 countries, with a good 10,000 young musicians.

The EMU will continue its policy of openness in the future, too. It offers its expertise, experience and the documents and statistics collated from 21 member states, for the benefit of all countries.

The EMU also wishes to take up initiatives for more intensive collaboration between all European musical organizations.

Josef Frommelt

In den vergangenen Jahren haben England, Irland, Kroatien, Litauen, Malta, Rumänien, Rußland, Slowenien, Slowakei, Tschechien, Ungarn und Polen von dieser Möglichkeit Gebrauch gemacht. Ungarn, Slowenien und Kroatien sind inzwischen bereits Mitglieder der EMU geworden. Der Präsident steht mit Musikschulvertretern in Rußland, Tschechien, Slowakei, Litauen, Malta, Polen und Rumänien in ständigem Kontakt, und es besteht die Hoffnung, daß die Gründung und der Aufbau von Musikschulverbänden in diesen Ländern schnelle Fortschritte macht und dadurch bald ein Beitritt zur EMU möglich wird.

In manchen Ländern mit langer Tradition schulischer und außerschulischer Musikerziehung und hoher Musikkultur sind die Kompetenzen und Verantwortlichkeiten nicht eigentlichen Musikschulen anvertraut. Der Instrumental- und Vokalunterricht ist in das Unterrichtsangebot öffentlicher Schulen integriert. Es kommt daher auch nicht zu Zusammenschlüssen von Musikschulen. Um auch diesen Ländern die Mitarbeit in der EMU zu ermöglichen, befaßt sich eine Arbeitsgruppe derzeit mit der Frage einer assoziierten Mitgliedschaft.

Die Offenheit der EMU zeigt sich besonders an den «Europäischen Musikfesten der Jugend», die alle drei Jahre durchgeführt werden. Für das 4. Musikfest, das 1995 in Budapest stattfinden wird, sind bereits 35 Länder mit rund 10 000 jungen Musikerinnen und Musikern angemeldet.

Die EMU wird ihre Politik der Offenheit auch in Zukunft fortsetzen. Sie bietet ihr Wissen, ihre Erfahrung und die aus 21 Mitgliedsländern gesammelten Unterlagen und Statistiken an, damit alle Länder davon profitieren können. Die EMU will auch Initiativen für eine intensivere Zusammenarbeit aller europäischen Musikorganisationen ergreifen.

Josef Frommelt

tions de l'EMU telles que, par exemple, les statuts et le règlement intérieur, les résolutions, les rapports spécialisés, les exposés, les rapports des différents pays, les statistiques etc...

Au cours des années précédentes, l'Angleterre, l'Irlande, la Croatie, la Lituanie, Malte, la Roumanie, la Russie, la Slovénie, la Slovaquie, la République Tchèque, la Hongrie et la Pologne ont profité de cette possibilité. La Hongrie, la Slovénie et la Croatie, sont, entre-temps, déjà membres de l'EMU. Le président est en contact permanent avec des représentants des écoles de musique en Russie, en République Tchèque, en Slovaquie, en Lituanie, à Malte, en Pologne et en Roumanie, et l'on espère que la fondation et le développement d'associations d'écoles de musique dans ces pays feront des progrès rapides et permettront bientôt leur adhésion à l'EMU.

Dans certains pays de longue tradition d'éducation musicale scolaire ou extrascolaire et de grande culture musicale, les compétences et les responsabilités ne sont pas confiées aux écoles de musique mêmes. L'enseignement instrumental et vocal est intégré au programme d'enseignement des écoles publiques. De ce fait, il ne se produit pas d'association d'écoles de musique. Afin de permettre la collaboration de ces pays avec l'EMU, un groupe de travail se penche en ce moment sur la question d'une adhésion assimilée.

L'ouverture de l'EMU se traduit en particulier par les «Fêtes Européennes de la Musique pour la Jeunesse», qui ont lieu tous les trois ans. Pour la 4ème fête de la musique, qui doit se dérouler en 1995 à Budapest, 35 pays et près de 10.000 jeunes musiciens et musiciennes se sont inscrits.

L'EMU poursuivra sa politique d'ouverture également à l'avenir. Elle offre ses connaissances, son expérience et les documentations et statistiques rassemblées provenant des 21 pays membres, afin que tous les pays puissent en profiter.

L'EMU veut également prendre des mesures pour une collaboration plus intense de l'ensemble des organisations musicales européennes.

Josef Frommelt

«La place que la musique occupe (ou devrait occuper) dans l'éducation des enfants et des adolescents est essentielle. Malheureusement, en ce qui concerne la Belgique, il me faut constater avec grande amertume la négligence et le désintérêt dont l'enseignement général (du niveau primaire comme du niveau secondaire) se rend coupable à l'égard de la musique. Par contre, mon pays dispose encore d'un réseau important d'écoles et d'académies de musique qui, le soir et lors des après-midis de loisir, dispensent un enseignement de grande qualité, tant dans les disciplines instrumentales qu'au niveau théorique. Ces écoles assurent ainsi la formation d'authentiques amateurs et préparent, par ailleurs, les élèves les plus doués à la fréquentation des Conservatoires royaux de musique.»

Jacques Leduc

Feldenkrais
Method

Die Feldenkrais-Methode
für Musiker und Dirigenten

Mit Hilfe einfacher, sanfter und interessanter Bewegungslektionen wird jenes entdeckend-neugierige Lernen gefördert, das für Klein-kinder selbstverständlich ist. Durch diese einzigartige Methode des Kernphysikers und Verhaltensphysiologen **Dr. Moshe Feldenkrais (1904–1984)** kann eine tiefgreifende Veränderung der Körperhaltung, Atmung, Koordination und Beweglichkeit erreicht werden.

Eine Entwicklung **des somatischen Selbstbilds** setzt schöpferische Kräfte des Musikers frei, die in der zeitgenössi-schen Musikpädagogik oft nicht ausreichend gefördert werden. Schüler von Moshe Feldenkrais waren z. B. Yehudi Menuhin, Narciso Yepes, Igor Markevitch, Carl Orff, Liselotte Orff, Peter Brooks, das Israelische und das Boston Symphonie Orchester.

Leitung: H. E. Czetczok, Dipl. Psychologe, Feldenkrais-Lehrer (Schüler von Dr. Moshe Feldenkrais)
Ort: im Raum Bielefeld
Informationen über Seminare, Einzelarbeit und Termine:
D-32120 Hiddenhausen · Wolfsweg 1 · Telefon 0 52 21/69 03 21

Literatur:

CZETCZOK, H. E.: Die Feldenkrais-Methode. In: M. Bühring, F. H. Kemper (Hrsg.): Naturheilverfahren und unkonventionelle medizinische Richtungen. Grundlagen/Methoden/Nachweissituation. Berlin/Heidelberg/New York 1993, Springer Verlag.

HANNA, Th.: Das Geheimnis gesunder Bewegung. Die Feldenkrais-Methode verstehen lernen (Einleitung von H. E. Czetczok) Paderborn 1993.

FELDENKRAIS, M.: Bewußtheit durch Bewegung. Der aufrechte Gang. Frankfurt/M. 1968

FELDENKRAIS, M.: Das starke Selbst. Anleitung zur Spontaneität. Frankfurt/M. 1989

Feldenkrais und Stimme

Auch unser Kommunikations-Instrument Stimme ist Bewegung und entsteht durch Bewegung. Wir können mit ihr in derselben Weise umgehen wie mit unseren Körperbewegungen und sie in derselben Weise entdecken und entwickeln. So findet jeder von uns **sein eigenes, zu optimaler Leistung fähiges Stimminstrument** durch Entwicklung der **eigenen Stimm-Identität**, durch das Entdecken der **eigenen Ordnungs-Strukturen** und der zum **künstlerisch-bewußten Stimmgebrauch geeigneten Feedback-Instrumente**.
Diese Arbeit wendet sich an **Gesanglehrer, Sänger, Gesangschüler und Gesangstudierende** und überhaupt an alle, die ihre Sprech- und Singstimme in Beruf und Privatleben besser gebrauchen wollen. Sie ist besonders wertvoll für Jugendliche, die Berufssänger werden wollen, als Grundlage eines späteren Gesangs-Studiums

Leitung: Prof. Peter Jacoby, Dirigent, Feldenkrais-Lehrer und Stimmbildner
Ort: Detmold-Hiddesen
Informationen über Seminare, Einzelstunden und Termine:
D-32760 Detmold · Dreimannstraße 6 · Telefon 0 52 31/8 97 02, Telefax 0 52 31/87 07 61

Literatur:

JACOBY, P.: Die Feldenkraismethode im Instrumental- und Gesangunterricht. In: PÜTZ, W. (Hrsg.): Musik und Körper, Musikpädagogische Forschung Bd. 11. Die blaue Eule, Essen 1990

JACOBY, P.: Unterricht als Weg zur Autonomie. Die Feldenkraismethode im Instrumental- und Gesangunterricht. In: EICHHORN, A. (Hrsg.): Festschrift Hans-Peter Schmitz zum 75. Geburtstag. Bärenreiter, Kassel-Basel-London-New York 1992

JACOBY, P.: Ganzheitliche Stimmbildung und Stimmtherapie. Die Feldenkrais-Methode als Wegweiser. In: LOTZMANN, G. (Hrsg): Das Prinzip der Ganzheit in Diagnose, Therapie und Rehabilitation mündlicher Kommunikationsstörungen. Wissenschaftsverlag Volker Spiess (Reihe: Edition Marhold), Berlin 1995

FELDENKRAIS, M.: Der Weg zum reifen Selbst. Phänomene menschlichen Verhaltens. Junfermann, Paderborn 1994

DOWANI™
INTERNATIONAL

THE LATEST EUROPEAN LEARNING AID

ORIGINAL TEMPO with solo instrument & piano accompaniment

SLOW, MEDIUM & ORIGINAL TEMPO with piano accompaniment only

WITH PIANO SELECTIONS the right or left hand can be heard separately

for Violin
F. Kuechler:
Concertino for Violin & Piano in G Major, Op. 11
Concertino for Violin & Piano, in the style of
A. Vivaldi, in D Major, Op. 15
O. Rieding:
Concertino for Violin & Piano in A Minor, Op. 21
Concerto for Violin & Piano in G Major, Op. 34
Concerto for Violin & Piano in B Minor, Op. 35
Concerto for Violin & Piano in D Major, Op. 36
H. Millies:
Concertino for Violin & Piano, in the style
of W. A. Mozart, in D Major
G. H. Fiocco:
Allegro for Violin & Piano in G Major
G. Ph. Telemann:
Sonatina No. 1 for Violin & Piano in A Major
A. Vivaldi:
Concerto No. 3 in G Major, for Violin & Piano, Op. 3
Concerto No. 6 in A Minor, for Violin & Piano, Op. 3
J. B. Accolay:
Concerto No. 1 for Violin & Piano in A Minor
J. S. Bach:
Concerto No. 1 in A Minor, for Violin & Piano

for Cello
J. B. Breval:
Sonata No. 1 for Cello & Piano in C Major
Concertino No. 1 for Cello & Piano in F Major

for Flute
W. A. Mozart:
Rondo in D Major, for Flute & Piano, K. 184
Andante in C Major, for Flute & Piano, K. 315
A. Vivaldi:
Concerto No. 2, "La Notte," for Flute & Piano, Op. 10

for Trumpet
J. Haydn:
Concerto in E Flat Major, for Trumpet & Piano

for Piano
J. S. Bach:
Anna Magdalena Notebook for Piano
J. B. Duvernoy:
Elementary Studies for Piano, Op. 176
Various composers:
Sonatinas for Piano
A. Diabelli:
Melodious Exercises for Piano, for 4 Hands, Op. 149

for Treble Recorder
(suitable also for flute, oboe, or violin)
G. F. Handel:
Four Sonatas from Op. 1
for Treble Recorder & Piano
Sonata No. 2 in G Minor
Sonata No. 4 in A Minor
Sonata No. 7 in C Major
Sonata No. 11 in F Major

for Descant Recorder
(suitable also for flute, oboe, or violin)
G. Ph. Telemann:
Partita No. 2 for Descant Recorder & Piano

for Clarinet
W. A. Mozart:
Concerto for Clarinet & Piano
in A Major, K. 622, Version for the A clarinet
W. A. Mozart:
Concerto for Clarinet & Piano
in A Major, K. 622, Version for the Bb clarinet
C. Stamitz:
Concerto No. 3 in B Flat Major,
for Clarinet & Piano

FOR FURTHER INFORMATION:
DOWANI Establishment, P.O. Box 252, Fl-9495 Triesen, Principality of Liechtenstein, Fax: (075) 392 11 44

MUSIZIEREN IM ENSEMBLE

UE für Ensemble – Streicher

für Streicher-Ensemble (Viola auch als 3. Violine)
herausgegeben von M. Radanovics
Partitur und Stimmen

1 „Winds and waves";
„Dorian Prelude" [1/2]
UE 19840   DM 24,–

2 „Scarborough Fair";
„Midnight Special" [2]
UE 19841   DM 24,–

3 „Lily of the West";
„Tom Dooley" [2/3]
UE 19842   DM 24,–

UE für Ensemble – Bläser

für Holzbläser-Ensemble herausgegeben von T. Kenny
Partitur und Stimmen

1 W. A. Mozart: „Reich mir
die Hand, mein Leben";
„Romanze" [2]
UE 19901   DM 26,–

2 G. F. Händel:
Air aus „Rinaldo";
E. Humperdinck: Tanzduett aus
„Hänsel und Gretel" [2]
UE 19902   DM 26,–

3 J. Haydn: Andante
aus der Symphonie Nr. 94;
W. A. Mozart:
Menuett aus „Don Giovanni" [2]
UE 19903   DM 26,–

4 W.A.Mozart: Non più andrai
aus „Le nozze di Figaro" [2]
UE 19904   DM 24,–

5 J. Strauß:
Champagnerpolka aus
„Die Fledermaus" [2/3]
UE 19905   DM 26,–

6 W. A. Mozart:
„Eine kleine Nachtmusik"
1. Satz [2]
UE 19906   DM 26,–

7 G. Bizet:
„L'Arlesienne" – Prelude
[2/3]
UE 19907   DM 20,–

8 W. A. Mozart:
Ein musikalischer Spaß" –
Finale
UE 19908   DM 19,–

UE für Ensemble – Jazz

für gemischtes Ensemble (Stimmen in C, B, Es, F, Klavier und
Schlagzeug) herausgegeben von J. Rae
Partitur und Stimmen

1 „Down by the Riverside"
[1/3]
UE 19680   DM 26,–

2 „Oh when the Saints . . ."
[1/3]
UE 19681   DM 26,–

3 „Swing low, sweet chariot"
[2]
UE 19682   DM 26,–

4 „Joshua fought the Battle
of Jericho" [2/3]
UE 19683   DM 26,–

UNIVERSAL EDITION · WIEN

vom Notenständer bis zur Akustikausstattung . . . beste Ausrüstungen für Musiker, Orchester, Chöre, Musikschulen, Schulen, Hochschulen . . .

ART TOUR GmbH
Garagenweg 5, Postfach 47
91088 Bubenreuth
Telefon 0 91 31/20 20 14
Telefax 0 91 31/20 20 13

GB-Verlag

Bearbeitungen jeder Art für Instrumentalgruppen und Orchester

Sie sind ständig auf der Suche nach spielbarer Literatur, die aber für die spezifische Besetzung Ihres Ensembles nicht gerade reichhaltig vorhanden ist? Sie würden gern bestimmte Stücke spielen, aber die Besetzung Ihres Ensembles entspricht nicht ganz den Forderungen der Partitur? Sie machen sich allmählich Sorgen um die Zukunft Ihres Ensembles?

Hier kann der **GB-Verlag** helfen.

Per Computer erhalten Sie Notenmaterial, das ganz auf Ihre speziellen Bedürfnisse abgestimmt ist; die kompositorische Qualität bleibt dabei soweit gewahrt wie irgend möglich.

Fordern Sie bitte Informationsmaterial unter dieser Adresse an:

GB-Verlag
Am Gogericht 27a
30855 Langenhagen
Telefon 05 11/74 32 66

Stefan Beck *bietet offers offre*

Instrumentenbau -Kurse -Seminare -Fortbildung -Beratung

Im Instrumentenbau habe ich seit 17 Jahren international einen Namen und gebe gerne mein Können und Wissen erfolgreich weiter.

Meine Angebote richten sich an alle MusikLiebhaber ; insbesondere an berufsausbildende Institutionen, Veranstalter; an Werklehrer, Musiklehrer, Berufsmusiker, Studenten. Auftraggeber sind Institutionen wie Volks -und Musikschulen; Berufs -Fortbildungszentren, Festivals.

Inhaltlich geht es um die Physik der Musikinstrumente um Bau und handwerkliche Umsetzung von Theorien. [Keine Bausatzmontage!]
(Als Fortbildungskurse für Lehrkräfte in Deutschland, Schweiz und Österreich anerkannt)

Termine und Veranstaltungsort vereinbare ich nach Ihren Wünschen.
•••••

instruments historiques en bois
NACHBAU HISTORISCHER HOLZINSTRUMENTE
Historical - Wood - Instruments
•

Rebecs -Einhandflöten mit Trommeln -Krummhörner-Comamusen-Mirlitons- Cornetti-Chalumeaux-Klarinetten -Traversflöten -Oboen und ethnische Instrumente anderer Kulturen.

Meine INSTRUMENTENBAU-KURSE SANTA MARIA(CH) finden in jedem Sommer in der 2.Hälfte Juli und in der 1.Hälfte August statt

bec musikhandwerk tel+fax:(D)-0241-405045
königstrasse 29   d - 52064 aachen

All that Jazz...
Jazz- und Rockmusik spielend lernen.

Praxisorientierte Fernlehrgänge bei freier Zeiteinteilung. Kursangebote mit unterschiedlichen Schwierigkeitsgraden in Theorie und Praxis für alle Instrumente.
Von der musikalischen Grundausbildung bis zur anspruchsvollen Improvisation.
Neu im Programm sind **Jazz Piano** und **Jazz Guitar** für den Musiker mit fortgeschrittenen Ansprüchen.
Umfangreiches Begleitmaterial und regelmäßige Anleitung durch erfahrene Musiker.
Teilnehmer-Workshops.

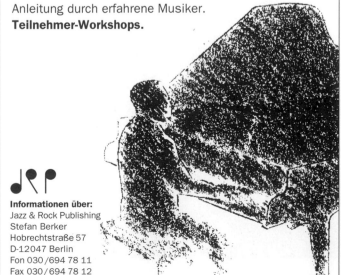

Informationen über:
Jazz & Rock Publishing
Stefan Berker
Hobrechtstraße 57
D-12047 Berlin
Fon 030 / 694 78 11
Fax 030 / 694 78 12

DIE ERSTE
GANZHEITLICHE
INTERPRETEN-SCHULE

Ein neuer Weg! Nutzen Sie die Macht Ihres Denkens, um ein erfolgreicher Interpret zu werden! Wer sein künstlerisches Potential bei Wettbewerben, Aufnahmeprüfungen oder Auftritten voll ausspielen will, muß Ängste ablegen, das Bewußtsein erweitern und seine Körpersprache entwickeln.

Konzertpianistin **Viviane Goergen** überzeugt durch jahrzehntelange Konzerterfahrung, Unterrichtspraxis und fundiertes psychologisches Fachwissen in ihren Tages-Seminaren

● Angst und Lampenfieber
Ängste ablegen, Blockaden abbauen, das Bewußtsein erweitern.

● Mentales Interpreten-Training
Sammlung aller Kräfte, Konzentration und Gelassenheit, von innen heraus musizieren, frei von Streß, optimale Übungsform.

● Der erfolgreiche Interpret
Körpersprache, Erkenntnis, Erfolgswissen, Aufbau der Künstlerpersönlichkeit, überzeugend auftreten, mitreißend konzertieren.

Weitere Informationen
und Anmeldeformular erhältlich
über das

INSTITUT FÜR
MUSIKALISCH-MENTALES
INTERPRETEN-TRAINING

Nelkenstraße 1,
D-63322 Rödermark bei Frankfurt,
Telefon/Telefax 0 60 74/9 88 60

Profile of the European Music School

Das Profil der europäischen Musikschule

Le profil de l'école de musique européenne

At the General Assembly of the EMU in March 1990 at Schloss Weinberg in Austria, a working team was created for «Research into Music Education». Its first undertaking was to gain an overall picture of the current position of music schools in Europe. Information was gathered from the member organizations of the EMU on «Musical Education and Legislation», «Professional Training for Instrumental and Singing Teachers at Music Schools», «Music Schools and Students» and «Music Schools and Their Teaching Staff».

The Organization and Structure of European Music Schools

Since music has a special place in the educational ideals of the countries of Europe, most of them have specialist music schools alongside general schooling: institutions wholly devoted to musical education, and chiefly geared towards practical music-making.

The term «music school» is commonly used in almost all the countries of Europe. The educational goals of music schools, with their pedagogical and artistic aims, are laid down in their statutes. There are no fixed and binding international commitments regarding the minimum requirements that a music school has to fulfil. However, membership of one of the national music associations affiliated to the EMU entails certain prerequisites and conditions. These concern the range of subjects offered, the qualifications of the teaching staff and numerous other aspects. In this way the EMU and its individual member associations vouch for the quality of education provided at their member schools and distance themselves from other, often commercial

Während der Generalversammlung der EMU in Schloß Weinberg (Österreich) wurde im März 1990 die Arbeitsgruppe «Musikpädagogische Forschung» gegründet. Sie stellte sich zunächst die Aufgabe einer Bestandsaufnahme der Musikschulrealität in Europa. Von den Mitgliedsorganisationen der EMU wurden Informationen zu den Bereichen «Musikerziehung und Gesetzgeber», «Berufsausbildung für Instrumental- und Gesangslehrer an Musikschulen», «Musikschulen und Schüler» sowie «Musikschule und Musikschullehrer» eingeholt.

Organisation und Struktur der europäischen Musikschule

Da Musik in den Bildungskonzeptionen europäischer Staaten eine besondere Rolle spielt, gibt es in den meisten von ihnen neben dem allgemeinen Bildungssystem Musikschulen: Einrichtungen, die sich ganz der musikalischen Ausbildung und hauptsächlich der praktischen Musikübung widmen.

Die Bezeichnung «Musikschule» ist in fast allen europäischen Ländern gebräuchlich. Der Bildungsauftrag der Musikschule sowie ihre pädagogischen und künstlerischen Ziele sind in Statuten (Satzungen) niedergelegt. Verbindliche internationale Festlegungen, welche Mindestanforderungen eine Musikschule erfüllen muß, gibt es nicht. Doch ist die Mitgliedschaft in einem der nationalen Musikschulverbände, die der EMU angeschlossen sind, an bestimmte Voraussetzungen und Bedingungen gebunden. Sie betreffen die Vielfalt des Fächerangebots, die Qualifikation der Lehrkräfte und zahlreiche weitere Aspekte. Auf diese Weise stehen die EMU und ihre Einzelverbände für die Qualität der in ihren Mitgliedschulen vermittelten Ausbildung ein und signalisieren eine Abgrenzung gegenüber anderen, oft kommerziellen Angeboten, die (weil der Name «Musikschule» nicht gesetzlich geschützt ist) nicht selten die gleiche Bezeichnung verwenden.

Die Nationalverbände der EMU sind gemeinnützig und erhalten in der Regel öffentliche Zuschüsse. Gleiches gilt für die in den Nationalverbänden organisierten Musikschulen. Es sind damit staatliche Vorgaben gekoppelt, die – häufig in Verbindung mit eigenen Richtlinien der Musikschulen – vergleich-

Au cours de l'Assemblée générale de l'EMU au château Weinberg (Autriche), a été fondé, en mars 1990, le groupe de travail «Recherche en pédagogie musicale». La première tâche qu'il se fixa fut d'établir un inventaire de la réalité de la situation des écoles de musique en Europe. Des informations ont été prises auprès des organisations membres de l'EMU sur les sujets suivants: «Education musicale et législation», «Formation professionnelle des professeurs d'instruments et de chant dans les écoles de musique», «Les écoles de musique et leurs élèves» ainsi que «L'école de musique et ses enseignants».

Organisation et structure de l'école de musique européenne

La musique jouant un rôle particulier dans les conceptions éducatrices des Etats européens, il existe, dans la plupart d'entre eux, parallèlement au système d'enseignement général, des écoles de musique, c'est-à-dire des institutions qui se consacrent entièrement à l'éducation musicale et, principalement, à la pratique de la musique.

Le terme d'«école de musique» est courant dans presque tous les pays européens. La mission éducative de l'école de musique ainsi que ses objectifs pédagogiques et artistiques sont fixés par des statuts. Il n'existe pas de définitions internationales contraignantes en ce qui concerne les exigences minimales à remplir pour une école de musique. Cependant, l'adhésion à l'une des associations des écoles de musique nationales rattachées à l'EMU est liée à un certain nombre de conditions concernant la variété des matières proposées, la qualification du personnel enseignant et de nombreux autres aspects. L'EMU et ses diverses associations se portent garants de la qualité de la formation transmise par les écoles membres et signalisent leur désolidarisation à l'égard d'autres établissements, à caractère souvent commercial, qui, le terme d'«école de musique» n'étant pas protégé, se servent fréquemment de la même dénomination.

Les associations nationales de l'EMU sont des associations d'intérêt public et elles reçoivent, en général, des subventions publiques. Ceci est également le cas pour les écoles de musique organisées au sein des associations nationales. Ces subventions sont grevées d'obligations qui, souvent en re-

«I want to draw attention to the necessity of developing the children's brains, who will be responsible for the world to come. Don't put in lots of data without much value, but attach the greatest attention to the faculty of being able to think originally without straining the memory to no use...

It is proved, that a musical education not only improves the cerebral capacity, but also the ability to guide, make influence and organize.»

Masaru Ibuka
Founder and director of SONY

enterprises, which frequently adopt the same name, «Music School», since the use of the term is not regulated by law.

The national associations of the EMU exist for the general good and, as a rule, they receive public funding. The same applies to the music schools which are organized into national associations. National requirements are linked to the provision of such funding – often in conjunction with the music schools' own guidelines – to ensure correspondingly high standards in these institutes. All music schools have a clearly defined organizational and curricular structure. Some are related to municipal or local authorities, while others are tied to a national curriculum. In some countries (Belgium, France, Finland, Iceland, Liechtenstein, Austria, Denmark, Greece and Switzerland) music schools, are taken into account by laws, which also regulate their financial basis. Comparison shows great similarities between the music schools of Europe, justifying the idea of a «profile of the European Music School». A «Music School» in Europe is a clearly defined institution which forms an integral part of European education systems.

Teacher Training

All over Europe, the training of music school teachers takes place at Conservatoires and Academies of music. We are therefore talking about academic studies at University level, with correspondingly high levels of attainment required. By laying down standards for the training of those intending to work as music school teachers, the State assumes responsibility for assuring the high quality of teaching at music schools. Courses usually last four or five years and lead to a state examination or diploma. These are courses of study which – unlike courses designed solely to promote an artistic career – contain appropriately structured components on teaching theory and methodology.

Education in Music Schools is still a fairly new field of specialization, and Colleges of Higher Education are still in the process of developing appropriate teacher training courses. New elements and new approaches are constantly being added, such as «Music in the Early Years», «Music in Adult Education», «Music with the Disabled». This means that teachers at music schools have an interest in

bar hohe Standards der Institute gewährleisten. Alle Musikschulen verfügen über eine klar umrissene organisatorische und inhaltliche Struktur. Sie ist zum Teil auf kommunaler Ebene verankert, teils auch auf nationaler Ebene mit verbindlichen Strukturplänen. In einigen Ländern (Belgien, Frankreich, Finnland, Island, Liechtenstein, Österreich, Dänemark, Griechenland und Schweiz) gibt es Musikschulgesetze, in denen auch finanzielle Grundlagen festgeschrieben sind. Der Vergleich zeigt, daß zwischen den Musikschulen Europas große Ähnlichkeiten vorhanden sind, die den Begriff eines «europäischen Musikschulprofils» rechtfertigen. «Musikschule» in Europa ist als eine klar definierte Institution integrativer Bestandteil der europäischen Bildungssysteme.

Die Ausbildung der Musikschullehrer/innen

Überall in Europa erfolgt die Ausbildung zum «Musikschullehrer» an Konservatorien und Musikhochschulen. Es handelt sich also um eine akademische Ausbildung mit universitärem Status und entsprechend hohen Leistungsanforderungen. Indem der Staat bestimmte Normen für das Studium mit dem Ziel «Musikschullehrer» vorschreibt, übernimmt er die Verantwortung für einen qualifizierten und hochwertigen Unterricht an den Musikschulen. Das Studium wird in der Regel nach einer Dauer von vier bis fünf Jahren mit einem staatlichen Examen bzw. Diplom abgeschlossen. Es handelt sich um eigenständige Studiengänge, die – anders als das rein künstlerisch ausgerichtete Musikstudium – eine intensive methodische und didaktische Komponente haben und entsprechende Studienfächer einschließen.

Die Musikschulpädagogik ist ein noch relativ junges Berufsfeld, dessen Ausbildungsinhalte an den Hochschulen sich noch in der Entwicklung befinden. Ständig kommen neue Bereiche und Ansätze hinzu: zum Beispiel die «Musikalische Früherziehung», «Musikalische Erwachsenenbildung», «Musik mit behinderten Menschen». Dies führt dazu, daß Lehrkräfte an Musikschulen ein Interesse an ihrer Fort- und Weiterbildung in einem Maße haben, wie man es etwa von Medizinern kennt. Die nationalen Musikschulverbände der EMU begrüßen dieses freiwillige Engagement und sehen in der Organisation und Durchführung solcher Fort-

lation avec les directives propres des écoles de musique, assurent un standard élevé de niveau comparable pour les diverses institutions. Toutes les écoles de musique disposent d'une structure claire sur le plan de l'organisation et des contenus. Celle-ci est, pour une part, ancrée au niveau communal, et d'autre part, également, au niveau national, avec des plans structurels fixes. Dans certains pays (Belgique, France, Finlande, Islande, Liechtenstein, Autriche, Danemark, Grèce et Suisse), il existe une législation sur les écoles de musique, en définissant également les bases financières. La comparaison montre qu'il existe de nombreuses ressemblances entre les différentes écoles de musique d'Europe, ressemblances qui justifient le concept d'un «profil européen de l'école de musique». L'«école de musique», en Europe, est, à titre d'institution clairement définie, partie intégrante des systèmes d'enseignement européens.

La formation des professeurs de musique

Partout en Europe, la formation au métier de professeur de musique s'effectue dans des conservatoires et des écoles supérieures de musique. Il s'agit donc d'une formation universitaire, de statut correspondant et répondant à des exigences de haut niveau. En prescrivant certaines normes pour les études devant mener au «professorat de musique», l'Etat a la responsabilité d'un enseignement qualifié et de qualité dans les écoles de musique. Les études se terminent, en général, au bout de quatre à cinq ans par un examen ou un diplôme d'Etat. Il s'agit de sections d'études indépendantes qui – à la différence des études de musique à orientation purement artistique – ont une composante méthodique et didactique importante et comprennent les matières correspondantes.

La pédagogie des écoles de musique est une branche relativement jeune encore dont les contenus sont encore en plein développement dans les établissements d'enseignement supérieur. Des domaines et des points de départs nouveau s'y ajoutent sans cesse – par exemple, «l'éducation musicale précoce», «l'éducation musicale des adultes», «la musique avec des handicapés». Ceci conduit à ce que les enseignants des écoles de musique s'intéressent vivement à leur formation continue, et ce avec un engagement tel qu'on le connaît dans le do-

further and continuing education on a par with that of medics. The national music school associations of the EMU welcome this voluntary commitment and see the organization and running of such courses on a national and regional level as one of their important functions.

What is available at Music Schools

It is a significant feature of European music schools that they try to offer a broad range of subjects (depending on the size of the school in question). Music schools are open, as a matter of principle, to all interested members of the public, for all forms of musical activity. As a rule, the «usual» instruments are taught and complementary subjects – ensemble playing in particular – are available.

While the starting point and chief emphasis in the work of music schools is still on «classical» (serious) music, other areas of study have been added over the years, such as folk music, rock/pop or jazz and various forms of ensemble, both traditional and modern. Contemporary music has its own place on the music school curriculum. Cultivation of national or folk music traditions results in variations of emphasis in individual countries. In addition, music schools are opening themselves to those disciplines in which music is linked with other arts: dance, ballet, musical, music theatre and film broaden the horizon of artistic activity and frequently lead to co-operation with other institutions.

In the majority of subjects, teaching takes the form of individual tuition or, where this is feasible and useful, in small groups. Schools however place a high value on the social aspect of music and the experience of making music together, and so group work acquires increasing importance. A good 40% of those studying an instrument play in an orchestra, a chamber music group, folk groups, Early Music ensembles, Big Bands, rock and pop groups – to give but a few examples. In their efforts to remain as open as possible, some music schools have introduced alternative approaches alongside the «traditional» forms of teaching: thus workshops, class teaching with various instruments and courses involving free accompaniment, improvisation or work with a music computer may figure on the timetable.

bildungsangebote auf nationaler und regionaler Ebene eine wichtige Aufgabe.

Die Angebote der Musikschulen

Ein wesentliches Merkmal der europäischen Musikschulen ist das Bemühen um eine große Vielfalt ihrer Unterrichtsangebote (abhängig von der Größe der jeweiligen Schule). Musikschulen sind grundsätzlich offen für alle Interessierten und für alle Formen musikalischer Betätigung. In der Regel werden die «heute gebräuchlichen» Instrumente unterrichtet und ergänzende Fächer, insbesondere Ensemblespiel, angeboten.

Ausgangspunkt und Akzent der Musikschularbeit liegen nach wie vor bei der «klassischen» (ernsten) Musik, doch sind im Laufe der Zeit andere Bereiche hinzugekommen, z.B. Folklore, Rock/Pop oder Jazz und verschiedene traditionelle und moderne Ensembleformen. Auch die zeitgenössische Musik hat ihren Platz im Angebot der Musikschulen. Unterschiedliche Schwerpunkte in einzelnen Ländern ergeben sich durch die Pflege ihrer nationalen oder volkstümlichen musikalischen Traditionen. Außerdem öffnen sich die Musikschulen solchen Disziplinen, in denen Musik mit anderen Künsten verbunden ist: Tanz, Ballett, Musical, Musiktheater, Film erweitern den Horizont künstlerischer Betätigung und geben häufig Anlaß zur Kooperation mit anderen Institutionen.

Der Unterricht findet in der Mehrzahl der Fächer als Einzelunterricht oder, wo dies möglich und sinnvoll ist, in kleinen Gruppen statt. Da den Musikschulen aber der soziale Aspekt der Musik, die Gemeinsamkeit beim Musikmachen, ein entscheidendes Anliegen ist, erhalten die Ensemblefächer wachsende Bedeutung. Rund 40% der Instrumentalschüler spielen in einem Orchester, einer Kammermusikgruppe, in Folklorespielkreisen, Ensembles für Alte Musik, Big Bands, Rock- und Popgruppen, um nur einige Beispiele zu nennen. Im Bemühen um größtmögliche Offenheit gibt es an Musikschulen Ansätze, neben den «herkömmlichen» Formen des Unterrichts Alternativen zu entwickeln und zu praktizieren: So finden sich etwa in den Stundenplänen Workshops, Klassenunterricht mit verschiedenen Instrumenten, Kurse mit freier Begleitung, Improvisation oder Umgang mit dem Musikcomputer.

Ziele der Ausbildung an Musikschulen

Die europäischen Musikschulen verfolgen im wesentlichen zwei Ziele. Zum einen wollen sie auf einen professionellen Umgang mit Musik vorbereiten: Sie vermitteln eine solide musikalische Ausbildung, die zu einem Studium an einer Musikhochschule oder einem Konservatorium befähigt. Zum anderen dienen sie der Förderung der musikalischen Breitenbildung und eines qualitativ hochstehenden Laienmusizierens. In einigen Ländern werden die beiden Ausbildungswege ab einer gewissen Stufe differenziert, und Studienanwärter werden in Form einer studienvorbereitenden Ausbildung gezielt und intensiv auf die Aufnahmeprüfungen zum Musikstudium vorbereitet.

Zur Gewährleistung eines hohen Gesamtniveaus – auch der nicht-professionellen Ausbildung – gibt es an den meisten europäischen Musikschulen (ausgenommen Dänemark, Schweden und Norwegen) regelmäßige Leistungsüberprüfungen. Sie sind in den einzelnen Ländern je nach den zugrundeliegenden pädagogischen Konzepten unterschiedlich in ihrer Form und Beurteilungsweise (vielerorts Zeugnisse oder Diplome). Sie gliedern zumeist die Struktur des Ausbildungsgangs (Stufenübergänge) und reichen von offziellen Examina (romanische Länder, Island, Finnland) über landesweit vergleichbare Prüfungen bis zu Regelungen einzelner Musikschulen (Niederlande, Schweiz). In den meisten Ländern erfolgen in unregelmäßigen Abständen auch Unterrichtsinspektionen durch den Direktor der Musikschule oder durch übergeordnete Gremien.

Die Lehrkräfte an den Musikschulen

Während das Ausbildungsniveau und damit das Berufsbild des «Musikschullehrers» in allen europäischen Ländern vergleichbar ist, gibt es noch erhebliche Unterschiede hinsichtlich der konkreten Arbeitsbedingungen. So differiert etwa die Dauer der Unterrichtseinheiten zwischen 40 und 60 Minuten, die Spanne der Vollbeschäftigung reicht von 20 bis 30 Wochenstunden. Außer der Vor- und Nachbereitungszeit des Unterrichts fällt Dienstzeit für Schüler- und Elterngespräche, Konferenzen, für das eigene Üben, Fortbildung usw. an. In den Niederlanden sind von einer 40-Stunden-Woche offiziell 14 Stunden für solche berufsbedingten Tätig-

croissante. Près de 40% des élèves apprenant un instrument jouent dans un orchestre, un groupe de musique de chambre, dans des cercles folkloriques, des ensembles de musique ancienne, des big bands, des groupes de rock et de pop, pour ne citer que quelques exemples.

Dans le cadre de leurs efforts en vue d'une ouverture maximale, les écoles de musique commencent à développer et à pratiquer des alternatives aux formes de cours «traditionnelles»: ainsi, on trouve dans leurs emplois du temps des ateliers de travail, des cours en classe avec plusieurs instruments, des cours avec accompagnement libre, improvisation ou utilisation de l'ordinateur musical.

Objectifs de la formation dans les écoles de musique

Les écoles de musique européennes poursuivent principalement deux objectifs. D'une part, elles veulent préparer à une appréhension et à une pratique professionnelles de la musique: elles transmettent une formation musicale solide ouvrant la porte à des études dans une école supérieure de musique ou un conservatoire. D'autre part, elles contribuent à la formation musicale de masse et à la pratique de la musique d'amateurs à un niveau qualitativement élevé. Dans certains pays, ces deux directions sont différenciées à partir d'un certain moment et les futurs étudiants sont préparés de manière ponctuelle et intensive aux examens d'admission aux études musicales sous forme d'une formation préparatoire.

Afin de garantir un niveau global élevé – même dans le cadre non professionnel -, la plupart des écoles de musique européennes (à l'exception du Danemark, de la Suède et de la Norvège) procèdent régulièrement à des contrôles de connaissances et de performances. Ils diffèrent dans les divers pays par leur forme (souvent certificats et diplômes) et leurs critères de jugement, en fonction des concepts pédagogiques sur lesquels ils reposent. Ils subdivisent la plupart du temps la structure de la formation (passages de classes) et s'étendent de l'examen officiel (dans les pays latins, en Islande et en Finlande) à des réglementations internes d'écoles de musique isolées (aux Pays-Bas et en Suisse) en passant par des contrôles comparables sur le plan national. Dans la plupart des pays, le directeur

teaching. In this, teachers make a significant contribution towards the attainment of educational goals; they also do much for the public image of the music school.

In most European countries, teaching salaries at such institutions are on a par with those of teachers at general schools (except in Germany, where they are considerably lower).

Conclusion

With their clear teaching objectives, standard organization and structure, the range of options they provide and the generally high standard of their work, music schools in Europe make a contribution to the musical training and education of young people and adults which cannot be matched by any other institution. The great demand for the services offered at music schools is evidence of this. Support for their work through national schemes and public funding is a mark and a measure of the cultural and educational importance of these institutions in European society.

keiten ausgewiesen. Zum Berufsbild des Musikschullehrers gehört es, sich über den unmittelba-
ren Unterricht hinaus in der Organisation von
Schülerkonzerten, Workshops oder Probenwo-
chenenden zu engagieren. Damit tragen die Lehrerinnen und Lehrer maßgeblich zum Erfolg der
pädagogischen Arbeit, aber auch zum Bild der Musikschule in der Öffentlichkeit bei. Die Vergütung
dieser Tätigkeit ist in den meisten europäischen
Ländern vergleichbar mit dem Gehalt von Lehrkräften an allgemeinbildenden Schulen (mit Ausnahme Deutschlands, wo sie deutlich darunter
liegt).

Fazit

Musikschulen in Europa haben mit ihren klaren
inhaltlichen Konzepten, ihrer einheitlichen Struktur und Organisation, der großen Vielfalt ihrer Angebote und dem allgemein hohen Niveau ihrer Arbeit einen wesentlichen, von keiner anderen Institution in gleicher Weise zu leistenden Anteil an der
musikalischen Bildung und Ausbildung junger und
erwachsener Menschen. Der rege Zuspruch zu den
Angeboten der Musikschulen bestätigt dies. Die
Förderung ihrer Arbeit durch staatlich garantierte
Strukturen und öffentliche finanzielle Zuschüsse ist
Ausdruck und Gradmesser der kultur- und bildungspolitischen Bedeutung dieser Einrichtung in
der europäischen Gesellschaft.

de l'école de musique ou des comités subordonnés
procèdent à des inspections des cours à intervalles
irréguliers.

Les enseignants des écoles de musique

Si le niveau de formation et le profil professionnel
du «professeur à l'école de musique» sont comparables dans tous les pays européens, il n'en reste
pas moins des différences majeures en ce qui
concerne leurs conditions de travail concrètes.
Ainsi, la durée des unités de cours varie de 40 à 60
minutes, le travail à plein temps va de 20 à 30 heures de cours par semaine. Outre les temps de préparation et de reprise des cours, s'y ajoutent les
conversations avec les élèves et les parents, les
réunions, le temps passé à la formation continue, à
s'exercer, etc... Aux Pays-Bas, 14 heures sont dé-
comptées officiellement de la semaine de 40 heures
pour des activités professionnelles de ce type. Le
profil professionnel du professeur enseignant à
l'école de musique implique, outre les cours di-
rects, d'être actif au niveau de l'organisation de
concerts des élèves, d'ateliers de travail ou de
week-ends d'exercice. Les enseignants contribuent
ainsi pour une grande part au succès du travail pédagogique, mais aussi à l'image de l'école de musique dans le grand public.

Cette activité est rémunérée de manière comparable au salaire des enseignants des écoles d'enseignement général dans la plupart des pays européens (à l'exception de l'Allemagne, où elle est net-
tement inférieure).

Résumé

Avec leurs concepts de fond clairs, leur structure
et leur organisation uniformes, la grande variété
des cours qu'elles proposent et le niveau généralement élevé de leur travail, les écoles de musique
jouent un rôle essentiel, et que l'on ne peut comparer avec celui d'aucune autre institution, dans
l'éducation et la formation musicale des jeunes et
des adultes. La réaction, extrêmement positive, aux
activités proposées par les écoles de musique le
confirme. Le soutien apporté à leur travail par des
structures d'Etat garanties et des subventions publiques est l'expression et le baromètre de l'importance culturelle et éducative de cette institution
dans la société européenne.

Austria

Austria is a federal State formed by nine rather autonomous Regions («Bundesländer»). As a result, music education is ruled by a large variety of different administrative structures and laws. In the Regions of Higher Austria, Carinthia and, since 1993, the Tyrol, the structure and financing of music education are governed by specific laws. Styria and Lower Austria have guidelines with regard to subsidies. Those responsible for music schools, i.e. the municipalities, are free to make their own provisions in respect of teachers' salaries, school fees and professional matters. Music school life develops best in those Regions where music teachers are covered by a scheme of social protection.

Furthermore, guidance and promotion of gifted children are well organized and ensured in good conditions by the authorities in the existing ten conservatoires and three higher education institutions for music and fine arts. Music education is also offered within the general education system in specialized primary, lower and upper secondary music schools. A few regions have developed models of cooperation between the general education system and the music schools. Cooperation between general upper secondary music schools and the conservatoires or higher music education institutions is regulated by law.

Österreich

Österreich ist ein föderalistischer Staat, bestehend aus 9 Bundesländern mit weitgehender Autonomie. Daher gibt es sehr unterschiedliche Organisationsformen und verschiedene gesetzliche Regelungen im Musikschulwesen. In den Bundesländern Oberösterreich und Kärnten und seit 1993 auch in Tirol sind Finanzierung und Struktur des Musikschulwesens durch eigene Gesetze abgesichert. In den Bundesländern Steiermark und Niederösterreich gibt es finanzielle Regelungen bzw. Förderungsrichtlinien. Die Gemeinden, die als Schulträger auftreten, können eigene Regelungen etwa bei der Besoldung der Lehrer, beim Schulgeld und bei fachlichen Entscheidungen treffen. In jenen Bundesländern, die den Musikschullehrern eine soziale Absicherung bieten, ist eine besonders positive Entwicklung des Musikschulwesens gegeben.

Dazu kommt – von öffentlicher Seite her gut organisiert und abgesichert – die Begabtenförderung in den 10 Konservatorien und in den 3 Hochschulen für Musik und Kunst. Schultypen wie Musikgymnasien, Musikhauptschulen und -volksschulen vermitteln ebenfalls musikalische Bildung. In einzelnen Bundesländern gibt es bereits Kooperationsmodelle zwischen den verschiedenen Formen des Regelschulwesens und den Musikschulen. Die Zusammenarbeit der «Oberstufenrealgymnasien für Studierende der Musik» mit den Konservatorien bzw. Musikhochschulen ist sogar gesetzlich geregelt.

Seit 1978 arbeitet die Dachorganisation der österreichischen Musikschulen – die Konferenz der österreichischen Musikschulwerke (KOMU) – an der Vereinheitlichung des Schultyps «Musikschule». Derzeit vertritt die KOMU gemeinsam mit dem Musikschulverband Südtirol ca. 750 Musikschulen, rund 7 000 Lehrer und 200 000 Musikschüler. 1994 hat die KOMU einen gesamtösterreichischen Rahmenlehrplan verabschiedet und publiziert. Zum ersten Mal haben sich die österreichischen Musikschulen damit einheitliche Richtlinien gegeben, die die Institution Musikschule, deren pädagogische Aufgaben und Grundsätze, die Struktur der Ausbildung und die Lerninhalte den letzten Erkenntnissen entsprechend definieren.

L'Autriche

L'Autriche est un Etat fédéral composé de neuf régions («Bundesländer») qui jouissent d'une autonomie relativement importante. Il en résulte une grande diversité quant aux structures administratives et juridiques qui régissent l'enseignement musical. Dans les régions de Haute-Autriche, de Carinthie et, depuis 1993, du Tyrol, le financement et la structure de l'enseignement musical sont règlementés par des lois spécifiques. En Styrie et en Basse-Autriche, il existe des règlements ou directives en matière de soutien financier. Les collectivités locales, responsables des écoles de musique, peuvent prendre leurs propres dispositions en matière de rémunération des professeurs, de droits d'inscription et dans toutes les questions professionnelles. Dans les régions dans lesquelles les professeurs de musique bénéficient d'une protection sociale, la vie des écoles de musique se développe de manière particulièrement positive.

Par ailleurs, la promotion et le suivi des enfants doués sont bien organisés et assurés dans de bonnes conditions par les pouvoirs public dans les dix conservatoires et trois établissements d'enseignement supérieur de musique et de beaux-arts que possède le pays. Une formation musicale est également dispensée dans les lycées, collèges et établissements primaires musicaux. Dans certaines régions, il existe des modèles de coopération entre les différentes formes d'enseignement musical scolaire et les écoles de musique. Quant à la coopération entre les lycées musicaux et les conservatoires ou établissements d'enseignement musical supérieur, elle fait même l'objet d'une réglementation juridique.

Depuis 1978, la Fédération des écoles de musique autrichiennes – la Conférence de l'oeuvre des écoles de musique en Autriche (la KOMU) – a oeuvré en faveur d'une harmonisation des «écoles de musique». Actuellement, le KOMU regroupe, avec l'Association des écoles de musique du Tyrol du Sud, environ 750 écoles de musique avec 7.000 professeurs et 200.000 élèves. En 1994, le KOMU a adopté et publié un programme cadre d'enseignement musical pour l'ensemble de l'Autriche. Les écoles de musique se sont ainsi dotées pour la première fois de directives uniformes qui définissent l'école de musique en tant qu'institution avec ses tâches et principes pédagogiques, ainsi que la

Since 1978, the Association of Austrian music schools (the KOMU) has been working towards harmonizing the music schools. Presently, 750 schools with 7,000 teachers and 200,000 pupils – including the Association from the South-Tyrol – belong to the KOMU. In 1994, the KOMU published a frame-work curriculum for the whole of Austria. For the first time in their history, music schools are defined as an institution and have uniform guidelines with regard to their tasks, pedagogigcs, training structures and syllabuses, inspired from the most recent findings.

The educational mission of the Austrian music schools follows the model set out by the EMU for «the European music school». The music schools have undertaken an educational mission which, in cooperation with the general school system, shall lead the pupil to a global understanding of culture and arts. The aim is to teach music as a whole and to help young people not only to master an instrument but also to reach an overall musical maturity. In some places, music schools carry out specific projects which link music to other forms of arts like literature and painting.

Beyond this ambitious mission, music schools play an increasing role as local cultural and artistic centers. Thanks to them, high level music performances which used to be reserved to major towns, may now be heard throughout the country.

The work of the music schools ranks high within Austrian cultural policy. And still, it is necessary to make sure that public opinion remains fully aware of their role.

Belgium

The Network of Music Academies within the French Community of Belgium is relatively dense: There are 94 «Académies de Musique» which teach 80,000 young people and adults in three fields: music, dance and the art of the word.

86 of these music schools depend on local governing bodies and eight on independent ones. These bodies represent the school before the subsidizing authority, they designate the directing, teaching and administrative staff and make sure that the legal provisions with regard to financing and teaching are respected. Their financial input is

Der Bildungsauftrag der österreichischen Musikschulen orientiert sich an den von den EMU formulierten wesentlichen Aufgaben der «europäischen Musikschule». Die Musikschule ist demnach einem Bildungsauftrag verpflichtet, der im Einklang mit dem allgemeinbildenden Schulwesen zu einem umfassenden Kultur- und Kunstverständnis führt. Musikschulen sollen Musik in ihrer Gesamtheit vermitteln, also neben der Ausbildung der instrumentalen Fertigkeiten auch die Heranreifung zu einer musikalischen Gesamtpersönlichkeit fördern. In Projektform stellt die Musikschule mancherorts auch die Verbindung zwischen Musik und anderen Künsten wie Literatur und Malerei her.

Über diesen umfangreichen und anspruchsvollen Bildungsauftrag hinaus fungiert die Musikschule als Träger örtlichen Kulturlebens. Die österreichischen Musikschulen entwickeln sich immer mehr zum kulturellen und musischen Zentrum ihrer jeweiligen Gemeinde. Veranstaltungen mit hochwertigen Darbietungen, die früher nur größere Städte bieten konnten, sind nun überall im Land anzutreffen.

Die Musikschularbeit besitzt in Österreich insgesamt einen hohen kulturpolitischen Stellenwert. Trotzdem bleibt die Verankerung im öffentlichen Bewußtsein ein ständiger Auftrag.

Belgien (französischsprachige Gemeinde)

Im französischsprachigen Landesteil gibt es ein relativ dichtes Netz von 94 «Académies de musique», in denen 80 000 Jugendliche und Erwach-

structure de formation et les contenus de l'enseignement, à la lumière des recherches les plus récentes.

La mission éducative des écoles de musique autrichiennes oriente son action sur le modèle des tâches principales de «l'Ecole de musique européenne» définies par l'EMU. L'école de musique souscrit ainsi à une mission éducative qui, en collaboration avec l'enseignement général, doit mener l'élève à une compréhension globale de la culture et de l'art. Elle lui transmet la musique dans sa globalité et vise, au delà de la maîtrise d'un instrument, le développement du jeune vers une maturité musicale globale. Dans certains endroits, l'école de musique développe également des projets qui créent des liens entre la musique et d'autres formes d'expression artistique telles la littérature ou la peinture.

Au delà de cette vaste mission ambitieuse, l'école de musique devient un lieu de rencontre et carrefour de la vie culturelle locale, en quelque sorte le centre culturel et artistique de la commune. Aussi, des représentations musicales d'un très haut niveau, naguère l'apanage exclusif des grandes villes, sont-elles maintenant proposées un peu partout dans le pays.

L'action des écoles de musique jouit d'une grande considération au sein de la politique culturelle du pays, mais il est important de veiller à ce que l'opinion publique en prenne et en garde pleinement conscience.

La Belgique (Communauté francaise)

Le réseau belge des académies de musique est relativement dense: 94 établissements en Communauté française (4,5 millions d'habitants) regroupent près de 80.000 jeunes et adultes dans les trois domaines: musique – danse – arts de la parole.

La majorité des académies de musique, à savoir 86 écoles, dépendent d'un pouvoir organisateur communal alors que 8 seulement dépendent d'un pouvoir organisateur libre. Ce pouvoir représente l'établissement face à l'autorité qui octroie les subventions, il nomme le personnel directeur, ensei-

limited to the management of the buildings and material and they partly finance the administrative staff.

The supervising authority is the «Ministry for the Teaching of Arts». It takes care of the salaries of the directors and teaching staff and grants operational subsidies per scholar: its participation amounts to approx. 95%. The courses are free. However, since 1993/94 a small inscription fee has been introduced. Children under 12 still do not pay – at least for the time being. The decision to charge a fee has been widely criticized by the corporation: foreseeable annual increases are likely to weaken the music school system for the benefit of private schools.

Strictly codified regulations set the frame for the general functioning of the «Académies de Musique», the organization of the courses, conditions for admission, criteria for subsidies, curricula and exams. These texts might be criticized for their rigidity, but they have the merit of setting reference values and standardizing the network of the music school system.

Music education in the «Académies de musique» whose overall organization is quite similar to the

sene in den drei Bereichen: Musik – Tanz – sprachgebundene Künste unterrichtet werden.

Von diesen Musikschulen unterstehen 86 einer kommunalen und 8 einer freien Verwaltungsinstanz. Diese vertritt die Schule gegenüber der zuschußgebenden Behörde, entscheidet über die Einstellung von Lehrkräften und Verwaltungspersonal und wacht über die Einhaltung rechtlicher Bestimmungen hinsichtlich der Finanzierung und Unterrichtsorganisation. Ihr finanzieller Anteil beschränkt sich auf Gebäude- und Sachmittel sowie teilweise Personalkosten in der Verwaltung.

Als übergeordnete Behörde trägt das «Ministère de l'Enseignement artistique» (Kunsterziehung) die Kosten für die Bezüge des leitenden Personals und der Lehrkräfte und zahlt pro Schüler einen Zuschuß: insgesamt etwa 95% der Gesamtkosten. Der Unterricht ist kostenlos; allerdings wird seit 1993/94 eine geringe pauschale Teilnehmergebühr erhoben. Für Kinder bleibt der Unterricht (vorerst) gebührenfrei. Die Einführung dieser Gebühr ist vom Berufsverband stark kritisiert worden; man befürchtet eine stetig zunehmende Erhöhung der Teilnehmerbeiträge, was langfristig das Musik-

gnant et administratif et veille au respect des normes pour l'attribution des subventions et l'organisation des études. Son investissement sur le plan financier est limité à la gestion du (des) bâtiment(s) et du matériel et à la prise en charge partielle du personnel administratif.

L'autorité de tutelle est le «Ministère de l'enseignement artistique». Il prend en charge environ 95% de l'ensemble des frais, à savoir les traitements du personnel directeur et enseignant ainsi qu'une subvention de fonctionnement par élève.

L'enseignement est gratuit. Cependant, un faible droit d'inscription forfaitaire a été introduit en 1993/94. Pour les enfants de moins de 12 ans, la gratuité reste (pour l'instant) acquise. L'introduction de ce droit d'inscription a été largement contestée par la corporation qui craint qu'une augmentation progressive de ces contributions ne défavorise à long terme le système d'écoles de musique par rapport aux écoles privées.

Une réglementation très codifiée fixe le fonctionnement général des académies de musique, l'organisation des cursus, les conditions d'admission des élèves, les normes pour l'attribution des subventions, les programmes d'études et d'examens, etc. Critiquables pour leur rigidité, ces textes ont au moins le mérite de fixer des valeurs de références et d'homogénéiser le réseau des académies de musique.

L'enseignement dans les académies de musique dont l'organisation générale est assez proche de celle de la France, est en général fort individualisé et compartimenté; le cursus habituel de l'élève instrumentiste comprend le cour de formation musicale (solfège) durant 5 années, couplé avec le cours individuel d'instrument étalé sur 8 à 10 années. A ceux-ci peuvent s'ajouter des cours optionnels, comme la musique de chambre, l'histoire de la musique, etc. A la fin des études, les élèves peuvent se présenter à un concours national qui est, pour beaucoup de jeunes, un tremplin vers les études supérieures et la carrière artistique.

French practice, is in general individualized and divided into separate compartments; the normal course for a pupil who learns an instrument includes five years of basic music education («solfeggio») parallel to an eight to ten years' individual instrumental course. These might be completed by optional courses on chamber music, history of music, etc. At the end of their studies, the pupils can take part in a national contest which for many young people is the starting point for higher studies and an artistic career.

However, in recent years, new initiatives have developed encouraging group activities (small choirs, small orchestras etc), introducing new, different instruments, different techniques, different styles (Jazz, music from all over the world, modern or contemporary dance etc). Since 1989, specific grants have been allocated to special projects: introduction of new courses (bagpipe, psycho-motor activities, oriental music,...), experiments in specific fields, scene plays, etc. In order to adapt the teaching to different contexts, the Ministry invited all Academies in June 1993 to develop individual concepts («projet école») setting out the pedagogical orientations and structures of the institution within a clearly set reference frame. 50 out of 85 applications were accepted. The idea is:

- to give more responsibility to the pedagogical team: each teacher shall have the opportunity to make suggestions with regard to the organization of the course, to the programme, to the objectives aimed at and to the methodology;
- to allow for a «local» colour (according to the social, cultural, geographical surroundings), whilst still safeguarding a global approach which all institutions have in common;
- to encourage a twofold orientation as from a certain study level onwards: a qualified branch applying to the majority of the pupils, a transitional branch for gifted and motivated children, and special offers adapted to the needs of the

schulsystem zugunsten privater Anbieter schwächen würde.

Die Arbeit der «Académies de musique» wird von verbindlichen Vorschriften bestimmt, von denen die Unterrichtsorganisation, die Zulassungsbedingungen, die Subventionsrichtlinien, die Lehrpläne und Prüfungen geregelt werden. Man kann sie sicher wegen ihrer Strenge tadeln, aber sie haben das Verdienst, klare Maßstäbe zu setzen und das Musikschulsystem zu vereinheitlichen.

Der Unterricht in den «Académies de musique», die den französischen Musikschulen sehr ähnlich sind, wird generell als Einzelunterricht in gesonderten Sparten erteilt; der normale Kursverlauf für Instrumentalschüler umfaßt eine fünfjährige Grundschulung («solfège») in Verbindung mit dem jeweiligen Instrumentalunterricht, der über acht bis zehn Jahre verläuft. Dazu kommen Wahlfächer wie Kammermusik, Musikgeschichte usw. Für Absolventen der Musikschulen gibt es einen nationalen Wettbewerb, der für viele ein Sprungbrett zu Hochschulstudium und künstlerischer Laufbahn ist.

Seit einigen Jahren gibt es neue Initiativen: gemeinsames Musizieren (Vokalensemble, Spielkreise usw.), neue Instrumente, moderne Spieltechniken, andere Stile (Jazz, außereuropäische Musik, Ausdruckstanz). Seit 1989 erhalten Musikschulen spezielle Förderungen für Sonderprojekte: Einführung neuer Angebote (Dudelsack, psychomotorische Aktivitäten, orientalische Musik u.a.), Experimente in bestimmten Bereichen, Durchführung besonderer Veranstaltungen. Um den Unterricht noch besser an Bedingungen des jeweiligen Umfelds anzupassen, hat das Ministerium 1993 die Musikschulen aufgefordert, individuelle Konzepte («projet école») zur pädagogischen Ausrichtung und Struktur der Schule im Rahmen bestimmter Richtlinien auszuarbeiten. Von 85 Vorschlägen wurden gut 50 angenommen. Folgende Tendenzen zeichnen sich ab:

■ Den Lehrkräften mehr Eigenverantwortung gewähren: Jeder Lehrer soll Konzepte zu Unterrichtsform, Zielsetzung, Inhalten und Methodik seiner Kurse vorschlagen können.

■ Ein eigenes Gesicht der Musikschulen zulassen, das örtlichen, gesellschaftlichen und kulturellen

Cela dit, depuis quelques années, de nouvelles initiatives ont vu le jour pour développer les pratiques collectives (ensembles vocaux, petits orchestres, etc.), aborder d'autres instruments, d'autres techniques, d'autres genres (jazz, musiques du monde, danse moderne ou contemporaine, etc.). Depuis 1989, des crédits spécifiques sont accordés aux établissement qui réalisent des projets particuliers: création de nouveaux cours (cornemuse, psychomotricité, musique orientale, etc.), expérimentation dans un domaine particulier, montage d'un spectacle, etc. Pour élargir encore les possibilités de moduler l'enseignement selon des critères contextuels, le Ministère a invité en juin 1993 toutes les académies à élaborer un «projet école» fixant les orientations pédagogiques et les structures de l'établissement dans les limites d'un cadre de référence. Sur les 85 demandes introduites, une cinquantaine ont été acceptées. Les intentions sont les suivantes:

■ Responsabiliser l'équipe pédagogique: chaque professeur remet un projet de classe dans lequel il propose l'organisation du cours, le programme, les objectifs poursuivis, la méthodologie,...

adults. Schools can choose freely the modalities for the exams and the evaluation of the pupils.

■ to give to everybody the necessary flexibility so as to implement his/her pedagogical aims within a sometimes reduced budget. This measure could be the starting point for the introduction of clear and strict rules concerning subventions on the basis of objective and adaptable criteria.

The liberty thus offered to all schools stands in a peculiar contrast to the rigid rules existing so far. But this liberty is limited to a one-year experiment and must respect the organizational and budgetary framework of the school. It should result in the drafting of a statute defining the form of the music schools and the role of the teachers. The aim is to define a just equilibrium between beneficial liberty and those reference criteria that are necessary to ensure a certain homogeneity in the education. Much is at stake for the future of music education in Belgium.

Bulgaria

There are about 30 schools that offer, in addition to current music education as foreseen in the school curriculum, a special branch with music as a compulsory subject. This intensive music education is state run and nearly entirely financed by the government. Presently, 4,500 pupils follow such courses.

Pupils who wish to enter this branch have to pass successfully an entrance examination where their music ear (i.e. the capacity of hearing and perceiving music consciously), their instrumental technical skill and their music level are tested. Admission to this branch is foreseen at the 1st, 4th and 8th grade.

Before entering this branch, children of the age of four and a half to five years can follow preparatory courses until the age of seven when they are admitted to the 1st grade.

Gegebenheiten Rechnung trägt, bei einer allen gemeinsamen Grundkonzeption.

- Zweigleisigkeit der Ausbildung ab einer bestimmten Stufe: für die Mehrheit der Schüler ein qualifizierter Unterricht, spezielle Förderung für die besonders Motivierten und Begabten, schließlich auch auf Erwachsene zugeschnittene Angebote. Prüfungsmodalitäten und Beurteilungsformen sollen jeder Musikschule überlassen werden.
- Auch innerhalb knapper Budgets jedem den nötigen Spielraum für die Realisierung seiner pädagogischen Konzepte geben. Anpassung der Subventionen nach objektiven und der jeweiligen Situation angemessenen Kriterien.

Die den Schulen hiermit gewährte Selbständigkeit kontrastiert stark zu den bisher gewohnten Reglementierungen. Sie ist zunächst auf ein «Versuchsjahr» beschränkt und muß im organisatorischen und finanziellen Rahmen der Schulen bleiben. Zielsetzung ist die Formulierung einer Satzung, die dann wieder verbindlicher die Form der Musikschulen definiert – und übrigens auch den Status der Lehrerschaft. Angestrebt wird ein praktikables Verhältnis zwischen fruchtbarer Eigenverantwortung und notwendigen Normen oder Maßstäben, die ein vergleichbares Niveau des Unterrichts sichern. Für die Zukunft der Musikerziehung in Belgien wird diese Reform außerordentlich wichtig sein.

Bulgarien

In Bulgarien gibt es an etwa 30 allgemeinbildenden Schulen neben dem normalen schulischen Musikunterricht einen Sonderzweig mit Musik als Pflichtfach. Träger dieser intensivierten Musikausbildung, an der zur Zeit etwa 4 500 Schüler teilnehmen, ist der Staat, der sie auch nahezu vollständig finanziert.

Die Schüler, die in diesen Fachbereich aufgenommen werden wollen, müssen eine Aufnahmeprüfung bestehen: Beurteilt werden die Bildung des Gehörs (das bewußte hörende Auffassen von Musik) sowie das technische Können und das musikalische Niveau auf einem Instrument. Eine Aufnahme in den Musikfachzweig ist im 1., 4. und 8. Schuljahr möglich.

- Permettre une empreinte «locale» (liée à des paramètres sociaux, culturels, géographiques,...), tout en préservant une conception de base commune à tous les établissements.

- Créer, à partir d'un certain niveau d'étude, une double orientation: une filière de qualification, destinée à la majorité des élèves, une filière de transition pour les élèves motivés et doués, et enfin un cycle d'études mieux adapté pour les adultes. Les modalités d'examen et d'évaluation sont laissées à l'appréciation de chaque école.

- Donner a chacun la souplesse nécessaire pour réaliser ses objectifs pédagogiques, à l'intérieur d'une enveloppe budgétaire quelquefois très réductrice, permettant ainsi l'attribution des subventions sur la base de critères objectifs et modulables.

Cette liberté donnée à chaque établissement contraste assez singulièrement avec la réglementation rigide qui a prévalu par le passé. Mais elle est limitée à une année expérimentale et soumise aux contraintes administratives et budgétaires des écoles, dans l'attente d'un décret fixant de manière plus définitive le fonctionnement général de l'enseignement et le statut du personnel enseignant. L'objectif est la réalisation d'un juste équilibre entre une liberté statutaire et des normes référentielles nécessaires à une certaine homogénéité de l'enseignement. Les enjeux sont importants pour l'avenir de l'enseignement de la musique en Belgique.

La Bulgarie

Il existe en Bulgarie une trentaine d'établissements scolaires qui proposent, à côté de l'enseignement musical prévu au programme scolaire, une branche spécialisée avec un enseignement musical obligatoire. Cet enseignement musical intensif dispensé actuellement à quelques 4.500 élèves, est assuré sous la tutelle de l'Etat qui assume la quasi-totalité de son financement.

L'admission à cette branche est subordonnée au passage d'un examen d'entrée qui comporte un test d'écoute musicale (la capacité d'entendre et de saisir consciemment la musique) ainsi qu'un test d'instrument permettant d'apprécier le niveau technique et musical de l'élève. L'accès se fait en 1ère, en 4ème ou en 8ème année.

In addition, there are 9 secondary music schools, two of which are specialized in folk music and teach traditional folk music instruments and folksongs. Admission to these secondary music schools is also subject to an entrance examination at the 1st, 4th or 8th grade. The tests include an instrumental performance and music theory («solfeggio»). Up to the 7th grade, the pupils follow the complete general school curriculum and have additional instrumental, «solfeggio» and elementary music theory classes: in the first years, this programme is identical to that of the specialized music branch of the general secondary schools, but it differs considerably as from the 8th grade.

Pupils who have successfully finished a secondary music school can enter higher education institutes for fine arts or humanities. There are two higher music education colleges, the State Academy in Sofia and the Academy for Music and Dance which also prepare for the profession of music teachers in kindergardens, schools and music schools.

Croatia

Music schools in Croatia are based on a strong and uninterrupted tradition. In 1804 the first music school was founded in Karlovac. Today, 60 elementary and 13 secondary music schools can be found in Croatia, together with the Academy of Music in Zagreb (with departments in Osijek, Rijeka, Split and Dubrovnik). In addition, there are four elementary and one secondary school for rhythm and dance, as well as two elementary and one secondary school for classical ballet.

These schools exist in addition to public schools which do teach music but do not carry instrumental courses. 90% of the costs of music education are covered by the government. Pupils only pay a small contribution to the equipment.

The basic concept of music education has not changed throughout these years: it aims at offering music education to all children who show interest in it, thereby enriching their own culture, as well as the culture of the whole country, and at stimulating

Es gibt vorbereitende Kurse hierzu, in die sich Kinder ab 4 1/2 bis 5 Jahren einschreiben können, bis sie mit 7 Jahren in die erste Stufe des Fachzweigs aufgenommen werden.

Außerdem gibt es in Bulgarien insgesamt 9 «Sekundar-Musikschulen», von denen zwei auf Volksmusik und ihre besonderen Instrumente spezialisiert sind. Der Eintritt in diese «Sekundar-Musikschulen» kann ebenfalls zur 1., 4. oder 8. Klasse erfolgen. Die Aufnahmeprüfung wird auf dem Instrument und in Musiklehre («solfeggio») abgelegt. Bis zur 7. Klasse machen die Schüler das komplette Programm der allgemeinbildenden Schule mit und haben zusätzlich Unterricht auf einem Instrument sowie in «solfeggio» und in Musiktheorie: Dieses Programm deckt sich anfangs mit dem an den Schulen mit Fachzweig Musik, unterscheidet sich aber dann deutlich davon ab der 8. Klasse.

Die Absolventen der Musikschulen haben die Möglichkeit, an einem Hochschulinstitut für Kunst oder für ein anderes humanwissenschaftliches Fach zu studieren. Bulgarien hat zwei Musikhochschulen: Die Staatsakademie in Sofia und die Akademie für Musik und Tanz, an der auch die Musiklehrer für Kindergärten, Schulen und Musikschulen ausgebildet werden.

Kroatien

Die Musikschulen in Kroatien können auf eine lange Tradition zurückblicken: 1804 wurde die erste Musikschule in Karlovac gegründet. Heute gibt es 60 «Grund»- und 13 «Sekundar»-Musikschulen sowie die Musikakademie in Zagreb (mit Instituten in Osijek, Rijeka, Split und Dubrovnik), daneben 4

Auparavant, les enfants de quatre ans et demi à cinq ans peuvent suivre des cours préparatoires jusqu'à leur admission au premier niveau de la branche spécialisée à l'âge de sept ans.

La Bulgarie dispose en outre de neuf écoles secondaires de musique dont deux spécialisées en musique traditionnelle avec enseignement d'instruments de musique et de chants traditionnels. L'entrée dans ces écoles se fait aussi au niveau de la 1ère, de la 4ème ou de la 8ème année après passage d'un examen d'admission qui porte sur la pratique d'un instrument et sur la théorie musicale («solfeggio»). Jusqu'à la 7ème année, les élèves suivent le programme complet des établissements d'enseignement général secondaire, avec en sus, des cours d'instrument, de solfège et de théorie musicale élémentaire. Pendant les premières années, le programme est identique à celui enseigné dans la branche musicale des établissements d'enseignement général. Mais à partir de la 8ème année, les programmes des deux filières divergent considérablement.

A l'issue de leur scolarité, les élèves des écoles secondaires de musique peuvent s'inscrire dans des établissements de formation supérieure pour suivre des enseignements artistiques ou de sciences humaines. Il existe, en Bulgarie, deux établissements d'enseignement musical supérieur: l'Académie d'Etat à Sofia et l'Académie de Musique et de Danse où sont également formés les enseignants de musique pour les établissement préscolaires, les écoles et les écoles de musique.

La Croatie

La tradition des écoles de musique en Croatie remonte loin et n'a jamais été interrompue: la première école de musique fut fondée en 1804 à Karlovac. A l'heure actuelle, il existe en Croatie 60 écoles de musique élémentaires et 13 écoles de musique secondaires à côté de l'Académie de Musique de Zagreb (avec des branches à Osijek, Rijeka, Split et Dubrovnik). En outre, il y a quatre écoles élémentaires et cinq écoles secondaires de rythme et de danse ainsi que deux écoles élémentaires et une école secondaire de ballet classique.

Ces écoles de musique fonctionnent à côté des établissements d'enseignement général où la musi-

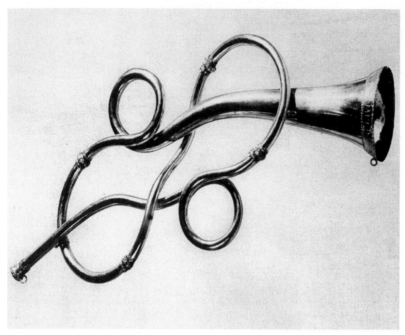

Grundschulen und eine Sekundar-
schule für Rhythmus und Tanz, sowie 2 Grundschulen und eine Se-
kundarschule für klassisches Ballett.

Diese Einrichtungen bestehen neben dem allgemeinen Schulsystem, das zwar auch Musikunterricht vermittelt, jedoch keine praktische Musikausbildung. Auch die
Kosten der Musikschulen trägt in
Kroation zu 90% der Staat. Die
Schüler zahlen einen geringfügigen Beitrag, den die Schulen für
eine zusätzliche Unterrichtsaus-
stattung verwenden.

talented children to continue their music education
and to become professional musicians.

The programme is divided into elementary (6
years), secondary (4 years) and academic education (4 years). Many music schools have their own
music kindergardens where children sing and play
children's instruments until they enter elementary
school. There are also post-graduate studies after
the Academy.

Children in elementary music schools are
between 6 – 10 years old. They learn an instrument
and the rudiments of musical theory («solfeggio»)
and take part in an ensemble (or choir). Besides the
classic instruments, «tamburitsa» – a typical folk
instrument with strings – is very popular. Additional music subjects are taught in secondary
grade. Most pupils who finish elementary and secondary grade continue playing in an amateur orchestra, a band, a folkmusic group, a chamber music orchestra or in an ensemble for early music.

There is close cooperation between music
schools and music academies. The Music School
Association organizes annually competitions to
identify and encourage talented children. Advanced training is also offered by numerous summer courses e.g. the International Camp for Music
Youth at Groznjan and the EPTA summer piano
school in Dubrovnik. Moreover, professional associations and the «Jeunesses Musicales» organize

Der Grundgedanke der Musiker-
ziehung war seit jeher, zum einen allen interessierten Kindern eine Musikausbildung zu bieten und
damit ihre eigene Kultur wie auch die des Landes
zu bereichern, zum andern begabte Kinder zu fördern und ihnen eine Berufsausbildung als Musiker
zu ermöglichen.

Der Ausbildungsgang gliedert sich in Grundausbildung (6 Jahre), Sekundarausbildung (4 Jahre)
und akademische Ausbildung (4 Jahre). Viele Musikschulen haben auch einen Musikkindergarten
(Singen und Spielen mit Kinderinstrumenten) vor
der Grundstufe. Außerdem gibt es Kurse für Absolventen der Akademie.

Die Schüler der Grund-Musikschule sind 6–10
Jahre alt. Sie lernen ein Instrument und Musiklehre («solfeggio») und nehmen an gemeinsamem
Musizieren (oder Chorsingen) teil. Neben den klassischen Instrumenten ist das volksmusikalische
Zupfinstrument «Tamburizza» sehr beliebt. In der
Sekundarstufe kommen dann andere Fächer
hinzu. Fast alle Schüler, die die Grund- und Sekundarstufe abschließen, spielen weiter in Laien-
orchestern, Bands, Volksmusikgruppen, Kammer-
orchestern oder Ensembles für Alte Musik.

Dem Finden und Fördern von besonders Begabten dient ein Wettbewerb, den der kroatische Musikschulverband jährlich veranstaltet. Außerdem
gibt es eine enge Zusammenarbeit zwischen den
Musikschulen und den Musik-Akademien. Inten-

que est enseignée comme un sujet parmi d'autres, mais non la pratique d'un instrument. Les écoles de musique sont financées à 90% par l'Etat alors que les élèves n'ont à payer qu'une contribution minime destinée à l'achat du matériel nécessité pour les cours.

Le concept de base de l'éducation musicale a toujours été d'offrir à tous les enfants qui s'y intéressent un enseignement musical, afin d'enrichir leur propre culture comme celle de l'ensemble du pays, et de stimuler les enfants doués afin qu'ils poursuivent leur formation musicale pour devenir des professionnels.

La formation est subdivisée en éducation élémentaire (6 ans), secondaire (4 ans) et académique (5 ans). Beaucoup d'écoles de musique possèdent leurs propres jardins d'enfants musicaux (où les enfants chantent et jouent sur des instruments d'enfants) qui précèdent l'école élémentaire. Il y a également des études post-universitaires pour ceux qui ont terminé l'Académie.

Les écoles de musiques élémentaires sont fréquentées par des enfants de 6 à 10 ans. Ils y apprennent à jouer un instrument, les règles de la théorie musicale («solfeggio») et apprennent à faire de la musique dans des ensembles (ou à chanter dans des chorales). A côté des instruments classiques courants, le «tambouritsa» (un instrument populaire à corde) est très en vogue. D'autres sujets musicaux viennent s'ajouter en formation secondaire. La plupart de ceux qui terminent la formation élémentaire et secondaire, continuent à faire de la musique dans des orchestres amateurs, dans des groupes musicaux, folkloriques, dans des orchestres de musique de chambre ou dans des ensembles de musique ancienne.

Les rapports entre les écoles de musique et l'Académie sont excellents: les écoles de musique s'efforcent d'identifier les enfants doués grâce à des concours annuels de musique, organisés par l'Association des écoles de musique. Des formations plus poussées sont offertes dans le cadre de nombreuses classes d'été, tel par exemple le camp international de musique de Groznan ou l'école d'été de piano EPTA à Dubrovnik. En outre, les associations professionnelles et les Jeunesses Musicales organisent des séminaires de musique et des

music seminars and concerts and also inform children in general educational schools on the programme of operas and concerts.

Great attention is being paid to the education of music teachers. A degree in music education is required from all professors who teach an instrument or particular music subjects in music or public schools. This degree can be acquired in a four years study course at the Academy where students are admitted after secondary school and after having passed an entrance exam.

Music schools have become the centres of music culture, in particular in small towns. The government does its best to expand the number of music schools and to keep up their high level of education. However there is some concern for the insufficient number of music teachers of whom a great number leave the country to work abroad.

In joining the EMU the Association of the Croatian Music Schools hopes to contribute considerably, thanks to the exchange of experiences, to the large community of music schools and to learn a great deal itself.

Denmark

Denmark was the first country in the world to adopt – as from 1976 – a comprehensive music law governing all music activities in the country, from the small provincial band to the Royal Opera. The purpose of the law was to decentralize and to encourage the practice of music throughout Denmark.

The law did actually give rise to an extraordinary increase in the number of music schools. And when the Music Act was extended by a specific Music School Act in 1990, music school activities gained even more importance due to the generous public support granted to music schools under the Act.

The Music School Act foresees in particular:

- The Government shall refund up till 25% of the teachers' salaries (incl. transport).
- Fees paid by the pupils may not exceed one

sive Ausbildung bieten auch zahlreiche Sommer-kurse, das internationale Jugend-Music-Camp in Groznjan und die EPTA-Sommerschule für Klavier in Dubrovnik. Die Berufsverbände und die «Jeunesse Musicale» veranstalten Seminare und Konzerte und informieren die Schüler über Konzert- und Opernangebote.

Große Bedeutung wird der Lehrerausbildung beigemessen. Die Musiklehrer an Musikschulen wie an allgemeinbildenden Schulen müssen ein musikpädagogisches Hochschul-Diplom besitzen. Nach Abschluß der Sekundarstufe und nach bestandener Aufnahmeprüfung kann dies durch ein vierjähriges Studium an der Musikakadmie erworben werden.

Musikschulen haben sich in vielen Städten, vor allem in kleineren, zu richtigen Zentren des Musiklebens entwickelt. Die Regierung tut daher ihr Möglichstes, die Zahl der Musikschulen in Kroatien zu erhöhen und das hohe Niveau der Ausbildung zu erhalten. Aber ein Problem ist die unzureichende Zahl von Lehrkräften, von denen viele ihr Land verlassen, um im Ausland zu arbeiten.

Mit seinem Beitritt zur EMU hofft der kroatische Musikschulverband, im Austausch von Erfahrungen sowohl vieles zu lernen als auch die große Gemeinschaft der Musikschulen durch seinen Beitrag zu bereichern.

Dänemark

Dänemark verabschiedete bereits 1976 – und damit als erstes Land der Welt – ein umfassendes Musik-Gesetz, das die gesamten musikalischen Aktivitäten des Landes, von der kleinen Provinz-Musikkapelle bis zur Königlichen Oper, gesetzlich regelte. Ziel des Gesetzes ist es, das Musizieren im ganzen Land zu dezentralisieren und zu fördern.

In der Tat hatte es eine außerordentliche Zunahme der Anzahl von Musikschulen zur Folge. Als es dazu im Jahre 1990 noch durch ein Gesetz über die Musikschulen erweitert wurde, wurde deren Tätigkeit nochmals aufgewertet, umso mehr, als die öffentliche Hand die Schulen seitdem in Anwendung des Gesetzes durch großzügige Zuwendungen unterstützt.

Dies sind die entscheidenden Passagen des Musikschul-Gesetzes:

concerts et informent les enfants, par le truchement des écoles, du programme d'opéras et de concerts.

Une grande priorité est accordée à la formation des enseignants. Les futurs enseignants de musique qui auront à enseigner un instrument ou d'autres sujets musicaux dans une école de musique ou dans un établissement d'enseignement général, doivent avoir un diplôme supérieur de formation musicale. Ce diplôme est décerné par l'Académie après une formation de quatre ans, accessible à l'issue de l'école secondaire et après le passage réussi d'un examen d'entrée.

Dans de nombreuses villes – surtout dans les petites communes – les écoles de musique sont devenues de véritables centres de culture musicale. Le gouvernement fait tout ce qui est en son pouvoir pour augmenter le nombre d'écoles de musique et pour maintenir le haut niveau de l'éducation musicale. Il reste, hélas, le problème du nombre insuffisant de professeurs de musique, dû en partie au fait que beaucoup d'entre eux partent travailler à l'étranger.

Maintenant que l'Association des écoles de musique croates est venue se joindre à l'EMU, le pays espère que les échanges d'expériences lui fourniront l'occasion d'apporter son patrimoine à la grande communauté des écoles de musique mais aussi, d'y apprendre beaucoup.

Le Danemark

Le Danemark a été le premier pays au monde à adopter – et ce dès 1976 – une loi globale sur la musique qui s'applique à toutes les activités musicales du pays, couvrant aussi bien les petits ensembles provinciaux que l'Opéra Royal. L'objectif poursuivi était de décentraliser et d'encourager les activités musicales à travers le pays.

Et en effet, les écoles de musique du Danemark ont connu un développement extraordinaire. Lorsque, de surcroît, une loi spécifique sur les écoles de musique est venue compléter en 1990 la loi sur la musique, les écoles s'en sont trouvées encore plus valorisées, notamment grâce à la subvention publique généreuse qui leur est accordée en vertu de cette loi.

third of the overall operational costs of the school.

- Central Government can contribute to the financing of up to one third of the gross expenses for basic music courses (i.e. the professional preparation for a conservatoire) provided that the remaining two thirds are covered by the relevant counties and local authorities.

Presently, Denmark has 225 music schools with 4,000 teachers, 110,000 students and 2,500 different school orchestras.

Finland

In Finland, satisfying the need for musical expression is regarded as one of the basic human needs. Music is therefore an important part of an all-round education. Music education should start as early as possible and give all pupils the opportunity to develop their talents up to a professional level, if they so wish.

- Die öffentliche Hand erstattet 25 % der Gehälter der Musikschullehrer (einschließlich Fahrtkosten).
- Die Schülergebühren dürfen nicht mehr als ein Drittel der gesamten Betriebskosten ausmachen.
- Die Bundesbehörden können bis zu einem Drittel der Brutto-Ausgaben für die musikalische Grundausbildung (das heißt hier: professionelle Vorbereitung auf ein Konservatorium) übernehmen, sofern die verbleibenden zwei Drittel von den jeweiligen Landkreisen bzw. Gemeinden getragen werden.

In Dänemark gibt es gegenwärtig 225 Musikschulen mit 4 000 Lehrern, 110 000 Schülern und 2 500 verschiedenen Schülerorchestern.

Finnland

Die Erfüllung des musikalischen Ausdrucksbedürfnisses gilt in Finnland als ein grundsätzlicher humaner Anspruch. Musik ist daher Bestandteil einer umfassenden Erziehung. Die Musikerziehung im besonderen sollte möglichst früh einsetzen, damit jeder Schüler seine Anlagen entwickeln kann, bis hin zum professionellen Musiker.

Es gibt Musik-Kindergärten, in denen 3–6jährigen Kindern eine grundlegende und vorbereitende Anleitung im Instrumentalspiel und in allgemeiner Musiklehre vermittelt wird.

Die Aufgabe der Musikschulen besteht darin, in Ergänzung zu der eher allgemeinen Musikerziehung in der Pflichtschule Finnlands nationale Musikkultur zu fördern und die aktive Beschäftigung mit Musik breiten Kreisen zu ermöglichen.

In den 92 Musikfachschulen, die dem Finnischen Musikschulverband angehören, werden Schüler auf Musikschul- und Musikfachschul-Niveau unterrichtet. Über Examina erreichen die Schüler die jeweils höhere Stufe. In den insgesamt 11 Konservatorien Finnlands, von denen 5 dem Musikschulverband angehören, werden die Absolventen der Musikfachschulen berufsorientiert ausgebildet.

Die Einrichtungen der Musikerziehung kommen ihrer Aufgabe durch folgende Lehrziele nach:

- breite Bevölkerungskreise zu aktivem Musikhören anregen,

La loi sur les écoles de musique stipule notamment:

- que les autorités publiques doivent rembourser les salaires des enseignants (y compris le transport) jusqu'à concurrence de 25 %,
- que les droits d'inscription des élèves ne doivent pas dépasser le tiers de l'ensemble des coûts opérationnels,
- que l'administration centrale peut prendre à sa charge le tiers (au maximum) des dépenses globales pour les cours de formation musicale de base (préparation professionnelle pour l'entrée au Conservatoire), à condition que les collectivités locales et régionales se chargent des deux tiers restants.

Il existe actuellement au Danemark 225 écoles de musique avec 4.000 enseignants, 110.000 élèves et 2.550 orchestres scolaires divers.

La Finlande

En Finlande, la satisfaction du besoin d'expression musicale est perçue comme un besoin fondamental de l'homme, et la musique constitue donc un élément important de la formation des jeunes. L'enseignement musical commence aussi tôt que possible, de façon à permettre à tout enfant de développer ses possibilités et, le cas échéant, de pouvoir accéder à la profession de musicien.

Il y a des jardins d'enfants «musicaux», où les enfants de trois à six ans reçoivent un enseignement de base préparatoire à la pratique d'un instrument et à la théorie musicale.

Les écoles de musique ont la double tâche de développer la culture musicale du pays, complétant ainsi l'enseignement musical de base dispensé par les établissements scolaires, et de renforcer l'intérêt général pour la musique.

Les 92 instituts de musique, membres de l'Association des écoles de musique de Finlande, comprennent deux niveaux d'enseignement, à savoir l'école de musique proprement dite et le collège de musique. Les élèves doivent passer des examens pour passer d'un niveau à l'autre.

Les conservatoires s'adressent aux étudiants issus des instituts de musique et aspirant à une formation professionnelle. Il y a, en tout, onze conser-

There are music-kindergardens where 3 to 6 years old children receive a basic and preparatory music education, introducing them to an instrument and to music theory.

Music schools have the task to supplement the basic music education provided under the compulsory school system in order to further Finland's national music culture and to broaden the pursuit of music.

The 92 Finnish music colleges belonging to the national music school association offer an education at music school and music college level. The passage from one level to the other is subject to an exam. Eleven conservatoires, five of which are members of the music school association, train future professionals after they have successfully finished the music college.

The music education establishments implement their goals by:

- encouraging the public at large to listen to music,
- providing basic instruction in composition and performance (at music school and music college level),
- preparing pupils for professional music studies (at music college level),
- training professional musicians (at conservatoire level).

In addition to their studies, pupils receive instruction in various subjects such as ear training, reading notes, music theory, musicology, figured bass and ensemble playing, and they can choose amongst numerous optional subjects.

The number of pupils in the various music schools and colleges is proportional to the funds available. Over 80% of the member establishments receive statutory state aid, so that their expenditure is covered to: 40–45% by statutory state aid, 40–50% by grants from local authorities, 10–20% by student fees.

The grants from local authorities as well as the student fees are higher in those establishments that do not receive statutory state aid.

The Sibelius Academy, Finland's only music academy at university level, trains musicologists and – in a special department – music pedagogues.

- grundlegende Anleitung zum Komponieren und Spielen von Musik geben (Musikschulen und Musikfachschulen),
- Vorbereitung auf ein Musikstudium (Musikfachschulen),
- Ausbildung in Musikberufen (Konservatorien).

Neben dem individuellen Instrumentalunterricht werden die Schüler in Gehörbildung, Musiklehre/ -theorie, Musikkunde, Generalbaß- und Ensemblespiel unterwiesen und haben zahlreiche weitere Ergänzungsfächer zur Auswahl.

Von der Höhe der öffentlichen Zuschüsse hängt ganz entscheidend die Zahl der Schüler an diesen Einrichtungen ab. Über 80% der im finnischen Musikschulverband zusammengeschlossenen Institute erhalten einen gesetzlich festgelegten staatlichen Zuschuß. Die Kosten verteilen sich zu 40–45% auf den gesetzlichen staatlichen Zuschuß, zu 40–50% auf kommunale Zuwendungen und zu 10–20% auf Unterrichtsgebühren. Bezieht die Schule keine staatlichen Zuschüsse, erhöhen sich die Anteile der Gemeinden und der Schüler entsprechend.

In der Sibelius-Akademie, Finnlands einziger Musikhochschule mit universitärem Rang, werden sowohl Musikwissenschaftler als auch – in einer besonderen Abteilung – Musikpädagogen ausgebildet.

Menschen, die eine sorgfältige Musikerziehung genossen haben, sind sich, wo auch immer ihr

vatoires dont cinq sont membres de l'Association des écoles de musique.

Les établissement d'éducation musicale répondent à leur vocation:

- en encourageant l'écoute de la musique à une large échelle
- en dispensant une formation de base en matière d'art musical créatif et d'interprétation (niveau de l'école et du collège musical)
- en préparant les élèves aux études supérieures de musique (collège de musique)
- en dispensant une formation préparant aux différentes professions musicales (conservatoire).

Outre l'enseignement individuel de la pratique instrumentale, le programme comprend, entre autres, la formation à l'écoute, des études de solfège, de théorie musicale, de musicologie et de basse continue, la participation aux exercices de musique d'ensemble ainsi que la possibilité de choisir de nombreuses disciplines supplémentaires.

Les subventions publiques ont une influence directe sur le nombre des élèves inscrits dans les écoles de musique. Sur la totalité des écoles affiliées à l'Association, plus de 80% bénéficient d'une subvention publique établie par la loi, tant et si bien que leur financement se présente comme suit: 40 à 45% sous forme de subvention de l'Etat stipulée par la loi, 40 à 50% sous forme de soutien apporté par les collectivités locales, 10 à 20% sous forme de droits d'inscription payés par les élèves.

Dans les écoles qui ne bénéficient pas de subventions de l'Etat, la part payée par les collectivités locales et par les élèves inscrits augmente en proportion.

L'Académie «Sibelius» est la seule école supérieure de musique de niveau universitaire: c'est ici que sont formés les musicologues ainsi que, dans une section particulière, les professeurs de musique.

Les personnes qui ont bénéficié d'un enseignement musical de qualité seront toujours conscientes – quelle que soit leur fonction – de l'importance de l'art musical pour le maintien d'une certaine harmonie dans la société; tout comme il est généralement admis que les amateurs de musique exer-

Persons with a good music education will always be aware of the importance of music in a well-balanced society, irrespectively of their place and role in the community. And the positive influence of persons with an active interest in music can be felt throughout society.

France

The situation of music education in France is ambiguous. The authorities responsible for the educational system – the «Education Nationale» – do not fulfil their mission in a satisfactory way, and the Government has progressively withdrawn from this field to the cost of local authorities (regions, districts, municipalities).

Mainly on the initiative of the municipalities, a network of some 3,000 institutes specialized in music education and dance was created; the Government does not give them any noteworthy financial support but still tries to control them. The majority of these institutes – i.e. slightly more than 1,000 schools representing 75 % of the pupils – are members of the French Association of Music Schools (the FNUCMU).

Platz im Gemeinwesen ist, des Stellenwerts bewußt, den Musik für eine harmonische Gesellschaft hat. Und von Menschen mit einem aktiven Interesse an Musik gehen spürbar positive Einflüsse aus.

Frankreich

Die Situation des Musikunterrichts in Frankreich ist nicht eindeutig geklärt. Die staatliche Erziehung in Form der allgemeinen Schulbildung erfüllt ihre Verpflichtung, allen jungen Franzosen eine musikalische Grundausbildung zu vermitteln, nur unzureichend. Vielmehr hat sich der Staat seiner Verantwortung auf diesem Gebiet zunehmend zu Lasten der Gebietskörperschaften (Regionen, Départements, Gemeinden) entledigt.

Hauptsächlich auf Initiative der Gemeinden ist ein Netz von Bildungsstätten entstanden, die auf Musik- und Tanzunterricht spezialisiert sind. Sie werden nicht vom Staat bezuschußt, aber er ist bestrebt, sie zu kontrollieren. Von insgesamt etwa 3 000 dieser Einrichtungen sind mehr als 1 000, die allerdings 75 % der Schüler und Lehrer stellen, im französischen Musikschulverband, der «Fédération Nationale des Ecoles et Conservatoires Municipaux de Musique des Danse et d'Art Dramatique» (FNUCMU), zusammengeschlossen.

Das gesamte Musikschulwesen in Frankreich ist institutionell folgendermaßen gegliedert:

- höhere staatliche Konservatorien (Paris und Lyon)
- staatliche regionale Konservatorien (32)
- staatliche Musikschulen (104)
- kommunale Musikschulen (etwa 2 000)
- Musikschulen von Gemeindeverbänden (etwa 1 000), darunter auch solche überörtlicher Institutionen.

Die höheren Konservatorien, bei denen die Ausbildung zu Musikberufen liegt, werden vollständig vom Staat unterhalten. Die staatlichen regionalen Konservatorien und Musikschulen werden zu höchstens 8 % aus der Staatskasse finanziert und sind daher – entgegen ihrer offiziellen Bezeichnung – ei-

cent une influence positive notable sur leur environnement.

La France

La situation de l'enseignement musical français est ambiguë. L'éducation Nationale – l'enseignement général – ne s'acquitte pas de façon satisfaisante de cette mission et l'Etat s'est progressivement dégagé de sa responsabilité dans ce domaine au détriment des collectivités territoriales (régions, départements, communes).

A l'initiative principale des communes, il s'est donc créé un réseau d'établissements d'enseignement spécialisé de la musique et de la danse – environ 3.000 –, que l'Etat ne subventionne pratiquement pas, mais qu'il cherche à contrôler. La majorité de ces établissements – un peu plus de 1.000 mais qui représentent 75 % des élèves et des professeurs – est fédérée par la «Fédération Nationale des Ecoles et Conservatoires Municipaux de Musique des Danse et d'Art Dramatique» (la FNUCMU).

Il existe cinq catégories d'établissements:

- les conservatoires nationaux supérieurs de musique (de Paris et de Lyon)
- les conservatoires nationaux des régions (32)
- les écoles nationales de musique (104)
- les écoles municipales de musique (2.000 environ)

There are five categories of institutes:

- the national higher music conservatoires (of Paris and Lyon)
- the national conservatoires of the regions (32)
- the national music schools (104)
- the municipal music schools (approx. 2,000)
- associative music schools (some 1,000) amongst which the intermunicipal institutes.

The higher conservatoires that form the future professionals are completely state-financed; despite their designation as «national» institutions, which in fact does not correspond to reality, regional conservatoires and the national music schools are only state-subsidized up to a max. of 8 % of their operational budget. The other institutes do not receive any state-subsidies.

The teachers of the national institutes are supposed to be paid according to a salary scheme established by the Government. However, due to there statute of local civil servants, they are liable to the authority (or to the good will) of the local politicians: according to the municipality they belong to, their salaries vary considerably (specific agreements, compensation systems applied with great differences,...). Moreover, recruitment of music teachers has been totally blocked since the 1991 decree which was issued by the Government but never implemented. In addition, the statute of the teachers of municipal schools does not correspond to reality. The situation of directors and teachers is highly precarious and 80 % of the profession is threatened with dismissal. But the various solutions put forward by the FNUCMU to ease the situation seem to have been favourably received by the public authorities.

The level of inscription and school fees is fixed by the municipality in which the school or the schools are located and varies therefore considerably. Some schools are cost-free whereas others are quite expensive. And it may occur that within one and the same institute, pupils pay different fees according to their place of residence.

gentlich auch Gemeindeeinrichtungen. Alle anderen Musikschulen erhalten überhaupt keine staatliche Unterstützung.

Auch die Lehrkräfte der staatlichen Institute, die ihrem Stand gemäß nach staatlichen Richtlinien besoldet werden müßten, sind als lokale Beamte dem Einfluß der Gemeinderäte unterworfen. Hier sind, je nach Gemeinde, sehr starke Unterschiede bei den Gehältern festzustellen (Sonderverträge, erheblich differierende Vergütungsregelungen). Außerdem besteht ein völliger Einstellungsstop seit den Dekreten, die der Staat 1991 erlassen, aber immer noch nicht umzusetzen begonnen hat. Die Stellung des Lehrpersonals der kommunalen Musikschulen ist ebenfalls nicht mehr den Realitäten angemessen. Die Situation der Direktoren und Lehrkräfte ist äußerst unsicher, und zur Stunde sind 80 % des Berufsstandes von Entlassung bedroht. Doch verschiedene von der FNUCMU vorgeschlagene Konzepte zur Lösung der verfahrenen Situation werden von den Behörden mit positivem Echo aufgenommen.

■ les écoles de musique associatives (environ 1.000) parmi lesquelles des établissements intercommunaux.

L'Etat finance entièrement les conservatoires supérieurs qui forment les futurs professionnels; il ne finance les conservatoires nationaux et écoles nationales de musique qu'à hauteur de 8% au maximum de leur budget de fonctionnement, malgré l'appellation «nationale» qui ne correspond guère à la réalité. Il ne finance pas du tout les autres établissements.

Les professeurs des établissements nationaux sont censés être rémunérés selon une grille indiciaire fixée par l'Etat. Cependant leur statut de fonctionnaires territoriaux les soumet à l'autorité (ou au bon vouloir) des élus locaux et on trouve une très grand disparité dans les traitements (contrats spécifiques, régime indemnitaire appliqué avec de grandes différences,...) selon la localité qui les emploie. Il faut ajouter que les recrutements de professeurs sont complètement bloqués depuis les décrets de 1991 que l'Etat a promulgué et qu'il n'arrive pourtant pas à appliquer. De plus, les enseignants dans les écoles municipales n'ont plus de statut correspondant à la réalité. La situation des directeurs et des professeurs est donc très précaire, et, actuellement, 80% de la profession sont menacés de licenciement. Mais, les différentes solutions avancées par la FNUCMU pour débloquer la situation semblent rencontrer un écho favorable de la part des pouvoirs publics.

Le montant des droits d'accès et des frais de scolarité est fixé par chaque commune siège d'une école de musique et est donc très disparate. Ces tarifs peuvent aller de la gratuité totale à des sommes tout à fait considérables. Il peuvent varier dans un même établissement selon le lieu de résidence des élèves.

L'absence de véritable direction de l'Etat dans la conduite de l'enseignement musical conduit à des situations particulières très diversifiées. Aussi, depuis 1991, l'Etat veut-il imposer un texte normatif

The absence of any state guidance with regard to the way music education is run has led to quite variegated situations. Since 1991, the Government has attempted to impose regulations – a so-called master plan – in order to strenghten its pedagogical control. But not only do the contents of the regulations meet with a poor reception by the profession, they are moreover supposed to apply to all insitutes, irrespectively of their diversity. Since overall state-subsidies for the specialized music education sector (the music schools) are limited to 8%, it is difficult to implement the regulations which might in addition lead to a dispersion of the teaching.

The FNUCMU is the only organization which ensures a really homogenous structure of the French music education, whilst giving its member schools the freedom they need to foster their pupils' self realization through music in an original and valuable way.

Germany

In Germany, there are some 1,000 music schools with approx. one million pupils. The network of music schools has strongly developed over the recent decades.

The Federal Länder are responsible for providing the overall conditions for the work of the music schools. But so far, only two Länder, Baden-Württemberg and Bavaria, made legal provisions with regard to the structure, the requirements and the financing of these schools.

Two-thirds of the music schools depend on municipalities and one-third on non-profit making organizations. The main part of the music schools' finances (some 60%) come from public, mainly municipal budgets as well as from student fees which vary according to the school and to the type of teaching.

An Association of Music Schools for the Young and for Everyone (Verband der Jugend- und Volksmusikschulen) was created in 1952 to develop music schools and to defend their interests. In 1966, the name of the association was changed into Association of German Music Schools (Verband deutscher Musikschulen – VdM). To be a member of the association, a music school will have to function as an institution of public utility and to comply with

Auch die Beitritts- und Unterrichtsgebühren werden von jeder Gemeinde individuell festgelegt und weichen sehr voneinander ab: Sie können von völliger Gebührenfreiheit bis zu einer erheblichen Summe reichen und sogar innerhalb einer Einrichtung je nach Wohnort des Schülers variieren.

Das Fehlen einer wirklichen staatlichen Leitung in der Ausrichtung der Musikerziehung führt zu im einzelnen sehr unterschiedlichen Situationen. Zudem will der Staat seit 1991 einen sogenannten «Richtlinienplan» durchsetzen, um seine pädagogische Vormundschaft zu behaupten. Jedoch findet der Inhalt dieses Papiers nicht die Zustimmung des Berufsstands; außerdem beansprucht es Geltung für die Gesamtheit der Musikschulen, wie unterschiedlich sie auch sein mögen. Die Bestimmungen sind nicht zuletzt schwer umzusetzen, da sich die staatliche finanzielle Beteiligung in den erwähnten 8% für den gesamten auf Musik spezialisierten Bildungssektor erschöpft. Eine Gefährdung des Unterrichts wäre die Folge.

Tatsächlich ist die FNUCMU die einzige Organisation, die eine wirklich einheitliche Struktur des französischen Musikschulwesens sicherstellt und dabei gleichzeitig den ihr angehörenden Musikschulen jene Freiheiten gewährt, die für eine echte und individuelle musikalische Entfaltung von entsprechender Qualität nötig sind.

Deutschland

Es gibt in Deutschland momentan über 1 000 Musikschulen, in denen insgesamt rund 1 Million Schüler unterrichtet werden. In den vergangenen Jahrzehnten wurde das Musikschulnetz systematisch ausgebaut, um ein möglichst flächendeckendes, bevölkerungsnahes Angebot an Musikschulen bereitzustellen.

In Deutschland, wo für die Rahmenbedingungen der Musikschularbeit die Bundesländer zuständig sind, gibt es gegenwärtig nur in Baden-Württemberg und Bayern gesetzliche Bestimmungen zu Struktur, Anforderungen und Landesfinanzierung. Etwa zwei Drittel der Musikschulen sind in kommunaler Rechtsträgerschaft, die anderen werden von gemeinnützigen Vereinen getragen. Die Finanzierung erfolgt zum größeren Teil durch öffentliche, überwiegend kommunale Mittel (im Gesamt-

– appelé schéma directeur – pour renforcer sa tutelle pédagogique. Or, le contenu de ce texte ne rencontre pas l'adhésion de la profession et il prétend, de plus, s'appliquer à l'ensemble des établissements, quelle que soit leur diversité. L'Etat ne donnant pas de financements si ce n'est pour une part de 8% du total du secteur de l'enseignement musical spécialisé (les écoles de musique), ce texte ne s'applique que difficilement et risque de créer un émiettement des enseignements.

De fait, la FNUCMU se retrouve la seule organisation qui assure une véritable structure homogène de l'enseignement musical français, tout en laissant à ses écoles adhérentes la liberté nécessaire à un épanouissement musical original et de qualité.

L'Allemagne

L'Allemagne compte plus de 1.000 écoles de musique fréquentées par plus d'un million d'élèves. Au cours des dernières années, le réseau des écoles de musique a été systématiquement développé pour permettre à tous les habitants d'avoir accès à des écoles de musiques de proximité.

Les conditions générales de fonctionnement des écoles de musique relèvent de la compétence des Länder. Seuls les Länder du Baden-Würtemberg et de Bavière ont introduit des dispositions juridiques pour règlementer les structures, les responsabilités et le financement de ces écoles.

Deux tiers, environ, des écoles de musique dépendent juridiquement des collectivités locales et un tiers d'associations reconnues d'utilité publique. Le financement des activités des écoles de musique est assuré en majeure partie par des fonds municipaux (en moyenne 60%) et par les droits d'inscription dont le montant varie selon les écoles et le type d'enseignement dispensé.

La défense des intérêts et le développement des écoles de musique relèvent d'une association créée en 1952 sous le nom de «Verband der Jugend- und Volksmusikschulen» (Association des écoles de musique pour les jeunes et chacun) et devenue en 1966 l'Association des écoles de musique allemandes («Verband deutscher Musikschulen» VdM). L'Association regroupe des écoles de musique qui opèrent comme établissements d'utilité publique et qui répondent à un certain nombre de critères. Elle

certain criteria: for instance, member schools do have to apply the structural plan adopted by the association, as well as the periodically revised range of syllabuses for the various subjects.

The structural plan describes the aims and tasks of music schools as follows: «Music schools are institutions devoted to the education of children, young people and adults. Their tasks include providing basic music training, training up-and-coming musicians for amateur and non-professional music practice, identifying and promoting the specially gifted as well as preparing them, as the case may be, for professional studies.»

As a rule, the instruction offered by music schools includes four levels. The basic level can start at preschool age with a precocious music education. The next level includes at least one main (instrumental of vocal) subject and one ensemble/complementary subject. Depending on the subject and the level, the instruction is provided in classes, groups or individual lessons. The educational goals and contents follow the framework syllabus of the association. The passage from the inferior to the middle and from the middle to the upper level is subject to a successfully passed exam. An additional «preparatory instruction for higher studies» is foreseen for those pupils who wish to dedicate themselves to music studies or for particularly gifted pupils.

The music school teachers have generally graduated from higher music schools with a special training for music teachers. There is a wide range of possibilities for recurrent and further education, part of which is also supported by the Music School Association. Since 1987, music school teachers are covered by a special collective agreement within the civil service.

The German Music School Association has taken numerous initiatives, which significantly influenced the contents of the music school activities:

- The «Curriculum for Early Music Training» had a decisive impact on the work with preschool children and serves as a model for a great number of music schools in other countries.

- As a result of a pilot programme carried out by the Association of German Music Schools en-

durchschnitt etwa 60%) sowie durch die von den Teilnehmern aufzubringenden Gebühren, die je nach Musikschule und Unterrichtsform verschieden hoch sein können.

Um die Interessen der Musikschulen wahrzunehmen und ihren Ausbau zu fördern, wurde 1952 der «Verband der Jugend- und Volksmusikschulen» gegründet, der sich seit 1966 «Verband deutscher Musikschulen» (VdM) nennt. Ihm gehören Musikschulen an, die als gemeinnützige Einrichtungen arbeiten und bestimmten Anforderungen entsprechen. So erarbeitete der VdM einen verbindlichen Strukturplan und verabschiedete für die meisten Unterrichtsfächer Rahmenlehrpläne, die regelmäßig aktualisiert werden.

Ziele und Aufgaben der Musikschulen werden im Strukturplan wie folgt umrissen: «Musikschulen sind Bildungseinrichtungen für Kinder, Jugendliche und Erwachsene. Ihre Aufgaben sind die musikalische Grundausbildung, die Heranbildung des Nachwuchses für das Laien- und Liebhabermusi-

a élaboré un plan structurel à caractère contraignant et adopté, pour la plupart des disciplines enseignées, des programmes cadre qui font l'objet d'une révision périodique.

Le plan structurel définit les objectifs et la mission des écoles de musique dans les termes suivants: «Les écoles de musique sont des établissements de formation s'adressant aux enfants, aux adolescents et aux adultes. Elles ont pour vocation de dispenser une formation musicale de base, de former de futurs musiciens non professionnels ou amateurs, d'encourager la découverte et promotion des talents, et de préparer, le cas échéant, à une formation professionnelle».

L'enseignement comporte quatre niveaux. Une éducation musicale précoce dispensée au niveau élémentaire qui peut débuter à l'âge préscolaire. Le prochain niveau comporte au moins une matière principale (instrument ou chant) et une matière d'ensemble/complémentaire. En fonction de la matière enseignée et du niveau, l'enseignement se fera

titled «Teaching the Disabled to play musical instruments», approx. one quarter of the schools
offer special courses for disabled children,
youngsters and adults.

- More and more music schools show interest in
non traditional instruments and styles, offer
interdisciplinary subjects such as dance and
music theater, and introduce other non-musical
cultural subjects such as dramatic arts, plastic
arts, photo, cinema and video.

- In future, music schools will be paying special
attention to the active participation of adults.
For this purpose, practical instructions have
been worked out and published for a series of
subjects.

zieren, die Begabtenfindung und -förderung sowie die eventuelle Vorbereitung auf ein Berufsstudium.»

Der Unterricht an der Musikschule ist in vier Stufen gegliedert. In der Grundstufe kann bereits im Kindergartenalter mit der «Musikalischen Früherziehung» begonnen werden. Daran schließt sich ein Unterricht in mindestens einem Hauptfach (vokal/instrumental) und einem Ensemble/Ergänzungsfach an. Er wird je nach Fach und Stufe als Klassen-, Gruppen- oder Einzelunterricht erteilt. Die jeweiligen Lernziele und Inhalte orientieren sich am Lehrplanwerk des VdM. Der Ausbildungsweg gliedert sich in Unter-, Mittel- und Oberstufe; jeweils am Stufenübergang sind Leistungsüberprüfungen vorgesehen. Der Vorbereitung auf ein beabsichtigtes Musikstudium bzw. der Förderung besonders begabter Schüler dient die «Studienvorbereitende Ausbildung».

Die berufliche Qualifikation der Lehrkräfte an Musikschulen erfolgt in der Regel durch ein Studium an einer Musikhochschule in besonderen Studiengängen für Musikschullehrer, das mit einem Diplom abgeschlossen wird. Es existiert ein breit gefächertes Angebot zur Fortbildung und Weiterqualifikation, zu dem auch der VdM beiträgt. Seit 1987 gibt es für Lehrer an Musikschulen einen speziellen Tarifvertrag im öffentlichen Dienst.

Der Verband deutscher Musikschulen hat zahlreiche Initiativen ergriffen, die die inhaltliche Arbeit der Musikschulen wesentlich beeinflußten:

- Das «Curriculum Musikalische Früherziehung» war wegweisend für die Musikschularbeit mit Vorschulkindern und wurde auch von vielen Musikschulen außerhalb Deutschlands übernommen.
- Aufgrund eines Modellversuchs «Instrumentalspiel mit Behinderten» wird zur Zeit an etwa einem Viertel der Musikschulen ein spezieller Instrumentalunterricht für behinderte Kinder und Jugendliche erteilt.
- Immer mehr Musikschulen öffnen sich den nicht-traditionellen Instrumenten und Musikstilen, machen fächerübergreifende Angebote wie Tanz oder Musiktheater und richten nicht-musikorientierte künstlerische Sparten wie darstellendes Spiel oder bildnerisches Gestalten/Foto/Film/Video ein.

soit en classe, soit en groupe ou encore par cours individuel. Les objectifs et contenus des enseignements suivent les orientation définies dans le programme cadre de l'Association des écoles de musique. Le passage du niveau inférieur au niveau moyen et, ensuite, au niveau supérieur est assujetti à un examen. Une formation préparatoire aux études musicales («studienvorbereitende Ausbildung») est réservée aux élèves souhaitant suivre des études supérieures de musique ainsi qu'aux élèves particulièrement doués.

Les enseignants des écoles de musique sont, en général, des diplômés d'écoles supérieures de musique où ils ont suivi une formation spéciale pour enseignants. Les possibilités de formation complémentaire sont multiples et en partie également soutenues par l'Association des écoles de musique. Depuis 1987, le personnel enseignant des écoles de musique bénéficie d'un contrat collectif particulier dans le cadre de la fonction publique.

L'Association des écoles de musique allemandes a pris de nombreuses initiatives qui ont marqué de façon sensible le contenu des enseignements des écoles de musique:

- le «Cursus d'éducation musicale précoce» a été déterminant pour le travail musical destiné aux enfants en âge préscolaire; il a été repris par de nombreuses écoles dans d'autres pays.

- Sur la base du projet pilote «Jeu instrumental avec jeunes handicapés», un quart environ des écoles de musique offrent aux enfants et adolescents souffrant d'un handicap des cours de musique instrumentale spécialement conçus pour eux;

- De plus en plus d'écoles de musique enseignent la pratique d'instruments et de styles non traditionnels, proposent des disciplines relevant d'autres secteurs comme par exemple, la danse, le théâtre musical et créent d'autres branches artistiques tels l'art dramatique, les arts plastiques, la photo, le cinéma, la vidéo etc.

- Enfin, les écoles de musique accorderont à l'avenir une attention toute particulière à la participation active des «adultes»; l'Association des écoles de musique a publié à cet effet des instructions pratiques pour diverses disciplines.

Greece

At the moment, there is no current report available.

Hungary

In 1950, there were only 32 mostly private music schools in Hungary. 1951 marked the starting point of a dynamic development with the creation of a national network of music schools. The impetus came probably from the new music education system invented by Kodaly, but also from an accelerated urbanization: In 1950, approx. 9,000 children followed music education in Hungary, in 1960 they were 32,000, in 1970 their number had increased to 48,000 and now, they are some 95,000. Presently there are 231 music schools in Hungary.

Music education has two objectives: to teach as many children as possible how to play an instrument and to prepare the most talented pupils for a musical career. The education follows a three-level system:

- basic teaching in music schools,
- secondary education in specialized secondary schools with extended music education (for future professionals),
- higher education in academies or in universities.

The syllabus, the regulations and the teaching material had difficulties to keep pace with the rapid development of the music schools and with the new teaching system. With regard to the traditional school system, music schools only used to be consi-

- Musikschulen werden künftig systematischer als bisher Erwachsene in ihre Arbeit einbeziehen; hierzu hat der VdM «Handreichungen» für verschiedene Fächer erarbeitet und veröffentlicht.

Griechenland

Es liegt im Moment kein aktueller Bericht vor.

Ungarn

Vor 1950 gab es in Ungarn insgesamt 32 überwiegend private Musikschulen. Doch 1951 begann eine dynamische Entwicklung des Aufbaus eines landesweiten Musikschulnetzes. Der Impuls hierzu ging wohl einerseits von dem neuen musikpädagogischen System Zoltan Kodálys aus, andererseits von der rasch zunehmenden Verstädterung der ungarischen Gesellschaft. Gab es 1950 in Ungarn etwa 9 000 Musikschüler, so waren es 1960 schon 32 000, sodann 1970 schon 48 000 und neuerdings rund 95 000. Momentan gibt es in Ungarn 231 Musikschulen.

Ziel der musikalischen Ausbildung ist es einerseits, einer immer größer werdenden Zahl von Kindern das Spiel auf einem Instrument beizubringen, andererseits gilt es, die Begabtesten auf eine Musikerlaufbahn vorzubereiten. Die Musikerziehung ist als ein dreistufiges System gegliedert:

- Die grundlegende Ausbildung erfolgt in den Musikschulen.
- Die weitere Ausbildung übernehmen spezialisierte Sekundarschulen (das sind Schulen mit erweitertem Musikunterricht) für künftige Berufsmusiker.
- Die höhere Ausbildung leisten Akademien und Hochschulen.

Das Unterrichtsprogramm, die Erstellung von Richtlinien und die Dokumentation haben mit der Ausbreitung und Entwicklung des Musikschulwesens kaum Schritt gehalten. Im Unterschied zum allgemeinen Bildungswesen galt die Arbeit der Musikschulen nur als eine Art Fachkursus. Die ersten gesonderten Bestimmungen für Musikschulen wurden 1980 erlassen, 1981 folgte das integrierte Bildungsprogramm. 1985 wurden die Musikschulen durch das neue Erziehungsgesetz dann in das allgemeine Bildungssystem eingegliedert.

Grèce

Pas de rapport disponible pour l'instant.

La Hongrie

Jusqu'en 1950, il n'existait en Hongrie que 32 écoles de musique dont la plupart étaient privées. L'année 1951 marqua le départ d'un nouveau dynamisme avec la mise en place d'un réseau national d'écoles de musique. Le nouveau système d'enseignement musical mis au point par Kodàly y fut certainement pour beaucoup, de même que l'accélération de l'urbanisation. Alors qu'en 1950, quelques 9.000 jeunes seulement suivaient un enseignement musical, leur chiffre passa en 1960 à 32.000 pour atteindre 48.000 en 1970; aujourd'hui, la Hongrie compte environ 95.000 élèves et 231 écoles de musique.

L'objectif que poursuit l'enseignement musical est double: il s'agit d' enseigner la pratique d'un in-

strument à autant d'élèves que possible et de préparer les plus doués à une carrière musicale. La formation comporte trois étapes:

- un enseignement de base dispensé par les écoles de musique,
- suivi d'une formation dans des écoles secondaires spécialisées qui préparent les futurs professionnels
- et enfin, une formation supérieure dispensée par les académies ou universités.

Alors que le système d'enseignement musical s'est développé à une vitesse impressionnante, l'élaboration du programme d'instruction et de la

dered as a sort of specialized courses. The first separate regulations on music schools were issued in 1980, while the integrated educational programme was elaborated in 1981. It was only in 1985 that the new Education Bill integrated the music schools into the general educational system.

Although music education could come up with outstanding results and met general recognition, it was only in the nineties with the creation of the Hungarian Federation of Music Schools (HFMS) and following cooperation with the trade union for music and dance that music schools were given their rightful place. The basic concept of HFMS is that music education is an organic part of the general educational system with a specific fundamental task. The concept is clearly formulated in the 1993 law on education: this is of great importance since the Government is responsible for the basic education and undertakes its financing.

The financing system has been operating since 1991 under a well-defined system of standards. The State allocates grants to local authorities in accordance with the school type and the number of pupils. Since governmental subsidies are not sufficient to cover all the costs, local authorities cover up to 30–40% from their own budget, which means that public subsidies adapt to the effective needs. Parental contributions have so far been only symbolic and were raised from 1% to 5% in 1994. A third source of support includes various foundations and subventions for specific objectives (e.g. competitions).

The HFMS was founded in 1990 mainly because no subsidies for music education had been foreseen in the State budget. An appropriate declaration of principles was signed by 57 music schools at the inaugural meeting. The development of HFMS shows an ever-increasing number of member schools: They are now 270, including the primary schools with a special music branch and the specialized secondary schools. The tasks of HFMS cover everything from the elaboration of fundamental guidelines and material (presently, 22

Trotz der außergewöhnlichen und allgemein anerkannten Erfolge, mit denen die Musikschulen aufwarten konnten, wurde ihnen erst nach der Gründung des ungarischen Musikschulverbands (HFMS) und der Zusammenarbeit mit der Gewerkschaft für Musik- und Tanzkunst in den 90er Jahren der ihnen gebührende Platz eingeräumt. Der Verband ist der Auffassung, daß Musikunterricht Bestandteil der allgemeinen Erziehung ist, und zwar als organischer Teil der Grundbildung. Diese Konzeption ist in dem neuen Gesetz über Bildung und Erziehung von 1993 klar formuliert. Dies ist wesentlich, da der Staat die Grundbildung trägt und finanziert.

Seit 1991 erfolgt die Finanzierung der Musikschulen in einem eindeutigen rechtlichen Rahmen: Der Staat sichert den kommunalen Behörden je nach Schultyp und Anzahl der Schüler entsprechende Mittel zu. Da diese nicht ausreichen, übernehmen die Kommunen einen Anteil an der Kostendeckung von 30–40%. Die Zuschüsse der öffentlichen Hand erfolgen also entsprechend den tatsächlichen Erfordernissen. Die Elternbeiträge, die sich 1994 von 1% auf 5% erhöhten, haben eher symbolischen Charakter. Eine weitere Finanzierungsquelle sind verschiedene Stiftungen und Beihilfen aus zweckgebundenen Zuwendungen (Wettbewerbe).

Der ungarische Musikschulverband HFMS wurde 1990 hauptsächlich deswegen gegründet, weil im Staatshaushalt die Finanzierung der Musikschulen damals nicht vorgesehen war. Auf der Gründungsversammlung wurde eine entsprechende Resolution von 57 Musikschulen unterzeichnet. Der zunehmende Erfolg der Arbeit des HFMS spiegelt sich in der wachsenden Zahl der Mitgliedsschulen:

Zur Zeit sind es 270 Musikschulen sowie Grundschulen mit musikalischem Fachzweig und spezialisierte Sekundarschulen. Der HFMS erarbeitet fachliche Perspektiven und Material – zur Zeit arbeiten 22 Arbeitsgruppen an den Lehrplänen der verschiedenen Fächer –, er organisiert Festspiele und Wettbewerbe und vertritt die Interessen der Musikschulen. Da es im Erziehungsministerium und im «Institut für öffentliche Erziehung» keinen Referenten für Musikerziehung gibt, ist diese Orga-

documentation appropriée ainsi que la mise en place d'un règlement n'ont pas suivi au même rythme. Au regard du système d'enseignement général, la formation musicale n'était rien d'autre qu'une simple série de cours spécialisés. Les premiers règlements spécifiques concernant l'enseignement musical ne virent le jour qu'en 1980; le programme intégré d'instruction suivit en 1981. En 1985 enfin, les écoles de musique furent intégrées au système d'enseignement général.

Le travail des écoles de musique était remarquable et largement reconnu. Et pourtant, ce ne fut qu'à partir des années 90 avec la constitution de l'Association hongroise des écoles de musique (HFMS) et grâce à la collaboration avec le Syndicat de l'art musical et de la danse que les écoles de musique trouvèrent leur place légitime dans l'enseignement général. Pour l'Association, l'éducation

musicale doit faire partie intégrante et organique du système éducatif général. Ce principe fondamental a trouvé son expression dans la nouvelle loi sur l'enseignement général, adoptée en 1993, qui confère à l'Etat la responsabilité pour la formation de base et pour son financement.

Le système actuel de financement qui est en cours depuis 1991, fonctionne dans un cadre juridique bien déterminé. L'administration centrale met à la disposition des collectivités locales une enveloppe dont le montant est fixé en fonction du type d'école et du nombre d'élèves. Cette contribution ne couvre cependant pas la totalité des dépenses, et les collectivités locales supportent de leur côté environ 30–40% des frais. Les subventions publiques

working teams are busy with the preparation of the syllabuses for the various subject matters), to the organization of festivals and competitions and the defence of professional interests. Since there are no referees for music education at the Ministry of Education or at the «Institute for public education», this form of association is particularly important. The creation of regional and county organizations is under way.

Iceland

The history of music schools in Iceland does not reach far back. The first music school in Iceland was founded in 1930 in Reykjavik by some young musicians led by an organist who had studied music in Germany. For a long time, the music school in Reykjavik was the only one in the country, and it was not until 1945 that the next school was established in the north of the country; additional schools followed over the years.

In 1963 the Parliament passed the first law on music education. According to this law, the Icelandic Government was to support the music schools financially to the extent of one third of the teachers' wages. School fees should cover one third of the costs and the District authorities another third. This legislation led to an increase in the number of music schools. In 1975 the legislation was improved. State support was extended to half of the teachers' wages and the District authorities were to pay the other half. The fees were to be used for other purposes such as accomodation, instruments, teaching equipment etc. In 1990 an additional Act was passed which ruled that music schools had to be entirely financed by the District authorities.

Today, there are 74 music schools in Iceland with some 11,000 students and 600 teachers. Much has been done within the schools to strengthen the school system and the quality of work. Syllabuses were published and a post of consultant, solely in charge of music education, was created within the Ministry of Education. In 1990, the Ministry appointed a committee to supervise the fonctioning of the schools as well as all pedagogical aspects. The committee decides under which conditions a music school can qualify for official recognition and it takes the examinations for the various degrees. It

nisation von besonderer Bedeutung. Auch die Gründung regionaler Musikschulverbände ist im Gange.

Island

Die Geschichte des Musikschulwesens in Island ist kaum sehr lang. 1930 wurde die erste Musikschule des Landes in Reykjavik von einigen jungen Musikern gegründet und von einem Organisten geleitet, der in Deutschland studiert hatte. Sie blieb lange Zeit die einzige Musikschule Islands, bis 1945 im Norden des Landes eine weitere eingerichtet wurde und in den folgenden Jahrzehnten weitere hinzukamen.

1963 wurde das erste Gesetz über Musikerziehung verabschiedet. Es bestimmte, daß der Staat die Musikschulen in Höhe eines Drittels der Personalkosten bezuschussen sollte, während die Unterrichtsgebühren ein Drittel nicht überschreiten durften und der Rest von den Bezirksbehörden übernommen wurde. Damals stieg die Zahl der Musikschulen rasch an, eine Entwicklung, die 1975 durch eine Verbesserung der gesetzlichen Bestimmungen weiteren Auftrieb erhielt: Der Staat und die Bezirksbehörden übernahmen nun jeweils die Hälfte der Lehrergehälter, und die Schulen konnten die Unterrichtsgebühren für andere Zwecke verwenden, etwa Unterbringung, Instrumente und Unterrichtsmittel. Seit 1990 schließlich bestimmt ein Gesetz, daß die Musikschulen vollständig von den Bezirksbehörden finanziert werden.

Island hat heute 74 Musikschulen mit rund 11 000 Schülern und 600 Lehrkräften. Es wurde eine Menge Entwicklungsarbeit geleistet, um das Musikschulwesen aufzubauen und die Qualität des Unterrichts zu steigern. So wurden zum Beispiel Lehrpläne veröffentlicht, und im Erziehungsministerium wurde die Position eines ausschließlich für die Musikerziehung zuständigen Referenten geschaffen. Das Ministerium setzte 1990 ein Komitee zur Kontrolle der Musikschulverwaltungen und zur Aufsicht über den Unterricht ein. Dieses entscheidet über die Voraussetzungen für die Anerkennung von Musikschulen und über die Bedingungen für die internen Prüfungen. Es fungiert als Berater des Ministers in allen relevanten Angelegenheiten einschließlich der Ausbildung von Musiklehrern. Unter Federführung des Komitees wird zur Zeit ein

s'adaptent donc aux besoins réels. La contribution des parents qui est passée en 1994 de 1% à 5%, est pour l'instant toujours symbolique. Les différentes fondations et les subventions destinées à des objectifs spécifiques (p. ex. concours) constituent une troisième source de financement

L'une des raisons principales à l'origine de la création de l'Association hongroise des écoles de musique en 1990 a précisément été la non-inscription au budget de subventions pour les écoles de musique: 57 écoles de musique on alors signé à l'occasion de l'Assemblée constitutive une déclaration de principe à cet effet. La HFMS a connu un succès remarquable: le nombre de ses adhérents n'a cessé d'augmenter, et aujourd'hui, 270 écoles de musique (y compris les écoles élémentaires à orientation musicale et les écoles secondaires spécialisées) sont fédérées dans l'Association. La HFMS élabore les orientations et le matériel d'enseignement (22 groupes de travail se penchent, en ce moment, sur l'élaboration de programmes cadre pour les diverses matières); elle organise des festivals et concours et se charge de la défense des intérêts de ses membres. En l'absence d'un représentant compétent en matière d'enseignement musical au sein du Ministère de l'éducation et de «l'Institut pour l'enseignement public», l'existence de la HFMS revêt une signification toute particulière. La mise en place d'associations régionales est en bonne voie.

L'Islande

L'histoire des écoles de musique d'Islande ne remonte pas bien loin. La première école de musique fut créée en 1930 à Reykjavik par quelques jeunes musiciens menés par un organiste qui avait fait ses études de musique en Allemagne. Cette école fut pendant des années la seule dans tout le pays et ce ne fut qu'en 1945 qu'une deuxième école fut installée au nord du pays. D'autres écoles suivirent au cours des années.

En 1963, le Parlement adopta une première loi sur l'enseignement de la musique. En vertu de cette loi, l'Etat devait subventionner les écoles de musique jusqu'à hauteur d'un tiers des rémunérations des professeurs. Les droits d'inscriptions étaient

acts as an advisor to the Ministry of Education on all relevant matters including the music teacher training. A subcommittee is preparing a general syllabus to be published in spring 1995.

Italy

Music education and the traning of professionals in Italy lags undoubtedly behind. There are various reasons to this, most of them linked to the country's cultural history and to the structure of the Italian society. For a long time, music education has been restricted to the sole public conservatoires, i.e. to the professional aspect; these conservatoires have old-fashioned structures and have been for several years in a severe crisis.

The Government persists nevertheless in considering the 80 conservatoires and similar institutes as the one and only place for music education. Still, over the last decades, things have changed following the introduction of compulsory music education in primary and lower secondary schools. But there is yet no overall plan.

However, under the pressure of an increasing demand from the population, music schools, run by municipalities or cultural associations, started appearing throughout the country. But they are having a hard time: having never been planned, they are not subsidized; they lack finances, their structures are not organized and they are not always in a position to respond to the increasing demand for music education.

With a view to giving guidance to this growing number of schools and to ensuring a minimum of coordination of their activities, an Italian Association of Music Schools (AISM) was created in 1985 under the initiative of the Experimental Research Center for Music Pedagogics in Fiesole and of ten music schools from various Italian regions. Today, 60 music schools have joined the Association which develops an impressive activity organizing seminars, symposia, discussions and events such as the annual «Giornale di musica», and fostering exchanges between teachers and pupils; not to forget the Association's participation in the «European Youth Music Festival» and in international meetings and its membership with the European Union of Music Schools.

Rahmenlehrplan ausgearbeitet, der Anfang 1995 herausgegeben werden soll.

Italien

Es ist nicht zu leugnen, daß Italien hinsichtlich der Musikerziehung und der Musikerausbildung in einem gewissen Rückstand ist. Die Ursachen sind vielschichtig; sie reichen weit in die italienische Kulturgeschichte zurück und liegen auch in der Struktur der italienischen Gesellschaft begründet. Die musikalische Ausbildung beschränkte sich lange auf die staatlichen Konservatorien, also den professionellen Bereich, und selbst hier befinden sich die ziemlich veralteten Strukturen seit einiger Zeit in einer Krise. Gleichwohl betrachtet der Staat weiterhin nur die rund 80 Konservatorien und gleichgestellte Institute als alleinige Stätten der Musikausbildung. In den letzten Jahrzehnten hat sich die Situation freilich – wenn auch ohne einen umfassenden Plan – insofern verändert, als Musikerziehung als Unterrichtsfach der Primar- und Sekundarstufe der Pflichtschule eingeführt wurde.

Um den verbreiteten Bedürfnissen der Bevölkerung nach musikalischer Anleitung entgegenzukommen, haben sich indes überall Musikschulen gebildet, die hauptsächlich von Gemeinden und kulturellen Vereinen getragen werden. Diese Musikschulen, unplanmäßig und ohne große finanzielle Unterstützung entstanden, führen eine schwierige Existenz und sind wegen fehlender Mittel und ungeordneter Strukturen oft nicht in der Lage, die steigende Nachfrage nach Musikunterricht zu bewältigen.

censés couvrir le deuxième tiers et les autorités départementales le dernier tiers. Cette législation fut à l'origine d'un accroissement du nombre des écoles de musique. Elle fut améliorée en 1975: le financement par l'Etat était porté à la moitié des coûts, l'autre moitié devant être assumée par les autorités départementales. Quant aux droits d'inscription, ils devaient servir à couvrir d'autres dépenses comme l'hébergement, les instruments, les équipements pédagogiques etc. Enfin, une loi adoptée en 1990 stipula que les écoles de musique devaient être entièrement financées par les autorités départementales.

Aujourd'hui, il existe en Islande 74 écoles de musique avec 11.000 élèves et 600 professeurs. Les écoles on pris de nombreuses initiatives pour renforcer le système et la qualité de l'enseignement. Des programmes ont été élaborés, et un poste de consultant uniquement chargé de l'enseignement de la musique, a été créé au Ministère de l'éducation. En 1990, le Ministère a institué une commission chargée de superviser le fonctionnement des écoles ainsi que divers aspects pédagogiques. La commission décide dans quelles conditions une école est agréée et c'est elle qui préside aux examens pour le passage entre les divers niveaux. Elle agit comme conseilleur du Ministère de l'éducation dans toutes les questions importantes, y compris la formation des professeurs. Une sous-commission prépare en ce moment un programme général qui sera publié au printemps 1995.

L'Italie

Il est incontestable que l'Italie a pris du retard dans son enseignement musical et dans la formation de ses professionnels. Les causes sont multiples et liées à l'histoire culturelle du pays ainsi qu'à la structure de la société italienne. Très longtemps, l'enseignement musical est resté limité aux seuls conservatoires publics, donc au volet professionnel, vétuste dans ses structures et depuis un moment déjà en crise. Néanmoins, l'Etat persiste à considérer les 80 conservatoires et établissements assimilés comme les seuls et uniques lieux de formation musicale. Au cours des dernières décennies, la situation a pourtant évolué, à la suite de

Since there is no governmental support, it is not easy to locate all the existing music schools (they are thought to be over one thousand, mostly in the north and in the center of the country), to contact them and to encourage them to join the AISM. Musicians and directors, often prisoners of an erroneous individualism, fear wrongly that because of their small size or the scarcity of their means, the Association might interfere with their work.

The AISM tries to gain support from the politicians for the recognition and development of the music schools on the basis of a regional planification which would be the only way to setting up successfully an appropriate network of music schools throughout the country. The first request of the AISM is to get the Government to delegate responsibility for music education and for professional training to the regions. This would allow for a legal basis to support the various individual intiatives of a few politicians and municipalities directly involved and more sensitive about the question.

As a direct consequence to the efforts of the AISM, the region of Tuscany adopted a law in 1994

Um das Wachstum der Schulen und ihre Arbeit einigermaßen zu steuern, wurde 1985 auf Initiative des Forschungs- und Experimentierzentrums für Musikdidaktik in Fiesole und von 10 Musikschulen aus verschiedenen Regionen Italiens der italienische Musikschulverband (AISM) gegründet. Schon heute gehören ihm 60 Musikschulen an. Die AISM hat in diesen Jahren eine beachtliche Aktivität entwickelt, Seminare, Symposien, Diskussionen und Veranstaltungen wie die jährlichen «Giornale di musica» durchgeführt, die dem Austausch zwischen Lehrern und Schülern der Mitgliedschulen dienen. Zu nennen sind auch die Beteiligung an den Europäischen Musikfesten der Jugend, internationale Begegnungen und nicht zuletzt der Beitritt zur Europäischen Musikschul-Union.

Aufgrund des fehlenden staatlichen Rückhalts ist es vor allem schwierig, die vorhandenen Musikschulen (wahrscheinlich an die 1 000 vorwiegend in Nord- und Mittelitalien) auszumachen, zu kontaktieren und sie zu einem Beitritt zur AISM zu bewegen. Wegen der Knappheit der Finanzmittel, der geringen Größe der Schulen und auch aufgrund eines falsch verstandenen «Individualismus» befürchten die Musiker und Musikschulleiter – zu Unrecht – ein Eingreifen in ihre Arbeit.

Die AISM richtet ihre Aufmerksamkeit daneben auch auf die politisch Verantwortlichen, um die Anerkennung und Unterstützung für die Entwicklung der Musikschulen auf Basis regionaler Planung zu erreichen. Nur durch eine solche Politik kann ein den Erfordernissen angemessenes Netz von Musikschulen in ganz Italien aufgebaut werden. Im Kern geht es der AISM darum, daß der Staat Zuständigkeiten im Bereich der musikalischen Erziehung und Ausbildung an die Regionen delegiert. Denn so könnte das, was heute mehr oder weniger als Ergebnis der Initiative einzelner Politiker oder Behörden dasteht, die solchen Forderungen offenbar offener gegenüberstehen, eine gesetzliche Grundlage erhalten.

Ein positives Signal ist jedenfalls, daß aufgrund der Bemühungen der AISM zunächst die Region Toskana 1994 ein Gesetz verabschiedet hat, das endlich die Arbeit der Musikschulen anerkennt und unterstützt. Sollten in absehbarer Zeit andere Regionen diesem Beispiel folgen, würde dies zu einer

l'introduction de l'enseignement musical obligatoire dans les écoles primaires et dans les collèges. Mais il n'y a toujours pas de plan d'ensemble.

Ceci étant, on a vu apparaître un peu partout, sous la pression d'une demande accrue de la part de la population, des écoles de musique mises en place sous l'égide de communes ou d'associations culturelles. Ces écoles de musique, nées à l'écart de toute planification et pratiquement sans subventions, n'ont pas l'existence facile: elles manquent de moyens et de structures organisées et ne sont pas toujours en mesure de répondre à l'intérêt croissant de la population pour un enseignement musical.

Afin de gérer ce nombre grandissant d'écoles et de coordonner et d'orienter tant soit peu leurs activités, une Association italienne des écoles de musique (AISM) a été créée en 1985 à l'initiative du Centre expérimental de recherches pour la pédagogie musicale de Fiesole et de dix écoles de musique de différentes régions italiennes. Aujourd'hui, l'Association fédère 60 écoles de musique. Elle a développé une activité considérable et organise des séminaires, des symposiums, des discussions et diverses manifestations, comme les annuelles «Giornale di musica» qui encouragent les échanges entre professeurs et élèves. A mentionner aussi, sa participation au Festival européen de la musique des jeunes, des rencontres internationales et surtout l'entrée dans l'Union Européenne des Ecoles de Musique.

En l'absence de tout soutien gouvernemental, il n'est pas facile de repérer toutes les écoles de musique en existence (on les estime à un millier, notamment réparties dans le nord et dans le centre de l'Italie), de les contacter et de les encourager à devenir membre de l'AISM. Les musiciens et les directeurs, enferrés dans un individualisme mal compris, craignent à tort et pour les raisons les plus diverses comme la pénurie des moyens ou la petite taille des écoles, que l'Association ne vienne s'immiscer dans leur travail.

L'AISM cherche également à gagner l'attention des responsables politiques, de manière à obtenir leur appui pour la reconnaissance et le développement des écoles de musique sur la base d'une planification régionale, condition indispensable à la

which recognizes and supports the music schools. If other regions would follow suit, this would mean a real turning point, providing a proper guarantee for music schools which they may demand to be able to fulfill the task of contributing decisively to Italy's social and cultural welfare.

Liechtenstein

The Music School of Liechtenstein was founded in 1963 as a private institution, to 50% state-subsidized, and became in 1973 a public Foundation. In 1991, the Parliament of Liechtenstein adopted a new law on Music Schools fixing the ratio for its financing (50% from the Government, 25% from local authorities and 25% from school fees) and giving the Foundation Council additional competence. The Music School of Liechtenstein is a member of the Swiss Association of Music Schools.

Since 1968, the permanent headquarters of the Music School have been located at the birthplace of the composer J.G. Rheinberger in Vaduz. In addition, music classes are offered in all eleven villages of the country.

According to the Music School Act, «the aim of the Foundation is to give instrumental and vocal instruction and to enhance music life throughout the country». To implement this objective of widening the basis, preschool music education was introduced in Kindergarden (1980), and basic music education is taught in the first two classes of elementary school (1993). At the present, 100 % of the children between 5 and 8 have early and basic music education. The central and local governments jointly bear the costs.

With regard to instrumental and vocal training, the Music School has extended its offer to all styles and areas of public and private music playing. Hence, all the instruments of the classic-romantic orchestra, all the traditional popular instruments and all keyboard instruments, including accordion and electronic keyboard, and electric guitar as well, are taught at the Music School.

Most of the lessons are individual, with the exception of the classes for certain wind instruments and of some group lessons, complementary to individual violin and cello lessons and to vocal education. The Music School supports numerous ensem-

regelrechten Wende führen: Die Musikschulen erhielten dann jene Existenzsicherung, die sie beanspruchen können, um in entscheidendem Maße zum sozialen, gesellschaftlichen und kulturellen Gedeihen Italiens beizutragen.

Liechtenstein

Die Liechtensteinische Musikschule wurde 1963 als Privatinstitut mit 50% staatlicher Unterstützung gegründet und erhielt 1973 den Status einer Stiftung des öffentlichen Rechts. 1991 hat der Liechtensteinische Landtag ein neues Musikschulgesetz erlassen, in dem die Finanzierung zu 50% durch den Staat, zu 25% durch die Gemeinden und zu 25% durch das Schulgeld festgelegt ist. Dem Stiftungsrat werden mehr Entscheidungsbefugnisse eingeräumt. Die Musikschule des Fürstentums Liechtenstein ist dem VMS («Verband Musikschulen Schweiz») angeschlossen.

Hauptsitz der Musikschule ist seit 1968 das Geburtshaus des Komponisten J. G. Rheinberger in Vaduz. Außerdem wird der Unterricht in allen elf Gemeinden Liechtensteins gegeben.

Das Musikschulgesetz formuliert als Zweck der Stiftung, «Instrumental- und Vokalunterricht zu erteilen und das musikalische Leben des Landes zu fördern». Die Zielsetzung einer breiten Basisarbeit führte dazu, die «Musikalische Früherziehung» in die Kindergärten zu integrieren (1980) und die

mise en place d'un réseau adéquat d'écoles de musique dans tout le pays. La revendication première de l'AISM est d'obtenir que l'Etat délègue la compétence pour l'enseignement musical et la formation professionnelle aux régions. Il serait alors possible d'asseoir sur une base juridique solide les initiatives individuelles de certains hommes politiques et de certaines collectivités locales, plus sensibles à cette visée.

Premier résultat positif, la région de la Toscane a adopté en 1994, à la suite des efforts de l'AISM, une loi qui apporte enfin reconnaissance et appui aux écoles de musique. Si d'autres régions pouvaient s'engager sur la même voie, ceci marquerait un véritable tournant: les écoles de musique se verraient alors attribuer cette garantie d'existence qu'elles réclament à juste titre en contrepartie de la contribution décisive qu'elles apportent au bien-être et à la croissance sociale et culturelle de la société italienne.

Le Liechtenstein

Créée en 1963 comme institution privée, subventionnée à 50% par l'Etat, l'Ecole de musique du Liechtenstein a reçu en 1973 le statut d'une fondation de droit public. Selon la nouvelle loi sur les écoles de musique, adoptée en 1991 par le Parlement du Liechtenstein, le financement de l'Ecole est assuré à 50% par l'Etat, à 25% par les communes et à 25% par les droits d'inscription. Par la même occasion, le Conseil de la Fondation s'est vu conférer des compétences accrues. L'Ecole de musique est membre de l'Association Suisse des Ecoles de Musique.

Depuis 1968, l'Ecole de musique est installée dans la maison natale du compositeur J. G. Rheinberger à Vaduz qui est son siège principal, mais les professeurs enseignent également dans les onze villages du pays.

Toujours selon la loi de 1991, l'objectif de la Fondation «est l'enseignement musical et vocal et la promotion de la vie musicale dans le pays». L'intention est de créer une très large base. Aussi, un enseignement musical précoce a-t-il été introduit dans les jardins d'enfants (1980) suivi d'un enseignement de base dispensé pendant les deux premières années de l'école primaire (1993). Grâce à

bles: string orchestras for children, a youth sinfonietta, a large school orchestra, orchestras for accordion, one Big-Band, a dance-orchestra, different Rock and Pop Groups, several folk music groups and chamber music ensembles, various song groups for children and a choir for adults.

Once a year, a national music competition is organized including several subjects for solo, chamber music, folk and amateur music, Rock, Pop and light music. As from 1971, international Master Classes have been organized every year in July with the participation of well-known artists who give high level classes to prepare the participants for solo careers, scene performance or participation in orchestras.

Teachers have the same social and job security schemes as teachers in public schools. They can be employed on the basis of long-term contracts. After ten years of teaching, they are entitled to one fully paid sabbatical semester for further training. According to the service regulations, teachers must regularly follow refresher courses and furnish yearly evidence that they have done so.

With hundreds of music events per year and in contributing music performance on various public and private occasions, the school leaves its mark

«Musikalische Grundschulung» in die ersten zwei Klassen der Primarschulen (1993). Damit werden im Alter von 5 bis 8 Jahren 100% aller Kinder erreicht. Die Kosten dafür tragen Staat und Gemeinden gemeinsam.

Im Instrumental-/Vokalunterricht faßt es die Musikschule als ihren Auftrag auf, alle Stile und Bereiche des öffentlichen und privaten Musizierens in ihr Angebot aufzunehmen. Deswegen werden alle Orchesterinstrumente, die traditionellen Volksinstrumente, alle Tasteninstrumente einschließlich Akkordeon und Keyboard sowie E-Gitarre unterrichtet.

Der Unterricht wird fast ausschließlich als Einzelunterricht erteilt. Gruppenunterricht wird teilweise bei Blasinstrumenten, manchmal zusätzlich zum Einzelunterricht für Streicher sowie in der Stimmbildung angeboten. Die Musikschule hat zahlreiche Ensembles: Kinderstreichensembles, eine Jugend-Sinfonietta, ein großes Schulorchester, Akkordeonorchester, eine Big Band, ein Tanzorchester, diverse Rock-/Popgruppen, mehrere Volksmusikgruppen, verschiedene Kammermusiken, Kindersinggruppen und einen Erwachsenenchor.

Jährlich wird ein Landesmusikwettbewerb durchgeführt, der jeweils für mehrere Solofächer, für Kammermusik, Volks- und Hausmusik sowie Rock-, Pop- und Unterhaltungsmusik ausgeschrieben ist. Seit 1971 finden jährlich internationale Meisterkurse statt, auf denen bekannte Künstler auf höchstem Niveau unterrichten, um die Teilnehmer auf eine Solo-Karriere, Orchester- oder Bühnentätigkeit vorzubereiten.

Die Lehrkräfte der Musikschule haben die gleichen sozialen Sicherheiten wie Lehrer an den öffentlichen Schulen. Sie können mit Langzeitverträgen beschäftigt werden; nach 10 Jahren kann ein Weiterbildungs-Semester bei voller Besoldung in Anspruch genommen werden. Das Dienstreglement verpflichtet alle Lehrkräfte zu regelmäßiger Weiterbildung, die jährlich nachgewiesen werden muß.

Mit Hunderten von Veranstaltungen und der musikalischen Gestaltung von öffentlichen und privaten Anlässen prägt die Musikschule das Musikleben in Liechtenstein. Mit 2 500 Schülern nehmen über 8% der Bevölkerung des Landes dieses Bil-

ce système, 100% des enfants entre 5 et 8 ans reçoivent un enseignement musical précoce et de base. Le gouvernement et les communes se partagent le coût de cette formation.

Du côté de l'enseignement instrumental et vocal, l'école propose tous les styles et domaines de la pratique musicale publique ou privée: y sont enseignés tous les instruments de l'orchestre classicoromantique, les instruments populaires traditionnels, de même que tous les instruments à touche y compris l'accordéon, le keyboard et la guitare E.

La plupart des leçons sont individuelles. Certaines leçons d'instruments à vent sont données en groupe ainsi que les cours proposés en complément des leçons individuelles de violon ou de violoncelle ou des cours de formation vocale. L'école entretient de nombreux ensembles: un ensemble d'instruments à corde pour enfants, une sinfonietta pour jeunes, un grand orchestre d'école, deux orchestres d'accordéon, un big-band, un orchestre de danse, divers groupes de rock et pop, plusieurs groupes de musique populaire et ensembles de musique de chambre, divers groupes vocaux pour enfants et une chorale pour adultes.

Tous les ans, l'école organise un concours musical national qui comporte plusieurs branches solo, de la musique de chambre, de la musique populaire et familiale ainsi que du rock et pop et de la musique de divertissement. Depuis 1971, des classes internationales de maîtrise sont organisées annuellement en été, avec la participation d'artistes internationaux de renom; les cours de haut niveau qu'ils proposent sont destinés à préparer les élèves à des carrières de solistes et à des activités scéniques ou à faciliter leur insertion dans un orchestre.

Les professeurs ont les mêmes droits sociaux que les professeurs des écoles publiques. Ils peuvent être engagés sur la base de contrats de longue durée. Après dix ans de carrière, ils peuvent prétendre à un semestre «sabbatique» avec salaire intégral, destiné à leur formation complémentaire. En vertu du règlement, tous les professeurs sont tenus à suivre des cours de formation continue et à en fournir l'attestation une fois par an.

Avec des centaines de manifestations musicales par an, l'Ecole de musique marque de son influence la vie musicale du pays. Comptant 2.500

on the country's music life. It has approx. 2,500 students which comes up to 8% of the population. From the very beginning, the Music School's philosophy was marked by the desire to introduce the country's whole population to music, starting at the very roots. Throughout the years, the school has tried to create as large as possible a soil, from which the most talented may emerge.

Luxembourg

The two main cities of the country, the capital Luxembourg, and Esch-Alzette each have their music Academy («Konservatorium»); in addition, there are eight music schools, each supported by a municipality: two of them call themselves Academies («Konservatorium»), some have branches in various towns.

The music schools have joined together to form the «Association of Music Schools of the Grand Duchy of Luxembourg» (AEM) in order to try to solve their problems jointly.

Furthermore, there is a regional music school and the music school of the «Union Grand Duc Adolphe» which is the association grouping the music and song clubs of the country. The latter has now 90 branches.

Thanks to the music schools of the AEM and to the various branches created throughout the country, everyone who wishes to learn music can do so in a place near to his/her home. In 1993, nearly 10,000 pupils were registered in music schools.

However, in consequence of this evolution the costs are rapidly increasing. It is hoped that the law on music, which has been under preparation for 16

dungsangebot wahr. Von Anfang an verfolgte die Musikschule die Philosophie einer «Musikalisierung» der Bevölkerung bis zu den Wurzeln. Bis heute wird die breitestmögliche Basis angestrebt, aus der die Spitzen in einer natürlichen Entwicklung herauswachsen.

Luxemburg

Neben den beiden Konservatorien, die die Hauptstadt Luxemburg sowie die Stadt Esch-Azette unterhalten, gibt es in Luxemburg 8 Musikschulen, die jeweils von einer Gemeinde getragen werden; zwei von ihnen nennen sich ebenfalls Konservatorium. Einige der Musikschulen haben noch weitere Zweigstellen in mehreren Ortschaften.

Die Musikschulen haben sich zu einem Dachverband, der «Association des Ecoles de Musique du Grand-Duché de Luxembourg» (AEM) zusammengeschlossen, um Probleme gemeinsam zu lösen.

Neben diesen Musikschulen gibt es eine weitere regionale Musikschule und die Musikschule der «Union Grand-Duc Adolphe», des Dachverbandes der Musik- und Gesangsvereine des Landes. Letztere hat gegenwärtig 90 Zweigstellen.

Dank der Musikschulen der AEM und der vielen über das ganze Land verteilten Zweigstellen hat jeder Interessierte die Möglichkeit, in unmittelbarer Nähe seines Wohnorts Musikunterricht zu erhalten. Fast 10 000 Schüler waren 1993 eingeschrieben.

Diese erfreuliche Entwicklung zieht allerdings eine regelrechte Explosion der Kosten nach sich. Große Hoffnungen setzt man auf das zu erwartende Musikschulgesetz, das nach mehr als 16jähriger Vorbereitungszeit vom Parlament nun bald in Kraft gesetzt werden soll. Es wird hoffentlich eine Absicherung des Musikschulunterrichts durch eine finanzielle Beteiligung des Staats bringen.

Neben den finanziellen Aspekten sieht der Gesetzentwurf Regelungen vor, die die Einrichtungen selbst sowie die Strukturen des Unterrichts und die Inspektion und Beratung in musikpädagogischen Fragen betreffen. Die Ernennung eines Kommissars soll die Koordinierung des Musikunterrichts gewährleisten. Ferner sieht das Gesetz eine Kom-

élèves, elle atteint 8% de la population. Dès ses débuts, elle s'est inspirée d'une politique visant à initier l'ensemble de la population à la musique, et ce dès le plus bas âge. Elle poursuit invariablement son objectif qui est d'élargir la base, favorisant ainsi le développement naturel des plus doués.

Le Luxembourg

La capitale, Luxembourg, ainsi que la ville Esch-sur-Alzette entretiennent chacune un conservatoire. A côté de ces deux conservatoires, le pays compte huit écoles de musique, chacune soutenue par une commune. Deux de ces établissements s'appellent d'ailleurs aussi «conservatoires». Certaines écoles ont des succursales dans d'autres localités.

Ces huit écoles de musiques se sont fédérées dans une Association, l'«Association des Ecoles de Musique du Grand-Duché de Luxembourg» (AEM), dans le but de résoudre ensemble un certain nombre de problèmes.

Il y a, en outre, une école de musique régionale ainsi que l'Ecole de Musique de «l'Union Grand-Duc Adolphe» qui regroupe tous les groupes de musique et de chant du pays. Cette école compte actuellement 90 succursales.

Grâce aux écoles de musique de l'AEM et des nombreuses succursales installées à travers l'ensemble du pays, toute personne qui le souhaite a la possibilité d'apprendre la musique à proximité de son domicile. En 1993, presque 10.000 élèves y étaient inscrits.

Ce développement tout à fait souhaitable a cependant entraîné une explosion des coûts. On espère pouvoir la maîtriser grâce à une loi sur l'enseignement musical, en préparation au Parlement depuis 16 ans et qui devrait prochainement entrer en vigueur. Il faut espérer que cette loi apporte, sous forme d'une participation financière gouvernementale, les garanties voulues pour l'enseignement musical.

Le projet de loi prévoit, par ailleurs, la réglementation des établissements et des structures de l'en-

years, should soon be approved by Parliament. According to this bill, state participation should bring an acceptable financial guarantee for music education.

In addition to these financial aspects, the bill will also deal with the institutions and structures for music education and ensure ways and means of advising and supervising the schools with regard to pedagogical questions. A commissioner will be nominated to guarantee the coordination of music education, and a commission entrusted with the preparation of a uniform syllabus for all branches. Finally, the law should allow for the adoption of a statute for all music schools teachers.

The Netherlands

There is no national law governing the music schools in the Netherlands; this makes it difficult to present a general picture of the Dutch music school system. Each local school has its own arrangements with regard to the organization and contents of the music education offered and to the financial contributions participants have to pay.

mission vor, die ein einheitliches Unterrichtsprogramm für alle Zweige des Musikunterrichts erarbeiten soll. Schließlich soll auf der Grundlage dieses Gesetzes endlich ein Statut für alle Lehrbeauftragten der Musikschulen geschaffen werden.

Niederlande

In den Niederlanden unterliegt die Arbeit der Musikschulen keinen gesetzlichen Regelungen. Ein allgemeiner Überblick über das niederländische Musikschul-System ist daher schwierig: Jede Schule bestimmt selbst, wie sie ihre Kurse organisiert, welchen Inhalt sie ihnen gibt und welchen Beitrag die Teilnehmer zu bezahlen haben. Im Durchschnitt erhalten die Musikschulen von den Gemeinden Subventionen in Höhe von 65% der Kosten.

Rund 95% der Musikschulen – das sind zur Zeit etwa 200 Schulen mit Hunderten von Zweigstellen – gehören der «Vereniging voor kunstzinnige vorming» (VKV) an, dem nationalen Verband der Amateur-Kunstschulen. Dieser fungiert als innerstaatliche Interessenvertretung der Musikschulen, als Tarifpartner für die Arbeitsbedingungen der Lehrkräfte, hat rechtsberatende Aufgaben und erarbeitet zusammen mit den Mitgliedern neue Tendenzen der Musikschularbeit. Die vom VKV angebotenen Modell-Lehrpläne werden weitgehend von den Musikschulen übernommen.

Jede Musikschule bietet für Anfänger ein 2–3jähriges Einführungsprogramm «Algemene muzikale vorming/orientatie» (AMV/AMO) an. Hier lernen die Schüler, bewußt Musik zu hören, und erhalten Informationen über alle Arten von Instrumenten, was ihre spätere Wahl erleichtern soll.

An die AMV schließt sich in der Regel ein 8jähriges Programm an, das in 4 Abschnitte gegliedert ist: Die Schüler werden in den Grundlagen der Musiklehre geschult und lernen, diese auf ihr jeweiliges Instrument anzuwenden. Über die technische Beherrschung hinaus geht es um ein Verständnis der Komposition und ihre künstlerische Interpretation. Der Instrumentalunterricht wird meist in Gruppen von 3 oder 4 Schülern erteilt. (Leider besteht aufgrund der Zuschußkürzungen die Tendenz, in immer größeren Gruppen zu arbeiten.) Bestandteil der Ausbildung ist auch das Zusammen-

seignement musical, ainsi que l'introduction d'un système permettant de superviser les écoles et de les conseiller au plan pédagogique. L'élaboration d'un programme de formation musicale uniforme pour toutes les branches de l'enseignement musical est confiée à une commission. Enfin, la loi devrait apporter un statut à toutes les personnes qui enseignent dans les écoles de musique.

Les Pays-Bas

Aux Pays-Bas, aucune loi ne régit les écoles de musique. C'est pourquoi il est difficile de présenter un aperçu général du système d'enseignement musical néerlandais. Chaque école est maîtresse de l'organisation et des contenus de l'enseignement qu'elle dispense et des droits d'inscriptions qu'elle demande à ses adhérents. En moyenne, les écoles tirent 65% de leurs recettes de subventions municipales.

Environ 95% des écoles de musique – c.a.d. à l'heure actuelle, 200 écoles avec des centaines de branches locales – sont fédérées dans la «Vereniging voor kunstzinnige Vorming» (VKV), l'Association nationale des écoles d'art pour amateurs. L'Association agit au plan national comme défenseur des intérêts des écoles d'art pour amateurs, elle conclut des accords salariaux pour les enseignants, conseille ses membres en matière juridique et élabore avec eux les nouvelles orientations du travail des écoles de musique. Les plans modèles qu'elle propose à ses membres sont largement suivis par les écoles de musique.

Chaque école de musique propose à ses débutants un programme introductif de deux ou trois ans appelé «Algemene muzikale vorming/orientatie» (AMV/AMO). Les élèves apprennent à écouter consciemment la musique et reçoivent des informations générales sur toutes sortes d'instruments, ce qui, le moment venu, facilitera leur choix.

Le AVM est suivi d'un programme d'une durée normale de 8 ans, subdivisé en quatre parties: les élèves sont formés à la théorie musicale et apprennent à appliquer ces connaissances à l'instrument de leur choix. Ils apprennent à maîtriser leur instrument et à comprendre la composition musicale de manière à pouvoir l'interpréter avec art. Les leçons d'instrument sont dispensées en groupe de

Approx. 95% of the schools – i.e. nearly 200 schools with their hundreds of local branches – adhere to the national association, «Vereniging voor kunstzinnige vorming» (VKV), the national Association of the Schools for Amateur Art. VKV acts as a national defender of the interests of the music schools, it negotiates the development of the teachers' salaries, advises its members on legal matters and develops with them new guidelines for the work of the music schools. The VKV provides its members with model-syllabuses which they follow to a large extent.

Each music school offers a two to three years programme for beginners, called «Algemene muzikale vorming/orientatie» (AMV/AMO), where pupils learn to listen to music and get general information on all sorts of instruments, so to be able to make a proper choice.

The AMV is usually followed by an eight years programme, divided into four parts: the pupils are introduced into basic music theory and learn to adjust this knowledge to a specific instrument. They are taught to master technically the instrument but also to understand the composition they are working with, in order to present an artistically valuable interpretation. The instrumental lessons take place in groups of three to four students (a number which tends to increase due to the decreasing subsidies). Making music with other pupils in an orchestra or an ensemble forms an integral part of this programme. Every second year, the progress of the pupil is tested in a more or less official way.

With regard to the actual matter of music teaching, music schools in the Netherlands operate to a large extent independently from the general school system. But in larger towns with a big population with relatively low incomes, music schools tend more and more to seek close cooperation with primary and lower secondary schools (basisscholen). As a result of this cooperation, music school teachers give AMV lessons in regular

spiel in Orchestern oder Ensembles. Alle zwei Jahre werden die Fortschritte der Schüler in mehr oder weniger offiziellen Prüfungen beurteilt.

Was den eigentlichen Musikunterricht angeht, arbeiten die Musikschulen weitgehend unabhängig von den allgemeinbildenden Schulen. Aber besonders in den großen Städten mit einem hohen Anteil von Geringerverdienenden versuchen die Musikschulen, mit den Grund- und Hauptschulen («basisscholen») enger zusammenzuarbeiten. Im Rahmen solcher Kooperationen unterrichten Musikschullehrer AMV-Stunden in der Schule, oder es kommt zu gemeinsamen befristeten Projekten. Auch beschäftigen einige Musikschulen seit jeher Berater, bei denen Schullehrer Anregungen für musikalische Aktivitäten im Unterricht bekommen können.

Die Musikschulen verstärken auch die Zusammenarbeit mit den staatlichen Konservatorien, auf denen die Berufsmusiker ausgebildet werden. Einige Musikschulen haben versuchsweise die Aufgabe übernommen, Schüler «offiziell» auf das Musikstudium vorzubereiten.

trois à quatre élèves (mais ces groupes ont, hélas, tendance à s'élargir du fait de la diminution des subventions). La pratique musicale en groupe – en orchestre ou en ensemble – fait également partie du programme. Tous les deux ans, les progrès des élèves sont testés de manière plus ou moins officielle.

En ce qui concerne l'enseignement musical en tant que tel, les écoles de musique fonctionnent plus ou moins indépendamment du système d'enseignement général. Mais, notamment dans les grandes villes à fortes populations à salaire modeste, les écoles cherchent à collaborer étroitement avec les écoles primaires et les collèges («basisscholen»): Les professeurs de musique donnent des leçons AMV dans les écoles publiques ou participent, pendant un temps limité, à des projets communs. Certaines écoles de musique emploient traditionnellement des personnes qui conseillent les instituteurs quant à la manière d'organiser des activités musicales à l'école.

La coopération entre les écoles de musique et les conservatoires publics qui préparent à la carrière professionnelle, se développe de plus en plus. A titre d'expérience, certaines écoles de musique préparent les élèves «officiellement» à une formation plus poussée.

Confrontée à une situation financière difficile, les autorités locales avancent un nouvel argument pour justifier la réduction des subventions accordées aux écoles de musique: elles posent la question de savoir si oui ou non les écoles de musique sont à considérer comme appartenant à la catégorie de ces installations de base qui doivent obligatoirement bénéficier d'un soutien public. Certaines municipalités considèrent qu'en dehors des dirigeants d'établissements, seules les leçons du type AMV devraient être subventionnées. D'autres ne veulent plus subventionner l'éducation des adultes.

C'est au vu de ces tendances que le VKV a engagé en 1993 des discussions sur l'avenir de l'enseignement artistique et musical, en poursuivant notamment deux objectifs:

schools or cooperate for a more limited time in joint projects. In some music schools, adequately trained persons advise school teachers on how to organize musical activities at school.

There is also growing cooperation between music schools and national conservatoires, i.e. the schools that prepare professional musicians. Experiments are under way whereby some music schools «officially» train those pupils who are wishing to enter these higher education establishments.

Faced with increasing financial difficulties, local governments try to justify reductions of subsidies for music schools with a new argument: they question the legitimacy of the claim of music schools to be considered as being one of those essential public facilities a local government has to maintain. Some local governments hold the view that apart from overheads of an institution, only lessons of the AMV type should continue to be subsidized. Others want to stop subsidies for adult education.

These tendencies have led VKV to initiate in 1993 a large-scale discussion on the future of amateur art education in the Netherlands. VKV expects two results from this discussion:

- a revitalization of amateur art education (and thus of music education, too) in the Netherlands, in order to resist more efficiently to the tendency of local governments to withdraw their subsidies;
- the acknowledgement of the fact that there are some common principles in music education, but that individually emphasis may be placed on various goals a music school might aim at (e.g. some schools might prefer to concentrate on the music education of children in school-age, others might rather choose to contribute primarily to local cultural life and to its organizations).

Norway

The huge economic development which Norway experienced in the seventies entailed an impressive growth of the number of municipal music schools: they increased from only 50 schools in 1973 to approx. 330 schools today. Public subsidies increased accordingly: they cover today approx. 80% of the

Die Gemeinden beginnen neuerdings angesichts ihrer schwierigen Finanzlage, Kürzungen der Musikschul-Zuschüsse mit Überlegungen zu begründen, ob die Musikschulen überhaupt noch zu jenen Grundstrukturen zählen sollen, die von der öffentlichen Hand zu unterstützen sind. Einige Gemeinden sind der Ansicht, daß neben der Musikschulleitung nur noch die AMV-Kurse bezuschußt werden sollten. Andere setzen den Rotstift bei der musikalischen Erwachsenenbildung an.

Diese Tendenzen veranlaßten die VKV im Jahr 1993, eine Diskussion über die Zukunft der Kunst- und Musikerziehung auszulösen. Von dieser Diskussion erhofft man sich im wesentlichen zwei Ergebnisse:

- ein verstärktes Wiederaufleben der Amateur-Kunsterziehung (also auch der Musikerziehung) in den Niederlanden, um den Kürzungsbestrebungen mehr Widerstand entgegenzusetzen;
- die Anerkennung der Tatsache, daß es einerseits bestimmte Grundprinzipien der Musikerziehung gibt, daß es auf der anderen Seite aber unterschiedliche Akzente und konkrete Zielsetzungen für jede einzelne Schule geben kann (zum Beispiel will die eine Musikschule sich auf den Unterricht schulpflichtiger Kinder konzentrieren, die andere sich mehr am örtlichen Kulturleben und seinen Organisationen beteiligen).

Norwegen

Der große wirtschaftliche Aufschwung Norwegens in den 70er Jahren brachte einen erfreulichen Anstieg der Zahl der kommunalen Musikschulen von 50 (1973) auf rund 330 bis heute. Entsprechend vervielfachten sich die Zuschüsse der öffentlichen Hand, die knapp 80% der Kosten abdecken. Ziel der Regierung ist es, in allen Gemeinden Norwegens Musikschulen zu haben und zu erreichen, daß mindestens 30% aller schulpflichtigen Kinder Angebote der Musikschulen wahrnehmen.

Musikschulen in Norwegen sind öffentliche Schulen, die zusätzlich zum Musikunterricht der allgemeinbildenden Schulen für Kinder, Jugendliche und Erwachsene Angebote der Musikausbildung machen. Grundsätzlich sollen alle Menschen des Landes Anspruch auf eine ihren Begabungen und

- le renouvellement de l'éducation artistique pour amateurs (donc aussi de l'éducation musicale) afin de pouvoir mieux s'opposer à une évolution qui s'oriente vers la diminution des subventions,

- la reconnaissance du principe selon lequel il existe un certain nombre de concepts fondamentaux à respecter dans l'enseignement musical, mais que, par ailleurs, chaque école est libre de choisir ses orientations particulières dans la poursuite de ses objectifs spécifiques (certaines écoles voudront, par exemple, se concentrer sur l'éducation musicale des enfants en âge scolaire, alors que d'autres choisiront de contribuer en premier lieu à la vie musicale locale ainsi qu'à son organisation).

La Norvège

La forte expansion économique qu'a connue la Norvège au cours des années 70 n'a pas manqué de profiter au développement des écoles de musique qui ont vu leur nombre passer de 50 en 1973 à environ 330 aujourd'hui. Les subventions publiques ont augmenté en proportion et couvrent actuellement environ 70% de leur coût. Le but du gouvernement est de voir chaque commune munie d'au moins une école de musique et de faire profiter au moins 30% des enfants en âge scolaire des possibilités qu'elles offrent.

Les écoles de musique norvégiennes sont publiques; elles proposent aux enfants, adolescents et adultes divers types de formation musicale, formation qui vient s'ajouter à celle offerte dans les établissements scolaires primaires et secondaires. En principe, chaque habitant du pays devrait pouvoir suivre une formation musicale adaptée à son talent et à ses qualifications, quel que soit son lieu de domicile ou sa situation financière. La formation est censée répondre au besoin inné de l'individu de pouvoir exprimer ses sentiments, pensées et rêves en musique. Il s'agit donc pour les écoles de musique de proposer des conditions d'enseignement favorables au développement personnel de l'élève pour qui la musique deviendra ainsi partie intégrante de sa vie.

overall costs. The Government's aim is to have at least one music school in each Norwegian municipality and to get at least 30 percent of all school children to participate in music school activities.

Music schools in Norway are public schools offering music education for children, adolescents and adults in addition to compulsory music education in primary and secondary schools. The basic concept is that everybody should be entitled to music education in accordance with his skills and qualifications, regardless of his place of residence and his financial means. The teaching must respond to the need of people to express their feelings, thoughts and imagination through music. Music schools must accordingly offer favourable conditions to enable music to foster the personal development of the pupil and to become a meaningful part of his life.

The mission of music schools is conceived in accordance with this philosophy. Their aim is to develop the musical and creative abilities of the pupils; to promote their understanding and experience of music as a universal means of expression; to further their instrumental/vocal skills in accordance with their capacities; and last not least, to offer them a meaningful and stimulating leisure activity as well as a solid basis for further (professional) training. Music schools should be able to educate active listeners, capable of enjoying and developing their own opinion on the large variety of music offered in today's society.

The teaching includes:

- elementary music education for children of pre-school age
- instrumental/vocal training for pupils of all age
- a manifold, comprehensive and high quality instruction
- numerous opportunities for ensemble playing
- music education for especially gifted children preparing them for higher music education and other music related professional education
- music education for disabled children

All municipal music education should be coordinated and integrated: this means that the music school, the compulsory school and the local music life must have their clearly defined tasks. Such

Fähigkeiten angemessene musikalische Bildung haben, ganz gleich, wo sie wohnen oder wie ihre finanziellen Mittel sind. Der Unterricht soll sich an dem Bedürfnis eines jeden einzelnen ausrichten, seine Gefühle, Gedanken und Vorstellungen durch Musik auszudrücken. Musikschulen müssen günstige Bedingungen bereitstellen, damit die Musik der Persönlichkeitsbildung des Schülers dienen und zu einem bedeutenden Bestandteil seines Lebens werden kann.

Hieran sind die Ziele der Musikschulen orientiert: Sie sollen die musikalischen und kreativen Anlagen der Schüler entwickeln und das Verständnis für bzw. die Erfahrung mit Musik als einem universellen Ausdrucksmittel fördern. Die instrumentalen und stimmlichen Begabungen der Schüler sollen ihren Fähigkeiten entsprechend ausgebildet werden, so daß sie eine sinnvolle Freizeitbeschäftigung und einen soliden Boden für eine weitere (professionelle) Ausbildung haben. Musikschulen sollen aktive Musikhörer heranbilden, die sich zu der großen Vielfalt an Musik ein eigenes Urteil bilden können.

Dementsprechend widmen sich die Musikschulen folgenden spezifischen Aufgaben:

- Musikerziehung im Vorschulalter
- Instrumental-/Vokalausbildung für Schüler aller Altersgruppen
- Bereitstellung eines vielfältigen und abwechslungsreichen Unterrichts mit möglichst großer Bandbreite und bestmöglicher Qualität
- ein reiches Angebot an Möglichkeiten zum gemeinsamen Musizieren
- Förderung besonders begabter Schüler und Vorbereitung auf das Musikstudium und andere Ausbildungswege, in denen Musik eine Rolle spielt
- Musikerziehung für behinderte Kinder

Die von den Gemeinden getragene Musikerziehung sollte insgesamt koordiniert und integriert sein. Das heißt, die Musikschulen, die allgemeinbildenden Schulen und das örtliche Musikleben sollen jeweils klar definierte Aufgaben haben. Und die enge Zusammenarbeit aller Beteiligten soll eine einheitliche, aufeinander abgestimmte Musikerziehung sicherstellen.

Les objectifs poursuivis par les écoles de musique s'inspirent des cette philosophie. Il s'agit notamment de développer les dispositions musicales et créatives des élèves, de susciter leur intérêt pour la musique et de faciliter leur accès à l'univers musical en tant que moyen d'expression universel. Leur talent pour un instrument ou leur talent vocal sera développé en fonction de leurs aptitudes, de sorte qu'ils y trouvent une occupation de loisirs riche et stimulante et, le cas échéant, une base solide pour une future formation (professionnelle). Les écoles de musique se proposent de former un public actif, capable de porter un jugement sur la multitude de produits musicaux qui lui sont, aujourd'hui, offerts.

Tels sont les principes à la base des objectifs des écoles de musique norvégiennes qui visent en particulier:

- l'éducation musicale pour enfants en âge préscolaire
- l'apprentissage d'un instrument et la formation vocale pour élèves de tous âges
- un enseignement riche et varié, comportant un large éventail de possibilités d'une qualité optimale
- de nombreuses possibilités de pratique musicale en groupe
- l'encouragement des enfants particulièrement doués, par une préparation à un niveau supérieur de formation musicale et à d'autres voies de formation professionnelle liées au secteur musical
- l'éducation musicale des enfants handicapés

L'enseignement musical dispensé sous la responsabilité des communes se veut coordonné et intégré; dans cette optique, les écoles de musique, les établissements scolaires et les organisateurs de manifestations musicales locales ont chacun leur rôle bien défini. Il s'agit de réaliser une coopération étroite entre toutes les personnes compétentes en la matière et d'assurer une éducation musicale cohérente et harmonisée au sein de la commune.

Ainsi, l'école de musique devient un lieu de rencontre, une instance centrale appelée à maintenir et à développer la compréhension et l'intérêt de la population pour la musique; l'école assume cette responsabilité de diverses manières, et notamment,

close professional coordination shall ensure a consistent and efficient music education.

The music school is seen as a professional resource centre for the local community, enhancing the population's understanding and interest in music. It is expected

- to assist other institutions/schools where music activities play an integral part in the development of the pupils
- to encourage the pupils' participation in the music life of their local community
- to seek the best possible cooperation with other institutions and organizations active in the field of art and culture.

Joint projects between music schools and primary or lower level secondary schools in the field of drama, dance, theatre and painting have shown new ways of creating an enjoyable school environment which is an essential basis for any successful learning.

Pioneering projects of this kind formed the basis for a music school philosophy that was to receive broad political support. Since 1993, the Government has granted subsidies for such pioneering projects which encourage cooperation between music schools and kindergardens, primary, secondary and high schools, and which are evidential of the cultural vitality of art in the development of young people.

Providing financially accessible music schools of high quality has become a first priority for the Norwegian authorities in their effort to encourage music education for children and young people.

Slovenia

The first music school in Slovenia was founded in 1807 in Ljubljana. A second one was created in1816: it was here that Franz Schubert applied unsuccessfully for the post of a music teacher. The school was organized on behalf of the Philharmonic Society as a «Deutscher Musikerschulverein» (German Association for Music Education). Similar schools existed in other towns. Ljubljana had in addition an organ school (1877), the first conservatoire (1919) and the music academy (1939).

In dieser Beziehung sollen Musikschulen in den Gemeinden eine zentrale Instanz darstellen, um das Musikverständnis und das Interesse an Musik wachzuhalten und zu entwickeln:

- Sie sollen den Musikunterricht der allgemeinbildenden Schulen und anderer Einrichtungen unterstützen, in deren Bildungsangeboten musikalische Aktivitäten vorkommen.
- Sie sollen die Schüler zur aktiven Teilnahme am Musikleben ihrer Gemeinde anregen.
- Musikschulen sollen mit anderen Institutionen und Organisationen des Kunst- und Kulturlebens zusammenarbeiten.

Gemeinschaftsprojekte von Musikschulen und allgemeinbildenden Schulen auf den Gebieten Tanz, Theaterspiel und bildender Kunst ließen erkennen, wie durch sie ein positives schulisches Umfeld, die Grundbedingung für jegliches Lernen, geschaffen werden konnte. Neue richtungsweisende Projekte dieser Art sind zur bestimmenden Grundlage für eine Philosophie der Musikschulen geworden, die landesweit politische Unterstützung gefunden hat: Die öffentliche Hand hat seit 1993 Subventionen für pädagogisch wegweisende Versuchsprojekte bereitgestellt und dabei vor allem solche Kooperationen von Musikschulen mit Kindergärten, Volks-, Sekundar- und Hochschulen gefördert, die die kulturelle Vitalität der Kunst im Bildungsprozeß junger Menschen aufzeigen.

Qualitativ anspruchsvolle und finanziell erschwingliche Musikschulen für alle sind zum entscheidenden Ziel der norwegischen Behörden bei ihrem Bemühen um die Musikausbildung von Kindern und Jugendlichen geworden.

Slowenien

Die erste öffentliche Musikschule in Slowenien wurde 1807 in Ljubljana gegründet. Eine weitere gab es ab 1816, an der sich unter anderen auch der junge Franz Schubert (übrigens erfolglos) als Musiklehrer bewarb. Sie wurde bis 1919 von der philharmonischen Gesellschaft als «Deutscher Musikschulverein» betrieben. Ähnliche Institute gab es auch in weiteren Städten. Zu erwähnen sind auch die Orgelschule (1877), das erste Konservatorium (1919) und die Musikhochschule in Ljubljana (1939).

- en soutenant les établissements scolaires ou autres institutions proposant des activités musicales comme partie intégrante de la formation des jeunes,

- en incitant les élèves à participer à la vie musicale de leur commune,

- en collaborant avec toutes les institutions et organisations actives dans le secteur artistique et culturel.

La coopération entre les écoles de musique et les établissements scolaires primaires et secondaires a donné naissance à bon nombre de projets communs dans les domaines de la danse, du théâtre et des beaux arts et créé de la sorte un environnement scolaire agréable et constructif, condition de tout apprentissage réussi.

Divers projets pilotes sont à la base d'une nouvelle vision des écoles de musique qui a rencontré le soutien des responsables politiques à travers le pays. Depuis 1993, les pouvoirs publics accordent des subventions à des projets pilotes novateurs et encouragent notamment les projets menés en coopération entre les écoles de musique et les établissements d'enseignement primaire, secondaire et supérieur, témoignant ainsi de l'importance et de la vitalité de la musique dans la formation des jeunes.

La création et l'entretien d'écoles de musique de grande qualité et financièrement accessibles à tous traduisent la volonté des autorités norvégiennes d'accorder la plus haute priorité à l'enseignement musical des enfants et des jeunes.

La Slovénie

La première école publique de musique en Slovénie fut créée en 1807 à Ljubljana; une deuxième école vit le jour dès 1816: ce fut ici que le jeune Franz Schubert se présenta – sans succès d'ailleurs – comme candidat au poste de professeur de musique. Jusqu'en 1919, l'école fut gérée par la Société Philharmonique sous le nom de «Deutscher Musikschulverein» (association d'éducation musicale de langue allemande). Des institutions d'un type semblable existaient aussi dans d'autres villes. A mentionner également, l'Ecole d'Orgue (1877), le premier Conservatoire (1919) et l'Ecole Supérieure de Musique à Ljubljana (1939).

Today, music schools ensure basic music education. Nearly 19,000 pupils, i.e. 7% of all children in compulsory school age participate in music education. In the lower secondary grades, music education is given in conservatoires which prepare for higher music education. At the highest (graduate and postgraduate) level, music is taught in various institutions: the Academy for Higher Music Education, the University Institute for Musicology and the Division for Music Pedagogics at the Faculty of Pedagogics in Maribor.

The 53 music schools of Slovenia are municipal schools; they are financed to 85% by public subsidies (the State covers all staff expenses). The remaining 15% are borne by the parents and the municipalities. Central and local government offer scholarships for particularly gifted students who have attained good results in contests. Such contests have been taking place in Slovenia since 1971. The new legislation on education also provides for the possibility of opening private music schools with an appropriate licence.

The music schools offer the following educational possibilities:
- the «infant music school» for preschool children over 5;
- teaching of instruments for children between 7 and 15; in addition, vocal training, and for all pupils, as a compulsory subject, music theory throughout all six years of education; in higher classes children also take part in chamber music education, play in orchestras and sing in choirs.

The schools offer preparation in various subjects (instruments) following the official curriculum: piano and accordion are the most popular instruments. Some music schools also teach folk instruments such as zither and the string instrument «tamburitsa», as well as electronic instruments. Thirteen music schools also teach ballet, but the preparation for the professional ballet study is only given in Ljubljana and Maribor.

Except for certain subjects (accordion, saxophone, ballet), teachers have to have a university preparation. Presently, some 1,200 teachers are working in music schools, out of whom two thirds have higher education diploma.

Heutzutage wird die Grundstufe der Musikausbildung von den Musikschulen übernommen, an deren Angeboten fast 19 000, das sind 7% aller schulpflichtigen Kinder, teilnehmen. Eine mittlere Stufe stellen die Konservatorien dar, die auf das Musikstudium vorbereiten. Die Diplom- und weiterführenden Studiengänge liegen bei der Musikhochschule, der musikwissenschaftlichen Abteilung der Universität und bei der musikpädagogischen Abteilung der pädagogischen Hochschule in Maribor.

Die insgesamt 53 Musikschulen Sloweniens werden von den Gemeinden getragen und zu 85% (sämtliche Personalkosten) vom Staat finanziert. Für die restlichen 15% kommen die Eltern oder die Gemeinden auf. Staat und Gemeinden vergeben Stipendien für besonders begabte Schüler, die bei den seit 1971 veranstalteten Wettbewerben gute Ergebnisse erzielen. Eine neue Schulgesetzgebung läßt auch private Musikschulen zu, die jedoch eine Konzession beantragen müssen.

Aujourd'hui, les écoles de musique assurent la formation musicale de base: 19.000 enfants, c.a.d. 7% de tous les enfants en âge scolaire fréquentent ces écoles. La formation de niveau moyen est dispensée par les conservatoires qui préparent aux études musicales. La formation de niveau supérieur (diplôme et études supérieures) se fait soit à l'Ecole Supérieure de Musique, soit à l'Institut de Musicologie de l'Université soit à l'Institut de Pédagogie Musicale de la Faculté de Pédagogie à Maribor.

Les 53 écoles de musique de Slovénie sont des institutions municipales, financées à 85% (tous les frais de personnel) par l'Etat. Les 15% restants sont assumés par les parents ou par la commune. Les autorités centrales et communales offrent des bourses aux élèves particulièrement doués qui ont obtenu de bons résultats aux concours organisés dans le pays depuis 1971. La nouvelle législation scolaire prévoit également la possibilité d'ouvrir

Once they have completed their basic music education and after having passed successfully the entrance examination, the most gifted children can attend one of the two music academies in Ljubljana or Maribor (which also teach jazz and light music). Here, they have two possibilities:

- either they take part in the complete programme of the music academy, where at upper secondary level, priority in general education is given to humanistic subjects (mother tongue, two foreign languages, philosophy, psychology),
- or they only follow the musical part of the curriculum and go to other upper secondary or high schools for the additional education.

In the Academies, priority is given to instruments and/or to harmony and counterpoint and to «solfeggio». Further specialized subjects are: piano, music history, chamber music, orchestra, choirs, accompanying songs, etc.

Music education and the music school system is an integral part of the nation's educational system; it creates an important basis for the cultural development; it contributes to the consolidation of the national cultural identity and opens the path to European cultural currents. Everything is done to provide equal educational opportunities for the young. With this new concept for the development of music education, Slovenia wishes to move closer to the well developed European educational system. But this does not mean that in euphoria or in sometimes uncritical imitation of European systems the country would ever forget or leave aside the achievements attained in the framework of its own traditions.

Musikschulen bieten folgende Ausbildungsmöglichkeiten an:

- «kleine Musikschule» für Vorschulkinder ab 5 Jahren
- Instrumentalunterricht (7–15 Jahre) sowie Gesang, dazu für alle Schüler Musiklehre als Pflichtfach während der ganzen 6 Ausbildungsjahre. In den höheren Klassen nehmen die Schüler auch an Kammermusik, Orchester oder Chor teil.

Der Unterricht erfolgt nach einem vorgeschriebenen Lehrplan in verschiedenen Fächern: allen voran Klavier und Akkordeon. In einigen Musikschulen werden auch Volksinstrumente wie Zither oder das Zupfinstrument «Tamburitsa» angeboten, aber auch elektronische Musikinstrumente. An 13 Musikschulen wird außerdem Ballettunterricht erteilt, an zweien gibt es eine intensive Vorbereitung auf das Ballettstudium.

Mit Ausnahme einiger Fächer (Akkordeon, Saxophon, Ballett) wird von den Pädagogen eine Hochschulausbildung verlangt. Zur Zeit unterrichten an den Musikschulen in Slowenien etwa 1 200 Lehrer, von denen zwei Drittel ein Hochschuldiplom haben.

Die begabtesten Schüler kommen nach abgeschlossener Grundausbildung und erfolgreich bestandener Aufnahmeprüfung an eines der beiden Konservatorien in Maribor oder Ljubljana (dort auch Jazz und Popularmusik). Hier gibt es zwei Wege:

- die Schüler nehmen am kompletten Programm des Konservatoriums teil, ihr Schwerpunkt in der allgemeinen («gymnasialen») Ausbildung liegt bei humanistischen Fächern (Sprachen, Philosophie, Psychologie usw.);
- die Schüler nehmen nur an der musikalischen Fachausbildung teil und besuchen daneben ein Gymnasium oder eine Mittelschule.

Im Konservatorium liegt der Schwerpunkt auf dem Instrumentalunterricht oder auf Harmonielehre/Kontrapunkt sowie auf «solfeggio». Daneben sind weitere Fächer wie Klavier, Musikgeschichte, Kammermusik, Orchester, Chor, Korrepetition usw. zu belegen.

– avec une licence appropriée – des écoles de musique privées.

Les écoles de musique proposent les formations suivantes:

- «petite» école de musique pour enfants en âge préscolaire à partir de 5 ans,
- formation aux instruments et au chant pour les enfants entre 7 et 15 ans, et théorie musicale pour tous les enfants comme matière obligatoire pendant les six années de formation; dans les classes plus avancées, les enfants participent également à des cours de musique de chambre, à des orchestres et à des chorales.

L'enseignement se fait selon un plan de formation agréé pour les différentes matières, avec en tête le piano et l'accordéon. Certains établissements proposent aussi des cours d'instruments populaires, par exemple, la cithare, l'instrument folklorique à corde «tambouritsa» et même des instruments électroniques. Treize écoles enseignent, en outre, le ballet, mais deux écoles seulement proposent la préparation intensive exigée pour les études de ballet.

A l'exception de quelques disciplines (accordéon, saxophone, ballet), les pédagogues doivent posséder une formation universitaire. Actuellement, sur les 1.200 professeurs qui enseignent dans des écoles de musique, deux tiers possèdent un diplôme universitaire.

Les élèves les plus douées passent, après la formation de base et après avoir réussi l'examen d'entrée, à l'un des deux conservatoires à Maribor ou Ljubljana (où sont également enseignés le jazz et la musique de divertissement). Ils ont alors deux possibilités:

- soit ils participent au programme complet du conservatoire, la priorité au niveau du programme du lycée étant donnée aux matières littéraires (langue maternelle, 2 langues étrangères, philosophie, psychologie),
- soit ils ne participent qu'à la partie musicale du programme, mais fréquentent, à côté du conservatoire, un lycée ou une autre école.

Au conservatoire, la priorité est accordée à la formation à l'instrument ou à l'harmonie et au contrepoint ainsi qu'au solfège. Autres matières ensei-

Spain

It is not easy to describe the situation of music education in Spain, given the great diversity that characterizes the country's cultural and political background. Another difficulty arises from the fact that the educational system as a whole is right now undergoing a fundamental reform. This reform is so significant that teachers and pupils have to do away with their old habits and that even the public is changing its views on music education and music practice.

Following the 1970 education reform which did not bring any noteworthy support to any of the possible music education systems, a new law on the general organization of the education system was passed in 1990, the LOGSE, and all over the country music education was set in motion. Hopefully, the prospective innovation the new law will bring might sraighten the so far rather confused situation.

Until adoption of this law, music education held a minor part within the general education system and music education for amateurs was simply reduced to a pure declaration of intent in the preamble of a decree.

Thanks to LOGSE, music is now a subject matter fully recognized within the general education system, just like all the other subjects; an additional law makes provision for music studies in specialist centres. Since the law does not make any distinction between regulated and non-regulated teaching, it allows for the opening of music schools of a new type on a legal basis.

Until the reform and whether they liked or not, music schools had to operate like small conservatoires; there were only a few schools which dared alternative teaching. All pupils, whether they wanted to become professionals or whether they just wanted to practice music as amateurs, were offered the same programme with high ambitions of professionalization. As a matter of fact, the result was unfair to both groups: the quality of music education for future professionals was diminished, whereas gifted potential amateur musicians were

Das Musikschulwesen ist ein integrierter Bestandteil des slowenischen Bildungssystems, und es schafft wichtige Voraussetzungen für die Kulturförderung des Landes: Es trägt zur Formung einer nationalen Identität ebenso bei wie zur Teilhabe an den europäischen Kulturströmungen. Das Bemühen geht dahin, gleiche Ausbildungsbedingungen für die Jugend zu schaffen. Und mit neuen Konzepten der Musikausbildung will Slowenien sich dem in Europa bestehenden Bildungs- und Ausbildungssystem annähern, ohne dabei in Euphorie und unkritischer Nachahmung die Vorteile des eigenen Systems zu verkennen oder zu vernachlässigen.

Spanien

Die Situation des Musikunterrichts in Spanien zu beschreiben ist nicht leicht: Zum einen bestehen im Land sehr unterschiedliche Realitäten in kultureller und politischer Hinsicht; zum andern wird zum gegenwärtigen Zeitpunkt das gesamte Bildungswesen reformiert. Die Reform der Musikerziehung ist so tiefgreifend, daß sich nicht nur Lehrer und Schüler von alten Gewohnheiten verabschieden müssen, sondern daß auch die Öffentlichkeit in Fragen des Musikunterrichts völlig umdenken muß. Nach der Bildungsreform von 1970, bei der keine Form des Musikunterrichts genügend berücksichtigt wurde, kam es 1990 zur Verabschiedung eines neuen Gesetzes zur allgemeinen Regelung des Bildungswesens («LOGSE»). Dieses brachte den Musikunterricht im ganzen Land in Bewegung. Es ist zu hoffen, daß die neuen Entwicklungsmöglichkeiten, die das Gesetz eröffnet, etwas Ordnung in die bislang recht unüberschaubare Situation bringen werden.

Vorher spielte der Musikunterricht neben dem allgemeinen Schulunterricht eher eine nebensächliche Rolle, und der Unterricht im Laienbereich mußte sich mit einer folgenlosen Absichtserklärung in der Präambel eines Dekrets begnügen.

Seit Inkrafttreten des «LOGSE» ist die Musik im allgemeinbildenden Unterricht ebenso anerkannt wie andere Fächer. Durch ein weiteres Gesetz wird auch die Möglichkeit einer Musikausbildung in «Fachzentren» eröffnet. Indem das Gesetz unterscheidet zwischen «geregeltem» und «nicht geregeltem» Unterricht, bietet es die Möglichkeit, Mu-

gnées, le piano, l'histoire de la musique, la musique de chambre, l'orchestre, la chorale, la corrépétition etc.

L'éducation musicale fait partie intégrante du système éducatif slovène. Elle crée d'importantes conditions pour le développement culturel du pays: elle contribue à consolider l'identité nationale et facilite en même temps l'accès aux grands courants culturels européens. A l'aide de nouveaux concepts d'éducation musicale, le pays souhaite se rapprocher des systèmes éducatifs européens, sans pour autant négliger, dans l'euphorie et l'imitation parfois inconditionnelle de ces systèmes, les résultats positifs réalisés par le passé par le système slovène de formation musicale.

L'Espagne

Ce n'est pas une tâche aisée que de présenter de façon succincte la situation de l'enseignement musical en Espagne: le pays est en effet marqué par de grandes diversités culturelles et politiques et connaît, en cet instant, une profonde réforme de son système d'enseignement. La réforme est d'une telle ampleur qu'elle oblige enseignants et élèves à changer leurs habitudes. Elle a même modifié la vision que l'opinion publique se faisait traditionnellement de l'éducation musicale.

La réforme de l'enseignement de 1970 n'avait guère fait une place équitable aux divers enseignements musicaux. L'adoption en 1990 d'une nouvelle loi sur l'ensemble du système éducatif (la «LOGSE») a par contre bouleversé l'enseignement musical dans tout le pays. Cette loi ouvre de nouvelles possibilités de développement qui permettront vraisemblablement de mettre de l'ordre dans une situation jusqu'alors plutôt confuse.

La place que tenait l'éducation musicale dans le système d'enseignement général antérieur était purement théorique. Il en allait de même pour l'enseignement musical destiné aux amateurs: il se limitait à une simple déclaration d'intention dans le préambule d'un décret resté lettre morte.

Depuis l'entrée en vigueur de la LOGSE, la musique tient la même place dans l'enseignement général que toutes les autres matières; une loi additionnelle prévoit par ailleurs un enseignement musical dans des centres spécialisés. La loi fait la distinc-

discouraged from learning music. This caused a certain vacuum.

On the other hand, the absence of planning resulted in the spontaneous creation of municipal music centres that tried to meet the increasing demand for music education from the population. But these centres did not have any pedagogical or organizational expertise. There were absolutely no guidelines nor models to which they could have had referred to.

The reform of music education not only requires the transformation of the centres but also a change of mentalities. The present reality, barely more than superficially structured, needs fundamental changes with regard to its foundation.

Out of the eight autonomous governments, each of which has full competence in educational matters, four passed a law on music schools and are now transforming their music centres following the music school model recommended by the EMU.

The legislation on music schools also sets the modes of their financing. In general, public music schools are municipal institutions; the way they are financed varies from region to region. Thus, Catalonia concluded several cooperation agreements

sikschulen eines neuen Typs auf rechtlich gesicherter Basis zu gründen.

Vor der Reform hatten die Musikschulen kaum eine andere Wahl, als zu kleinen Konservatorien zu werden; nur wenige wagten alternative Unterrichtsformen. Für alle Schüler, egal ob sie Berufsmusiker werden oder nur als Liebhaber musizieren wollten, gab es ein und dasselbe Lehrangebot mit höchst professionellen Ambitionen. Dadurch kamen beide Gruppen zu kurz: Die Qualität der Ausbildung der Berufsmusiker ging zurück, und viele begabte potentielle Musikliebhaber fühlten sich entmutigt oder abgeschreckt. So ist hier eine große Lücke entstanden.

Darüber hinaus kam es aufgrund mangelnder Planung zur spontanen Bildung kommunal getragener «Musikzentren», die bemüht waren, der immer größeren Nachfrage der Bevölkerung nach Musikunterricht gerecht zu werden. Doch standen diesen Zentren weder pädagogische noch organisatorische Fachleute zur Seite. Es gab keine Richtlinien oder Modelle, an denen man sich hätte orientieren können.

Die Reform der Musikerziehung wird also nicht allein eine Umwandlung dieser Zentren erforder-

tion entre l'enseignement réglementé et l'enseignement non réglementé permettant ainsi l'ouverture d'écoles de musique d'un type nouveau sur une base légale.

Dans l'état de droit antérieur, c.a.d. avant la réforme, les écoles de musique n'avait guère d'autre choix que d'agir comme des petits conservatoires; peu d'écoles seulement se hasardaient à offrir des programmes alternatifs. Tous les élèves, aussi bien ceux qui visaient une carrière musicale que ceux qui voulaient faire de la musique à titre d'amateur, se voyaient offrir un seul et même apprentissage avec des visées hautement professionnelles. Et en fin de compte, personne n'était vraiment satisfait. D'un côté, le niveau de la formation professionnelle baissait, de l'autre, de possibles amateurs doués étaient découragés par des exigences trop poussées. Toute une génération musicale en a fait les frais.

Par ailleurs, l'absence de planification a suscité la création spontanée de nombreux centres municipaux de musique qui tentaient ainsi de répondre à une demande toujours accrue de formation musicale de la part de la population. Cependant, ces centres ne pouvaient s'appuyer sur aucune expérience pédagogique ou administrative, ni se référer à des théories ou modèles à suivre.

La réforme de l'enseignement musical exige donc, au delà de la transformation des centres musicaux, un véritable changement des mentalités. Toute une réalité demande à être redéfinie, réalité qui existe dans les structures de surface, mais dont les fondements doivent être entièrement renouvelés.

Les gouvernements de quatre d'entre les huit régions autonomes qui ont compétence en matière d'éducation, ont adopté des lois sur les écoles de musique et se sont mis à transformer les centres musicaux pour en faire des écoles de musique du type recommandé par l'EMU.

La législation sur les écoles de musique réglemente également leur financement. En principe, les écoles de musique publiques dépendent des communes; les modèles de financement varient d'une ré-

with the municipalities, and the autonomous government undertook to cover up to one third of the costs for music education of children of school age. In other regions, the system of subsidies is more complicated. There is a problem with regard to private music schools, some of which act as public schools but do not receive any support.

Generally, participants contribute up to 15–30% to the budget of the music school, but their contribution should as a rule not exceed 30%. In some regions, there is a trend towards music education free of charge.

The teachers' working conditions as well as their social prestige vary throughout the country – just like the overall situation of the music schools. There is a multitude of different employment contracts. A research project including the collection of relevant data is presently under way which hopefully will result in considerable advance in this field, too. The claim for a better ranking of music teachers in the wage index might be a first step towards a better social and professional recognition of music teachers.

The Association of Catalan Music Schools (ACEM), created in 1992, has become a competent partner of negotiation and consultation with the educational authorities. Other autonomous regions

lich machen, sondern einen Mentalitäts-
wandel: Hier wird eine in ihrer Ober-
flächenstruktur zwar bereits vorhandene, in ihren Grundlagen jedoch ände-
rungsbedürftige Realität neu definiert.

Die Hälfte der Regierungen der acht
autonomen Regionen des Landes, bei
denen die Zuständigkeit für die Erziehung liegt, haben Gesetze über Musikschulen verabschiedet und sind daran
gegangen, die «Musikzentren» nach
dem Modell der von der EMU empfohle-
nen Musikschule umzuwandeln.

Die Musikschulgesetze regeln auch die
Finanzierung. In der Regel sind die Musikschulen
Einrichtungen der Gemeinden, und so sind die Fi-
nanzierungsmodelle – auch je nach Region – verschieden: In Katalonien wurden beispielsweise
Verträge über die Zusammenarbeit mit den Gemeinden geschlossen, und die Regierung verpflichtet sich, bis zu einem Drittel für die Kosten der Mu-
sikschulausbildung schulpflichtiger Kinder aufzu-
kommen. Auch in anderen Regionen gibt es teilweise komplexe Subventionssysteme. Ein Problem
stellen die privaten Musikschulen dar, die zur Zeit
gar keine Unterstützung erhalten, aber in vielen
Fällen die Funktionen öffentlicher Musikschulen
ausüben.

In der Regel tragen die Schüler mit etwa 15–30%
zu den Kosten der Musikschule bci. Auf 30% soll
der Teilnehmerbeitrag auch beschränkt bleiben. In
einigen Regionen geht die Tendenz hin zu einem
kostenlosen Unterricht.

Wie das gesamte Musikschulwesen, sind auch
die Sozial- und Arbeitsbedingungen der Lehrer von
einer Vielfalt von Vertragsmodellen geprägt. Gegenwärtig werden in einem Forschungsprojekt Da-
ten gesammelt und verglichen, um hier – wie auch
in anderen Bereichen des Musikschulwesens – mit
den Reformen weiterzukommen. Die Forderung
nach einer höheren Einstufung der Musiklehrer ist
ein erster Schritt zur sozialen und leistungs-
gemäßen Anerkennung ihrer Arbeit.

Der 1992 in Katalonien gegründete Musikschulverband (ACEM) ist längst zum kompetenten Ansprechpartner der Erziehungsbehörden geworden.

gion à l'autre. En Catalogne, par exemple, des
contrats conclus entre municipalités et gouvernement autonome engagent ce dernier à financer
pour un tiers l'éducation musicale des enfants en
âge scolaire. Dans d'autres régions, on trouve des
systèmes de subvention parfois très complexes. Les
écoles de musiques privées posent un problème
particulier dans la mesure où elles assument souvent les fonctions d'écoles publiques sans pour autant recevoir de subventions.

De manière générale, les élèves contribuent à
15–30% au budget des centres. La contribution
des élèves doit, en principe, rester plafonnée à 30%
du coût de l'enseignement. Et plusieurs régions
s'orientent même vers la gratuité totale de l'enseignement.

Les conditions sociales et de travail des enseignants, et par conséquent leur prestige, sont déter-
minés par une multitude de contrats qui, à l'instar
de la situation des écoles de musiques, varient
d'une région à l'autre. Des recherches sont en
cours dans le but de réunir un maximum de données afin de faire progresser ce dossier. La demande d'intégration des enseignants de musique
dans un catégorie salariale supérieure pourrait représenter un premier pas vers leur véritable reconnaissance sociale et professionnelle.

L'Association des écoles de musique de la Catalogne (ACEM) créée en 1992, est devenue un interlo-
cuteur compétent des autorités éducatives en matière musicale. D'autres régions autonomes se proposent de fonder des associations similaires. On es-

plan the creation of similar associations, and it is to be hoped that finally a large network of music schools will be spread all over the country.

Sweden

In Sweden, there are 284 music schools – nearly one in each municipality – with over 300,000 pupils.

In recent years, major administrative changes have taken place. Music schools mostly depend on the same organizations as the general schools and the institutes for cultural education or leisure activities. But like many other sectors of municipal services, also the music schools have undergone budget cuts. Compared to other services, the situation of the music schools is by far not a privilged one. In large cities, they have suffered the most severe cuts. On the other hand, even higher grants have been allocated in some cases.

Faced with these recessions, music schools had to think about alternative solutions and changes other than the mere increase of fees, as for instance:

- more group education,
- reduction in the number of substitute teachers,
- reduction in the number of partner teachers.

So far, music schools had been financed up to 90%, and sometimes even more, by public subsidies. Many music schools have maintained their relatively low level of fees, and, increases never went beyond 10–20%.

As a consequence, music schools had to look into their own organization and had to try to find new structures. A few music schools have founded companies with money from the municipality. A few more music schools plan to do alike. In some municipalities, adult education associations run the music schools. Several music schools cooperate with the compulsory schools, the upper secondary schools and the Music Academies. This cooperation usually consists in paid services offered by the music schools and in teacher training programmes proposed by Music Academies.

There is a tendency that music schools offer other subjects, such as dance, drama, theatre, rhythm and art. Some music schools have started

In den anderen autonomen Regionen plant man die Gründung ähnlicher Verbände und hofft, letztlich im ganzen Land ein alle verbindendes großes Netz von Musikschulen zu schaffen.

Schweden

In Schweden gibt es 284 Musikschulen – fast in jeder Gemeinde eine – mit insgesamt 300 000 Schülern.

In den letzten Jahren kam es zu größeren verwaltungstechnischen Veränderungen. Musikschulen unterstehen oft derselben Organisation wie die Schulen oder wie Kultur- und Freizeitaktivitäten.

Wie für viele Gebiete der städtischen Dienstleistungen mußte auch für die Musikschulen das Budget gekürzt werden; und im Spektrum der städtischen Angebote rangiert die Musikschule kaum an erster Stelle. Vor allem in den großen Städten waren die Kürzungen einschneidend. Andererseits gibt es auch einige Fälle, in denen Gemeinden höhere Zuschüsse zugeteilt haben.

Aufgrund der Etatkürzungen haben sich Musikschulen Gedanken über Konsequenzen machen müssen. Neben der Anhebung der Unterrichtsgebühren gibt es andere Maßnahmen:

- mehr Unterricht in Gruppen,
- Reduktion von Vertretungen,
- weniger Unterricht, bei dem eine Gruppe/ Klasse von zwei Lehrern betreut wird.

In Schweden wurden die Musikschulkosten bislang zu über 90 % im Gesamtdurchschnitt durch öf-

père ainsi créer à travers le pays un grand réseau réunissant toutes les écoles de musique.

La Suède

Il existe en Suède 284 écoles de musique avec un total de 300.000 élèves. En fait, pratiquement chaque commune possède au moins une école.

Au cours des dernières années, le système a subi d'importants changements administratifs.

Les écoles de musique dépendent pour la plupart de la même organisation que les établissements scolaires et les instituts de formation culturelle ou de loisirs.

La plupart des budgets des services municipaux ont été fortement réduits. Or, les écoles de musique font partie de ces services mais n'y figurent guère en tête de liste. Aussi leurs budgets ont-ils fortement diminué, notamment dans les grandes villes. Dans quelques cas isolés, pourtant, les communes ont augmenté les subventions accordées aux écoles de musique.

Confrontées à ces diminutions budgétaires, les écoles de musique on dû engager une réflexion sur des solutions alternatives. Il existe en effet d'autres possibilités que la pure et simple augmentation des droits d'inscription, à savoir:

- davantage de formation en groupe,
- la réduction du nombre d'enseignants engagés à titre de remplaçants,
- moins de cours (en groupe ou en classe) assurés à la fois par deux enseignants.

Jusqu'à présent, les écoles de musique ont été financées à plus de 90 % par des subventions publiques. Beaucoup d'écoles n'ont, pour l'instant, pas touché aux droits d'inscription dont le niveau est toujours relativement bas; lorsqu'il il y a eu augmentation, elle a été de l'ordre de 10 à 20 %.

Il a donc fallu que les écoles de musique revoient leur système d'organisation et recherchent de nouvelles structures. Quelques écoles de musique se sont constituées en association à l'aide de subventions municipales. D'autres prévoient d'en faire au-

«culture schools», others are planning to do so. These schools offer a great variety of subjects and cooperate with other schools.

For all these reasons music schools are now expanding, and in exploring new grounds they contribute in enriching the cultural life of the community.

Switzerland

Music education involves the whole human being. It engages spirit, soul and body and plays an important cultural and social role. Therefore, music schools have to be accessible to everybody.

Music schools are expected to promote their pupils' musical talents and abilities and to help them to relate themselves to music in a positive, independent and critical way. Music schools aspire to form competent listeners as well as active amateur musicians. They also have to cater for a rising generation of professional musicians. The three main pillars of the music schools are the general music orientation (elementary music education), instrumental lessons and ensemble playing.

The music schools are part of the Swiss educational system and they co-ordinate their tasks with similar institutions. They cooperate in particular with the public primary and secondary schools.

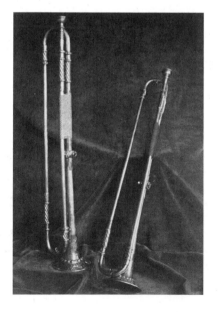

There is no legal regulation with regard to music education which might be compulsory upon the whole country. Each of the 26 cantons of Switzerland is autonomous and can issue its own laws for schools as well as for music schools. The teachers' salaries vary from one canton to the other. Many cantons make contributions to the music schools. These may vary between 1% and 50%. In many cantons, there is still a long way to go to reach an equal (i.e. a one third) contribution to the costs from each of the three partners: the parents, the municipality and the canton. But in other cantons, parents pay approx. 20% of the costs only.

The music schools are mainly supported by the local authorities or by associated municipalities.

fentliche Zuschüsse abgedeckt. Viele Schulen haben ihre relativ geringen Teilnehmergebühren zunächst beibehalten; ansonsten stieg der durchschnittliche Teilnehmeranteil um 10–20%.

Eine weitere Konsequenz war, daß Musikschulen ihre Verwaltung und Organisation überprüfen und nach neuen Wegen suchen mußten. Einige Musikschulen haben mit finanziellen Mitteln der Gemeinde Gesellschaften gegründet, was zunehmend Nachahmer findet. In einigen Gemeinden werden die Musikschulen vom Verein für Erwachsenenbildung getragen. Mehrere Musikschulen arbeiten mit den allgemeinen Pflichtschulen, den Sekundarschulen und den Musikhochschulen zusammen. Diese Kooperation besteht in der Regel in bezahlten Dienstleistungen der Musikschulen und in der Lehrerfortbildung innerhalb der Musikhochschulen.

Immer häufiger bieten Musikschulen auch andere Fächer wie Tanz, Theater und Rhythmus sowie bildende Kunst an. Einige Musikschulen haben «Kulturschulen» eröffnet oder planen dies zu tun. Solche Einrichtungen bieten eine Vielzahl verschiedener Fächer an und kooperieren mit anderen Schulen.

Aus all diesen Gründen expandieren die Musikschulen und betreten neue Felder, was wiederum ein Mehr an Kultur für die Gemeinden bedeutet.

Schweiz

Musikerziehung erfaßt den ganzen Menschen. Sie spricht Geist, Seele und Körper an. Musikerziehung hat eine wichtige kulturelle, bildungspolitische und soziale Bedeutung. Darum soll das Unterrichtsangebot der Musikschulen in der Schweiz allen Bevölkerungsschichten offenstehen.

Die Schüler der Musikschulen sollen in ihren musikalischen Anlagen und Fähigkeiten gefördert werden. Sie sollen ein positives, selbständiges und kritisches Verhältnis zur Musik aufbauen. Die Musikschulen wollen kompetente Musikhörer und aktive Laienmusiker ausbilden sowie den Nachwuchs an Berufsmusikern sicherstellen. Die drei Hauptpfeiler der Musikschulen sind: die Musikalische Grundausbildung (elementare Musikerziehung), der Instrumentalunterricht sowie das gemeinsame Musizieren.

tant. Dans un certain nombre de communes, les associations de formation d'adultes ont pris en main l'enseignement musical. Plusieurs écoles de musique collaborent avec les établissements d'enseignement scolaire primaire et secondaire et avec les instituts de formation musicale supérieure. Cette collaboration se fait sous forme de services rémunérés, offerts par les écoles de musique et sous forme de formation complémentaire dispensée aux enseignants par les établissements d'enseignement supérieur de musique.

Il est de plus en plus fréquent de voir les écoles de musique proposer aussi d'autres formations tels la danse, le théâtre, le rythme et les beaux arts. D'autres écoles encore ont ouvert des «écoles de culture» ou sont sur le point de le faire. Ces établissement offrent une grande variété de formations et entretiennent entre eux une excellente coopération. Ainsi peut-on assister à une véritable évolution des écoles de musique qui, en faisant irruption dans de nouveaux secteurs, enrichissent la vie culturelle des communes.

La Suisse

L'éducation musicale englobe l'être humain dans sa totalité: son esprit, son âme et son corps. Elle revêt un aspect culturel, social et politique. Il est donc important que toutes les couches de la population aient accès aux écoles de musique.

Dans ces établissements, les élèves ont la possibilité de développer leurs facultés et leurs dispositions musicales; ils y acquièrent une vision positive, indépendante et critique de la musique. Le rôle des écoles de musique est de former des auditeurs compétents ainsi que des amateurs avertis et d'assurer la relève des musiciens professionnels. Les trois buts principaux des écoles de musique sont la formation élémentaire, l'enseignement instrumental et la pratique de la musique d'ensemble.

Les écoles de musique font partie intégrante du système suisse de formation et cordonnent leurs tâches avec d'autres institutions semblables. Elles travaillent surtout avec les écoles publiques primaires et secondaires.

En Suisse, il n'y a pas de réglementation relative à l'enseignement musical. Chacun des 26 cantons est autonome et promulgue les lois pour les écoles

30% are ruled by civil law, 70% by public law. Many music schools are placed under the same authorities as public schools. Others are directly subordinated to the municipality or are supported by an independent association. In difficult times, music schools that are firmly rooted in public law are financially better off.

Most of the Swiss music schools are members of the Swiss Music School Association (VMS). Many cantons also have a cantonal Association of Music Schools. Their representatives are members of the Conference of the delegates of the VMS. The VMS publishes a two-month magazine, «Animato». The VMS also establishes contacts, informs, publishes documents, organizes recurrent and further training courses (congresses, sessions, courses for music school directors etc.) and advises the music schools.

Turkey

At the moment, there is no current report available.

Die Musikschulen gehören zum schweizerischen Gesamtbildungssystem und koordinieren ihre Aufgaben mit ähnlichen Institutionen. Vor allem aber arbeiten sie mit den öffentlichen Volksschulen und Gymnasien zusammen.

Es gibt keine schweizerischen gesetzlichen Regelungen für das Musikschulwesen. Jeder der 26 Kantone ist autonom und kann eigene Gesetze sowohl für die öffentlichen Schulen als auch für die Musikschulen erlassen. Die Besoldungen der Lehrkräfte sind in jedem Kanton unterschiedlich. Auch die Zuschüsse, die viele Kantone den Musikschulen zahlen, können zwischen 1% und 50% schwanken. In vielen Kantonen ist man noch weit davon entfernt, die Kosten für die Musikschulen zu je einem Drittel durch Beiträge der Eltern, der Gemeinde und des Kantons zu finanzieren. Andererseits gibt es Kantone, in denen die Eltern nur noch etwa 20% zu den Kosten beitragen müssen.

Die Musikschulen werden hauptsächlich von den Gemeinden oder von Gemeindeverbänden getragen. 30% sind privatrechtlich und 70% öffentlich-rechtlich organisiert. Viele Musikschulen sind den Behörden der Volksschulen unterstellt. Andere unterstehen direkt der Gemeinde oder werden von einem selbständigen Verein getragen. Je besser die Musikschulen im öffentlichen Recht verankert sind, desto sicherer ist ihre Finanzierung auch in schwierigen Zeiten.

Die meisten Musikschulen der Schweiz sind im «Verband Musikschulen Schweiz» (VMS) zusammengeschlossen. Viele Kantone haben auch einen kantonalen Musikschulverband. Deren Vertreter bilden die Delegiertenkonferenz des VMS. Der Verband gibt eine zweimonatlich erscheinende Zeitschrift «Animato» heraus. Er betreibt eine Altersvorsorge-Versicherung für alle Musiklehrkräfte. Der VMS pflegt Kontakte, informiert, gibt Dokumente heraus, veranstaltet Aus- und Fortbildungen (Kongresse, Tagungen, Kurse zur Ausbildung von Musikschulleitern usw.) und berät die Musikschulen.

Türkei

Es liegt im Moment kein aktueller Bericht vor.

publiques comme pour les écoles de musique. La rétribution du corps enseignant diffère d'un canton à l'autre. Plusieurs cantons apportent une contribution aux écoles de musique, oscillant entre 1% et 50%. Dans certains cantons, on est encore loin d'atteindre une répartition égale entre parents, commune et canton (chacun contribuant pour un tiers aux dépenses globales), alors qu'ailleurs la part des parents est limitée à 20%.

Les écoles de musique sont soutenues principalement par les communes ou associations de communes. 30% d'entre elles sont régies par des règles de droit privé et 70% par des règles de droit public. Beaucoup d'entre elles sont subordonnées aux autorités des écoles publiques, d'autres dépendent directement des communes ou d'associations indépendantes. Plus les écoles de musique sont régies par le droit public, mieux leur financement est-il assuré, même en période difficile.

La plupart des écoles de musique suisses font partie de l'«Association Suisse des Ecoles de Musique» (ASEM). Plusieurs cantons ont également une association cantonale des écoles de musique dont les représentants forment l'assemblée des délégués de l'ASEM. Cette dernière publie une revue bimestrielle, «ANIMATO». Elle gère aussi son propre fonds de prévoyance pour tous les professeurs de musique. L'ASEM établit des contacts, informe, édite des documents, dispense des cours de formation et de perfectionnement (congrès, sessions, cours de formation pour directeurs d'écoles de musique) et apporte ses conseils aux écoles de musique.

Turquie
Pas de rapport disponible pour l'instant.

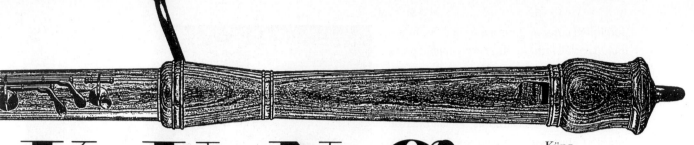

·K·Ü·N·G·
Blockflöten

Ein gutes Instrument. Von Anfang an.

Küng
Blockflötenbau
CH-8200 Schaffhausen
Grabenstrasse 3

Gitarren-Unterricht kann schon im Vorschulalter beginnen. Unsere kindgerechten „Junior"-Gitarren sind erschwinglich und klingen gut.

Die angebotenen Modelle eignen sich für Körpergrößen von 100 cm bis 160 cm.

Alle Instrumente sind leicht spielbar und vertragen schon mal rauhe Behandlung.

Die Ausstattung ist komplett, mit schöner Schalloch-Verzierung, mit Kantenschutz um Decke und Boden, pflegeleichter Hochglanz-Politur und servicefreundlichem Griffbrett.

Als kleinen Beitrag zum Schutz des Regenwaldes haben wir weitgehend auf exotische Edelhölzer verzichtet und verwenden dafür einheimisches Material, das ständig wieder aufgeforstet wird.

Modell Junior I

Mensur 44 cm
Altersgruppe 5 – 8 Jahre
Körpergröße 100 –130 cm

Modell Junior II

Mensur 53 cm
Altersgruppe 8 – 11 Jahre
Körpergröße 120 –140 cm

Modell Junior III

Mensur 57 cm
Altersgruppe 10 –13 Jahre
Körpergröße 130 –150 cm

Modell Junior IV

Mensur 62 cm
Altersgruppe 11 –14 Jahre
Körpergröße 140 –160 cm

Die „Junior"-Serie:

Gitarren für kleine Leute

Carl Hellweg

Was fasziniert an originalen Blockflöten der Barockzeit?
Das charakteristisch obertönige Timbre,
die für Blockflöten so dynamische Tonbildungsmöglichkeit,
doch vor allem das Spielgefühl, mit einem Instrument solcher Art
auf besondere Weise eins sein zu können.

*

Wir bieten – neben unseren Rottenburgh-Flöten –
folgende Barockkopien an:

Sopran- und Altblockflöten
nach

Jan Steenbergen

(1675-1728, Amsterdam)

Originale in der Sammlung Frans Brüggen, Amsterdam
a' = 440 oder 415 Hz. Aus Birnbaum, Indisch Buchs oder
Grenadill, geölt und gewachst. Im Lederfutteral.

Altblockflöte
nach

Thomas Stanesby senior

(1668-1734, London)

Original in der Sammlung Frans Brüggen, Amsterdam.
Die wohl berühmteste überlieferte Altflöte aus der Barockzeit.
Rekonstruktion Ralf Ehlert – a' = 440 oder 415 Hz. Aus Indisch
Buchs, natur oder antik gebeizt, geölt. Im Lederfutteral.

*

Die Steenbergen-Kopien werden bei uns von Gabriele Grünewald,
die Stanesbys von Ralf Ehlert – beide Blockflötenbaumeister –
sowohl in der Herstellung als auch im Service betreut. Jedem
Instrument liegt ein entsprechendes Zertifikat bei.

Bitte Sonderprospekt anfordern, oder rufen Sie einfach unser
Informationstelefon an: 0 51 41 / 88 53 23.

MOECK

VERLAG + MUSIKINSTRUMENTENWERK
Postfach 3131, D-29231 Celle

Achten Sie beim Kauf Ihres Pianos auf die Mechanik...

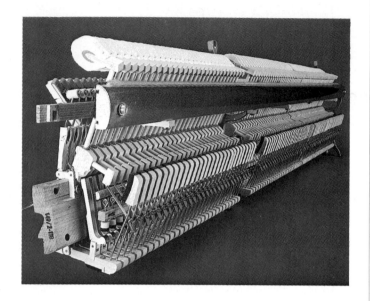

Denn ohne Spielwerk, ohne dessen 6000 präzise Einzelteile, wäre auch das schönste Piano nur ein klangloses Gehäuse.

Alle großen bedeutenden Klavierhersteller bauen Mechaniken von Renner ein.

Warum aber gerade die von Renner?

Weil keiner der großen, bedeutenden Klavierhersteller sich auch nur den kleinsten Fehler leisten kann.

Die Mechanik von Renner.

Louis Renner GmbH & Co., Fritz-Reuter-Straße 18, D-70193 Stuttgart, Tel. (07 11) 6 56 51-0, Telegramm-Adresse: Mechanikrenner

FRANK HAMMERSCHMIDT KLARINETTEN

MEISTERWERKSTATT FÜR HOLZBLASINSTRUMENTE

AUGSBURGER STRASSE 46 · 89331 BURGAU / SCHWABEN
POSTFACH 1271 · 89326 BURGAU / SCHWABEN
TELEFON 0 82 22 / 76 25 · TELEFAX 0 82 22 / 81 13

PYRAMID®
Saiten · Strings · Cuerdas

Saiten- und Stimmpfeifenfabrik Junger GmbH
Postfach 6, P.O.Box 6
Tel. (09131) 2 40 64 • Fax (09131) 20 66 42
D-91088 Bubenreuth

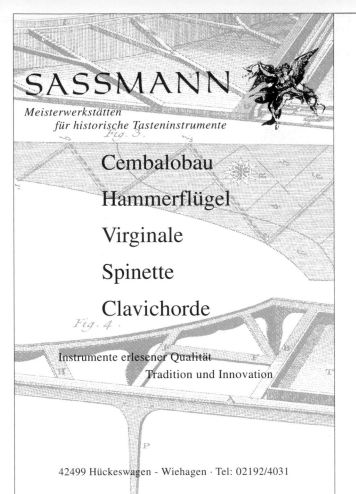

SASSMANN

Meisterwerkstätten
für historische Tasteninstrumente

Cembalobau

Hammerflügel

Virginale

Spinette

Clavichorde

Instrumente erlesener Qualität
Tradition und Innovation

42499 Hückeswagen · Wiehagen · Tel: 02192/4031

1955–1995

Die Firma SASSMANN
feiert in diesem Jahr
ihr 40jähriges Bestehen
und hat somit großen Anteil
an der Renaissance des historischen
Tasteninstrumentenbaus.
Diese Tradition bleibt,
da sie verpflichtet!

Deutscher Musikinstrumenten-Preisträger 1994

Studio for Doublebasses

Sven-Henrik Gawron

— Bassist —

Doublebasses — on hire · purchase · sale · repair
all accessories · strings · pickups · selected amplification systems

Marktstraße 5 · 41751 Viersen (Dülken)
Telefon 0 21 62/5 33 09 · Telefax 0 21 62/4 56 92

Contrabasses
JOCHEN BIEN
— Violinmaker —

Old and new
double basses

Repairs and
accessories

Pupil basses
down to $\frac{1}{8}$ size

D-22587 Hamburg
Frahmstraße 15

Fax: +49 (0)40/86 96 49
Phone: +49 (0)40/86 99 18

ATLANTIS MUSIKBUCH

Aktualisierte 1994 Neufassung

Vierte, vollständig überarbeitete und erweiterte Auflage 1994

KLAUS WOLTERS
Handbuch der Klavierliteratur zu zwei Händen

Ein zuverlässiger Führer durch die gesamte Klavierliteratur, ein riesiges Panorama, das sich vom Spanier Cabezòn bis zu seriellen Komponisten erstreckt und jeden der Meister mit klug abgewogenen Urteilen nahebringt.

Inhalt
• Klavierschulen
• Anleitung zur Improvisation
• Methodische und historische Schriften
• Technische Studienwerke - Etüden Anthologien
• Die Meister der Renaissance und Barockzeit
• Die klassischen Meister
• Die Nachfolge der Klassiker Das frühe Virtuosentum
• Die großen Klaviermeister des 19. Jahrhunderts
• Kleinmeister im Bereich der deutschen Romantik
• Nationale Schulen im 19. Jhd. und ihre Fortsetzung bis zur Gegenwart
• Die Musik unserer Zeit
• Personenregister

Best.-Nr. ATL 6119, 699 Seiten mit Notenbeispielen, Leinenausgabe mit Schutzumschlag, DM 98,- / öS 765,- / sFr 98,-

Informationen über das Gesamtprogramm finden Sie im ATLANTIS Musikbuch-Katalog, erhältlich im Fachhandel.

ATLANTIS MUSIK-BUCH

Für nur 99,33 DM mtl. 20 Bände GROVE sofort komplett und MGG neu 8 Bände!

Ihnen biete ich Rundum-Information zur Musik in Geschichte & Gegenwart jetzt besonders wohlfeil!

Antworten Sie rasch, Kombi-Angebot gilt nur bis zum 30.04.1995!

Verehrte Leserin, lieber Musikfreund, natürlich kennen Sie die berühmte MGG: jetzt kommt sie neu, die „Musik in Geschichte & Gegenwart", angelegt auf 20 Bände. Wenn Sie schon sehnlichst auf die Neu-Ausgabe gewartet haben, greifen Sie zu. Wählen Sie ob Sie sich volle 1.000,– DM-Subskutionsvorteil sichern wollen für 8 Bände Sachteil und 12 Bände Personenteil, 20 Bände gesamt (Band 1 ist lieferbar, Band 2 erscheint in wenigen Tagen)

Und wenn Sie bisher den großen GROVE in 20 Bänden noch entbehren, ist jetzt der richtige Moment für Sie, sich die „große Kombi" zu sichern: Man höre & staune – ich liefere Ihnen GROVE

in 20 Bänden zusammen mit Band 1 MGG neu sofort · Ihre Investiton im Monats-Schnitt ist gerade mal 99,33 DM. Sie zweifeln? Sollen Sie! Fragen Sie nach – Ihre Antwort per Coupon verpflichtet Sie zu gar nichts, sichert Ihnen alles (vorausgesetzt, Sie antworten schnell). Mein Angebot gilt bis zum 30.04.95: GRATIS-Info kommt per Post · dann erst entscheiden Sie. Das garantiert Ihnen Ihr Partner für Musik-Literatur & Nachschlage-Werke Hans-D. Blatter

Gratis-Info über das Aktions-Angebot „Kombi": GROVE komplett 20 Bände + MGG neu Sachteil 8 Bände jetzt für Sie nur 99,33 DM monatlich ohne Zins-Aufschlag! Coupon am besten gleich einsenden an:
Akademischer Lexikadienst
Dipl.-Vw. H.D. Blatter, Rosenstraße 12-13, D 48143 Münster, Tel. 0251-42882, Fax 0251-518565

Ja, Ihre Gratis-Info interessiert mich. Zugleich sichere ich mir die Option auf Ihr Kombi-Angebot, das Sie mir bis 30. April offenhalten. Wenn ich mich dazu entscheide, kann ich MGG & GROVE schon für nur DM 99,33 monatlich erhalten, wie beschrieben. Und spare mindestens 1.000,– durch die Subskription MGG. Jetzt verpflichte ich mich zu nichts. Mein Kontakt:

_____   _____
Name, Vorname   Telefon für Info

_____
Straße, PLZ, Ort

Haast music publishers

99 Prinseneiland: 1013 LN Amsterdam
tel. (31)020-623 97 99; fax. (31)020-6243 53 34
Holland

Willem Breuker

Ragtime
Concert Band
Circus Knieval
Concert Band
Aanpakken en wegwezen
Symphony Orchestra
Onleesbaar
Symphony Orchestra
Chain and Clay
Brass-band
Woody Wood
Big-band
Overture Little Amsterdam Rhapsody
Big-band
Summer Music
Big-band
Lost Ground
Organ
Joy of fishing
Guitar
Washed-up
Bassoon
Guts
Chime
Strijkkwartet van de week
String Quartet
Pilot light
Harpsichord/Chamber Orchestra
Han de Vries
Oboe/Chamber Orchestra
For Yo-Yo Ma
Oboe/Chamber Orchestra

Bernard Hunnekink

De eindeloze slof
Concert Band
Veur den blaos weg
Concert Band
Hout en hars
Concert Band
Hè, hè, effe sitte
Bassoon Quartet

Fachkundige
Gesprächs-
partner
informieren,
beraten,
vermitteln
Orchester-
musiker und
Musikschul-
lehrer.

10719 Berlin	Kurfürstendamm 210 Tel. 030/88 43 05-0 Durchwahl -50 Fax 030/88 43 05-13 zuständig für die neuen Bundesländer
40476 Düsseldorf	Schwannstraße 3 Tel. 02 11/43 06-0 Durchwahl -298, -568 Fax 02 11/43 06-643 zuständig für die alten Bundesländer

Künstlerdienste
der Bundesanstalt für Arbeit

MILO   der Stuhl für
kleine und große Musiker

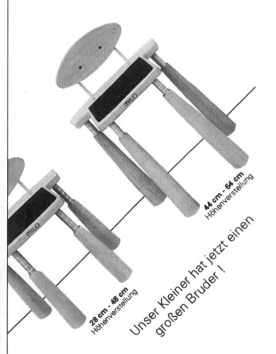

44 cm - 64 cm
Höhenverstellung

28 cm - 48 cm
Höhenverstellung

Unser Kleiner hat jetzt einen
großen Bruder !

Gute
Industrie
Form 95

MILO - Tannenweg 9 - D 73525 Schwäbisch Gmünd
Telefon 07171/ 61553 - Telefax 07171/ 64450

HENLE
STUDIEN-EDITION

Urtext-Ausgaben
großer Komponisten
im handlichen Buchformat

17 × 24 cm, 157 Seiten
HN 9001   DM 14,–   öS 122,–   sFr. 16.80

Eine neue Serie
preisgünstiger Notenbände
von höchster Qualität
zum Mitlesen und Studieren!

Die ersten sieben Titel sind bereits erschienen.
Weitere befinden sich in Vorbereitung.

Sonderprospekt lieferbar!

G. HENLE VERLAG

Buildings to House Music Schools

Häuser für Musikschulen

Des maisons pour les écoles de musique

«A music school – what's that?» Of course, we all know that a music school is not a thing, but an area of activity: the joining and working together of people with the aim of learning and teaching music – wherever this may take place. Alongside the students and teachers, the music school is also made up of those who organize this meeting together: that is, the directors and administrative workers. The music school's influence is extended by the inclusion of the pupils' parents, families and friends of those who show their interest by coming to concerts and music school festivals, and of those people who sometimes read something about a music school in the newspaper or who only know of it by reputation.

A typical question put by outsiders gives an indication of the importance to a music school of having a building of its own: «The music school – where's that?» The identification of the work and activities of a music school with a particular location, most obviously achieved through having its own building, makes people aware that «there is a Music School». If music schools are truly to become centres of musical life in their environment, then their presence needs to be established in a place belonging to them and them alone, where people can spot them and visit them. These premises must also be central in their geographical location: a central focus of musical activity in their town or region.

Not only for the sake of its public image, but for those people engaged in activity within the music school, such a building is a visible symbol of the whole. Here people are brought together under the banner of music and it is here where they communicate with one another: teachers discuss educational questions and problems; students find others to join them in music-making; rehearsals, concerts, administrative business, staff meetings and parents' meetings – all are brought together here under one roof. A special music school building gives a feeling of belonging, of cohesion, which is to be considered an important prerequisite for success in the teaching of music and the experience of music as a source for social harmony.

«Musikschule – was ist das?» Freilich wissen wir alle, daß Musikschule nicht etwas «ist», sondern «sich ereignet»: im Zusammenkommen und Zusammenarbeiten von Menschen mit dem Ziel, Musik zu lernen und zu lehren – wo auch immer dies stattfinden mag. Neben den Schülern und Lehrern «sind Musikschule» auch diejenigen, die das Zusammenkommen organisieren, also die Schulleitung und die Mitarbeiter der Verwaltung. Weitere Kreise zieht Musikschule durch Einbeziehung ihres Publikums: die Eltern, Familien und Freunde der Schüler, Neugierige und Interessierte, die zu Konzerten und Musikschulfesten kommen, und Leute, die in der Zeitung manchmal über die Musikschule lesen oder sie nur vom Hörensagen kennen.

Gerade an einer typischen Frage von Außenstehenden kann man jedoch die Bedeutung ablesen, die ein eigenes Haus für eine Musikschule hat: «Musikschule – wo ist denn die?» Die Identifikation der Arbeit und der Inhalte einer Musikschule mit einem räumlichen Bezugspunkt, wie ihn am deutlichsten ein eigenes Haus sichtbar machen kann, prägt das Bewußtsein, «daß da eine Musikschule ist». Wenn Musikschulen in ihrem örtlichen Umfeld wirklich zu Zentren des Musiklebens werden sollen, dann brauchen sie auch einen festen, ihnen allein gehörenden Ort, an dem sie «präsent» sind, wo man sie aufsuchen kann und wo sie auch zu finden sind. Der Ort dieser Repräsentanz muß auch in seiner geographischen Lage «zentral» sein: als Mittelpunkt der Musikschulaktivität in der Stadt oder der Region.

Und nicht nur nach außen, der Öffentlichkeit zugewandt, sondern auch für die innerhalb der Musikschule engagierten Menschen ist ein solches Haus sichtbares Sinnbild für das Ganze. Hier kommt man im Zeichen der Musik zusammen, hier findet Kommunikation statt: Lehrer besprechen pädagogische Fragen und Probleme, Schüler finden Partner zum gemeinsamen Musizieren, Proben, Konzerte, Verwaltungsgeschäfte, Konferenzen und Elterngespräche – hier sind «alle unter einem Dach». Das gemeinsame Haus Musikschule vermittelt ein Wir-Gefühl, das als wichtige Voraussetzung für den musikpädagogischen Erfolg, für das Erleben der sozialen, verbindenden Kraft der Musik gelten kann.

«Une école de musique – qu'est-ce que c'est?». Bien évidemment, nous savons tous qu'une école de musique n'est pas quelque chose, mais qu'elle «se produit», qu'elle «a lieu»: par la rencontre et la collaboration d'individus ayant un même but: apprendre et enseigner la musique – où que ce soit. Outre les élèves et les professeurs, «sont» aussi l'école de musique ceux qui organisent cette rencontre, c'est-à-dire la direction de l'école et les collaborateurs de l'administration. L'école de musique s'étend plus encore par l'inclusion de son public: les parents, les familles et les amis des élèves, les curieux et les personnes intéressées qui viennent à des concerts et des fêtes de l'école et les gens qui, dans le journal, lisent quelquefois des articles sur l'école de musique ou ne la connaissent que par des on-dits.

C'est justement l'une de ces questions typiques posées par des profanes qui permet de définir l'importance que revêt une maison propre pour l'école de musique: «L'école de musique – c'est où, ça?» L'identification du travail et des contenus d'une école de musique avec un point de référence spatial, visualisé de manière optimale par une maison propre empreint la conscience du fait «qu'il y a là une école de musique». Si les écoles de musique, avec leur environnement local, veulent vraiment devenir des centres de la vie musicale, il leur faut un lieu fixe, qui n'appartienne qu'à elles, où elles seront «présentes», où l'on pourra leur rendre visite et où on les trouvera. Le lieu de cette représentation doit également être «central» sur le plan de sa situation géographique: au centre de l'activité musicale de la ville ou de la région.

Une telle maison est un symbole visible de l'ensemble, et ce non seulement vers l'extérieur, vers le grand public, mais également pour les individus qui s'engagent au sein de l'école de musique. Ici, on se rassemble sous le signe de la musique, ici, on communique: les enseignants discutent de questions et de problèmes pédagogiques, les élèves trouvent des partenaires avec lesquels ils peuvent faire de la musique, s'exercer, donner des concerts, il y a une administration, des conférences, des discussions avec les parents – ici, tout le monde est «sous le même toit». La maison commune de l'école de musique communique un sentiment du «Nous», la condition la plus importante, sans

«The house» has a wider emotional symbolism than its purely practical importance in people's lives, a value that needs to be exploited to establish a positive environment for music learning and music-making: the feeling of having a «home», a special place for music, a refuge, a shelter and a shell, where individuals have room to develop their musical talents. Old and historic buildings seem best suited to generating the kind of atmosphere which also increases motivation by stimulating an awareness of cultural tradition.

Of course, a house of this kind for musicians, whether the building is old or new, needs to be properly furnished and equipped. It must meet the usual standards required of school buildings with regard to safety and suitability; it must have a large number of rooms, a hall for rehearsals, concerts or auditions; it must be equipped with instruments (pianos, simple instruments for work with young children, percussion setups etc.) and it must also have a staff room and offices. Lastly, its acoustic suitability has to be considered and it needs to be furnished in a way that is both pleasant and functional.

Where music schools are obliged to carry out their teaching in ordinary school buildings where normal school-teaching takes place in the mornings, conditions are far from ideal. Organizational problems arise through overlapping of timetables; the ambience of rooms and the manner in which they are furnished is usually quite unsuitable for instrumental lessons or for work with small children. What is worse, the atmosphere of the classroom, which for children and adolescents is their place of work, a place of cognitive and strictly assessed learning, does not suit the «freer» character of a music school as a place which nurtures creative artistic development and individual expression.

On the other hand, it will not always be practicable to concentrate all the teaching activities of a music school in one single building, for these need to be readily accessible to all the residents of a town. With small children in particular, it is very important that they should not have too far to go to get to the music school. There is also the need to accommodate socially disadvantaged groups by bringing music to them and to the areas where they

Im Leben aller Menschen hat «das Haus» an sich einen weiteren, als existentiell zu bezeichnenden emotionalen Symbolwert, der für ein positiv besetztes Musiklernen und Musikmachen genutzt werden muß: das Gefühl, ein «Zuhause» zu haben, einen ganz speziellen Schutzraum für die Musik, ein sicheres «Gehäuse», das einen Spiel-Raum bietet für die individuelle Ausbildung der musikalischen Anlagen. Vor allem alte, historische Häuser strahlen eine solche Atmosphäre aus, die zudem das Bewußtsein kultureller Tradition als Motivationsfaktor wirksam werden läßt.

Es versteht sich, daß ein solches Musiklern-Haus – ob alt oder modern – über eine vernünftige Ausstattung verfügen muß. Es muß hinsichtlich Sicherheit und Funktionalität den üblichen Anforderungen an ein Schulgebäude entsprechen, es muß zahlreiche Räume bieten, einen Saal für Proben und Konzerte oder Vorspiele, es muß mit Instrumenten bestückt sein (Klaviere, elementare Instrumente für die Früherziehung, Schlagzeuge usw.), und es sollte auch ein Lehrerzimmer und Verwaltungsräume haben. Schließlich ist die akustische Tauglichkeit zu bedenken und für eine angenehme und zugleich zweckmäßige Einrichtung zu sorgen.

Dort, wo Musikschulen gezwungen sind, ihren Unterricht in Schulgebäuden zu erteilen, in denen vormittags normaler Schulunterricht stattfindet, herrschen dagegen schlechte Bedingungen. Organisatorische Probleme treten bei den Nutzungszeiten durch Überschneidung der Stundenpläne auf; meist ist die Ausstattung und Beschaffenheit der Räume völlig unzweckmäßig für Instrumentalunterricht oder gar die musikalische Früherziehung. Schlimmer noch ist, daß die Atmosphäre des Klassenzimmers, das ja der Arbeitsraum der Kinder und Jugendlichen, ein Ort kognitiven und streng benoteten Lernens ist, dem «Frei»-Zeit-Charakter von Musikschule substantiell entgegenwirkt – wo es doch gilt, die musischen, kreativen Kräfte und eine freie Entfaltung des Schülers zu fördern.

Auf der anderen Seite wird es nicht immer möglich und sinnvoll sein, den gesamten Unterricht einer Musikschule auf ein einziges Haus zu konzentrieren. Denn die Musikschule muß und will ja auch ein wohnortnahes Angebot machen. Vor allem für die kleinen Kinder der musikalischen Grundstufe

doute, du succès musico-pédagogique, de l'expérience de la force sociale et relationnelle de la musique.

«La maison», dans la vie de tous les hommes, a, en soi, une autre valeur symbolique émotionnelle que l'on caractérisera d'existentielle, valeur qui peut être utilisée avec profit pour un apprentissage positif de la musique et de la pratique musicale: le sentiment d'avoir un «chez-soi», un refuge tout particulier pour la musique, un «boîtier» protégé qui offre un espace pour la formation individuelle des dons musicaux naturels. Ce sont surtout les maisons anciennes, historiques, qui respirent cette atmosphère qui, de plus, fait agir la conscience de la tradition culturelle comme facteur de motivation.

Il va de soi qu'une telle maison de la musique – qu'elle soit ancienne ou moderne – doit disposer d'un équipement raisonnable. Elle doit répondre, sur le plan de la sécurité et de la fonctionnalité, aux exigences habituelles posées à un établissement scolaire, elle doit avoir des salles nombreuses, une salle de répétition et de concert ou de représentation, elle doit être équipée d'instruments (pianos, instruments élémentaires pour l'éducation précoce, percussions, etc...) et elle devrait également disposer d'une salle des professeurs et de locaux administratifs. Enfin, il conviendra de considérer ses qualités acoustiques et de veiller à un ameublement agréable et fonctionnel à la fois.

Là où les écoles de musique sont contraintes de donner leurs cours dans des bâtiments scolaires où des cours normaux ont lieu le matin, les conditions de travail sont mauvaises. Des problèmes d'organisation apparaissent au niveau des heures d'occupation des locaux, les emplois du temps se coupant; la plupart du temps, l'équipement et la nature des locaux sont totalement inadaptés à l'enseignement d'un instrument ou même à l'éducation musicale précoce. Pis encore, l'atmosphère de la salle de classe – lieu de travail pour les enfants et les jeunes, lieu de l'étude cognitive et sévèrement notée – va à l'encontre du caractère de temps «libre» de l'école de musique de manière substantielle, alors qu'il s'agit de développer et d'encourager les forces poétiques et créatives et l'épanouissement libre de l'élève.

«Jahr für Jahr treffen sich viele tausend junge Musiker in Internationalen Music-Camps und Chortreffen, bei Schüleraustauschen, Kursen und Wettbewerben oder bei den großen „Europäischen Musikfesten der Jugend", die von der Europäischen Musikschul-Union in verschiedenen Ländern veranstaltet werden. Die Musik führt sie zusammen, läßt sie einander über Sprachgrenzen hinweg verstehen, ihre kulturelle Eigenart kennen- und schätzenlernen, ihre nationale Verschiedenheit akzeptieren, Vorurteile abbauen und Vertrauen ineinander fassen. Je besser ein jeder die gemeinsame Sprache, die Musik, beherrscht, um so schneller und direkter funktioniert die Kommunikation.

Ich persönlich wünsche mir, daß diese Art der Kommunikation auch dazu beiträgt, daß die Menschen Frieden finden.»

Fürstin Marie von und zu Liechtenstein

live, as near as possible. Finally, there is never room in one building to teach all the most popular instruments, such as piano, guitar or recorder, at once. So the music school has to go out into the various districts of a town and the surrounding villages. This will always involve sharing the use of rooms in schools or other institutions. But the music school should always make sure that its own interests are properly represented and that its needs are met. It should for instance have sole use of certain rooms, with a proper right to use facilities in other rooms, with sufficient space to move about in, cupboards and pianos that can be locked, etc.

In large towns that have grown together out of several smaller communities, or in large districts with a number of centres, it may even be desirable to provide the music school with several of its own buildings. The feeling people have of identifying with a particular residential zone includes the desire for «their» community to develop a cultural life of their own.

For a music school to have its own premises is surely not an extravagant demand, and a funding authority which provides a music school with its own home is being anything but wasteful. Rather it is creating the basic organizational and teaching conditions which encourage both personal motivation and «efficiency», doing much to help increase the effectiveness of music schools and promote the attainment of their cultural and educational goals.   *uw.*

ist ein kurzer Weg zur Musikschule ausschlagge-
bend. Auch ist es wichtig, sozial schwächeren Be-
völkerungsgruppen mit Angeboten des Musizierens
und der Anleitung dazu soweit als möglich schon
räumlich «entgegenzukommen». Schließlich sind
stark frequentierte Fächer wie Klavier, Gitarre oder
Blockflöte niemals alle in einem Haus unterzubrin-
gen. Die Musikschule muß also in die verschiedenen Stadtteile gehen, in den verschiedenen Ortschaften einer Gemeinde präsent sein. Dabei wird
es immer zu einer Gemeinschaftsnutzung von Räumen in Schulen oder anderen Einrichtungen kommen. Doch in jedem Fall sollte die Musikschule auf
ihre besonderen Belange Anspruch erheben und
diesen Anspruch auch durchsetzen. So etwa sollte
sie wenigstens einzelne Räume zur alleinigen Nut-
zung erhalten, in anderen Räumen ihre geschütz-
ten Plätze haben (genügend Bewegungsfläche, ab-
schließbare Klaviere, Schränke usw.).

In größeren Städten, die aus verschiedenen Or-
ten zusammengewachsen sind, oder in großen
Kreisen mit mehreren Hauptorten kann es sogar
erstrebenswert sein, der Musikschule mehrere eigene Häuser zu geben. Denn zu der auch im Bewußtsein der Menschen gewachsenen Siedlungs-
struktur gehört der Wunsch, in «ihrem» Ort ein
Kulturleben eigener Prägung zu entfalten.

Ein eigenes Haus für die Musikschule – dies ist
keine überzogene Forderung; und ein Musikschul-
träger, der seinem Institut ein eigenes Domizil zur
Verfügung stellt, ist alles andere als ein Verschwen-
der. Vielmehr wird damit eine fachliche und organisatorische Grundvoraussetzung geschaffen, die
durch Momente der persönlichen Motivation wie
auch der «betrieblichen Effizienz» die Wirksamkeit
der Musikschularbeit im Hinblick auf ihre kultur-
und bildungspolitische Zielsetzung enorm steigern
hilft. *uw.*

D'autre part, il ne sera pas toujours possible et
bon de concentrer l'ensemble des cours d'une école
de musique dans un seul bâtiment. Car l'école de
musique doit et veut offrir un éventail de possibilités à proximité des lieux d'habitation. Pour les petits enfants des classes de musique primaires, surtout, il est de caractère décisif que le trajet jusqu'à
l'école de musique soit court. Il est également important de venir, le plus possible, «au-devant»,
dans l'espace, des groupes de la population plus
faibles avec des possibilités de faire de la musique
et d'y être introduit. Enfin, des matières à fréquentation importante telles que le piano, la guitare ou
la flûte à bec, ne peuvent en aucun cas être logées
toutes dans une seule maison. L'école de musique
doit donc se rendre dans les différents quartiers,
être présente dans les différentes localités d'une
même commune. Et il se produira toujours une utilisation collective des locaux dans des écoles ou
d'autres institutions. Mais, dans chaque cas, l'école
de musique devra revendiquer et imposer ses intérêts propres. Ainsi, par exemple, elle devrait obtenir au moins quelques salles isolées utilisées par
elle seule, disposer, dans les autres salles, d'espa-
ces protégés (avec suffisamment de liberté de mouvement, des pianos et des armoires pouvant être
fermés à clé, etc...).

Dans les grandes villes nées de plusieurs localités
différentes, ou dans les grandes circonscriptions
avec plusieurs localités principales, il sera même
souhaitable de donner à l'école de musique plusieurs maisons propres. Car le désir de développer
dans «leur» localité une vie culturelle portant leur
empreinte propre fait partie de la structure de l'ha-
bitat qui a grandi, aussi, dans la conscience des
hommes.

Une maison propre pour l'école de musique – il
ne s'agit pas là d'une revendication exagérée; et un
responsable qui donne à son institution un domicile propre n'est pas un gaspilleur. Bien plus, ceci
permet de créer la condition technique et d'organisation de base qui, par des moments tant de motivation personnelle que d'«efficience interne»,
contribue à augmenter l'efficacité du travail de
l'école de musique au sens de ses objectifs culturels
et éducatifs. *uw.*

Musical Training and Education in the Early Years

Musikalische Früherziehung und musikalische Grundausbildung

Education musicale précoce et formation musicale élémentaire

Bearing in mind the cultural and political role of music schools, the years of primary musical education – and the early years in particular – are an important field of work. A fundamental goal here is to make available to all children the opportunity for musical training appropriate to their interests and abilities, but also to their individual development.

The significance of early musical training in the whole process of a child's education has been scientifically proven: the positive influence of such training on the development of personality, general capacity for learning and development of social skills constitutes an advantage which ought to be made available to all young people.

For the sake of equal chances for everybody there is a need to tear down barriers which prevent many from turning to cultural activity: the question of fees is as important as adopting the right approach in order to establish contact with families. It is decided within the family whether a child takes up the offer of music lessons, so anyone who wishes to assure the child's musical future must win the parents' support and encourage their interest. This understanding the pedagogical approach of Early Music Learning takes account of.

The general aims of music teaching at primary level are the following:

- Children should, first of all, exercise their senses and compile a repertoire of musical experiences in a playful way with others of the same age.
- Surrounded by a musicbound atmosphere, children should develop elementary musical skills and acquire those abilities which form the basis for musical activity.
- Children should gain a real interest which may lead them to learn an instrument later on or to become involved in music in some other way.
- Musical gifts should be recognized very early on and receive all possible support and encouragement.

In the early years, the aim of promoting musical abilities has to be balanced with the need for teaching-methods appropriate for children aged 4–6. Children at nursery level have to be taught through games related to their environment and

Gerade in Hinsicht auf den kulturpolitischen Auftrag der Musikschule zu musikalischer Breitenarbeit ist die musikalische Grundstufe – und hier insbesondere die musikalische Früherziehung – ein bedeutendes Arbeitsgebiet. Ein fundamentales Ziel ist es dabei, prinzipiell allen Kindern eine Option auf eine musikalische Ausbildung zu eröffnen, die ihren Wünschen und Fähigkeiten, aber auch ihren Entwicklungen angemessen ist.

Die Bedeutung, die einer musikalischen Früherziehung für den gesamten Bildungsprozeß eines Kindes zukommt, ist wissenschaftlich erwiesen: Die positive Beeinflussung der Persönlichkeitsstruktur, des allgemeinen Lernvermögens und des Sozialverhaltens durch frühes Musiklernen sind Startchancen, die allen jungen Menschen offenstehen sollen.

Im Sinne der Chancengleichheit gilt es daher auch, die bei vielen Menschen vorhandenen Barrieren gegenüber kulturellen Angeboten abzubauen: Der Kostenfaktor ist dabei ebenso entscheidend wie eine attraktive und einladende Ansprache der Familien. Die Familie ist der Ort, an dem es sich entscheidet, ob ein Kind die von außen herangetragene Chance einer Musikausbildung nutzen kann. Wer den musikalischen Weg des Kindes sichern will, muß also die positive Einstellung, das Interesse und die Mitwirkung der Eltern fördern. Die Didaktik der musikalischen Früherziehung trägt dieser Erkenntnis Rechnung.

Allgemein hat der Musikunterricht in der Grundstufe der Musikschule folgende Zielsetzung:

- Die Kinder sollen zunächst im gemeinsamen Spielen mit Gleichaltrigen ihre Sinne schärfen und einen Erfahrungsschatz an musikalischen Erlebnissen sammeln.
- Die Kinder sollen in einer von Musik geprägten Atmosphäre elementare musikalische Fähigkeiten entwickeln und die grundlegenden Voraussetzungen erwerben, mit Musik umgehen zu können.
- Die Kinder sollen ein dauerhaftes Motiv ausbilden, später ein Musikinstrument zu erlernen oder in anderer Weise musikalisch aktiv zu sein.
- Musikalische Begabungen sollen sehr früh erkannt und optimal gefördert werden.

Dans le cadre de la mission politico-culturelle de l'école de musique en vue d'un travail musical de masse, la formation musicale primaire – et, en particulier, l'éducation musicale précoce – constitue un domaine de travail important. L'un des buts fondamentaux en est d'ouvrir à tous les enfants, par principe, une option à une formation musicale adaptée à leurs souhaits et à leurs capacités.

L'importance d'une éducation musicale précoce pour le processus éducatif global de l'enfant est scientifiquement prouvée: l'influence positive exercée par un apprentissage musical précoce sur la structure de la personnalité, la faculté générale à l'étude et le comportement social sont des chances de départ qui doivent être mises à la disposition de tous les jeunes.

Au sens d'une égalité des chances, il s'agit donc d'abolir, chez beaucoup de gens, les barrières existant vis-à-vis des offres culturelles: le facteur des frais est, ici, tout aussi décisif qu'un appel attrayant et attirant à l'égard des familles. La famille est le lieu où l'on décide si l'enfant peut saisir la chance, venue de l'extérieur, d'une formation musicale. Si l'on veut donc assurer à l'enfant une voie musicale, il faut encourager l'attitude positive, l'intérêt et la participation des parents. La didactique de l'éducation musicale précoce rend compte de cette conclusion.

En général, les cours de musique de la classe primaire de l'école de musique poursuivent les buts suivants:

- Les enfants doivent tout d'abord, en jouant avec d'autres enfants du même âge, aiguiser leurs sens et amasser un trésor d'expériences musicales vécues.
- Les enfants doivent, dans une atmosphère empreinte de musique, développer des facultés musicales élémentaires et acquérir les conditions de base leur permettant d'appréhender et de pratiquer la musique.
- Les enfants doivent développer une motivation durable d'apprendre, plus tard, un instrument ou d'exercer une activité musicale sous une autre forme.
- Les dons musicaux doivent être décelés très tôt et être encouragés de manière optimale.

matching their abilities. Psychologists have known for a long time that the ability and willingness to learn are particularly great at pre-school age. On the whole, cognitive development can be stimulated early on; however, abstract subjects should not be introduced too soon. Written music and theory are of little importance and less interest to small children; indeed, they could put a child off and cause it to turn away from music altogether. The child's learning through enjoyment, its primary motivation, should not be disturbed by the intrusion of elements apparently alien. With pre-school music groups, the teacher's most important approach must be to appeal to the children's sense of voice, movement and play.

The primary school age group of 6–8 is quite different: They have interest in trickier questions, relations and systems, a dawning understanding of symbols and structures, and are familiar with teaching methods encountered at school. The meaning of musical forms, written music and other rules and principles may now be understood. Then again, children of this age have an unbound desire to play an instrument for themselves. An occasional bash on a xylophone is no longer anything like enough! There should be an interesting collection of simple instruments ready at hand in the classroom. The best thing, of course, is for a child to have its own musical instrument.

One of the chief tasks of primary music education is to train the ear. In the last two decades perception of music has undergone a great change: background music and constant exposure to this brand of «listening» has become the dominant mode of musical experience, even for children of pre-school age. In this respect, music education is to establish a foundation for attentive and careful listening and to practise these skills. Learning to listen, though, also means training and refining a musical ear: the training of a more acute ear, sensitive to pitch, intervals, rhythm and harmony, can and must be prepared and begun in the nursery and reinforced at primary school age. It is right to link structured training of children's listening skills closely to every

Bei der musikalischen Früherziehung muß die Absicht der musikalischen Förderung mit den Besonderheiten eines Unterrichts mit 4–6jährigen Kindern in Einklang gebracht werden: Vorschulkinder brauchen spielerische Methoden des Lernens, die ihrem Umfeld entlehnt sind und ihren Fähigkeiten entsprechen. Seit langem weiß die entwicklungspsychologische Forschung, daß die Lernfähigkeit und auch die Lernbereitschaft von Kindern im Vorschulalter besonders hoch ist. Einerseits kann also die kognitive Leistungsfähigkeit frühzeitig geweckt werden, andererseits darf es kein zu frühes Lernen abstrakter Dinge sein. Notenschrift und Musiklehre sind in diesem Alter weniger wichtig und interessant. Es droht im Gegenteil die Gefahr des Desinteresses und einer Abkehr von der Musik. Das kindliche Lernen aus Freude an der Sache, die primäre Motivation, sollte nicht durch fremd anmutende Elemente verschüttet werden. Im Mittelpunkt des vorschulischen Musikunterrichts müssen als wichtigste Helfer des Lehrers stehen: Die Stimme, die Bewegung und das Spiel.

Das entscheidend andere in der Altersstufe der Grundschulkinder (6–8 Jahre) ist ihr Interesse an kniffligen Fragen, Zusammenhängen und Systemen, das beginnende Verständnis für abstrakte Zeichen und Strukturen und die Vertrautheit mit Methoden des schulischen Lernens. Musikalische Formen, die Notenschrift und andere Ordnungsprinzipien und Regeln können nun in ihrer Bedeutung richtig erfaßt werden. Andererseits drängen Kinder in diesem Alter heftig zu eigener Aktivität am Instrument. Ein gelegentlich angeschlagenes Xylophon reicht bei weitem nicht mehr aus! Im Unterrichtsraum muß eine anspruchsvolle Sammlung elementarer Instrumente bereitstehen. Am besten ist natürlich ein eigenes Musikinstrument.

Eine zentrale Aufgabe der musikalischen Grundschulung ist es, den Gehörsinn zu entwickeln. Das Musikhören war in den letzten beiden Jahrzehnten einem starken Wandel unterzogen: Musik im Hintergrund und als Dauerberieselung zu «hören», ist zum dominierenden musikalischen Verhalten vieler Kinder geworden – auch schon im Vorschulalter! Aufgabe der Musikerziehung ist es hier, die Haltung des «Hinhörens», des «Horchens» vorzubereiten und aktiv einzuüben. Hörenlernen bedeutet aber auch die Ausbildung und Differenzierung

Au niveau de l'éducation musicale précoce, l'intention de l'encouragement musical doit être adaptée aux particularités d'un enseignement avec des enfants de 4 à 6 ans: les enfants en âge préscolaire ont besoin de méthodes éducatives ludiques, dérivées de leur environnement et correspondant à leurs capacités. La recherche sur la psychologie du développement sait depuis longtemps que l'aptitude à l'apprentissage, et, également, la disposition à l'apprentissage, est particulièrement importante chez les enfants en âge préscolaire. Il est donc possible, d'une part, d'éveiller très tôt la faculté performative cognitive. Mais, d'autre part, il ne doit pas s'agir là de l'apprentissage prématuré de choses abstraites. La notation et la théorie musicales sont, à cet âge, d'importance et d'intérêt moindres. Au contraire, on court le danger d'un désintérêt et d'un détournement de la musique. L'apprentissage enfantin par plaisir, la motivation primaire, ne devrait pas être remise en question par des éléments perçus comme étrangers. Au centre de l'enseignement musical préscolaire doivent se placer la voix, le mouvement et le jeu, les auxiliaires les plus importants du professeur.

Ce qui différencie la catégorie des enfants allant à l'école primaire (6–8 ans) de manière fondamentale, c'est leur intérêt pour des questions délicates, des rapports et des systèmes, le début de la compréhension de signes et de structures abstraits et l'habitude des méthodes de l'apprentissage scolaire. La signification des formes musicales, de la notation et d'autres principes d'ordre et règles peuvent alors être saisis correctement. D'autre part, les enfants réclament avec véhémence, à cet âge, de jouer eux-mêmes d'un instrument. Un xylophone sur lequel on frappe à l'occasion ne suffit plus, loin s'en faut! La salle de cours doit renfermer une collection d'instruments élémentaires bien composée. Le mieux est, naturellement, de posséder un instrument propre.

L'une des tâches centrales de l'éducation musicale primaire est de développer l'ouïe. L'écoute de la musique a subi, au cours des deux dernières décennies, un changement important. «Entendre» de la musique à l'arrière-plan, en bruit de fond constant, est devenu le comportement musical dominant de beaucoup d'enfants – dès l'âge préscolaire! Le rôle de l'éducation musicale est donc de prépa-

occuring occasion for musical activity. This close link is fundamental for sensitive listening, prepares for musical activities in later life and shields against having the ears flooded by the media, too.

As well as working with children of nursery and primary school age, teachers of beginners' classes at music schools are turning their skills to new areas.

- Not only children, but adults, too, can begin to develop a musical awareness that has been neglected, or never yet been tapped. Here, the transmission of musical knowledge is the main focus of teaching. But even the basic practical abilities such as rhythmic and melodic awareness can still be trained in adults.
- Elementary music teaching for the disabled is a subject which has become established at music schools in recent years. What matters here is to discover and encourage the musical talents of the disabled as far as possible and to integrate these people into the social life of the music school. Music lessons in mixed groups of disabled and non-disabled participants have an important part to play in such integration, and these are particularly successful where people are involved in making music together.
- The transition from the beginners' level to instrumental lessons is a challenge for every music school. Parents and children should be given information on the special characteristics, problems and opportunities commonly associated with learning a particular musical instrument. Likewise, instrumental teachers should

des musikalischen Hörsinns selbst: Ein verfeinertes Hören, das für Tonhöhen, Intervalle, Rhythmen und Harmonien empfänglich ist, kann und muß im Vorschulalter vorbereitet und begonnen und im Grundschulalter gefestigt werden. Richtig ist es, die methodischen Bemühungen um das bewußte Hören der Kinder eng mit allen Gelegenheiten musikalischer Aktivität zu verknüpfen. Diese Verbindung legt die Grundlage für ein sensibles Hören, bereitet auf späteren aktiven Umgang mit Musik vor und wappnet auch gegen die akustische Flut der Medien.

Neben der Arbeit mit Kindern im Vor- und Grundschulalter wenden sich die Elementarlehrerinnen und -lehrer der Musikschulen manchen neuen Aufgaben zu.

- Nicht nur Kinder, auch Erwachsene können beginnen, ihr brachliegendes oder noch nie beanspruchtes musikalisches Vermögen zu entwickeln. Hier steht die Vermittlung von musikbezogenen Kenntnissen im Mittelpunkt. Aber auch praktische Grundfähigkeiten wie Rhythmusgefühl und Melodiebewußtsein können noch im Erwachsenenalter ausgebildet werden.
- Elementarer Musikunterricht mit Behinderten ist ein weiterer Bereich, der sich in der letzten Zeit an Musikschulen etabliert hat. Hier geht es darum, die musikalischen Anlagen der Behinderten, so weit es geht, zu entdecken und zu fördern und diese Menschen in das Leben der Musikschule zu integrieren. Der elementare Musikunterricht in gemischten Gruppen von Behinderten und Nichtbehinderten hat eine wichtige integrative Funktion, die gerade im gemeinsamen Musizieren erfolgreich ist.
- Eine Herausforderung für jede Musikschule ist der Übergang von der Grundstufe zum nachfolgenden Instrumentalunterricht. Eltern und Kinder müssen Informationen dazu bekommen, mit welchen Eigenarten, Problemen und Chancen der Schüler beim Erlernen eines bestimmten Musikinstruments rechnen muß. Andererseits müssen die Lehrkräfte der Instrumentalfächer

rer et d'exercer activement à l'attitude de «l'écoute», de «l'écoute attentive». Mais apprendre à écouter signifie aussi former et différencier le sens auditif musical même: une écoute affinée, sensible aux hauteurs de tons, aux intervalles, aux rythmes et aux harmonies, peut être préparée et amorcée à l'âge préscolaire et consolidée à l'âge de l'école primaire. Il est bon de relier étroitement les efforts méthodiques et l'audition consciente des enfants avec toutes les occasions de l'activité musicale. Cette relation sera le fondement d'une écoute sensible, elle prépare à la pratique ultérieure active de la musique et arme l'enfant contre le flot acoustique des médias.

Parallèlement au travail avec des enfants d'âge préscolaire et de l'école primaire, les enseignants et enseignantes des cours élémentaires se vouent à bien d'autres tâches nouvelles.

- Non seulement les enfants, mais également les adultes peuvent commencer à développer leurs aptitudes musicales en friche ou n'ayant jamais été travaillées. Ici, la transmission de connaissances liées à la musique est au centre des préoccupations. Mais les facultés pratiques de base telles que le sens du rythme et de la mélodie peuvent elles aussi, encore, être formées à l'âge adulte.
- L'enseignement musical élémentaire avec des personnes handicapées est un autre des domaines qui, ces derniers temps, se sont établis dans les écoles de musique. Il s'agit ici de découvrir et d'encourager, dans la mesure du possible, les dons musicaux des handicapés et d'intégrer ces individus à la vie de l'école de musique. L'enseignement musical élémentaire en groupes mixtes d'handicapés et de non handicapés a une fonction d'intégration importante qui connaît son succès justement dans la pratique commune de la musique.
- Le passage du niveau primaire à l'enseignement instrumental qui lui fait suite constitue un défi pour toute école de musique. Les parents et les enfants doivent être informés sur les particularités, les problèmes et les chances avec lesquels l'élève devra compter dans le cadre de l'apprentissage d'un certain instrument. D'autre part, les enseignants des matières instrumentales doivent intégrer les connaissances et

«Dans mon cas, c'est la musique (univers sonore) qui m'a conquis plutôt que les autres arts; peut-être parce que je suis mieux formaté génétiquement et aussi plus fortuné (privilégié) culturellement par mes aieux paternels et mes parents. De plus la musique associe spontanément les grandes sciences dans des rapports approchés mais encore à découvrir. J'oserais risquer qu'aujourd'hui en particulier, la musique est peut-être l'art le plus central, le plus globalisant. Soleil de la pensée obscure.»

Dominique Bodson

take account of children's knowledge and experience gained in these elementary classes, when considering their methodology. Lastly, a smooth transition should be effected in the move from a large group to a small group or individual tuition.

Teaching music lessons at beginners' level requires special training and years of study. In addition to requiring practical musical skills, it takes a competent teacher, capable of working with groups of about 12 very young children in such a way that it is by her/his «charisma» how the subjects of learning are transmitted.   *mg.*

Teaching to Play an Instrument Nowadays

Instrumentalunterricht heute

L'enseignement d'un instrument aujourd'hui

For a long time instrumental tuition has been a core element, a «classic» part of the tuition offered at music schools. In how far does «instrumental teaching today» differ from «instrumental teaching yesterday»? What are the problems and challenges that instrumental teachers currently have to deal with in music schools? What new requirements do today's teachers have to meet in order to fulfil the wishes and expectations of their pupils?

If one looks at trends in instrumental teaching at music schools in recent years, a few basic observations can be made.

1. The variety of styles in the musical repertoire covered in lessons has increased enormously. The «classical» teaching repertoire, which clung to the traditions of the 19th Century well over half way into our own century, has given way to a diverse pluralism of musical styles and forms from all kinds of cultural origins. This includes jazz, pop and rock, as well as various kinds of New Music. (Post-Modernism in music has long since put an end to the persistent Avant-garde aversion to genuine, simply-structured New Music, either written for or suitable for teaching purposes.) This musical diversity is

die Kenntnisse und Erfahrungen der Kinder aus dem elementaren Unterricht in ihre Methodik einbeziehen. Schließlich sollte der Wechsel vom Lernen in der großen Gruppe zu den Formen des Kleingruppen- und Einzelunterrichts als gleitender Übergang gelingen.

Die Aufgabe, elementaren Musikunterricht zu erteilen, erfordert eine spezifische Ausbildung, ein qualifiziertes Studium. Zu dem Anspruch an die musikalische Kompetenz der Lehrkraft tritt der an die pädagogische Fähigkeit: mit Gruppen von etwa 12 Vorschulkindern so arbeiten zu können, daß die persönliche «charismatische» Ausstrahlung die fachlichen Inhalte zu vermitteln vermag.   *mg.*

Les expériences des enfants provenant des cours élémentaires dans leur méthodologie. Enfin, le passage de l'apprentissage dans un groupe de dimensions relativement importantes aux formes du cours en petits groupes ou du cours particulier doit, pour réussir, se faire sans accroc.

La tâche de donner un enseignement musical élémentaire exige une formation spécifique, des études qualifiées. Aux exigences de compétence musicale viennent s'ajouter les facultés pédagogiques: il s'agit de pouvoir travailler avec des groupes d'environ 12 enfants d'âge préscolaire de telle sorte que le rayonnement «charismatique» personnel soit en état de transmettre le contenu.   *mg.*

Seit langem ist der Instrumentalunterricht ein Kernbereich, ein «klassischer» Teil des Lehrangebots von Musikschulen. Wodurch unterscheidet sich «Instrumentalunterricht heute» von «Instrumentalunterricht gestern»? Was sind die aktuellen pädagogischen Probleme und Herausforderungen, mit denen Instrumentallehrerinnen und -lehrer an Musikschulen derzeit zu tun haben? Welche neuen Anforderungen müssen Lehrende heute erfüllen, um den veränderten Wünschen und Erwartungen der Lernenden an den Instrumentalunterricht in unserer Zeit gerecht zu werden?

Überblickt man die Tendenzen des Instrumentalunterrichts an Musikschulen in der jüngeren Vergangenheit, so ergeben sich einige prinzipielle Feststellungen.

1. Die stilistische Bandbreite der im Unterricht behandelten Musikliteratur hat sich enorm ausgeweitet. Die lange über die Jahrhundertmitte hinaus dominierende Beschränkung auf die den Traditionen des 19. Jahrhunderts verhaftete «klassische» Unterrichtsliteratur ist einem vielfältigen Pluralismus von Stilen und Musikarten aus diversen musikalischen Teilkulturen gewichen. Dazu gehören Jazz, Pop, Rock ebenso wie

Depuis longtemps, l'enseignement d'un instrument est un domaine central, une partie «classique» de la palette des cours proposés par les écoles de musique. En quoi «l'enseignement d'un instrument aujourd'hui» se différencie-t-il de «l'enseignement d'un instrument hier»? Quels sont les problèmes et les défis pédagogiques actuels auxquels se trouvent confrontés, aujourd'hui, les professeurs des écoles de musique enseignant un instrument? A quelles exigences nouvelles les enseignants et enseignantes doivent-ils satisfaire aujourd'hui afin de répondre aux désirs et aux attentes nouveaux des élèves participant à des cours d'instruments de nos jours?

Si l'on considère l'ensemble des tendances de l'enseignement d'un instrument dans les écoles de musique dans un passé récent, il en résulte quelques constatations de principe.

1. La palette stylistique de la littérature musicale traitée pendant les cours s'est énormément élargie. La limitation longtemps dominante, au-delà des années 50, au matériel de cours «classique» attaché aux traditions du XIXème siècle a fait place à un pluralisme varié de styles et types de musique provenant de sub-cultures

reflected in the curricular variety of the newer schools of instrumental teaching and in the content of teaching materials. More than ever before, teachers need a broad knowledge of repertoire suitable for the purposes of tuition, so as to be able to respond to the various musical preferences of their students.

2. Improvization, which had definitely been neglected in instrumental teaching since the 19th Century and latterly abandoned altogether, has made a startling recovery in the last few years. This includes not only genuine jazz improvization, but a tendency, at least, towards improvization and embellishment in most styles. The desire to be able to improvize is a driving impulse for many people to learn to play an instrument. A wide range of materials now being available for use in developing the ability to improvize, many teachers still lack skills in improvization and in teaching the same.

3. In addition to their «traditional» work with children and teenagers, instrumental teachers now play an important role in working with preschool children on the one hand and adults (including retired people) on the other. While the methods of elementary musical training generally used and well established in music schools are a source of plenty of ideas for teaching methods and games suitable for young children, the field of adult education, which is likely to expand enormously in the «leisure society» of the future, represents largely new territory which is only gradually being explored.

4. Alongside the traditional form of individual tuition, group tuition is proving to be of considerable value, particularly in the early stages of learning an instrument. This must not be dismissed as a cost-saving measure, but regarded as a useful complement to individual tuition. It requires particular teaching methods and skills that many teachers have not covered sufficiently in the course of their training.

Instrumental teachers not only teach music, but have a general influence on their pupils' education

verschiedene Richtungen Neuer Musik. (Die musikalische Postmoderne hat längst die zählebige Avantgarde-Aversion gegen pädagogisch motivierte bzw. geeignete, einfach strukturierte Neue Musik, die diesen Namen verdient, abgelegt.) Die musikalische Vielfalt spiegelt sich in der inhaltlichen Buntheit der in jüngerer Zeit erschienenen Instrumentalschulen und Unterrichtsmaterialien. Mehr als früher müssen Lehrende heute über weitgespannte Kenntnisse auf den Gebieten der für Unterrichtszwecke geeigneten Literatur verfügen, um auf die unterschiedlichen Musizierbedürfnisse ihrer Schüler eingehen zu können.

2. Das seit dem 19. Jahrhundert in der Instrumentalausbildung zusehends vernachlässigte und schließlich preisgegebene Improvisieren hat in den letzten Jahren im Unterricht eine geradezu verblüffende Wiederbelebung erfahren. Dies gilt über den genuin improvisatorischen Jazz hinaus zumindest tendenziell für die meisten Musizierbereiche. Der Wunsch, improvisieren zu können, ist für viele Instrumentalschüler ein starker Lernimpuls. Während mittlerweile vielerlei improvisationsmethodische Unterrichtsmaterialien vorliegen, mangelt es vielen Lehrern (noch) an Fähigkeiten des Improvisierens und der Vermittlung von Improvisationmöglichkeiten im Unterricht.

3. Zum «traditionellen» Unterricht mit Kindern und Jugendlichen im Schulalter sind als wichtige pädagogische Aufgaben einerseits der Frühinstrumentalunterricht und andererseits der Unterricht mit Erwachsenen (bis ins Seniorenalter) hinzugekommen. Während die an den Musikschulen allgemein verbreitete und eta-

musicales diverses. Le jazz, le pop, le rock, en font tout autant partie que différents courants de Musique Nouvelle. (Le postmodernisme musical s'est défait depuis longtemps déjà de l'aversion avant-gardiste envers une Musique Nouvelle de structure simple à motivation pédagogique, ou, tout au moins, adaptée à la pédagogie et digne de ce nom). La variété musicale se reflète dans la diversité multicolore des contenus des méthodes instrumentales et du matériel pédagogique qui ont fait leur apparition récemment. Les enseignants, plus qu'autrefois, doivent disposer de connaissances étendues dans les domaines de la littérature adaptée aux cours afin de pouvoir aborder avec compréhension les différents besoins musicaux de leurs élèves.

2. L'improvisation, négligée de plus en plus dans la formation instrumentale depuis le XIXème siècle avant d'être abandonnée complètement, a connu un renouveau on ne peut plus étonnant au cours des dernières années. C'est le cas tout au moins, au-delà de l'improvisation naturelle du jazz, de manière tendancielle pour la plupart des domaines musicaux. Le désir d'improviser constitue pour beaucoup d'élèves une motivation à l'apprentissage non négligeable. Alors qu'il existe entre-temps une foule de matériel pédagogique de méthodologie de l'improvisation, il manque encore à beaucoup d'enseignants l'aptitude à l'improvisation et à la transmission des possibilités de l'improvisation en cours.

3. Aux cours «traditionnels» pour les enfants et les jeunes en âge scolaire sont venus s'ajouter d'une part l'éducation instrumentale précoce, d'autre part les cours pour adultes (jusqu'au troisième âge), tâches pédagogiques importantes. Tandis que l'éducation musicale élémentaire établie et répandue de manière générale dans les écoles de musique a apporté de nombreuses suggestions pour des cours adaptés à l'âge des élèves et, surtout, ludiques pour les enfants d'âge préscolaire et scolaire précoce, les cours pour adultes – dont l'importance ira sans doute croissante encore à l'avenir dans la «société de loisirs» – restent une terre pédagogique inconnue qui commence seulement à être explorée peu à peu.

through their role as teacher. In instrumental tuition, especially in the individual tuition that is still the norm, a close personal relationship frequently develops between pupil and teacher. Individual tuition makes it possible for the teacher to focus on each pupil and concentrate on their individual needs. For many pupils, children, adolescents and adults alike, it is invaluable for the development of their personality and emotional stability to have an hour a week of undivided attention from the teacher they relate to so closely. Here instrumental teachers often assume a very important function in influencing the development of personality, beyond the immediate practical scope of instrumental tuition: they become role models, mentors, educators, partners or personal advisors.

In considering the extensive range of an instrumental teacher's responsibilities, there is another aspect whose importance is becoming increasingly evident. Every pupil learning an instrument not only has his own personal interests, abilities and difficulties, but also his own particular physical identity. In many cases this includes physical problems, usually of psychological origin: tensions, inhibitions, blocks etc. These soon reveal themselves as obstacles in learning an instrument and need to be dealt with judiciously in lessons. Many experienced instrumental teachers agree with observations by pedagogues, therapists and doctors that psychosomatic problems in all age groups have increased considerably in recent years and over the last couple of decades. This tendency is also reflected in the increased demand among music students for special lessons in body awareness and correction of physical problems (e.g. Alexander Technique, Feldenkrais Method, Eutonie and breathing techniques). Dealing with psychosomatic blocks, which represent an urgent problem for many pupils, sometimes requires the teacher to take on the role of therapist. In this area, instrumental teachers can make an important contribution to the overall physical and mental health of the individual.

«Instrumental teaching today» is thus a demanding and many faceted field of activity whose scope is likely to expand further in the future. The work of teachers capable of meeting the needs of aspiring musicians in today's society can hardly be valued too highly.

blierte elementare Musikerziehung viele Anregungen für einen altersgemäßen, vor allem spielerischen Unterricht mit Kindern im Vorschul- und im frühen Schulalter vermittelt hat, ist der – in der zukünfigen «Freizeitgesellschaft» wahrscheinlich enorm zunehmende – Unterricht mit Erwachsenen noch weithin pädagogisches Neuland, das erst allmählich erkundet wird.

4. Neben dem traditionellen Einzelunterricht wird als vielfach bewährte und vor allem in der ersten Ausbildungszeit produktive Unterrichtsform der Gruppenunterricht praktiziert. Dieser darf allerdings nicht zur Sparmaßnahme entfremdet werden, sondern rechtfertigt sich als pädagogisch sinnvolle Ergänzung zum Einzelunterricht. Dies setzt besondere pädagogische und methodische Fähigkeiten voraus, die viele Lehrkräfte in ihrem Studium nicht in hinreichendem Maße erworben haben.

Instrumentalpädagogen vermitteln nicht nur Musik, sondern wirken im Zusammenhang damit auch allgemeinerzieherisch. Im Instrumentalunterricht, besonders in dem bis heute dominierenden Einzelunterricht, entsteht häufig eine enge zwischenmenschliche Beziehung zwischen Schüler und Lehrer. Der Einzelunterricht ermöglicht dem Lehrenden, sich dem jeweiligen Schüler intensiv zuzuwenden und ganz auf seine Individualität einzugehen. Vielen Schülern – Kindern, Jugendlichen wie Erwachsenen – ist es ein unschätzbarer Wert für die Entwicklung ihrer Persönlichkeit und für ihre psychische Stabilität, eine Unterrichtsstunde pro Woche die vertraute Bezugsperson des Lehrers bzw. der Lehrerin ganz für sich zu haben. Hier gewinnen Instrumentalpädagogen häufig fundamentale persönlichkeitsbildende Funktionen, die über die unmittelbare instrumentalpraktische Lehre hinaus wirksam sind: Sie werden zu Vorbildern, Mentoren, Erziehern, Partnern oder zu persönlichen Beratern.

Im Blick auf das weitgefächerte Aufgabenfeld der Instrumentallehrer gewinnt noch ein weiterer Gesichtspunkt erheblich an Bedeutung. Jeder Instrumentalschüler hat nicht nur seine persönlichen Lernwünsche, -fähigkeiten und -schwierigkeiten, sondern auch seine besondere, individuelle «Körperlichkeit». Dazu gehören vielfach auch körperli-

4. Parallèlement aux cours particuliers traditionnels, on pratique également la forme du cours en groupe, qui a fait ses preuves à maints égards et s'avère surtout particulièrement productive dans la première période de la formation. Celle-ci, toutefois, ne doit pas dégénérer en mesure d'économie, elle est justifiée à titre de complément pédagogique utile au cours particulier. Cette forme de cours suppose des capacités pédagogiques et méthodiques que beaucoup d'enseignants n'ont pas acquises de manière suffisante au cours de leurs études.

Les pédagogues enseignant un instrument ne transmettent pas seulement des connaissances musicales, ils ont également une fonction éducatrice générale. Le cours d'apprentissage d'un instrument, et plus précisément le cours particulier, qui domine encore aujourd'hui, permet souvent l'établissement d'une relation humaine étroite entre l'élève et le professeur. Le cours particulier permet à l'enseignant de se consacrer de manière intensive à chaque élève et de s'adapter entièrement à son individualité. Pour beaucoup d'élèves – enfants, adolescents et adultes – le fait d'avoir, une heure par semaine, la personne de référence du professeur pour soi tout seul est d'une valeur inestimable pour le développement de leur personnalité et leur stabilité psychique. Les pédagogues assument ici une fonction souvent fondamentale dans l'évolution de la personnalité, fonction ayant une influence dépassant l'apprentissage direct de la pratique de l'instrument: ils deviennent des modèles, des mentors, des éducateurs, des partenaires ou des conseillers privés.

Si l'on considère le large éventail des tâches du professeur enseignant un instrument, un autre point de vue prend une place plus importante encore. Chaque élève apprenant à jouer d'un instrument a non seulement ses désirs, ses aptitudes et ses difficultés d'apprentissage propres, mais aussi son «caractère corporel» individuel particulier. En font également partie à plus d'un titre les problèmes corporels (souvent psychophysiques): les tensions musculaires nerveuses, les complexes, les blocages, etc... Lorsque l'on apprend à jouer d'un instrument, ils se révèlent bientôt à titre d'obstacles et doivent être traités avec précaution pendant le cours. Beaucoup d'enseignants expérimentés

The heading «instrumental teaching today» not only indicates current challenges to adapting teaching methods, but also raises the question which has been posed so often in recent times as to the legitimacy of providing public funding for instrumental tuition at music schools. Can a society which is in economic difficulties and which will be compelled to make massive cuts in the foreseeable future afford the «luxury» of publicly subsidized instrumental teaching? Is it the responsibility of government to support the personal hobbies of those people interested in music, without considering any general social benefit?

It may already have become clear that music-making and the associated training are far from being «useless» activities. Even beyond those merits already identified here, educational experts and researchers cite a whole series of additional, «transferred» benefits to be gained from playing an instrument: music-making is said to stimulate intelligence and creativity, increase powers of concentration and thresholds of tolerance in confronting problems, develop communicative skills and

thus improve standards of behaviour, helping both young people and adults to cope with the threats that exist in contemporary society in the face of decaying values, lack of direction, loneliness, increasing recourse to violence, drugs etc. All these are without doubt weighty arguments in favour of funding by the state and local authorities for instrumental tuition.

Beyond the kind of answer that adopts a utilitarian standpoint, the question provokes a challenge on a matter of principle: an artistic activity as fulfilling and as complex as playing and learning to play an instrument, one which promotes the development of the individual's whole personality, cannot and must not be evaluated according to criteria of some determinable «usefulness».

Like all art forms, music is not to be defined solely in terms of its usefulness to society, for it has

che (meist psychophysische) Probleme: Verspannungen, Hemmungen, Blockaden etc. Sie werden beim Erlernen eines Instruments bald als Hindernis offenbar und müssen im Unterricht umsichtig behandelt werden. Viele erfahrene Instrumentallehrer bestätigen die Beobachtungen von Pädagogen, Therapeuten und Ärzten, daß in den letzten Jahren und Jahrzehnten psychosomatische Störungen in allen Altersgruppen beträchtlich zugenommen haben. Diese Tendenz spiegelt sich auch in der vermehrten Nachfrage von Musikstudierenden nach speziellem Unterricht auf dem Gebiet der Körperwahrnehmung und -therapie (z.B. Alexander-Technik, Feldenkrais-Methode, Eutonie, Atemtherapie). Die bei vielen Instrumentalschülern dringliche pädagogische Arbeit an der Lösung psychophysischer Blockaden verlangt dem Lehrenden bisweilen therapeutische Qualitäten ab. Hier leisten Instrumentalpädagogen einen wichtigen Beitrag zur leibseelischen Gesundung der betreffenden Menschen.

«Instrumentalunterricht heute» ist also ein anspruchsvoller, vielgestaltiger und in Zukunft sich weiter differenzierender Aufgabenbereich. Die pädagogische Leistung von Lehrerinnen und Lehrern, die sich den in der gegenwärtigen Gesellschaft bestehenden Musizierwünschen stellen und sie erfüllen, kann kaum überschätzt werden.

Die Formel «Instrumentalunterricht heute» verweist aber nicht nur auf die aktuellen pädagogischen Herausforderungen, sondern auch auf die in jüngster Zeit häufig gestellte Frage nach der Legitimation öffentlicher Förderung von Instrumentalunterricht an Musikschulen: Kann eine ökonomisch gefährdete, auf absehbare Zeit zu massivem Sparen gezwungene Gesellschaft sich den «Luxus» eines öffentlich subventionierten Instrumentalunterrichts leisten? Ist es Aufgabe der öffentlichen Hand, ohne Rücksicht auf gesellschaftlichen Nutzen individuelle Privathobbys musikinteressierter Menschen zu fördern?

Es dürfte bereits deutlich geworden sein, daß Musizieren und die Anleitung dazu keineswegs «nutzlose» Tätigkeiten sind. Über die genannten Werte hinaus führen Pädagogen und Lernforscher aber noch eine Reihe weiterer «Transfer-Qualitäten» des Instrumentalspiels an: Musizieren fördere

confirment les observations des pédagogues, des thérapeutes et des médecins selon lesquelles les troubles psychosomatiques ont augmenté considérablement dans toutes les classes d'âge au cours des dernières années et des dernières décennies. Cette tendance se reflète également dans la demande croissante des étudiants en musique, qui réclament des cours spécialisés dans les domaines de la perception et de la thérapie corporelles (par exemple la technique d'Alexandre, la méthode Feldenkrais, l'eutonie, la thérapie respiratoire). Le travail pédagogique urgent auprès de nombreux élèves apprenant à jouer d'un instrument au niveau de l'élimination de blocages psychophysiques exige quelquefois de l'enseignant des qualités thérapeutiques. Les pédagogues enseignant un instrument apportent ici une contribution importante à la guérison psychosomatique de l'individu concerné.

«L'enseignement d'un instrument aujourd'hui» est donc un domaine d'activité de haut niveau, aux facettes multiples, et qui se différenciera plus encore à l'avenir. La performance pédagogique des enseignants et enseignantes qui font face et répondent aux désirs musicaux de la société actuelle ne peut être surestimée.

Mais la formulation «l'enseignement d'un instrument aujourd'hui» ne renvoie pas seulement aux défis pédagogiques actuels, mais également à la question, posée fréquemment ces derniers temps, de la légitimation du subventionnement public des cours d'enseignement d'instruments dans les écoles de musique: une société exposée à des dangers économiques, condamnée à court terme à des économies massives, peut-elle se permettre le «luxe» d'un enseignement instrumental subventionné publiquement? Est-ce le devoir de la main publique d'apporter son soutien aux passe-temps privés individuels de personnes intéressées par la musique sans égard pour l'utilité sociale de la chose?

Nous avons déjà démontré clairement que la musique et son apprentissage ne sauraient en aucun cas être des activités «inutiles». Outre les valeurs mentionnées, les pédagogues et les chercheurs sur les problèmes de l'apprentissage avancent une série d'autres «qualités de transfert» de la pratique d'un instrument: la musique favorise le développement de l'intelligence et de la créativité, elle contri-

an «aesthetic» value of its own which cannot be measured. This special value should not be denied or played down by music schools, instrumental teachers and pupils, but defended boldly.

Instrumental tuition which equips people for genuine music-making opens the way for an immeasurable potential for artistic development. I have two final comments on this. Playing a musical instrument is an ideal means of educating the combined powers of the human «heart, mind and hand» (Pestalozzi), that is, of feeling, thought and activity. «Educating» here means not simply «training» or «developing» skills, but far more than this, increasing those powers through their interaction. Combining these three areas of strength through instrumental teaching certainly calls for excellent qualities in a teacher. Tuition which only focuses on a narrow-minded kind of activity, without really involving the «mind» and «heart», falls short of the ideal. This happens only too often when teachers strive towards the wrong kind of professionalism with their pupils, aiming for the perfection of a smoothly functioning machine. True education through instrumental teaching should include thinking about music, encouraging people to talk about music and thereby to experience it more intensely, trying out, describing, comparing and evaluating various possible angles of interpretation.

die Intelligenz und die Kreativität, erhöhe die Konzentrationsfähigkeit und die Frustrationstoleranz beim Bewältigen von Problemen, entwickle kommunikative Fähigkeiten und verbessere somit das Sozialverhalten, stabilisiere Jugendliche wie Erwachsene gegen aktuelle Bedrohungen in der gegenwärtigen Gesellschaft wie Wertezerfall, Orientierungslosigkeit, Einsamkeit, zunehmende Gewaltbereitschaft, Drogen usw. Dies alles sind zweifellos gewichtige Argumente zur Rechtfertigung staatlicher und kommunaler Finanzierung von Instrumentalunterricht.

Über eine solche (den utilitaristischen Standpunkt anerkennende) Antwort hinaus fordert die gestellte Frage aber zu einer prinzipiellen Kritik heraus: Eine so komplexe, die Persönlichkeit des einzelnen vollständig fordernde und erfüllende künstlerische Aktivität wie das Instrumentalspiel sowie der entsprechende Unterricht können und dürfen nicht nur nach Kriterien einer vermeßbaren «Nützlichkeit» bewertet werden. Wie alle Kunst geht Musizieren nicht auf in gesellschaftlichem Nutzen, sondern hat einen nicht vermeßbaren «ästhetischen Eigenwert». Diesen Eigenwert sollten Musikschulen, Instrumentalpädagogen und auch die Schüler nicht verleugnen und nicht schüchtern verkleinern, sondern offensiv verteidigen.

Instrumentalunterricht, der zu einem authentischen Musizieren befähigt, eröffnet ein kaum auslotbares Potential an künstlerischer Bildung. Dazu zwei abschließende Gedanken. Instrumentales Musizieren bildet in geradezu exemplarischer Weise die menschlichen Kräfte von «Herz, Geist und Hand» (Pestalozzi), also von Empfinden, Denken und praktischem Tun. «Bilden» bedeutet hier nicht nur «entwickeln», sondern überdies ein Vereinen, ein wechselseitiges Stimulieren, ja Potenzieren. Die Ermöglichung eines sinnvollen Miteinander- und Ineinanderwirkens der drei Kräfte durch Instrumentalunterricht erfordert allerdings wiederum hohe pädagogische Qualitäten. Zu kritisieren wäre ein Unterricht, der sich ohne intensive Beteiligung von «Geist» und «Herz» auf ein engstirniges Machen beschränkt. Dies geschieht nicht selten, wenn Lehrer bei ihren Schülern einen schlechten Professionalismus erstreben, der auf das Ideal einer perfekten, reibungslos funktionierenden Maschine

bue à augmenter la faculté de concentration et la tolérance de la frustration lorsqu'il s'agit de surmonter des problèmes, elle développe la faculté de communiquer et améliore ainsi le comportement social, stabilise les jeunes et les adultes face aux menaces de la société actuelle telles que la décadence des valeurs, le manque d'orientation, la solitude, la disposition croissante à la violence, la drogue etc... Ce sont là sans nul doute des arguments de poids justifiant le financement national et communal de l'enseignement instrumental.

Mais, au-delà du cadre de cette réponse, reconnaissant le point de vue utilitariste, la question posée appelle à une critique de principe: une activité artistique si complexe, réclamant et emplissant entièrement la personnalité d'un individu, comme le fait de jouer d'un instrument, et l'enseignement correspondant, ne peuvent et ne doivent être jugés d'après des critères d'«utilité» mesurable. Comme toute forme d'art, la musique ne trouve pas sa raison d'être dans une utilité sociale, elle a une «valeur esthétique propre» immesurable. Les écoles de musique, les pédagogues qui se consacrent à l'apprentissage des instruments et les élèves eux-mêmes devraient ne pas renier ou minimiser cette valeur propre, mais, au contraire, la défendre de manière offensive.

L'apprentissage d'un instrument, ouvrant la porte à une pratique authentique de la musique, dégage un potentiel de formation artistique presque insondable. Pour finir, deux réflexions à ce sujet. La pratique instrumentale de la musique forme d'une manière pour ainsi dire exemplaire les forces humaines du «coeur» de «l'esprit et» de «la main» (Pestalozzi), c'est-à-dire de la sensibilité, de la pensée et de l'activité pratique. «Former» ne signifie pas seulement ici «développer», mais, de plus, une union, une stimulation mutuelle, une élévation à une puissance énième. La possibilité d'une action commune et d'une interaction judicieuses de ces trois forces par l'intermédiaire de l'apprentissage d'un instrument exige, il est vrai, des qualités pédagogiques de haut niveau. Un enseignement qui se limiterait à un travail borné, sans participation de «l'esprit» et du «coeur» serait critiquable. Ceci n'est pas rare, si les professeurs veulent que leurs élèves parviennent à un professionnalisme, mal compris, orienté vers l'idéal d'une machine au

Furthermore, playing an instrument offers a unique mode of musical experience. Special aspects of personal identity can be discovered and developed through the medium of music, through encountering the «other self» (the characteristics, gestures, styles, messages, etc.) which a piece of music represents to the person performing it. Through discovering and developing, refining and presenting this «other self», playing an instrument can free the individual from his own limitations, letting him out of the cage of «That's just the way I am». By equipping people with the means to make music, instrumental tuition makes it possible for them to discover themselves and their own creative abilities through the process of music-making. *um.*

Group Teaching for Instrumentalists

Instrumentaler Gruppenunterricht

L'enseignement de groupe dans l'apprentissage d'un instrument

Instrumental teaching at music schools has traditionally been orientated to the training of professional musicians. This means having in mind the way of study at music college and thus demanding a high level of technical and artistic accomplishment, with individual tuition as the norm. For some time now, though, group teaching has been discussed and put to the test in music schools as an alternative mode of instrumental tuition. Two facts have prompted this new approach:

For one thing, it has been recognized that individual tuition alone is not capable to answer the students' need to make music and learn in collaboration with others. The high percentage of students who abandon their instrumental studies after only a short time shows that concentrating on a style of teaching alike to preparing students for careers as soloists and professional performers is neither realistic nor appropriate to the capabilities and ex-

ausgerichtet ist. Zu einem qualifizierten, «bildenden» Instrumentalunterricht gehören nicht zuletzt auch das Nachdenken über Musik, die Anregung, Musik differenziert zu versprachlichen und damit gesteigert zu erleben, das Erfahren, Ausprobieren, Beschreiben, Abwägen, Beurteilen von Interpretationsmöglichkeiten. Überdies ist Instrumentalspiel ein einzigartiges Medium musikalischer Erfahrung. Es ermöglicht eine spezifische Persönlichkeitsfindung und -erweiterung im Medium der Musik: In der Auslieferung an das «Andere» (an die Charaktere, Gesten, Stile, Botschaften etc.), was die jeweilige Musik der sie ausführenden Persönlichkeit gegenüber darstellt, im Erschließen und Vollziehen, im Üben und Darstellen dieses «Anderen» befreit das Instrumentalspiel den Einzelnen aus seiner individuellen Begrenztheit, aus dem Käfig des «So bin ich nun einmal». Indem Instrumentalunterricht Menschen dazu anleitet, Musik zu gestalten, ermöglicht er ihnen, sich selbst durch die gespielte Musik gleichermaßen als «gestaltet» und als gestaltungsfähig zu erfahren.   *um.*

Traditionell war und ist auch der Instrumentalunterricht an Musikschulen noch vielfach am Bild des Berufsmusikers orientiert. Damit ist zugleich die Vorstellung einer konservatorialen Musikausbildung im Spiel: mit dem Anspruch eines künstlerischen Niveaus auf hoher Ebene der technischen Perfektion und dem Einzelunterricht als regulärer Form der Unterweisung. Doch schon seit geraumer Zeit wird an den Musikschulen Gruppenunterricht als alternative Form des Instrumentalunterrichts diskutiert und erprobt. Diese neue Orientierung wurde von zwei Seiten her ausgelöst:

Zum einen erkannte man, daß der ausschließliche Einzelunterricht das Bedürfnis der Schüler nach gemeinschaftlichem Musizieren und Musiklernen zu wenig berücksichtigt. Der hohe Prozentsatz von Schülern, die den Instrumentalunterricht schon nach kurzer Zeit wieder abbrechen, zeigt, daß die einseitige Orientierung am solistischen und

fonctionnement parfait et sans accroc. Un apprentissage qualifié et «formateur» d'un instrument comprendra également la réflexion sur la musique; la suggestion de rendre la musique langage et de la vivre ainsi à un plus haut niveau; l'expérience, l'essai, la description, l'examen attentif et le jugement des possibilités d'interprétation. De plus, jouer d'un instrument est un médium unique d'expérience musicale, qui permet de se trouver et d'élargir sa personnalité dans le médium de la musique; dans le fait de se livrer à «l'Autre» (aux personnages, aux gestes, aux styles, aux messages, etc...), que représente la musique face à la personnalité qui la joue, dans l'ouverture et l'accomplissement, l'exercice et la représentation de cet «Autre», le fait de jouer d'un instrument libère de la limite de son propre individu, de la cage du «je suis comme ça». L'apprentissage d'un instrument, invitant l'individu à donner forme à la musique, lui permet de faire l'expérience de la musique jouée comme d'une musique «mise en forme» et formable.   *um.*

Traditionnellement, l'apprentissage d'un instrument était et est encore, dans les écoles de musique, orienté en fonction de l'image du musicien professionnel. Ceci implique l'idée d'une formation musicale de conservatoire, avec l'exigence d'un haut niveau artistique à un haut degré de perfection technique et des cours particuliers comme forme régulière d'enseignement. Pourtant, depuis un certain temps déjà, l'enseignement de groupe est discuté et mis à l'épreuve dans les écoles de musique comme forme alternative de l'enseignement d'un instrument. Cette orientation nouvelle a été déclenchée par deux côtés.

D'une part, on a compris que l'enseignement en cours particuliers seul ne tient pas suffisamment compte du besoin des élèves d'exercer et d'apprendre la musique en commun. Le pourcentage élevé d'élèves qui cessent les cours au bout de quelques temps déjà montre que l'orientation unilatérale

«Norway has 320 munici-
palities with music schools,
we have almost 80,000
children at these schools,
nearly 20% of Norwegian
children and adolescents
attend music schools. This is
fantastic! Children and
young people need a place
where they can get instruction and the opportunity to
learn to play an instrument.
The most important preven-
tive measure is to provide
children with leisure activities. The Norwegian Council
of Music Schools is doing a
marvelous job in this area.»

Jon Lilletun
Member of the Norwegian
Parliament and chairman of
Committee for Education

pectations of many of them, and ultimately leads to discouragement and frustration.

Another important factor in the move towards group tuition has been the matter of financial and organizational problems faced by music schools: where there is a shortage of teachers, or where cuts are necessary, group tuition seems to offer an alternative to reducing the number of student places. However, this pragmatic measure, made necessary by political decisions, has prompted teachers to take a closer look at the particular merits and drawbacks of both group and individual tuition.

In evaluating the educational merits of the two forms of teaching, two aspects must be distinguished: that of technical musicianship, and the social aspect of group dynamics.

In musical terms, group teaching offers many opportunities which lend themselves to the spirit of communication through music. Playing together with others has to occupy a central place on the curriculum, whether it be in the form of ensemble playing or in working out musical compositions and engaging in improvization. Playing together with others demands musical precision from every player, as well as stimulating them to more imaginative music-making. Students learn to adapt musically to a group, but also to play solos in front of the others and overcome performance nerves. Working on solo repertoire as a group has also proved to be a valuable exercise, enabling students to learn from one another, consider various possibilities of interpretation and extend their knowledge of the repertoire.

Exercises for posture and correct movement, which are particularly necessary with beginners, can be taught very effectively through group work: movement games played in a group can often be of more help than technical exercises taught in isolation in individual lessons. Group lessons generally provide a positive environment for making use of games: in a group of pupils of about the same age, conditions for introducing a «game» are more favourable than in the relationship between an individual pupil and his or her teacher, characterized as it is by authority and markedly different levels of competence. Games of this kind can also be used in

professionellen Musizieren weder den realistischen Möglichkeiten noch den Erwartungen vieler Schüler angemessen ist und letztlich demotivierend und frustrierend wirkt.

Zum andern waren und sind die Tendenzen zum Gruppenunterricht vielfach durch finanzielle und organisatorische Probleme der Musikschulen bestimmt: Bei Lehrermangel oder notwendigen Sparmaßnahmen scheint sich Gruppenunterricht als Lösung für fehlende Unterrichtsplätze anzubieten. Doch auch diese pragmatische kulturpolitische Notlösung provozierte das pädagogische Interesse an einer intensiveren Auseinandersetzung mit den spezifischen Chancen und Problemen sowohl des Gruppen- wie auch des Einzelunterrichts.

Bei der pädagogischen Bewertung der beiden Unterrichtsformen müssen zwei Ebenen voneinander unterschieden werden: die musikalisch-fachlichen und die gruppendynamisch-sozialen Aspekte.

In musikalischer Hinsicht bietet der Gruppenunterricht vielfältige, dem kommunikativen Wesen der Musik entsprechende Möglichkeiten. Ein zentraler Lerninhalt ist natürlich das Zusammenspiel, sei es als Ensemblespiel oder in Form von musikalischen Gestaltungsaufgaben und Improvisationen. Das Spiel mit anderen verlangt vom einzelnen Genauigkeit der Ausführung und fördert seine musikalische Vorstellungskraft. Die Schüler lernen, sich musikalisch in eine Gemeinschaft einzufügen, aber auch, vor der Gruppe solistisch zu spielen und Vorspielängste abzubauen. Ebenso erweist es sich als vorteilhaft, solistische Literatur gemeinsam in der Gruppe zu erarbeiten. Dabei können die Schüler voneinander lernen, werden mit verschiedenen Möglichkeiten der Interpretation konfrontiert und können ihre Repertoirekenntnis erweitern.

Gruppenunterricht begünstigt Haltungs- und Bewegungsübungen, wie sie vor allem im Anfangsunterricht notwendig sind: Bewegungsspiele in der Gruppe können das Erlernen eines Bewegungsablaufs oft besser unterstützen als isolierte Technikübungen im Einzelunterricht. Generell eignet sich der Gruppenunterricht für spielerische Ansätze: In einer Gruppe von etwa gleichaltrigen Schülern sind bessere Grundbedingungen für ein «Spiel» gegeben als in dem von Autorität und Leistungsgefälle geprägten Verhältnis eines Einzelschülers zu sei-

vers un exercice de la musique professionnel et en soliste n'est adapté ni aux possibilités réalistes ni aux attentes de nombreux élèves, et qu'elle a, en fin de compte, un aspect démotivant et frustrant.

D'autre part, les tendances à un enseignement en groupes étaient et sont déterminées par les problèmes de financement et d'organisation des écoles de musique: dans le cas d'un manque de professeurs ou d'une nécessité de mesures d'économie, l'enseignement de groupe semble se présenter comme étant la solution au manque de places dans les cours. Mais cette solution pragmatique, elle aussi, a provoqué l'intérêt pédagogique pour une discussion plus approfondie sur les chances et les problèmes spécifiques liés tant aux cours en groupes qu'aux cours particuliers.

Dans le jugement de valeur pédagogique de ces deux formes d'enseignement, il faut distinguer deux niveaux: les aspects spécialement musicaux et les aspects sociaux et de dynamique de groupe.

Sur le plan musical, les cours en groupes offrent des possibilités variées, correspondant bien à l'essence communicative de la musique. Un contenu central en est naturellement le fait de jouer en commun, que ce soit sous la forme d'ensembles ou sous la forme d'activités de création musicale ou d'improvisations. Le fait de jouer avec les autres exige de chacun une exactitude d'exécution et contribue au développement de sa faculté d'imagination musicale. Les élèves apprennent à s'intégrer musicalement dans une communauté, mais aussi, à jouer en soliste devant le groupe et à surmonter leur peur du public. De même, il s'avère être un avantage de travailler ensemble, en groupe, de la littérature pour solistes. Les élèves peuvent alors apprendre l'un de l'autre, sont confrontés aux diverses possibilités d'interprétation et peuvent enrichir leurs connaissances du répertoire.

Les cours en groupes favorisent les exercices de maintien et de mouvement, nécessaires principalement au début: des jeux de mouvements en groupe peuvent être un soutien meilleur à l'apprentissage du déroulement d'un mouvement que des exercices techniques en cours particulier. En général, les cours en groupes sont adaptés aux points de départs ludiques: dans un groupe d'élèves à peu près du même âge, les conditions de base pour «jouer»

other subjects, for example in aural training and in the study of music and music history.

Group tuition not only makes it possible to spread lesson content and variety of teaching method more widely; there are also psychological advantages to be gained from this method of learning. The small group typically used for instrumental teaching is an ideal forum for learning social skills: the individual adapts to fit in with the group, becomes aware of himself through relating to others, learns – with the help of «musical role plays» – to take on a series of different roles: that of leader, of accompanist, of equal partner, and even that of teacher. Examples set by the peer group often provide more effective motivation than the unattainably high standard set by the teacher in individual lessons. The group environment offers real opportunities to learn through imitation. By comparing themselves with others, students learn to assess the level of their own playing and develop standards for measuring their own achievements and those of others. Group tuition favours the development of communication skills and co-operation, thus contributing to the general education of the individual and their behaviour.

This exposition of the positive benefits and potential of group teaching is, admittedly, based on ideal conditions. The many problems which can arise with group tuition however should not be ignored.

A central problem in group teaching is the time management. Group lessons require different time allocation than individual lessons – unfortunately, this is not attended to in many cases where music schools are chiefly concerned with economy or where they cling to a rigid timetable. But, of course, it takes a larger amount of time for a teacher to attend to the needs of a whole group than of a single pupil.

nem Lehrer. Solche Spiele können auch andere Lerninhalte wie z.B. Gehörbildung, Musiklehre oder Musikgeschichte betreffen.

Der Gruppenunterricht ermöglicht nicht nur eine breitere Streuung der Lerninhalte und der Methoden, sondern es ergeben sich auch lernpsychologische Vorteile. Die Kleingruppe, wie sie im Instrumentalunterricht charakteristisch ist, ist ein idealer Ort sozialen Lernens: Der einzelne gliedert sich in ein Gruppengefüge ein, er baut sein Selbstbild in Gegenüberstellung mit Fremdbildern auf, er lernt – unterstützt durch «musikalische Rollenspiele» – wechselnde Rollen einzunehmen: die des Anführers, des Begleiters, des ebenbürtigen Partners, auch die des Lehrers. Das Beispiel Gleichaltriger motiviert oft mehr als das unerreichbare Vorbild des Lehrers im Einzelunterricht. Die Gruppe bietet Identifikationsmomente für ein Lernen durch Imitation. Im Vergleich mit anderen lernen die Schüler, sich selbst einzuschätzen, und entwickeln Maßstäbe zur Beurteilung eigener und fremder Leistungen. Gruppenunterricht fördert die Kommunikations- und Kooperationsfähigkeit und trägt somit zur Persönlichkeits- und Verhaltensbildung bei.

Diese Darstellung der positiven Möglichkeiten und Chancen des Gruppenunterrichts geht zugegebenermaßen von idealen Bedingungen aus. Mancherlei Probleme, die sich beim Gruppenunterricht ergeben, sollen darüber nicht unberücksichtigt bleiben.

Ein zentrales Problem des Gruppenunterrichts ist der Zeitfaktor. Gruppenunterricht bedarf anderer zeitlicher Strukturen als der Einzelunterricht – leider wird dies oft nicht berücksichtigt, wo Musikschulen vorrangig ökonomisch denken oder an einem starren Stundenplanschema festhalten. Die pädagogische Betreuung einer Gruppe benötigt jedoch naturgemäß einen größeren zeitlichen Rahmen als die eines Einzelschülers.

Die Arbeit in der Gruppe bringt es mit sich, daß dem einzelnen Schüler insgesamt weniger individuelle Zuwendung eingeräumt werden kann. Diese Möglichkeit, auf individuelle Probleme und Bedürfnisse eingehen zu können, zeichnet den Einzelunterricht vor dem Gruppenunterricht aus. Dies kann zu einer Nivellierung der Leistungen der einzelnen Gruppenmitglieder führen. Darunter haben vor al-

sont meilleures que dans une relation, empreinte par les disparités de l'autorité et de l'exigence de performance, d'un seul élève avec son professeur. De tels jeux peuvent également concerner d'autres points de fond tels que, par exemple, le développement de l'ouïe, la théorie musicale ou l'histoire de la musique.

L'enseignement de groupe ne permet pas seulement une distribution plus large des contenus et des méthodes, il a également des avantages sur le plan de la psychologie de l'apprentissage. Le petit groupe, caractéristique des cours où l'on apprend à jouer d'un instrument, est un lieu idéal d'apprentissage social: l'individu s'intègre dans le groupe, il élabore son image propre par rapport aux images des autres, il apprend – à l'aide des «jeux de rôles musicaux» – à glisser dans des rôles différents: celui du chef, de l'accompagnateur, du partenaire égal, et même celui du professeur. Le groupe offre des moments d'identification pour un apprentissage par l'imitation. En se comparant avec les autres, les élèves apprennent à se juger et développent des jalons pour le jugement de leurs propres performances et de celles des autres. Les cours en groupes contribuent au développement des facultés de communication et de coopération et, par là même, de la personnalité et du comportement.

Cette présentation des possibilités positives et des chances du cours en groupe suppose, il faut l'avouer, des conditions idéales. Nombre de problèmes qui apparaissent au cours de l'enseignement en groupe, ne doivent cependant pas être oubliés.

Un problème central des cours en groupes est le facteur temporel. L'enseignement de groupe nécessite des structures temporelles différentes de celles des cours particuliers – hélas, ceci, souvent, n'est pas pris en considération, les écoles de musique devant penser avant tout à l'aspect économique ou respecter un schéma d'emploi du temps rigide. L'encadrement pédagogique d'un groupe nécessite cependant, de par sa nature, un cadre temporel plus important que celui d'un élève de cours particulier.

Le travail dans le groupe a pour conséquence qu'on ne peut accorder autant d'attention individuelle à chaque élève en particulier, dans l'ensemble. Cette possibilité d'aborder les problèmes et des

Working with a group means that less personal attention can be given to each individual student; the opportunity to address individual problems and needs is the distinguishing merit of individual tuition. This can lead to a degree of levelling out in the attainment of the various members of group. Pupils who are higher achievers suffer particularly here through not being sufficiently stretched. Weaker pupils, on the other hand, soon feel out of their depth and react with frustration. As a rule, the feeling within a group is decisive in determining the progress of that group: what can encourage a healthy competitive spirit in one group may lead to rivalry and conflict in another. It is the task of the teacher to attend to the group dynamic and to ensure, by varying group activities, that a hierarchy does not become fixed and affect the working of the group.

Another decisive factor in the success of group work has to be the size of the group. No general guidelines or recommendations can be given in this matter; however, differences between particular instruments are one factor to be borne in mind. The composition of the group is important in terms of age, level of attainment, aptitude, family background, personality and existing emotional links such as friendships. But it is not even possible to say whether, as a matter of principle, either homogeneity or variety create better conditions for work in a group.

All these questions make demands on a teacher's personal experience and his or her ability to react with sensitivity and flexibility to a variety of situations. Such teachers need a broad knowledge of their subject, as well as having special skills for working with groups: they must be aware of all that is going on within the group and manage to steer pupils into different roles, supporting them as initiator, fellow music-maker, observer or co-ordinator. Group teaching requires a high degree of flexibility, imagination, energy and preparation from the teacher. In addition to all this, attention should be paid to the wishes of teachers for a more flexible timetable and the provision of rooms and equipment suitable for group lessons. Improved training opportunities and further training courses should also be made available, along with suitable teaching materials.

lem leistungsstarke Schüler zu leiden, die zu wenig gefordert werden. Leistungsschwächere Schüler fühlen sich dagegen schnell überfordert und reagieren mit Frustration. Insgesamt spielt das spezifische Gruppenprofil für die Leistungsfähigkeit einer Gruppe eine entscheidende Rolle: Was in der einen Gruppe den gesunden Wettbewerbsgeist fördern kann, führt in einer anderen vielleicht zu Leistungs- und Konkurrenzkampf. Aufgabe des Lehrers ist es dann, durch differenzierte Aufgabenstellungen das Gruppenprofil beweglich zu halten, so daß Rangordnungen, die Gruppenprozesse wesentlich prägen, sich nicht verhärten.

Entscheidend für den Erfolg der Gruppenarbeit ist sicher auch die Gruppengröße. Hierzu gibt es aber keine allgemeinen Richtlinien oder Empfehlungen; zu beachten sind aber instrumentenspezifische Unterschiede. Eine große Rolle spielt die Zusammensetzung der Gruppe im Hinblick auf Alter, Ausbildungsstand, Begabung, soziale Herkunft, Persönlichkeitsmerkmale und vorhandene emotionale Bindungen wie z.B. Freundschaften. Aber selbst ob Homogenität oder Verschiedenheit bessere Voraussetzungen für die Arbeit in der Gruppe sind, kann nicht prinzipiell gesagt werden.

In all diesen Fragen ist die persönliche Erfahrung des Lehrers gefordert sowie seine Fähigkeit, sensibel und flexibel auf diverse Situationen zu reagieren. Er bedarf eines fachlich weiten Horizonts und muß über spezielle gruppenpädagogische Fähigkeiten verfügen: Es geht darum, Gruppenprozesse differenziert wahrzunehmen und sie behutsam in unterschiedlichen Rollen zu steuern bzw. zu unterstützen, sei es als Impulsgeber, Mitagierender, Beobachter oder Koordinator. Gruppenunterricht erfordert vom Lehrer ein hohes Maß an Flexibilität, Phantasie, Energie und Vorbereitung.

Dazu sollten auch die Wünsche der Lehrer nach einer größeren Flexibilität der Stundenpläne und einer dem Gruppenunterricht angemessenen räumlichen und materiellen Ausstattung berücksichtigt werden. Außerdem sind verbesserte Ausbildungs- und Fortbildungsmöglichkeiten sowie die Bereitstellung geeigneter Unterrichtsmaterialien zu wünschen.

Instrumentaler Einzelunterricht und Gruppenunterricht sind keineswegs zwei einander aus-

besoins individuels distingue le cours particulier du cours en groupe. Ceci peut conduire à un nivellement des performances des divers membres du groupe.

En souffrent particulièrement les bons élèves, pour qui les activités sont trop faciles. Les élèves plus faibles, par contre, se sentent vite dépassés et réagissent avec frustration. Dans l'ensemble, le profil du groupe joue un rôle décisif pour sa performance: ce qui, dans un groupe, peut favoriser une saine concurrence peut, dans un autre, conduire à un combat de performance et de concurrence. Le rôle du professeur est alors de veiller à ce que le profil du groupe reste mobile, par des exercices différenciés, de sorte que les classements, qui déterminent pour une grande part les processus de groupes, ne se figent pas.

L'importance du groupe est sans nul doute, elle aussi, un facteur décisif de succès. Mais il n'existe pas de directives ou de recommandations à ce sujet; il convient de respecter cependant les différences spécifiques liées aux divers instruments. La composition du groupe sur le plan de l'âge, du niveau de formation, des dons, des origines sociales, des caractéristiques personnelles et des relations émotionnelles existantes, par exemple des amitiés, joue également un grand rôle. Mais il n'est pas possible de dire par principe si l'homogénéité ou la variété constituent des conditions meilleures pour le travail de groupe.

Dans toutes ces questions, il faut faire appel à l'expérience personnelle de l'enseignant ainsi qu'à son aptitude à réagir de manière sensible et flexible aux diverses situations. Il lui faut avoir un horizon large sur le plan de la matière et disposer de facultés spéciales pour la pédagogie de groupe: il s'agit là de percevoir de manière différenciée les processus de groupes et de les conduire ou de les aider avec précaution dans des rôles divers, que ce soit à titre de donneur d'impulsion, d'acteur, d'observateur ou de coordinateur. L'enseignement de groupe exige de l'enseignant une grande flexibilité, de l'imagination, de l'énergie et une bonne préparation.

Pour ce faire, il convient de tenir également compte des désirs des professeurs au niveau d'une plus grande flexibilité des emplois du temps et d'un

«L'éducation musicale est un moyen pédagogique plus puissant que tout autre. Car le rythme et l'harmonie font leur chemin jusque dans les recoins les plus profonds de l'âme et confèrent à cette âme grâce et vertu.»

Socrate

Individual tuition and group tuition are certainly not to be seen as two mutually exclusive alternatives. What can represent an advantage in the one can be a drawback in the other. Schools should aim for a combination of both forms of teaching, making the most of the personal attention provided in individual tuition whilst fully exploiting the potential of group tuition. *ub.*

Adults at Music Schools

Erwachsene an der Musikschule

Les adultes à l'école de musique

Teaching in music schools or academies was originally chiefly oriented towards the training of future professional musicians. A next step in their evolution – representing part of a general trend towards open access in education – was the inclusion of educational provision for children and adolescents destined to become amateur musicians. A third step in this process of development may be identified now that adults of various ages are expressing the wish to learn an instrument or develop a singing voice, either from scratch or to recall half-forgotten skills, in order to participate in active music-making.

The reasons for this surge in interest are that, for one thing, the amount of time taken up in adult life by earning a living has diminished, leaving people with increased leisure time. For another thing, people's average life expectancy has increased significantly: there are more older people, and their capabilities and desire for activity are now much greater. The effects on society of this demographic development are manifold. New ways have to be found, not only of funding activities for older people, but of ensuring they have a place in society and opportunities for leisure and cultural pursuits.

This opens up what is, for the most part, a new kind of involvement for music schools. A steadily growing number of adults want their enjoyment of music to go beyond that of the consumer: this is shown by surveys where almost 15% of those ques-

schließende Alternativen. Was der Vorzug der einen Unterrichtsform ist, kann Nachteil der anderen sein. Anzustreben ist eine Kombination beider Möglichkeiten. So kann die individuelle Betreuung des Schülers durch den Einzelunterricht ebenso genutzt werden wie die vielfältigen Möglichkeiten im Gruppenunterricht. *ub.*

Ursprünglich war der Unterricht an Musikschulen oder Konservatorien in der Hauptsache auf die Vorbereitung künftiger Berufsmusiker ausgerichtet. In einem historisch nächsten Schritt – und im Zuge einer allgemeinen Demokratisierung des Bildungswesens – ist in den Ländern Europas die Ausbildung vor allem von Kindern und Jugendlichen zum Amateurmusizieren hinzugekommen. Als dritte Stufe dieser Entwicklung ist zu sehen, daß heute auch Erwachsene unterschiedlichen Lebensalters den Wunsch haben, ein Instrument oder den Umgang mit ihrer Stimme ganz neu zu erlernen oder wieder aufzufrischen und hierdurch eine Möglichkeit zum gemeinsamen Musizieren zu erhalten.

Die Gründe hierfür sind, daß zum einen die zeitliche Inanspruchnahme der Erwachsenen durch ihre berufliche Tätigkeit zurückging und ihnen also mehr Freizeit zur Verfügung steht. Zum anderen hat sich die durchschnittliche Lebenserwartung der Menschen erheblich gesteigert: Es gibt mehr ältere Menschen, und ihre Leistungsfähigkeit und Aktionswilligkeit haben entscheidend zugenommen. Die gesellschaftlichen Auswirkungen dieser demographischen Entwicklung sind vielfältig. Neue Lösungen sind gefordert, wenn es darum geht, neben einer finanziellen Grundversorgung älterer Menschen ihre generelle gesellschaftliche Teilhabe zu sichern und Angebote zur Freizeitgestaltung und zur Teilnahme am geistigen Leben bereitzustellen.

équipement matériel et spatial adapté à l'enseignement de groupe. De plus, une amélioration des possibilités de formation et de formation continue ainsi qu'une mise à disposition de matériel scolaire adapté serait souhaitable.

Le cours particulier et le cours en groupe en vue de l'apprentissage d'un instrument ne sont en aucun cas des alternatives qui s'excluent mutuellement. Ce qui est l'avantage d'une des formes de cours peut être un désavantage pour l'autre. Il faut tendre à une combinaison de ces deux possibilités. Ainsi, l'encadrement individuel d'un élève par le cours particulier pourra tout aussi bien être utilisé que la variété des possibilités des cours en groupe. *ub.*

Au départ, les cours des écoles de musique ou des conservatoires tendaient principalement à la préparation des futurs musiciens professionnels. Dans un second temps – et dans le courant de la démocratisation de l'éducation –, la formation principalement d'enfants et d'adolescents est venue s'ajouter, en Europe, à la musique d'amateur. La troisième étape de cette évolution peut être considérée comme le fait que, aujourd'hui, les adultes de tous âges éprouvent eux aussi le désir d'apprendre à jouer d'un instrument ou à se servir de leur voix, ou de rafraîchir leurs connaissances. L'école de musique leur donne la possibilité de faire de la musique en commun.

Les raisons en sont d'une part le fait que les adultes sont moins pris qu'autrefois par leur activité professionnelle et qu'ils ont donc plus de loisirs. D'autre part, l'espérance de vie a sensiblement augmenté: il y a plus de personnes âgées, et leur vitalité et leur désir d'action se sont accrus de manière décisive. Les conséquences sociales de cette évolution démographique sont multiples. Il s'agit de chercher des solutions nouvelles pour assurer – outre les pensions de vieillesse des personnes âgées – leur intégration générale dans la société et leur offrir des possibilités de loisirs et de participer à la vie intellectuelle.

La tâche qui revient ici aux écoles de musique est d'un type pour la plus grande part nouveau. Le nombre des adultes qui ne veulent pas se contenter

tioned expressed great interest in opportunities for active music-making. In many cases the parents or grandparents of young music school pupils are roused by the example of their children or grandchildren into doing likewise and making music themselves.

The European Union of Music Schools dealt with this subject at its 1988 conference in Florence and passed a resolution entitled «Music Training for Adults at Music Schools», identifying the need for availability of special music teaching for adults at music schools. This can mean either taking up a new instrument – or singing lessons – or renewing acquaintance with an instrument previously studied, but it may also involve participation in various forms of group music-making in chamber music ensembles, orchestras and choirs. It should also be made possible for adults to participate in newer forms of music-making using simple percussion, dance or musical theatre. An introduction to an appreciation of musical works and instruction in the principles of music theory are other possible areas that might be developed.

Discussion of the educational principles applying to adult music education tends to focus on two questions: – Are those adults who express an interest, particularly the more elderly, still capable of learning an instrument or developing their voice in the role of a «pupil»? – Are the teachers at music schools properly equipped by their training and professional experience to teach adults? The two questions are naturally interrelated.

The first question may be answered with a «yes». Recent research into learning and development psychology has established that intellectual powers do not normally stop developing or deteriorate in adults, but continue to develop throughout a person's life. Capacity for learning is great, even in old age. In everyday life, however, it is rarely used to its full extent. It is therefore possible to learn an instrument or study singing even in old age. However, the greatest progress is generally to be

Hier sind auch die Musikschulen mit einer überwiegend neuen Aufgabe gefordert. Immer größer wird die Zahl auch der Erwachsenen, die sich nicht allein konsumorientiert mit Musik befassen möchten: Das zeigen Umfragen, bei denen fast 15% der Befragten ein starkes Interesse an Möglichkeiten aktiven Musizierens äußerten. Oft sind es die Eltern oder Großeltern jugendlicher Musikschul-Schüler, die sich von ihren Kindern oder Enkelkindern angeregt fühlen, es ihnen gleichzutun und selber zu musizieren.

Die Europäische Musikschul-Union hat sich 1988 auf ihrem Kongreß in Florenz mit diesem Thema befaßt und eine Resolution «Musikunterricht mit Erwachsenen an Musikschulen» verabschiedet. Darin wird auf die Notwendigkeit «spezieller musikpädagogischer Angebote für Erwachsene an Musikschulen» hingewiesen. «Dabei kann es sich entweder um die Neuaufnahme oder eine Wiederaufnahme von Instrumental- oder Gesangunterricht handeln, ebenso aber um eine Teilnahme an verschiedenen Formen des gemeinsamen Musizierens in kammermusikalischen Ensembles, Orchestern und Chören. Auch eine Teilnahme erwachsener Bürger an neuen Formen des Musizierens auf elementaren Musikinstrumenten, des Tanzes oder des Musiktheaters sollte ermöglicht werden. Eine Einführung in das Verständnis musikalischer Werke und die theoretischen Grundlagen der Musik sind gleichfalls mögliche Arbeitsfelder».

Die pädagogische Diskussion über musikalische Erwachsenenbildung konzentriert sich zunächst auf zwei Fragen: – Sind interessierte Erwachsene, vor allem in fortgeschrittenem Alter, überhaupt noch in der Lage, als «Schüler» ein Instrument spielen zu lernen oder ihre Stimme auszubilden? – Sind die Musikschulpädagogen aufgrund ihrer Ausbildung und ihrer bisherigen beruflichen Tätigkeit in der Lage, Erwachsene sinnvoll und erfolgversprechend zu unterrichten? Beide Fragestellungen hängen natürlich miteinander zusammen.

Die erste kann grundsätzlich mit «Ja» beantwortet werden. In Forschungen der Entwicklungs- und Lernpsychologie ist neuerdings festgestellt worden, daß beim Erwachsenen normalerweise kein Stillstand oder genereller Abbau der geistigen Kräfte erfolgt, sondern sich Entwicklungen bis zum Ende

de consommer de la musique s'accroît également sans cesse. Des sondages le montrent: près de 15% des personnes interrogées ont exprimé un vif intérêt à l'égard de possibilités d'exercer une activité musicale. Ce sont souvent les parents ou les grands-parents de jeunes élèves de l'école de musique qui sont incités à les imiter et à faire de la musique eux aussi.

L'«Union Européenne des Ecoles de Musique» s'est préoccupée de ce sujet en 1988 lors de son congrès de Florence et a rédigé une résolution intitulée «l'éducation musicale des adultes dans les écoles de musique». Celle-ci souligne la nécessité d'offres pédagogiques musicales spéciales pour adultes dans les écoles de musique. Il peut s'agir là soit de commencer à prendre des cours d'instrument ou de chant, soit d'en reprendre, mais il s'agit également de participer à diverses formes de l'exercice commun de la musique au sein d'ensembles de musique de chambre, d'orchestres ou de choeurs. La participation d'adultes à des formes nouvelles de l'exercice de la musique telles que la musique sur les instruments élémentaires, la danse ou le théâtre musical devrait également être rendue possible. Une introduction à la compréhension d'oeuvres musicales et aux rudiments théoriques de la musique sont également des domaines de travail à envisager.

La discussion pédagogique sur l'éducation musicale des adultes se concentre tout d'abord sur deux questions: – Les adultes intéressés, surtout les adultes d'un âge avancé, sont-ils encore capables comme des «élèves» d'apprendre à jouer d'un instrument ou de former leur voix? – Les pédagogues enseignant dans les écoles de musique sont-ils capables, de par leur formation et leur activité professionnelle, de donner des cours judicieusement et avec succès à des adultes?

Les deux questions sont bien entendu dépendantes l'une de l'autre.

On peut systématiquement répondre par «oui» à la première. Les recherches récentes sur la psychologie du développement et de l'apprentissage ont permis de constater que les aptitudes intellectuelles des adultes ne sont normalement pas soumises à un statu quo ou à une détérioration générale, mais que leur développement se poursuit jusqu'à la fin

des Lebens vollziehen. Die Lernkapazität ist auch im Alter noch hoch. Sie wird jedoch im Alltag nur selten in ganzem Umfang genutzt. Es ist daher bis ins Alter möglich, ein Instrument oder das Fach Gesang zu erlernen. Vor allem aber ist eine Erweiterung der Fertigkeiten bei denjenigen zu erwarten, die bereits in früheren Lebensjahren ein Instrument oder das Singen gelernt hatten und nun an diese vorhandenen, aber lange brachliegenden Grundlagen wieder anknüpfen können.

achieved by those who learned an instrument or had singing lessons in their youth and who can now build on the foundation of these neglected skills.

Adults have a different approach to learning from children or adolescents, though. Children's learning is generally extrinsic or secondary in its motivation: directed towards a goal which brings measurable rewards, challenged by their immediate environment to seek praise and recognition, to communicate with other people or to secure advantages for later life. An adult, on the other hand, tends to have intrinsic or primary motivation: the wish to pursue his own interests, possibly involving the discovery and employment of hidden talents.

The different character of their motivation is not the only noticeable difference to mark adults' approach to learning. They do not normally learn through imitating what the teacher demonstrates, but need to see and grasp the purpose of a step and a procedure. Without such conscious acceptance, learning is impossible for them. This means that a teacher must adopt methods for working with adults which differ significantly from those customarily used with children and adolescents. With an adult, teaching aims and contents have to be discussed and agreed beforehand. In general an adult, who may not in any event find it easy to step into the role of a «pupil» again, should be treated far more as a «partner» and involved in the planning and delivery of lessons. Since adults are very self-

Erwachsene haben jedoch ein anderes Lernverhalten als Kinder und Jugendliche. Kinder lernen im allgemeinen extrinsisch oder sekundär motiviert: auf ein Ziel hin gerichtet, das sich messen läßt und Vorteile bringt, herausgefordert durch ihre Umwelt und auf Lob und soziale Anerkennung aus, bestrebt, Kommunikation zu anderen Menschen herzustellen oder Chancen für das spätere Leben zu erhalten. Ein Erwachsener hingegen ist überwiegend intrinsisch oder primär motiviert: Seine Motivation ist es, den eigenen Interessen nachzugehen oder eventuell verborgene Talente zu entdecken und zu mobilisieren.

Die andersartig ausgeprägte Motivation ist nicht der einzige markante Unterschied, der das Lernverhalten Erwachsener kennzeichnet. Sie lernen normalerweise nicht durch Imitation dessen, was der Lehrer ihnen vormacht, sondern müssen den Sinn einer Maßnahme und eines Schrittes kennen und erkennen. Ohne diese bewußte Akzeptanz ist ein Lernen für sie nicht möglich. Dies bedeutet also für die Lehrkraft gegenüber Erwachsenen ein Unterrichtsverhalten, das von dem im Unterricht mit Kindern und Jugendlichen gewohnten entscheidend abweicht. Mit dem Erwachsenen müssen die Unterrichtsziele und -inhalte vorher besprochen und abgestimmt werden. Überhaupt sollte der Erwachsene, dem es an sich schon nicht leichtfällt, wieder in die Rolle eines «Schülers» zu wechseln, viel eher als «Partner» betrachtet und in die Planung und Durchführung des Unterrichts einbezogen werden. Da Erwachsene sehr selbstkritisch

de la vie. La capacité à l'apprentissage est encore très élevée même au troisième âge. Cependant, elle n'est exploitée que rarement dans toute son amplitude dans la vie quotidienne. Il est donc possible d'apprendre un instrument ou le chant jusque dans la vieillesse. Mais on peut avant tout s'attendre à un élargissement des facultés acquises chez les adultes ayant déjà appris à jouer d'un instrument ou appris le chant dans leur jeunesse et pouvant donc renouer avec ces bases, présentes, mais longtemps négligées.

Cependant, les adultes ont un comportement à l'apprentissage différent de celui des enfants ou des adolescents. Les enfants apprennent généralement par motivation extrinsèque ou secondaire: en fonction d'un objectif mesurable et apportant des avantages, poussés par leur environnement et les compliments et la reconnaissance sociale, avides d'établir une communication avec autrui ou de se créer des chances pour l'avenir. Un adulte, au contraire, est principalement motivé de manière intrinsèque ou primaire: sa motivation est de donner libre cours à ses intérêts ou, éventuellement, de découvrir et de mobiliser ses talents cachés.

Cette motivation, de caractère totalement différent, n'est pas la seule différence marquante caractérisant le comportement à l'apprentissage de l'adulte. Normalement, les adultes n'apprennent pas par imitation de ce que leur montre l'enseignant, ils ont besoin de comprendre le sens des mesures ou des étapes pédagogiques. Sans cette acceptation consciente, l'apprentissage, pour eux, n'est pas possible. Ceci implique donc, pour l'enseignant placé face à des adultes, un comportement d'enseignement fondamentalement différent des cours habituels avec des enfants ou des adolescents. Les objectifs et les contenus des cours pour adultes doivent être discutés auparavant. De manière générale, l'adulte – qui a déjà des difficultés à passer dans le rôle de «l'élève» – devra être bien plus considéré comme un partenaire et associé à la planification et à l'exécution du cours. Les adultes étant très autocritiques, il convient de louer beaucoup leurs bons résultats et leurs progrès partiels. Une atmosphère détendue et joyeuse pendant le cours joue également chez les adultes un rôle décisif pour un apprentissage réussi.

«People playing an instrument are always in a good mood because it is impossible to be sour and play at the same time.»

Birgitte Arendt

«Musik steht im Zentrum meines beruflichen und meines privaten Lebens. Ich kann mir ein Leben ohne Musik so wenig vorstellen, wie ein Leben ohne Wälder und ohne Vegetation. Heute, wo sich meine berufliche Tätigkeit gegen die Seite der Kulturpolitik verschoben hat, nehme ich die existentielle Bedeutung der Musik eher noch stärker wahr. Die Turbulenzen des heutigen Lebens, und die zum Teil fast unlösbaren Schwierigkeiten auf dem kulturellen Gebiet sind nur zu ertragen und zu bewältigen, wenn der Kraftstrom aus der Musik nicht versiegt, der das Lebensgefühl und die Lebensfreude ebensosehr nährt wie den Geist.

Wenn ich die Schwerpunkte meiner beruflichen Tätigkeit vom aktiven Musizieren zugunsten der Verbesserungen der Rahmenbedingungen verschoben habe, so geschah es gegen meine eigene Natur und aus der Erkenntnis, daß Musiker sich auch außerhalb ihrer eigentlichen Tätigkeit auf allen Ebenen und mit allen Mitteln für die Wahrung und Erhaltung der musikalischen Erziehung einsetzen müssen, die im Augenblick aufs schwerste bedroht ist.»

Urs Frauchiger

critical, much praise should be given for good results and for every small step forward. A relaxed atmosphere of enjoyment in lessons is a decisive element in ensuring successful learning for adults, too.

The answer to the second question raised above, as to whether music school teachers have appropriate training for a task so fundamentally different as working with adults, has to be: «only to a limited extent, in most cases». As a rule, teachers have not been trained for the task of teaching adult non-professionals. Even where they have good teaching qualifications as well as being good musicians, the demands of this kind of teaching are new to most of them.

Yet it may be expected that more and more music schools will turn to the new task of adult education, extending their range of courses considerably in this respect. In order to deal with any uncertainty regarding teaching methods and lesson content, teachers need effective support.

There may be a place for running practically oriented training projects at the music schools themselves, for example. The Association of German Music Schools ran a project lasting several years at more than 50 music schools. The result of this has been the development and publication of so-called «recommendations» for a number of popular instrumental options, such as piano, guitar, recorder german flute or violin, as well as for singing, primary music teaching and a wide range of ensemble options and subsidiary subjects, for example groups of elderly people playing together with diverse instruments or music – moving – dance. These «recommendations» are intended as a useful addition to the curriculum in each subject and provide a framework of basic advice on teaching adults at music schools, including the special requirements of such teaching, with advice on teaching methods and suggestions regarding suitable teaching material.

Work with adults should also figure more frequently among the further training opportunities offered by music school associations and other authorities; there is unlikely to be a lack of demand for such courses. Lastly, particular attention might be given to special features of working with adult

sind, ist bei guten Ergebnissen und auch bei erfolgreichen Teilschritten viel Lob angebracht. Eine gelöste und freudvolle Atmosphäre während des Unterrichts spielt für ein erfolgreiches Lernen auch bei Erwachsenen eine entscheidende Rolle.

Die Antwort zu der zweiten oben aufgeworfenen Frage, ob die Musikschulpädagogen für eine fundamental so verschiedene Arbeit mit Erwachsenen angemessen ausgebildet sind, lautet: «Grundsätzlich nur bedingt». In aller Regel sind die Lehrkräfte auf die Aufgabe, erwachsene Nicht-Profis zu unterrichten, nicht vorbereitet worden. Auch wenn sie neben einer guten künstlerischen auch eine gute pädagogische Ausbildung gehabt haben, sind diese Anforderungen doch zumeist neu für sie.

Es steht aber zu erwarten, daß sich immer mehr Musikschulen der neuen Aufgabe des Erwachsenenunterrichts zuwenden und ihre entsprechenden Angebote wesentlich ausweiten werden. Um der Unsicherheit zu begegnen, wie ein solcher Unterricht methodisch und inhaltlich gestaltet werden soll, brauchen die Lehrkräfte wirksame Hilfestellungen.

Hier ist beispielsweise an praxisorientierte Modellversuche an den Musikschulen selbst zu denken. Der Verband deutscher Musikschulen führte an über 50 Musikschulen ein mehrjähriges Projekt durch. Ergebnis war die Erarbeitung und Veröffentlichung sogenannter «Handreichungen» für mehrere wichtige Instrumentalfächer wie Klavier, Gitarre, Blockflöte, Querflöte und Violine sowie für Gesang, elementaren Musikunterricht und für eine breite Palette von Ensemble- und Ergänzungsfächern wie Seniorengruppen, Zusammenspiel mit beliebigen Instrumenten oder Musik–Bewegung–Tanz. Diese «Handreichungen» sind als Ergänzung zu den Lehrplänen der entsprechenden Fächer gedacht und bieten grundsätzliche Informationen zur musikalischen Erwachsenenbildung an Musikschulen und zu den Besonderheiten des Unterrichts mit Erwachsenen, methodische und didaktische Hilfen für die Lehrenden sowie Literaturvorschläge.

Die Arbeit mit Erwachsenen sollte auch in den Fortbildungsangeboten der Musikschulverbände und anderer Veranstalter zunehmend vertreten sein. Über mangelnde Resonanz wird man kaum zu klagen haben. Schließlich wäre zu wünschen,

La réponse à la deuxième question posée ci-dessus, à savoir si la formation des pédagogues des écoles de musique est adaptée à un travail si fondamentalement différent avec les adultes, est la suivante: «Par principe, dans une certaine limite seulement». En règle générale, les enseignants n'ont pas été préparés à enseigner à des adultes non professionnels. Même s'ils ont reçu, outre une bonne formation artistique, une bonne formation pédagogique, ces exigences sont, la plupart du temps, nouvelles pour eux.

Mais il faut s'attendre à ce que de plus en plus d'écoles de musique se tournent vers cette tâche nouvelle de l'enseignement pour adultes et élargissent de manière correspondante la palette des matières proposées. Afin de compenser les doutes concernant la conception méthodologique et substantielle de ce type d'enseignement, les enseignants ont besoin d'un soutien efficace.

Il faudra envisager ici des essais de modèles orientés vers la pratique dans les écoles de musique mêmes. L'Association Allemande des Ecoles de Musique a réalisé un projet sur plusieurs années au niveau de 50 écoles de musique. Le résultat en fut l'élaboration et la publication de «trucs» pour plusieurs matières instrumentales importantes – telles que le piano, la guitare, la flûte à bec, la flûte traversière et le violon –, ainsi que pour le chant, l'enseignement élémentaire de la musique et pour une large palette de matières d'ensembles et de matières complémentaires telles que les groupes du troisième âge, la musique commune avec des instruments quelconques ou le complexe de musique – mouvement – danse. Ces «trucs» se veulent constituer des compléments aux matières correspondantes et présentent des informations fondamentales sur l'éducation musicale des adultes dans les écoles de musique et sur les particularités de l'enseignement pour adultes, des auxiliaires méthodologiques et didactiques pour les enseignants ainsi que des conseils de littérature.

Le travail avec des adultes devrait également être représenté de manière croissante dans les offres de formation continue des associations des écoles de musique et autres organisateurs. On ne saurait se plaindre du manque de demande. Enfin, il serait souhaitable que les particularités de l'enseigne-

students as part of the training of teachers to work in music schools.

This new subject area, the new task of educating adults at music schools, is a cultural and educational issue of great contemporary importance, requiring a real commitment from music schools and related organizations. *dw.*

Music with the Disabled at Music Schools

Musik mit Behinderten an Musikschulen

La musique avec des handicapés dans les écoles de musique

Children, adolescents and adults who are disabled have the right to education and support for their development like anyone else. Disabled people enjoy music-making like anyone else; involvement with music occupies an important place in their leisure time. Where this means playing an instrument, they too are best catered for in a music school.

The general term «disabled» is extremely vague and includes people who are affected by damage to their senses or limits on their ability to learn, their social behaviour, their powers of spoken communication or their psycho-motor co-ordination, to the extent that participation in the life of the community becomes far more difficult for them. Various kinds of disability can be distinguished here: there are the physically handicapped, the blind and those with impaired vision, the deaf and those with hearing impairments, those with speech problems, learning difficulties, mental disabilities or behavioural problems. Often, several of these occur together, and slight variations are generally to be observed between one case and another.

A person disabled in this way is now introduced to music – and reacts just like an able-bodied person: he or she enjoys listening to music, preferring some kinds of music and rejecting others, and also has a desire to make music by singing or playing an instrument. Able to experience music like anyone else and in that sense innately musical, this person like any other will experience «the urge to express himself through music» (Friedrich Klausmeier). This human characteristic is far from being fixed and immutable, but can be and needs to be devel-

daß auch in der Ausbildung der Musikschullehrer an den Hochschulen die Besonderheiten des Unterrichts mit Erwachsenen berücksichtigt und weiterentwickelt werden.

Das neue Thema, die neue Aufgabe «Erwachsene an Musikschulen», ist gesellschaftspolitisch und pädagogisch hochaktuell und braucht die Initiative und das Engagement der Musikschulen und ihrer Organisationen. *dw.*

Behinderte haben wie nichtbehinderte Kinder, Jugendliche und Erwachsene das Recht auf Bildung und Förderung. Behinderte haben wie Nichtbehinderte Freude am Musizieren. Die Beschäftigung mit Musik nimmt in ihrer Freizeit einen großen Raum ein. Wenn es um das Instrumentalspiel geht, ist die Musikschule auch für sie der richtige Ort.

Der Sammelbegriff «Behinderte» ist höchst unscharf und umfaßt Menschen, die durch die Schädigung ihrer Sinne oder die in ihrem Lernen, im sozialen Verhalten, in der sprachlichen Kommunikation oder in ihren psychomotorischen Fähigkeiten so weit beeinträchtigt sind, daß ihre Teilhabe am Leben der Gesellschaft wesentlich erschwert ist. Es lassen sich verschiedene Arten der Behinderung differenzieren: Körperbehinderte, Blinde und Sehbehinderte, Gehörlose und Hörgeschädigte, Sprachbehinderte, Lernbehinderte, geistig Behinderte, Verhaltensgestörte. Oft liegt eine Mehrfachbehinderung vor, und graduelle Unterschiede sind die Regel.

Der so beschriebene Behinderte wird nun mit Musik in Verbindung gebracht – und er verhält sich so wie der Nichtbehinderte: Er hört gerne Musik, nimmt bestimmte Stilrichtungen an oder lehnt sie ab; auch er hat den Wunsch, Musik zu machen, zu singen oder zu musizieren. Er ist wie jeder Mensch in der Lage, Musik zu erleben, ist in diesem Sinne musikalisch, ihm ist wie allen Menschen «die Lust» eigen, «sich musikalisch auszudrücken» (Friedrich Klausmeier). Diese Eigenheit des Menschen ist keineswegs statisch, unveränderbar, sondern entwicklungsfähig und entwicklungsbedürftig, insbe-

ment pour adultes soient prises en compte et développées dans la formation des professeurs des écoles de musique.

Le nouveau sujet, la nouvelle tâche intitulée «les adultes à l'école de musique», est on ne peut plus actuelle sur le plan de la politique sociale et de la pédagogie, et elle a besoin de l'initiative et de l'engagement des écoles de musique et de leurs organisations. *dw.*

Les handicapés, tout comme les enfants, les adolescents ou les adultes non handicapés, ont le droit de recevoir une formation et d'être encouragés et soutenus. Les handicapés, tout comme les non handicapés, éprouvent du plaisir à jouer de la musique. La musique occupe une place importante dans leurs loisirs. Et s'il s'agit de jouer d'un instrument, l'école de musique est le lieu idéal pour eux.

Le concept fourre-tout de «handicapé» est extrêmement flou et flottant; il renferme des gens dont les sens sont remis en question ou qui sont handicapés au niveau de la communication linguistique ou dans leurs facultés psychomotrices dans une proportion telle que leur participation à la vie sociale en est rendue difficile. On différencie divers types de handicapés: les handicapés physiques, les aveugles et les malvoyants, les sourds et les malentendants, les handicapés de la parole, les handicapés à l'apprentissage, les handicapés mentaux, les troubles du comportement. Souvent, le handicap est multiple, et les différences de degrés constituent la règle générale.

Le handicapé ainsi décrit est alors mis en relation avec la musique – et il se comporte comme un non-handicapé: il aime écouter de la musique, il apprécie ou refuse certains styles, il éprouve lui aussi le désir de faire de la musique, de chanter ou de jouer d'un instrument. Comme n'importe quel autre être humain, il est capable de vivre la musique, il est donc, à ce sens du terme, «musical», «l'envie de s'exprimer par la musique» lui est propre, comme à tout autre être humain (Friedrich Klausmeier). Cette particularité de l'être humain n'est aucunement statique, immuable, mais au

oped, particularly in the case of musical skills and abilities. This is the starting point for musical education, for skills and abilities can be trained.

A disability may sometimes affect these skills and abilities, making it more difficult or preventing people from making music. There may be limited movement in the arm or hand, blindness or limited vision, or deficiencies in perception and understanding. Obstacles of various kinds stand in the way of realizing the inherent desire to make music. Ways therefore have to be found of getting round the disability, or of giving it special consideration in choosing suitable teaching methods.

Let us first assume that the instrument chosen by the child or young person is to be played without the aid of special appliances and additional equipment. This will often mean setting aside the strictest precepts of schools of instrumental technique: hand and arm positions will be determined by what is possible. Another approach is to adapt the instrument to the handicap: special recorders have been developed with a system of keys allowing for the whole range of the instrument to be played with the use of a single hand. Descriptions of possible ways of adapting instruments and various aids to playing can be found in the relevant specialist journals*.

Many children and young people are mentally handicapped or have recognised learning difficulties. Here it requires imagination on the part of the teacher to get around difficulties in understanding verbal explanations: simple clarity in demonstrating what has to be learned, sparing use of words, brief and clear instructions, repetition where appropriate, and the communication of plenty of enjoyment in playing are all important in the teacher's approach.

All this would be in vain, however, without a real desire to learn this particular instrument. Motivating people, giving them a real desire to work at an instrument – a desire strong enough to help them overcome problems as they arise: this is a central aim of work with the disabled at music schools. However, in many cases disabled people have already experienced so much frustration through not being able to do things as they wish, that they have lost the confidence to say: I want to play the piano

sondere sind dies die musikalischen Fähigkeiten und Fertigkeiten. Hieraus leitet sich die musikpädagogische Aufgabe ab, denn Fähigkeiten und Fertigkeiten sind trainierbar.

Eine Behinderung wirkt sich möglicherweise auf Fähigkeiten und Fertigkeiten aus und erschwert oder verhindert somit ein Musikmachen. Das können Lähmungserscheinungen im Arm- und Handbereich sein, das können Blindheit oder Sehschwächen sein oder Schwächen in der Wahrnehmung und im Verstehen. Dem immanenten Wunsch zum Musizieren stehen Hindernisse unterschiedlicher Art, ihn zu verwirklichen, gegenüber. Es sind also Wege zu finden, die Behinderung zu umgehen oder sie beim Lernvorgang besonders zu beachten.

Man wird zunächst davon ausgehen, daß das vom Kind oder Jugendlichen gewählte Instrument ohne spezielle Spielhilfen gespielt wird. Dabei muß man sich von den Idealvorstellungen der Instrumentalschulen oftmals lösen: Hand- und Armhaltung richten sich nach der Möglichkeit, das Instrument trotz der Behinderung zu bedienen. Ein anderer Weg besteht darin, Instrumente der Behinderung anzupassen. Bekannt wurden Einhand-Blockflöten, bei denen ein Klappensystem erlaubt, den gesamten Tonumfang des Instruments mit der funktionsfähigen Hand zu spielen. Beschreibungen von Umbau- und Anpassungsmöglichkeiten und Spielhilfen finden sich in der einschlägigen Fachliteratur*.

Manche Kinder und Jugendliche sind geistig behindert oder gelten als lernbehindert. Hier ist in erster Linie der Einfallsreichtum der Lehrerin oder des Lehrers gefragt, die Schwierigkeiten im Aufnehmen verbaler Erläuterungen zu umgehen: durch Anschaulichkeit im Darstellen des zu Erlernenden, durch sparsame Anwendung der Sprache, durch kurze einprägsame Anweisungen, durch sinnvolle Wiederholung, durch das Vermitteln von viel Freude am Spiel.

All dies würde aber nichts bringen, wenn der unbedingte Wunsch, gerade dieses Instrument spielen zu wollen, fehlen würde. Die Motivation zur intensiven Beschäftigung mit dem Instrument zu erreichen, die auch aufkommende Schwierigkeiten überwinden hilft, ist ein zentrales Ziel der Arbeit

contraire capable de développement, bien plus, elle a besoin de se développer, en particulier en ce qui concerne les facultés et aptitudes musicales. En découle la tâche de la pédagogie musicale, car facultés et aptitudes peuvent être développées par l'exercice.

Un handicap peut influencer ces facultés et aptitudes et rendre difficile ou même impossible la pratique de la musique. Il peut s'agir là de paralysies dans le domaine du bras et de la main, de cécité ou d'un défaut visuel, ou de défauts de perception et de compréhension. Les obstacles s'opposant à la réalisation du désir immanent de faire de la musique peuvent être de nature différente. Il faut donc trouver des méthodes permettant de contourner le handicap ou de lui accorder une attention particulière au cours du processus d'apprentissage.

Il faut tout d'abord partir du principe que l'instrument choisi par l'enfant ou l'adolescent est joué sans auxiliaires spéciales. Il faut souvent rompre ici avec les conceptions idéales des méthodes d'instruments: la position du bras et de la main sont fonction de la possibilité d'utiliser l'instrument malgré le handicap. Une autre méthode est d'adapter l'instrument au handicap. On connaît des flûtes à bec à une main, dans lesquelles un système de clapets permet de jouer l'ensemble de la gamme de l'instrument avec la main saine. On trouvera des descriptions des possibilités de modifications et d'adaptation ainsi que des auxiliaires de jeu dans la littérature se rapportant à ce sujet*.

Certains enfants et adolescents sont handicapés mentaux ou sont considérés comme handicapés à l'apprentissage. C'est l'imagination du professeur qui doit aider à contourner les difficultés d'assimilation des explications verbales: par l'expressivité de la présentation de la matière à apprendre, par l'économie de l'expression linguistique, par des ordres brefs et facilement mémorisables, par une répétition à bon escient, par la transmission du plaisir de l'exercice de la musique.

Mais tout ceci ne servirait à rien si le désir inconditionnel d'apprendre justement cet instrument là venait à manquer. La motivation à l'exercice intense de l'instrument, motivation qui aide à surmonter les difficultés qui ne manqueront pas de surgir, est un objectif central du travail avec des

*

de Bruijn, *Muziek in de Kinderrevalidatie,* Nijkerk 1984

Clark/Chadwick, *Clinically Adapted Instruments for the Multiply Handicapped,* St. Louis 1980

Probst, *Instrumentalspiel mit Behinderten. Ein Modellversuch und seine Folgen,* Mainz 1991

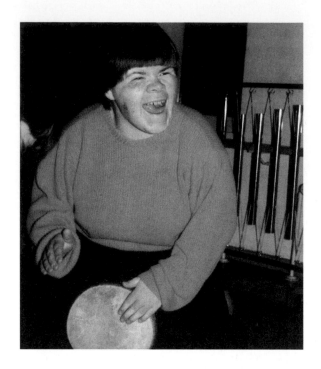

like my sister, I want to play the guitar like my friend, I want to play the drums like the drummer in a rock group – «now I want to do it, too». The parents, who often feel frustrated, too, think they are being realistic in not crediting their child with the capability of learning an instrument.

Our first task is therefore to convince the children that they are indeed able to do this. They need to experience a range of instruments and the sounds they can make for themselves, to understand the principles of each by constructing models and then taking hold of the instrument itself and playing it, so as to realize: «I can do it, too». The choice of an instrument will take the form of a definite preference after this preparatory motivation, and children and young people should then be allowed to learn to play the instrument of their choice. Experience has shown that when a child has found the instrument he wants to learn, following this process of intensive familiarization, he makes good progress and succeeds in overcoming periods of frustration through persistent effort.

This motivation phase is best organized in association with special schools for the disabled, through co-operation between Special Needs teachers and Music School teachers. Through simple music-making together in class or in smaller groups where the focus is on instruments, students discover the desire to play a particular instrument.

mit Behinderten an Musikschulen. Behinderte haben jedoch in der Regel so viel an Frustration erlebt, weil sie Dinge nicht so tun können, wie sie es möchten, daß sie das Selbstbewußtsein verloren haben zu sagen: Klavier spielen wie die Schwester, Gitarre wie der Freund, Schlagzeug wie der Drummer in der Rockgruppe – «das will ich jetzt auch». Die Eltern, ebenfalls oft frustriert, glauben realistisch zu sein und trauen ihrem Kind das Erlernen eines Instruments nicht zu.

Wir müssen daher die Kinder zuerst überzeugen, daß sie es können. Sie müssen eine Reihe von Instrumenten und deren Musiziermöglichkeiten hautnah erleben, im Nachbau der Instrumente das Prinzip erkennen und das originale Instrument in die Hände, an den Körper nehmen und spielen, um dann festzustellen: «Das kann ich auch». Die Instrumentenwahl nach dieser Motivationsphase wird sehr gezielt ausfallen, und das gewünschte Instrument sollten die Kinder und Jugendlichen dann erlernen können. In der Praxis zeigt sich, daß immer dann, wenn das Wunschinstrument nach solch intensivem Vertrautwerden gefunden wurde, die Schüler erfolgreich lernen und mit andauerndem Bemühen auch Durststrecken überwinden.

Diese Motivationsphase erfolgt am besten in Kooperation mit den Sonderschulen für Behinderte, und zwar in Zusammenarbeit von Sonderschullehrer und Musikschullehrer. Über gemeinsames elementares Musizieren im Klassenverband oder in Gruppen, in dessen Mittelpunkt immer Instrumente stehen, wird bei den Schülern der Wunsch, ein bestimmtes Instrument zu spielen, geweckt.

Der anschließende Unterricht, der die Fertigkeiten für das Spiel dieses Instruments entwickeln soll, darf nicht hinter diese erreichte Spielfreude zurückgehen. Das bedeutet, daß nach Möglichkeit in Gruppen unterrichtet wird und daß das Instrument von vornherein in ein gemeinsames Musizieren eingebunden wird. Es ist eine Frage der Musikauswahl und des Arrangements, Musik zu machen, auch wenn die Schüler erst ein oder zwei Töne spielen können. Worauf es ankommt, ist das überzeugte und überzeugende Musizieren. Wenn alles, was klingt, Musik werden kann, ist die Bandbreite unendlich groß: Klangspiele, Vertonungen von Geschichten, Stücke der Klassik und der Moderne, Folklore und Pop.

handicapés dans les écoles de musique. Les handicapés, cependant, ont, en règle générale, connu tant de frustrations parce qu'ils ne peuvent pas faire ce qu'ils veulent comme ils le veulent, qu'ils ont perdu la confiance en eux-mêmes leur permettant de dire: jouer du piano comme ma soeur, de la guitare comme mon ami, de la batterie comme le batteur du groupe de rock – «je veux aussi». Les parents, souvent frustrés eux aussi, pensent être réalistes et ne croient pas que leur enfant soit capable d'apprendre à jouer d'un instrument.

Il nous faut donc convaincre tout d'abord les enfants qu'ils le peuvent. Ils doivent pouvoir faire l'expérience directe d'une série d'instruments et des possibilités d'en jouer, comprendre le principe des instruments en les reproduisant, tenir dans leurs mains, contre eux, l'instrument et en jouer pour pouvoir constater ensuite «je peux moi aussi». Le choix d'un instrument, succédant à cette phase de motivation, sera très ponctuel, et les enfants et adolescents devraient ensuite pouvoir apprendre l'instrument choisi. La pratique a montré que, lorsque l'instrument souhaité a été trouvé après une telle familiarisation intense, les élèves l'apprennent avec succès et surmontent également avec constance des périodes difficiles.

Cette période de motivation devrait se dérouler de préférence en collaboration avec les écoles spécialisées pour handicapés, et par une collaboration entre les enseignants des écoles spécialisées et les enseignants des écoles de musique. L'exercice commun élémentaire de la musique dans la classe ou en groupe, exercice de la musique au centre duquel devra toujours se trouver l'instrument, éveille chez les élèves le désir de jouer d'un instrument précis.

Les cours, qui, ensuite, développent les facultés à jouer de cet instrument, ne doivent pas être en retrait de ce plaisir à jouer. Ceci signifie que les cours devront, dans la mesure du possible, avoir lieu en groupe et que l'instrument doit être inclus dès le départ dans l'exercice commun de la musique. Faire de la musique est une question du choix de la musique et de l'arrangement, même si les élèves ne peuvent jouer qu'une ou deux notes. L'important, c'est un exercice de la musique convaincu et convaincant. Si tout ce qui est son peut devenir musique, la palette des possibilités est infinie: jeux de

«De tous les arts, c'est la musique qui a la plus profonde influence sur l'âme, c'est donc l'art qu'un législateur devrait le plus encourager.»

Napoléon Bonaparte

The teaching programme which follows, with the aim of developing those skills necessary for playing the instrument, must not be allowed to undermine this sense of fun in playing. This means that teaching should be in groups wherever possible and the instrument used to make music with others from the very beginning. The choice of music and the manner of music-making is crucial, even when pupils can still only play one or two notes. What matters is confident and convincing music-making. If everything that produces sound can be used to generate music, the scope is infinitely wide: playing with sounds, setting stories to music, classical and modern pieces, folk and pop music.

Instrumental lessons are given by Music School teachers, for this does not come under the responsibilities of Special Needs teachers, nor, in most cases, are they equipped for it by their training. Music school teachers can attend training courses to prepare them for this kind of teaching. Lessons will take place at the Music School, unless problems of access to the school preclude this, and where there are wheelchair users, the building should be properly equipped to cater for their needs. In this, too, disabled students should feel that they belong and are not being marginalized.

Numerous music groups have been formed in which the disabled and able-bodied make music together – jazz, pop and rock groups, as well as ensembles with a classical repertoire. It is repeatedly demonstrated that the able-bodied do not take the role of «Good Samaritans» here, but must contribute as equal partners. This is a process of integration which cannot be imposed by regulations.

There is also a need for integration when handicapped children are included in pre-school or primary-school music groups. The involvement of parents or a support teacher will be needed in order to cope with special problems and to ensure that all children are treated fairly. Mother and child groups have proved successful, particularly when all the children in the group are disabled.

No mention has yet been made of the large field of music therapy. Here the influence of music is used to achieve other, non-musical goals associated with the treatment of the consequences or the causes of a disability. Work with instruments with

Der Unterricht auf dem Instrument wird von Musikschullehrern erteilt, denn der Sonderschullehrer ist weder von seiner Aufgabe noch in den meisten Fällen von seiner Ausbildung her dazu in der Lage. In berufsbegleitenden Lehrgängen können sich Musikschullehrer auf diesen Unterricht vorbereiten. Der Unterrichtsort wird die Musikschule sein, wenn nicht ungünstige Schulwege dagegen sprechen, und bei Rollstuhlfahrern sollte das Gebäude behindertengerecht ausgestattet sein. Die behinderten Schüler sollen auch hier merken, daß sie dazugehören und nicht ausgegrenzt sind.

Es haben sich zahlreiche Musikgruppen gebildet, in denen Behinderte und Nichtbehinderte gemeinsam musizieren – Jazz-, Pop- und Rockgruppen sowie Ensembles mit klassischem Repertoire. Immer wieder zeigt sich, daß die Nichtbehinderten hier keine «Samariter-Rolle» spielen, sondern sich als gleichberechtigte Partner einbringen müssen. Hier entwickelt sich die Integration, die man nicht verordnen kann.

Integration ist ebenso angesagt, wenn in der musikalischen Früherziehung oder Grundausbildung behinderte Kinder einbezogen werden. Die Mitwirkung von Eltern oder einer weiteren Lehrkraft wird notwendig sein, um besondere Probleme zu regeln und allen Kindern gerecht zu werden. Mutter-Kind-Guppen haben sich bewährt, vor allem, wenn nur behinderte Kinder in der Gruppe sind.

Nicht angesprochen wurde das breite Feld der Musiktherapie. Hier wird die Wirkung der Musik auf den Menschen genutzt, um außermusikalische

sons, mises en musique d'histoires, morceaux classiques et modernes, folklore et pop.

L'apprentissage d'un instrument est assuré par des enseignants de l'école de musique, car les enseignants des écoles spécialisées n'en sont pas capables: ce n'est pas leur tâche et ils ne disposent pas, dans la plupart des cas, de la formation nécessaire. Les enseignants des écoles de musique peuvent se préparer à ce type de cours au sein de cycles de formation continue. Le lieu de cours peut être l'école de musique, si des trajets inopportuns ne s'y opposent pas, et l'établissement devrait être équipé pour les handicapés dans le cas de handicapés en fauteuils roulants. Les élèves handicapés doivent voir qu'ils ne sont pas exclus, mais acceptés.

De nombreux groupes de musique se sont formés dans lesquels handicapés et non handicapés font de la musique ensemble – des groupes de jazz, de pop, et de rock ainsi que des ensembles au répertoire classique. La pratique montre que les non handicapés ne jouent pas le rôle du «bon Samaritain», mais qu'il leur faut s'inclure à titre de partenaires égaux en droit. S'y développe une intégration qu'il n'est point besoin d'ordonner.

L'intégration est donc à l'ordre du jour si des enfants handicapés sont inclus à l'éducation musicale précoce ou à l'éducation musicale élémentaire. La collaboration des parents ou d'un autre enseignant sera nécessaire pour régler des problèmes particuliers et tenir compte de tous les enfants. Les groupes mères-enfants ont fait leurs preuves, surtout si le groupe est constitué exclusivement d'enfants handicapés.

Le vaste domaine de la thérapie musicale resterait à traiter. Ici, on utilise l'effet de la musique sur l'être humain pour parvenir à des buts non musicaux résidant dans le traitement des effets ou des causes d'un handicap. On constate des modifications positives du comportement, une amélioration de la perception, une élimination de paralysies spastiques pendant l'exercice de la musique avec un instrument. Cet effet secondaire est enregistré

the disabled has as well been observed to bring about positive changes in behaviour, improved powers of perception and freedom from spastic reflexes while the instrument is being played. Within the context of work with the disabled at music schools this is noted and exploited as a welcome by-product. However, this is not to be described as music therapy, which calls for other methods, other goals and, above all, therapists with a different kind of training. The Music School teacher who works with the disabled remains a music teacher – one who is specially qualified for this kind of teaching.   *wp.*

Ensemble Playing

Ensemblespiel

Jouer dans un ensemble

What particularly distinguishes European music culture is its polyphonic quality; compositions with just one musical line are the exception in the spectrum of musical styles. This polyphony is a (more or less) elaborate combination of a number of different parts, each of them necessary to the whole. The saying that one could never get an orchestra together if everyone wanted to play the first violin is born of the nature of our music. An orchestral piece – or even a duet – cannot be performed if only one part or another is played. By far the greater part of European music relies on the cooperation of a number of players. The consequence of this is that I can only «perform» on my instrument as part of a whole piece – with the help of others. Admittedly, it is quite possible on keyboard instruments for a single player to fill in all the harmonies without assistance: pianists or organists are perfectly capable of playing in «splendid isolation». But then again, keyboard instruments are a vital feature of many musical combinations – the harpsichord continuo, the grand piano that accompanies instrumental soloists or singers in chamber music, the piano that features so prominently in jazz, and the electronic keyboards of modern light entertainment.

On the other hand players and singers have to be capable of using their instrument or voice in such a

Ziele zu erreichen, die in der Behandlung von Auswirkungen oder Ursachen einer Behinderung liegen. Auch beim Instrumentalspiel mit Behinderten sind positive Verhaltensänderungen, Erweiterungen der Wahrnehmungsfähigkeit, Aufhebung spastischer Lähmungserscheinungen während des Musizierens festzustellen. Im Rahmen der Arbeit mit Behinderten an Musikschulen wird dies als erfreuliche Nebenwirkung registriert und genutzt. Doch sollte hier nicht von Musiktherapie gesprochen werden, denn hierzu sind andere Verfahren, andere Zielsetzungen und vor allem Therapeuten vonnöten. Der Musikschullehrer, der mit Behinderten arbeitet, bleibt ein für diesen Unterricht besonders qualifizierter Musikpädagoge. *wp.*

Was Musik im europäischen Kulturraum besonders auszeichnet, ist ihre Mehrstimmigkeit – einstimmige Stücke sind im Spektrum der Musikstile die Ausnahme. Und es ist ein (mehr oder weniger) kunstvolles Zusammenwirken verschiedener substantieller Stimmen, bei dem auf keine verzichtet werden kann. Die Einsicht, daß man kein Orchester zusammenbekäme, wenn alle die erste Geige spielen wollten, beruht auf diesem Wesen unserer Musik. Ein Orchesterstück – auch nur ein Duett – wird nicht realisiert, wenn man nur die erste oder eine andere einzelne Stimme spielt. Der weitaus größte Teil europäischer Musik wird erst existent im partnerschaftlichen Zusammenspiel. Und in weiterer Konsequenz: Ich kann mit meinem Instrument nur dann «auftreten», wenn ich eine vollständige Musik vortrage – unter Mitwirkung anderer. Freilich sind etwa auf Tasteninstrumenten durchaus komplette mehrstimmige Stücke von nur einem Spieler auszuführen: Pianisten oder Organisten können durchaus in «splendid isolation» für sich bestehen. Andererseits sind Tasteninstrumente als Bestandteil vieler Besetzungen unverzichtbar – im Continuo-Part des Cembalos, im kammermusikalischen Verbund des Flügels mit Instrumentalsolisten oder Sängern, bei der Rolle des Klaviers im Jazz und der Keyboards in der neueren Unterhaltungsmusik.

avec joie et exploité dans le cadre du travail avec des handicapés dans les écoles de musique. Mais on ne saurait parler ici de thérapie musicale, car on nécessite pour cela d'autres procédés, d'autres objectifs et, surtout, des thérapeutes. L'enseignant à l'école de musique qui travaille avec des handicapés reste un pédagogue musical particulièrement qualifié pour ce type de cours. *wp.*

Ce qui caractérise particulièrement la musique dans l'espace culturel européen, c'est sa polyphonie – dans le spectre des styles de musique, les morceaux à une voix sont une exception. Et il s'agit là du concours (plus ou moins) artistique de diverses voix substantielles, c'est-à-dire que l'on ne peut renoncer à aucune d'entre elles. Le fait de comprendre et d'admettre que l'on ne pourrait jamais réunir un orchestre si tous voulaient jouer le premier violon repose sur cette nature de notre musique. Un morceau pour orchestre – et ne serait-ce qu'un duo – n'est pas réalisé si l'on n'en joue que la première voix ou une autre voix isolée. La partie de loin la plus importante de la musique européenne ne devient existante que dans le jeu commun de partenaires. Autre conséquence: je ne peux «me produire» avec mon instrument que si je présente une musique complète – avec la collaboration d'autres personnes. Les instruments à touches, il est vrai, permettent à un interprète isolé d'exécuter des morceaux complets à plusieurs voix: les pianistes ou les organistes peuvent tout à fait exister à part entière pour eux-mêmes en une «splendid isolation». Mais, d'autre part, les instruments à touches sont indispensables en tant que composantes de nombreuses distributions – dans la partition de continuo du clavecin, dans l'association du piano à queue aux instrumentistes solistes ou aux chan-

way that they are able to contribute to the success of a combined performance, not undermining the success of the whole through a lack of skill.

These fundamental insights into the nature of our musical tradition form the basis for the approach adopted by music schools in the broad area of en-

semble training, which should not be considered as being separate from instrumental tuition. Ever since the emergence of the «virtuoso» and the specialist professional musician, music teaching institutions up to and including our modern music schools have dedicated themselves chiefly to the goal of «soloistic» perfection in instrumental playing: even today, an instrument studied at a Music School, Conservatoire or Music College is identified as the «First Study», while participation in music groups, orchestras, chamber music etc. is reckoned to be a «complemental» activity.

For some time now, though, professional attitudes among music school teachers have been undergoing a noticeable change: music schools today aim to offer both kinds of teaching as mutually complementary. Playing in groups and ensembles «complements» instrumental lessons by providing students with motivation, challenges, opportunities for making comparisons, and by helping to develop skills such as rhythmic precision, articulation and phrasing, dynamic differentiation and intonation. Ensemble playing provides the student with opportunities to use the skills learned in instrumental lessons and to share in the experience of creating a musical whole. But should this be seen as a «complemental» subject? Is it not rather the essence of music; is not music-making the goal in learning an instrument in the first place?

From this perspective, instrumental lessons may be seen as a «complement» to ensemble playing: providing the basic skills, working on technique, offering the advantages of individual attention, establishing a solid foundation to be used in making music. Of course, they also enable the pupil to become familiar with the specific repertoire for that

Auf der anderen Seite muß es natürlich Spieler und Sänger geben, die auch in der Lage sind, mit ihrem Instrument bzw. ihrer Stimme so umzugehen, daß sie als Partner des Zusammenspiels sinnvoll zu einem Gelingen des Ganzen beitragen können und dies nicht durch mangelnde Fertigkeiten stören oder gar zerstören.

In diesen grundsätzlichen Einsichten in das Wesen unserer Musik liegen die Ansatzpunkte für die Arbeit der Musikschule auf dem großen Feld der Ensemblefächer, die nicht unabhängig vom Instrumentalunterricht zu sehen sind. Seit dem Aufkommen des «Virtuosen» und des spezialisierten Berufsmusikers hat sich die institutionelle Musikausbildung bis in die heutigen Musikschulen hinein vorwiegend der «solistischen» Perfektion am Instrument verschrieben: Bis heute werden die Instrumentalfächer an Musikschulen, Konservatorien und Musikhochschulen als künstlerische «Haupt»-Fächer bezeichnet, eine Teilnahme an Spielkreisen, Orchestern, Kammermusik usw. gilt dagegen als «Ergänzungsfach».

Im Bewußtsein der Musikpädagogen vollzieht sich jedoch seit einiger Zeit eine entschiedene Wandlung: Musikschulen wollen heute beide Unterrichtsangebote im Sinne einer gegenseitigen Ergänzung vermitteln. Die Mitwirkung in Ensembles und Spielkreisen «ergänzt» den Instrumentalunterricht, indem sie die Schüler motiviert, herausfordert, ihnen Vergleiche ermöglicht und Fähigkeiten wie etwa rhythmische Genauigkeit, Artikulation und Phrasierung, dynamische Differenzierung und Intonation entwickeln hilft. Sie zeigt ihm konkrete Anwendungsmöglichkeiten für die im Instrumentalunterricht erlernten Fertigkeiten und läßt ihn als Mitwirkenden ein musikalisch Ganzes erleben. Doch ist dies eine «Ergänzung»? Ist dies nicht vielmehr «die Musik» an sich, «das Musizieren», also das Ziel, für das man das Instrument überhaupt lernt?

In dieser Perspektive «ergänzt» der Instrumentalunterricht das Ensemblespiel: Er schafft die Voraussetzungen, vermittelt die Techniken, bietet eine individuelle Betreuung, baut systematisch und längerfristig auf, was beim Spiel eingesetzt werden soll. Freilich ermöglicht er auch das Kennenlernen von spezieller Literatur für das jeweilige Instru-

teurs dans la musique de chambre, par le rôle du piano droit dans le jazz ou des claviers électroniques dans la musique légère moderne.

D'autre part, il doit bien entendu y avoir des interprètes et des chanteurs capables de se servir de leur instrument ou de leur voix de telle sorte qu'ils puissent contribuer, par leur participation, à la réussite de l'ensemble et ne dérangent ou ne détruisent pas ce dernier par manque de savoir-faire.

Le travail des écoles de musique dans le vaste domaine des matières touchant à la musique d'ensemble – qui ne peuvent être considérées indépendamment de l'enseignement des instruments – repose sur ces connaissances fondamentales de l'essence de notre musique. Depuis la naissance du «virtuose» et du musicien professionnel spécialisé, la formation musicale institutionnelle s'est vouée principalement, jusqu'aux écoles de musique actuelles, à la perfection de la pratique de l'instrument «en soliste»: aujourd'hui encore, les matières d'enseignement des instruments, dans les écoles de musique, les conservatoires et les écoles supérieures de musique, sont désignées comme étant les matières artistiques «principales», la participation à des cercles de jeu, des orchestres, des ensembles de musique de chambre, etc..., par contre, sont considérées comme des matières «complémentaires».

Cependant, un changement se produit depuis quelques temps dans l'esprit des pédagogues de la musique: les écoles de musique veulent, aujourd'hui, offrir les deux possibilités de cours au sens d'un complément mutuel. La participation à des ensembles et des cercles de jeu «complète» les cours d'apprentissage de l'instrument, car elle motive les élèves, elle constitue un défi, elle leur permet de comparer, et elle les aide à développer certaines aptitudes telles que par exemple l'exactitude rythmique, l'articulation et le phrasé, la différenciation dynamique et l'intonation. Elle leur montre des possibilités d'application concrète du savoirfaire acquis dans les cours d'apprentissage de l'instrument et leur fait vivre un tout musical auquel ils participent. Mais s'agit-il là d'un «complément»? N'est-ce pas plutôt «la musique» en soi, le fait de «faire de la musique», le but, donc, en vue duquel on apprend à jouer d'un instrument?

instrument. But in dealing with music written for more than one player, again this goal can only be reached through rehearsing and playing together with others. One cannot warn too often against the dangers of learning and practising in «isolation». Piano lessons, in particular, should not be allowed to lead to a sort of »solitary confinement» – not least because thousands of people learning to sing or play an instrument need a good piano accompanist for the major part of their repertoire: a «good» pianist here is one who is able and willing to serve as an accompanist. This, however, has to be learned and should be taught at music schools.

Having recognized this, music schools are making increasing efforts to encourage their pupils to play together with others from the outset: group games in nursey education already have this end in mind. Group singing and playing with simple percussion instruments are good ways of filling the «gap» which can be left after first years of music teaching, when children are sometimes still too young to learn an instrument. Children's choirs also serve to teach the basics of making music with others. At the beginner's stage of instrumental tuition, group tuition with two or three pupils then offers valuable opportunities for playing together. Fundamental musical skills such as responding to one another, rhythmic awareness, a feeling for dynamics, listening to oneself and to other players – all this can be begun at this early stage.

Then there is a need for music groups where beginners can be helped to develop these skills: string, wind or brass groups where very simple

ment. Doch wo es sich um Musik für mehr als einen Spieler handelt, ist auch hier das Ziel erst im gemeinsamen Proben und Spielen erreicht. Vor der Gefahr, in einer gewissen «Vereinzelung» zu lernen und zu üben, ist nicht genug zu warnen. Vor allem der Klavierunterricht sollte nicht in «Einzelhaft» ausmünden. Schon deswegen nicht, weil Tausende von Menschen, die ein Melodieinstrument spielen oder singen, bei dem größten Teil ihres Repertoires auf einen guten Klavierpartner angewiesen sind und bleiben – wobei sich ein «guter» Partner durch die Fähigkeit und Bereitschaft zum Zusammenspiel definiert. Das aber muß in der Musikschule gelernt und gelehrt werden.

In dieser Einsicht versuchen die Musikschulen zunehmend, ihre Schüler von Beginn an zum Zusammenspiel anzuleiten: Schon in der musikalischen Früherziehung dienen Gruppenspiele diesem Ziel. In der manchmal schwer zu überbrückenden «Lücke» nach Abschluß der Grundstufe, wenn Kinder für den Instrumentalunterricht manchmal noch zu klein sind, empfehlen sich Sing- und Spielgruppen mit elementaren Instrumenten. Auch Kinderchöre vermitteln elementares Zusammen-Musizieren. Im Anfängerstadium des Instrumentalunterrichts bietet dann die Form des Gruppenunterrichts mit zwei oder drei Schülern wichtige Chancen des Zusammenspiels. Grundlegende «musikalische» Verhaltensweisen wie aufeinander reagieren, rhythmische Orientierung, Lautstärkeempfinden, die Mitspieler und sich selber hören – das alles kann hier schon begonnen werden.

Andererseits sollten auch Spielkreise vorhanden sein, die auf leichtestem Niveau diese Fähigkeiten entwicklen helfen: Streicher-, Holz- oder Blechbläsergruppen, wo in homogener Klangbesetzung einfach strukturierte Stücke zu einem schnellen Erfolgserlebnis verhelfen. Mit zunehmendem Alter und Können der Schüler kann im Ensemble auf eine regelrechte Probenarbeit übergegangen werden, die eine längerfristige Erarbeitung auch anspruchsvollerer Stücke zum Ziel hat. Um jeden Schüler wirklich optimal fördern zu können, ist eine Verständigung zwischen Instrumentallehrer und Ensembleleiter notwendig. Dem Schüler muß der Vorteil der gegenseitigen Ergänzung von Instrumentalunterricht und Ensemblespiel einsichtig werden.

Dans cette perspective, c'est le cours d'apprentissage de l'instrument qui «complète» la pratique musicale au sein d'un ensemble: il crée les conditions nécessaires, transmet les techniques, offre un encadrement individuel, construit de manière systématique et à long terme ce qui devra être mis en pratique dans l'exécution. Il permet également, bien entendu, de faire connaissance avec la littérature spécialisée de l'instrument respectif. Mais, dans la mesure où il s'agit d'une musique pour plus d'un interprète, le but sera également, ici, l'exercice et l'interprétation en commun. On ne saurait mettre suffisamment en garde contre le danger d'apprendre et de s'exercer dans un certain «isolement». Le cours de piano, en particulier ne devrait pas dépérir en «cellule d'isolation», ne serait-ce que parce que des milliers de gens qui jouent d'un instrument mélodique ou chantent sont et restent, pour une grande part de leur répertoire, dépendants d'un bon partenaire au piano – le «bon» partenaire se caractérisant par le fait qu'il est capable de jouer avec quelqu'un d'autre et qu'il est prêt à le faire. Mais ceci devra être appris et enseigné à l'école de musique.

A cet égard, les écoles de musique tentent de plus en plus à apprendre à leurs élèves, dès le départ, à jouer avec d'autres: dans l'éducation musicale précoce, déjà, des jeux en groupe poursuivent cet objectif. Dans «le vide», parfois difficile à franchir, qui fait suite à la fin du niveau primaire, lorsque les enfants sont quelquefois trop petits encore pour apprendre un instrument, on peut recommander des groupes de chant et de jeu avec des instruments élémentaires. Les chœurs d'enfants, eux aussi, introduisent aux rudiments de la musique pratiquée en commun. Au stade de départ de l'apprentissage d'un instrument, la forme de l'enseignement de groupe avec deux ou trois élèves offre des possibilités d'exercice commun importantes. Il est possible de commencer ici à assimiler des comportements «musicaux» de base tels que la réaction à autrui, l'orientation rythmique, le sentiment du volume, d'apprendre à s'écouter soi-même et à écouter les autres.

D'autre part devraient également exister des cercles de jeu aidant à développer ces capacités à un niveau extrêmement simple: des groupes de cordes, de bois, ou de cuivres, dans lesquels des mor-

«The aim is, that every smith shall be able to speak one foreign language and play a music instrument.»

Georg Poulsen
(former head of the federation of metalworkers in Denmark)

pieces for groups of similar instruments lead to rapid success as a reward for their efforts. Older and more able pupils can move on to proper rehearsal work in an ensemble, taking more time to work on more demanding pieces. In order to give every pupil the best possible support and encouragement, there needs to be communication between instrumental teachers and the directors of these ensembles. Each pupil needs to understand the advantages of combining instrumental lessons with playing in an ensemble.

There is no room here to give a list of every imaginable type and combination of instrumental or vocal ensemble. Alongside «classical» ensembles, music schools will provide opportunities for groups playing music of other styles, in order to meet the needs and requirements not only of their students, but also of teaching staff with their «special preferences»: Early Music, traditional and folk music, jazz, percussion groups, wind bands, light entertainment bands, Big Bands and rock groups, other groups working with electronic instruments and musical computers – perhaps improvization groups, too. Music schools are now beginning to reach even outside their own territory and establish links with musical theatre. The idea of «playing together» includes bringing music together with words, movement, dance, pantomime and ballet.

«Making music together: bringing people out of isolation» – this, the motto of a music schools' congress, provides the theme for a conclusion. It addresses the great importance of music as a social force – something which should certainly not be played down, but recognized as part of the essence of our musical tradition: bringing people together for a successful performance and drawing others in to join them as an audience of listeners. Admittedly, only the musicians are able to experience those forces in music, that require the commitment of every player for the production and the quality of the whole; responding to one another, «helping each other out», playing down in an accompanying role, playing out in solo passages as a «representative» of the rest, blending in with other parts of equal importance, being carried along by other players, carrying others oneself – the whole person, body, mind and spirit, totally involved in a process of giving and receiving.

Es können hier nicht sämtliche denkbaren Formen und Zusammensetzungen von instrumentalen/vokalen Ensembles aufgelistet werden. Neben den «klassischen» Besetzungen wird die Musikschule auch Spielgruppen anderer Musikstile in ihr Angebot aufnehmen, um den Bedürfnissen und Interessen ihrer Teilnehmer, aber auch ihrer Lehrkräfte und deren «Spezialgebieten» entgegenzukommen: Alte Musik, Volksmusik, Folklore, Jazz, Percussionsgruppen, Blasorchester, Unterhaltungsorchester, Big Band, aber auch Rockgruppen oder Arbeitsgruppen mit elektronischen Instrumenten und Musikcomputern, vielleicht auch Gruppenimprovisation. Schließlich beginnen Musikschulen auch, über ihr eigentliches Gebiet hinaus Brücken zu schlagen zu Formen des Musiktheaters. Der Begriff «Zusammenspiel» bezieht die Koordinierung von Musik und Wort, Bewegung, Tanz, Pantomime, Ballett mit ein.

«Gemeinsam Musizieren. Wege aus der Vereinzelung» – dieses Motto eines Musikschul-Kongresses soll als Schlußgedanke aufgegriffen werden. Es spricht die soziale, die gesellschaftsbildende Kraft der Musik an, die aber durchaus keine nachgeordnete «Funktion» ist. Vielmehr entspricht es dem anfangs genannten Wesen unserer Musik, daß sie zu ihrer Ausführung und zu ihrem Gelingen musizierende Menschen versammelt und weitere Menschen als zuhörendes Publikum vereinigt. Nur den Musizierenden freilich erlebbar sind jene Kräfte der Musik, die an die gemeinsame Verantwortung der Beteiligten für das Zustandekommen und die Qualität des Ganzen appellieren: Aufeinander eingehen, sich «einhelfen», sich begleitend zurücknehmen, solistisch als «Stellvertreter» des Ganzen hervortreten, im gleichberechtigten Stimmenverband integriert sein, von andern getragen werden, selbst mittragen – mit Körper, Seele und Geist als ganzer Mensch in Geben und Nehmen begriffen.

Das Ausbilden von Menschen zur aktiven musikalischen Betätigung beinhaltet unverzichtbar ihre Zusammenführung zum gemeinsamen Musizieren. Und das heißt auch: über das «Zusammenproben» eines Programms hinaus jene ganzheitlichen Kräfte der Musik, jene soziale Komponente pädagogisch zu vermitteln – nicht als Theorie, sondern auf dem Wege der Anleitung zum gemeinsamen Musikmachen. Musikschulen haben die Ver-

ceaux de structure simple, dans une distribution sonore homogène, conduisent à un sentiment de succès rapide. En grandissant et au fur et à mesure des connaissances des élèves, l'ensemble pourra passer à un travail d'exercice au sens propre du terme, travail ayant pour but l'assimilation, à long terme, de morceaux plus complexes. Afin d'encourager chaque élève de manière vraiment optimale, il est nécessaire que le professeur responsable de l'apprentissage de l'instrument et le directeur de l'ensemble se concertent. L'élève doit prendre conscience de l'avantage d'une complémentarité mutuelle entre l'apprentissage de l'instrument et le fait de jouer dans un ensemble.

Il n'est pas possible d'évoquer ici toutes les formes et compositions imaginables d'ensembles instrumentaux et vocaux. Outre les distributions «classiques», l'école de musique proposera également des groupes de styles musicaux différents afin de répondre aux besoins et aux intérêts des participants et des enseignants et aux spécialités de ces derniers: musique ancienne, musique populaire, folklore, jazz, groupes de percussions, orchestres à vent, orchestres de musique légère, big band, mais aussi groupes de rock ou groupes de travail avec des instruments électroniques et des ordinateurs, peut-être aussi groupes d'improvisation. Enfin, les écoles de musique commencent aussi à dépasser leur domaine propre pour rejoindre des formes du théâtre musical. Le concept de «jouer ensemble» implique la coordination de la musique et de la parole, du mouvement, de la danse, de la pantomime et de la danse classique.

«Faire de la musique ensemble. Pour sortir de l'isolement»: Nous reprendrons ici pour finir ce slogan d'un congrès des écoles de musique. Il se réfère à la force sociale et constitutive de la musique, qui ne saurait être une «fonction» secondaire. Bien plus, le fait de rassembler des musiciens qui l'interprètent et assurent son succès et d'unir d'autres gens en un public d'auditeurs correspond à l'essence, mentionnée au début, de notre musique. Seuls les musiciens, bien entendu, peuvent faire l'expérience de ces forces de la musique qui font appel à la responsabilité commune des participants pour la réalisation et la qualité de l'ensemble: chercher à se comprendre l'un l'autre, s'aider à «rentrer», se tenir en retrait, à l'accompagnement, se

Educating people to engage in musical activity must necessarily include bringing them together to make music. This also means not merely «rehearsing» a programme, but conveying the integral power of music, including the social aspect, through teaching – not presenting it as theory, but demonstrating it through the whole approach to making music with others. Music schools have a responsibility, which they recognize, to train their pupils to play in instrumental ensembles so that they are in a position to get together with other people to make music on their own initiative: to make music within the family, to join chamber music groups, bands and orchestras, in churches and local societies. In the world of today, «bringing people out of isolation» is an especially important task for music schools in creating a humane society in Europe.   *uw.*

Choirs, Vocal Training and Solo Singing

Chor, Stimmbildung und Gesang

Le choeur, l'éducation de la voix, le chant

Any music teacher devoted to his work would like his pupils' world to revolve around his subject before all else. As a singing teacher, I am no different in this. I even go so far as to dream that each person's whole life might mean a continual encounter and lasting practical involvement with singing. This would – I am sure of it – be to the benefit of my instrumental teacher colleagues, too.

The ideal musical career really begins even before birth. The unborn child not only hears every song its mother sings, but shares in the experience as it feels her breathing. The effect of singing on a small child's sensibilities and emotions I know from my mother's accounts of how she used to sing her favourite arias to me: she assures me that I responded to mournful arias with tears. – But times

antwortung und nehmen sie wahr, ihre Schüler durch Ausbildung im instrumentalen Zusammenspiel in die Lage zu versetzen, sich aus eigener Initiative mit anderen musizierenden Menschen zusammenzutun: zum Musizieren in der Familie, zu Hausmusikvereinigungen, zu Gruppen und Orchestern in Kirchen und Vereinen. «Wege aus der Vereinzelung» zu weisen ist besonders in der heutigen Zeit eine wichtige Verantwortung der Musikschulen für eine humane Lebenswelt in Europa.   *uw.*

distinguer en soliste, «représentant» l'ensemble, être intégré à l'association des voix, sur le même plan, être porté par les autres, porter les autres – tout homme avec le corps, l'âme et l'esprit, prenant et donnant à la fois.

La formation à une activité musicale active comprend, c'est indispensable, leur réunion dans le but d'une pratique commune de la musique. Ceci signifie aussi: transmettre par la pédagogie, au-delà de «l'exercice commun» sur un programme, ces forces d'ensemble de la musique, ces composantes sociales, non point à titre de théorie, mais sur la voie d'une introduction à la pratique commune de la musique. Les écoles de musique ont la responsabilité, et elle l'assument, de rendre leurs élèves capables, par la formation à une pratique commune de la musique, de se rassembler de leur propre initiative avec d'autres musiciens: pour faire de la musique en famille, dans des associations musicales privées, en groupes et en orchestres dans des églises et des sociétés. Montrer des voies «pour sortir de l'isolement», c'est là une responsabilité importante des écoles de musique, aujourd'hui surtout, pour un monde humain en Europe.   *uw.*

Jeder Musikpädagoge, der seiner Aufgabe mit Leib und Seele nachgeht, wünscht sich, daß sich die Welt seiner Schüler vor allem um sein Fachgebiet dreht. Und bei mir als Gesanglehrer ist dies auch nicht anders. Ich gehe sogar so weit, davon zu träumen, daß der ganze Lebensweg jedes Menschen eine ständige Begegnung und ein dauernder praktischer Umgang mit dem Singen sei. Davon würden – dessen bin ich sicher – auch meine Instrumentalkollegen nebenan profitieren.

Der ideale musikalische Lebensweg beginnt eigentlich schon vor der Geburt. Das ungeborene Baby hört nicht nur jedes Lied, das die Mutter singt, sondern erlebt es, ihren Atem fühlend, mit. Wie sensibilisierend und emotionalisierend das Singen schon auf ein Kleinkind wirkt, weiß ich aus

Tout pédagogue de la musique prenant son travail à coeur souhaite que l'univers de ses élèves tourne surtout autour de sa matière. Et il en va de même pour moi, en ma qualité de professeur de chant. Je vais même jusqu'à rêver que toute la vie de chaque individu serait une rencontre constante avec le chant, une pratique durable. Mes collègues d'à côté, les instrumentistes, en profiteraient aussi, j'en suis certain.

La carrière musicale idéale commence en fait dès avant la naissance. Le bébé, dans le ventre de sa mère, n'entend pas seulement chaque chanson qu'elle chante, il les vit aussi, en sentant son souffle. Je sais de ma mère à quel point le chant éveille à la sensibilité et aux émotions pour un petit enfant: elle me chantait toujours ses airs préférés;

have changed, and young mothers to-day have no such experiences. They belong to a generation that has grown up consuming music passively; their mothers had already listened to the latest hits on the radio, and they themselves now see and hear the latest video clips on television.

And yet it is so important for parents to begin singing with their children at an early age; there are three clear reasons that can be given to show the value of singing with children. First of all, singing is the most basic form of music-making and thus the most natural way of expressing feelings through music. But as people grow older, they become less ready to express themselves in this way and to allow their emotions to be touched by song. What opportunities these people miss!

Secondly, singing is the first and best way of training the ear, for listening is of primary importance in singing: after all, a note can only be sung when it has been heard within and when the pitch of the note is monitored and adjusted as it is sung, by listening. Thus complex neuro-muscular processes are stimulated, trained and refined by singing. One cannot begin to do this early enough.

Thirdly, this ability to co-ordinate complex physiological processes in singing diminishes in the course of time – indeed, relatively early on, even in children. In our work in music schools we frequently encounter children who have never heard singing at home and who have hardly sung at all, even at Kindergarten – or if they have, then in the wrong way. «Wrong», in this context, means that songs have been sung in keys too low for the child's voice. This can damage the voice, and these children are often not capable of picking up even one note, or else they can only sing notes that lie below the proper physiological range of a child's voice. When they come to sing at music school – in nursery groups and primary classes, in singing lessons and children's choirs – these children actually have to be «brought back» from the lower register to have their range adjusted upwards.

Erzählungen meiner Mutter, die mir immer ihre Lieblingsarien vorsang: Auf traurige Arien soll ich zuverlässig mit Tränen reagiert haben. – Die Zeiten haben sich geändert. Den jungen Müttern heute fehlen solche Erfahrungen. Sie gehören schon zu einer Generation, die in den Zeiten des passiven Musikkonsums groß geworden ist. Schon ihre Mütter hörten die neuesten Schlager im Radio, und sie selber sehen und hören sich die neuesten Video-Clips im Fernsehen an.

Dabei wäre es so wichtig, daß Eltern schon früh beginnen, mit ihren Kindern zu singen. Drei Gründe machen den Wert des Singens mit Kindern leicht einsehbar. Zuallererst ist das Singen die ursprünglichste Form des Musizierens und damit auch der natürlichste Weg, Gefühle musikalisch auszudrücken. Aber mit zunehmendem Alter läßt die Bereitschaft nach, sich singend auszudrücken und auch sich emotional durch Gesang ansprechen zu lassen. Welche Möglichkeiten fehlen solchen Menschen!

Zum zweiten ist das Singen die erste und beste Schule des Gehörs, denn vor und beim Singen ist das Hören die Hauptsache: Ein Ton kann schließlich nur gesungen werden, wenn er vorher innerlich gehört wurde und wenn während des Singens immer wieder eine Kontrolle und Korrektur der Tonhöhe durch das Gehör stattfindet. So werden komplizierte neuromuskuläre Vorgänge durch das Singen gefordert, geschult und verfeinert. Man kann nicht früh genug damit anfangen.

Drittens verkümmert im Laufe der Zeit – und zwar relativ früh auch schon bei Kindern – diese Fähigkeit zur Koordination der komplexen physiologischen Vorgänge beim Singen. In der Musikschulpraxis begegnen uns häufig Kinder, in deren Elternhaus nicht gesungen wurde, die selbst im Kindergarten kaum gesungen haben – und wenn, dann falsch. In diesem Zusammenhang heißt «falsch», daß Lieder in Tonarten gesungen werden, die für die Kinderstimme zu tief liegen. Das führt zu Stimmschäden, und die Kinder sind oft nicht fähig, auch nur einen Ton richtig nachzusingen. Oder sie können nur Tonfolgen singen, die unterhalb des physiologisch richtigen Tonumfangs der Kinderstimme liegen. Beim Singen in der Musikschule – in der Früherziehung und Grundausbil-

j'aurais réagi invariablement par des larmes, dit-elle, aux airs tristes. – Les temps ont changé. Il manque cette expérience aux jeunes mères d'aujourd'hui. Elles font déjà partie d'une génération qui a grandi à l'époque de la consommation passive de musique. Leurs mères, déjà, écoutaient les derniers hits à la radio, et elles-mêmes regardent les derniers clips à la télévision.

Et pourtant, il serait important que les parents commencent, très tôt déjà, à chanter avec leurs enfants. Le fait de chanter avec les enfants est d'une grande valeur pour trois raisons qu'il sera aisé de comprendre. Le chant est, en tout premier lieu, la forme d'exercice de la musique la plus originelle, et donc la manière d'exprimer ses sentiments la plus naturelle qui soit. Mais, avec l'âge, on est de moins en moins prêt à s'exprimer par le chant et à se laisser toucher émotionnellement par le chant. Quelles possibilités manquent à ces gens-là!

En second lieu, le chant est la première et la meilleure école de l'ouïe, car avant le chant et au cours du chant, le principal est l'écoute: un ton ne peut être chanté que s'il a été, auparavant, écouté intérieurement, et si, pendant le chant, il se produit un contrôle et une correction continus de la hauteur du ton par l'ouïe. Le chant permet ainsi de développer, de former et d'affiner des processus neuromusculaires complexes. Il n'est jamais trop tôt pour commencer.

Troisièmement, la capacité de coordination des processus physiologiques complexes qui se produisent au cours du chant diminue avec le temps – et ce relativement tôt, chez l'enfant déjà. Dans la pratique quotidienne, à l'école de musique, nous rencontrons souvent des enfants dont les parents n'ont pas chanté, qui n'ont pour ainsi dire pas chanté, même au jardin d'enfants, ou, si oui, ont chanté faux. On entend par faux, dans ce contexte, le fait que les chansons sont chantées dans des tonalités trop basses pour la voix des enfants. Ceci conduit à des lésions de la voix, et les enfants, souvent, ne sont pas capables de répéter un seul ton juste. Ou alors, ils ne peuvent que chanter des suites de tons situées au-dessous du registre physiologiquement correct de la voix enfantine. Lors des cours de chant à l'école de musique – dans l'éducation précoce et la formation élémentaire, les cours de chant

The general decline of singing in society is reflected in the approach of many music teachers. I recall a conversation with a young lady colleague who, in answer to my question: «What do you sing with the children in the nursery classes?», answered readily: «I don't sing with the children, because I myself don't have a singing voice». Once I had explained to her that one does not need to be an opera singer in order to be able to sing with children, she started taking chances. Today she is a subject specialist in Musical Education for the Early Years, and one of the first conferences she organized was entitled: Singing in the Early Years.

A conversion of this sort is still necessary in many cases, I am sure, but singing is on the whole becoming more popular. There are regions in Europe where there is no need for a «renaissance of singing», where all music teaching is done through singing, and where voice training and speech training accompany this to ensure that voices develop correctly.

It is a particularly good idea to establish singing classes or children's choirs at music schools, so that children can move on to these from their nursery groups or primary music classes, just as they begin instrumental lessons. From the singing teacher's point of view, this keeps the voice in training and maintains the habit of singing. Instrumental teachers also reap the benefits of this, however. In singing groups like these, children discover the joy of making music with others while they are still not sufficiently advanced with their instrumental skills to be able to play in an ensemble. Singing trains the ear and therefore helps with learning to play an instrument. How thankful a piano teacher feels, for instance, if he does not have to explain to a pupil what is meant by a phrase and how to breathe between phrases, because the child has already learned this through singing in a choir.

Let all my instrumental teacher colleagues therefore be encouraged to think of including singing in their instrumental teaching – and simply to sing more often with their pupils. Telemann was quite right when he said: «Singing is the foundation for music in every respect.» He also had in mind: for music on every instrument.

While instrumental teaching has always figured on the curriculum of music schools, the subject

dung, in Singklassen und Kinderchören – müssen solche Kinder regelrecht aus der tiefen Lage «abgeholt» werden, um ihren Tonumfang wieder nach oben hin zu korrigieren.

Der allgemeine Rückgang des Singens in der Gesellschaft spiegelt sich auch im Bewußtsein vieler Musikpädagogen. Ich erinnere mich an ein Gespräch mit einer jungen Kollegin. Auf meine Frage: «Was singst Du denn mit den Kindern in der musikalischen Früherziehung?», antwortete sie frank und frei: «Ich singe nicht mit den Kindern, weil ich selbst keine Stimme habe». Als ich ihr klargemacht hatte, daß man selbst keine Opernsängerin sein muß, um mit Kindern zu singen, hat sie Mut gefaßt. Heute ist sie Fachleiterin für den Früherziehungsbereich, und eine der ersten Konferenzen, die sie einberief, hatte das Thema: Singen in der musikalischen Früherziehung.

Ein solcher Gesinnungswandel ist sicher noch in vielen Fällen notwendig, aber das Singen ist wohl insgesamt im Aufwind. Und es gibt Regionen in Europa, wo eine «Renaissance des Singens» gar nicht erforderlich ist. Die gesamte Vermittlung der allgemeinen Musiklehre geschieht dort über das Singen. Außerdem wird ganz nebenbei Stimmbildung und Sprecherziehung betrieben, wird darauf geachtet, daß die Stimmen richtig geführt sind.

Besonders sinnvoll ist die Einrichtung von Singklassen oder Kinderchören an Musikschulen, die die Kinder im Anschluß an die musikalische Früherziehung oder Grundausbildung parallel zu ihrem ersten Instrumentalunterricht besuchen sollten. Vom gesangpädagogischen Standpunkt aus bleibt so die Stimme im Training und der Kontakt mit dem Singen erhalten. Aber vor allem profitieren auch die Instrumentallehrer. In solchen Singgemeinschaften erfahren die Kinder schon dann die Freude am gemeinschaftlichen Musizieren, wenn sie mit ihren instrumentalen Fertigkeiten noch nicht so weit sind, um in einem Ensemble mitspielen zu können. Singen schult das Gehör und erleichtert so den Instrumentalunterricht. Und wie dankbar ist beispielsweise ein Klavierlehrer, wenn er seinem Schüler nicht nur theoretisch erklären muß, was eine Phrase ist und wie sie atmet, weil das Kind dies schon im Chorsingen erfahren hat.

et les chorales d'enfants – il faut littéralement «récupérer» ces enfants pour les faire sortir de ce niveau bas afin de corriger vers le haut leur registre.

La régression générale du chant dans la société se reflète également dans la conscience de nombreux pédagogues de la musique. Je me souviens d'une conversation avec une jeune collègue. A ma question: «Qu'est-ce que tu chantes avec les enfants dans les cours d'éducation précoce?», elle me répondit carrément: «Je ne chante pas avec les enfants, parce que je n'ai pas de voix». Après que je lui eu fait comprendre qu'il n'était pas nécessaire d'être une chanteuse d'opéra pour chanter avec des enfants, elle prit courage. Aujourd'hui, elle est chef de section de l'éducation précoce, et la première réunion qu'elle organisa avait pour thème: le chant dans l'éducation précoce.

Un tel volte-face est certainement nécessaire dans de nombreux cas, mais le chant, dans l'ensemble, semble être en progression. Et il y a des régions d'Europe où il n'est point besoin d'une «renaissance du chant». L'ensemble de l'enseignement de la théorie musicale générale s'y effectue par l'intermédiaire du chant. De plus, on y pratique, en passant, l'éducation de la voix et des organes de la phonation, on y veille à une bonne conduite des voix.

L'instauration, dans les écoles de musique, de classes de chant ou de chœurs d'enfants, que les enfants devraient fréquenter parallèlement à leurs premiers cours d'apprentissage d'un instrument, à la suite de l'éducation musicale précoce ou de la formation élémentaire, est particulièrement judicieuse. Du point de vue de la pédagogie du chant, la voix continue ainsi d'être exercée et le contact avec le chant se maintient. Mais, surtout, les professeurs enseignant un instrument en profitent. Dans des communautés de chant de ce type, les enfants font une première expérience des joies de la pratique commune de la musique si leur savoir-faire instrumental n'est pas encore suffisant pour leur permettre de jouer dans un ensemble. Le chant éduque l'oreille et facilite ainsi l'apprentissage d'un instrument. Et le professeur de piano qui, par exemple, n'aura pas besoin d'expliquer dans la théorie à son élève ce que c'est qu'une phrase et comment elle respire parce que l'enfant l'a déjà appris en chantant dans une chorale, en sera fort reconnaissant.

«Ich war froh, daß ich mal in der Knabenmusik Luzern mit Piccolo und Flöte mitspielen durfte. Somit weiß ich, was es heißt, ein Zusammenspiel zu erleben. Ich hatte oft Hühnerhaut dabei. Ich möchte dieses Erlebnis allen jungen Menschen gönnen. Wer Musik spielt, kennt keine Drogen, denn Musik allein kann beflügeln.»

Emil Steinberger

«solo singing» is among the options more recently made available, though one which is in constantly increasing demand. In the routine task of advising those interested in taking singing lessons, the question of motivation is always of primary importance: why does this person want to have singing lessons? Someone who only wants to sing for his own pleasure at home does not necessarily need to have his voice fully trained; singing as an amateur musician in a choir does not call for training as a soloist. But anyone who comes up against vocal problems when singing in a choir – difficulty with breath control, for instance – may find that singing lessons help to solve the problem and enrich his experience.

Then one has to sort out what students hope to gain from singing lessons. Many people do not realize that basic training has to precede specialization. There is the singer from a rock band, for example, who finds his voice continually becoming hoarse and now comes looking for help; or the 28 year old office worker filled with enthusiasm for musicals and determined to give up her job and become a musical star. It has to be made clear to both of them that there is no specific vocal technique for rock singing or musicals, but that the voice is an instrument, a combination of body, mind and spirit working together according to certain natural laws. Discovering and developing the balance of these vital elements, a balance unique in each individual, forms the basis of what is generally known as classical voice training. There is no way round this, even if one later wishes «only» to sing rock or musicals.

A few other points need to be mentioned in this context: if singing lessons are to be successful, one should learn to read music; one also needs a keyboard instrument at home for practice (an electronic keyboard will do). One of the most important prerequisites for satisfactory progress often comes as a surprise to would-be students: in order to be able to sing oneself, one needs a precise idea of what «singing» sounds like. Basically, a person learns to sing through imitation: without an idea of the sounds that can be produced by the human voice, nobody will succeed in discovering the full range of his or her own vocal potential. Therefore the student must not only work on his own voice,

Darum seien alle Instrumental-Kollegen ermutigt, sich Gedanken über eine Einbeziehung des Singens in den Instrumentalunterricht zu machen und mit ihren Schülern einfach mehr zu singen. Wie recht hatte doch Telemann, wenn er sagte: «Das Singen ist das Fundament zur Musik in allen Dingen.» Und damit meinte er auch: zur Musik auf allen Instrumenten.

Während der Instrumentalunterricht von jeher den Fächerkanon der Musikschulen prägte, gehört das Fach «Sologesang» zu den jüngeren Unterrichtsangeboten, erfreut sich aber einer stetig wachsenden Nachfrage. In der täglichen Praxis der Beratung von Interessenten für den Gesangunterricht steht zunächst immer die Frage der Motivation im Vordergrund: Warum will jemand überhaupt Gesangunterricht nehmen? Wer nur für sich zu Hause singen möchte, braucht nicht unbedingt eine regelrechte Ausbildung seiner Stimme; auch um als Musikliebhaber in einem Chor zu singen, ist zusätzlicher Sologesangunterricht nicht notwendig. Wer aber beim Chorsingen an stimmliche Grenzen stößt, etwa Schwierigkeiten mit dem Atemverbrauch hat, für den kann der Gesangunterricht eine große Erleichterung und Bereicherung sein.

Dann sind die Erwartungen zu klären, die der Schüler an den Gesangunterricht hat. Vielen ist überhaupt nicht klar, daß vor der Kür die Pflicht kommt. Zum Beispiel kommt der Sänger einer Rockband, der immer heiser wird und nun Rat und Hilfe sucht; oder es kommt die musicalbegeisterte 28jährige Büroangestellte, die fest entschlossen ist, ihren Beruf an den Nagel zu hängen und Musical-Star zu werden. Beiden muß zunächst deutlich gemacht werden, daß es keine spezielle Rock- oder Musical-Gesangtechnik gibt, sondern daß die Stimme als Instrument eine Einheit von Körper, Seele und Geist ist, die nach bestimmten Naturgesetzen zusammenwirken. Die bei jedem Menschen unterschiedliche Balance dieser Naturgesetze auszuloten und zu trainieren – das ist es, was man im allgemeinen als klassischen Gesangunterricht bezeichnet. Und darum kommt man nicht herum, auch wenn man später «nur» Rock oder Musical singen will.

Auch andere Zusammenhänge sind zu klären: So sind für einen erfolgreichen Gesangunterricht No-

C'est pourquoi il faudrait encourager tous les collègues enseignant un instrument à réfléchir sur l'inclusion du chant dans l'enseignement instrumental et à chanter plus souvent avec leurs élèves. Telemann avait ô combien raison de dire: «Le chant est la base de la musique en toutes choses». Il voulait également dire par là: de la musique sur tous les instruments.

Tandis que l'enseignement d'un instrument a, de tout temps, empreint le canon des matières des écoles de musique, le «chant en solo» fait partie des matières proposées plus récemment, mais il est de plus en plus demandé. Dans la pratique des conseils quotidiens donnés aux personnes intéressées par des cours de chant, la question de la motivation se place toujours au premier plan: pourquoi quelqu'un veut-il prendre des cours de chant? Qui ne veut que chanter pour lui, à la maison, n'a pas forcément besoin d'une formation vocale dans les règles de l'art; même pour l'amateur de musique qui veut chanter dans une chorale, il n'est pas nécessaire de prendre des cours de chant en solo supplémentaires. Mais pour qui chante dans une chorale et arrive aux limites de sa capacité vocale ou a des problèmes de souffle, le cours de chant peut être un grand soulagement et un enrichissement.

Il faut déterminer ensuite ce que l'élève attend du cours de chant. Beaucoup n'ont pas du tout conscience du fait que le programme obligatoire précède le programme libre. C'est par exemple le cas du chanteur d'un groupe de rock, qui est toujours enroué et cherche conseil et secours; ou l'employée de bureau de 28 ans, fan de musical, bien décidée à laisser tomber son travail pour devenir une star de musical. Il faut, dans un premier temps, faire comprendre à tous deux qu'il n'existe pas de technique de chant particulière pour le rock et le musical, mais que la voix, en tant qu'instrument, est une unité du corps, de l'âme et de l'esprit, qui se conjuguent selon des lois naturelles précises. Sonder et exercer cet équilibre, différent chez chaque individu, c'est là ce que l'on appelle, en général, le cours de chant classique. Et l'on ne peut y échapper, même si l'on ne veut, plus tard, «que» chanter du rock ou du musical.

Il faut également déterminer d'autres éléments cadres: ainsi, il est nécessaire, pour prendre des

but study other voices and a variety of musical styles. The rock singer or musical singer who refuses to listen to an opera for once, or to sing just one Schubert song for himself, is holding himself back from unlocking the potential of his own voice.

Following the preliminary interview, then, the office worker who loves musicals is ready for anything: she not only gets a piano, she even takes piano lessons, goes to a theory course once a week, is now starting to go to the opera more frequently and has – with her singing teacher's approval – joined a good choir. She even practises and is making good progress with her voice. But there is a problem: at the age of 28, the young lady should no longer be thinking of a career as a stage performer. This example shows, however, what we have to deal with in music schools: people who are seeking to enrich their lives through music, through singing. It can be very difficult for singing teachers at music schools to help people who may have set their sights too high to get their feet back on the ground and yet still find enrichment through singing. If they succeed, though, it is the most rewarding job I can imagine.   *rt.*

tenkenntnisse erforderlich; auch ein Tasteninstrument benötigt man zu Hause für das Üben (es darf auch ein Keyboard sein). Eine der wichtigsten Voraussetzungen für ein zufriedenstellendes Vorwärtskommen löst immer wieder Überraschung bei den Interessenten aus: Um selber singen zu können, ist es nämlich unerläßlich, daß man eine genaue innere Vorstellung davon hat, wie «Singen» klingt. Grundsätzlich lernt der Mensch auch das Singen durch Imitieren: Ohne eine Vorstellung davon, welche klanglichen Möglichkeiten die menschliche Stimme überhaupt haben kann, gelingt es niemandem, seine eigenen stimmlichen Fähigkeiten ganz zu entdecken. Darum muß der Schüler sich zusätzlich zu seiner eigenen Stimme mit anderen Stimmen und mit verschiedenen Musikstilen beschäftigen. Der Rocksänger oder die Musicalsängerin, die sich weigern, auch einmal eine Oper anzuhören oder selbst einmal ein Schubertlied zu singen, behindern sich selbst im Erschließen ihrer eigenen Stimme.

Nach dem Beratungsgespräch ist also die musicalbegeisterte Büroangestellte zu alldem bereit: Sie schafft nicht nur ein Klavier an, sondern nimmt auch Klavierunterricht, besucht einmal wöchentlich einen Theoriekurs, neuerdings auch immer öfter die Oper und wirkt – mit Genehmigung ihrer Gesanglehrerin – in einem guten Chor mit. Sie übt sogar und macht stimmlich entsprechend gute Fortschritte. Aber es gibt ein Problem: Mit 28 Jahren sollte sich die junge Dame in ihrer Lebensplanung nicht mehr auf eine Bühnenkarriere einstellen. Doch macht dieser Fall sichtbar, womit wir es in der Musikschulpraxis zu tun haben: Mit Menschen, die für ihr Leben eine Bereicherung durch Musik, durch Gesang suchen. Es ist allerdings eine schwierige Aufgabe für die Gesanglehrer an Musikschulen, Menschen, deren Ziele zu hoch gesteckt sind, auf den Boden der Tatsachen zurückzuholen und ihnen trotzdem zu einer Bereicherung durch das Singen zu verhelfen. Wenn dies aber gelingt, ist es auch die schönste Arbeit, die ich mir vorstellen kann.   *rt.*

cours de chant avec succès, de savoir lire les notes; on a également besoin d'un instrument à touche, chez soi, pour s'exercer (il peut s'agit d'un synthétiseur). L'une des conditions les plus importantes d'une progression satisfaisante provoque toujours l'étonnement des personnes intéressées: pour pouvoir chanter soi-même, il est en effet indispensable d'avoir une idée intérieure précise de ce qu'est le chant. Par principe, l'homme apprend le chant par imitation: si l'on n'a aucune idée des possibilités sonores que la voix humaine peut avoir, personne ne réussira à découvrir entièrement ses propre aptitudes vocales. C'est pourquoi l'élève devra étudier non seulement sa propre voix, mais également d'autres voix et des styles musicaux différents. Le chanteur de rock ou la chanteuse de musical qui se refusent à écouter une seule fois un opéra, ou à chanter eux-mêmes une seule fois un Lied de Schubert, se font obstacle à eux-mêmes dans la découverte de leur propre voix.

Après une consultation d'orientation, l'employée de bureau fan de musical est prête à tout: elle ne s'achète pas seulement un piano, elle prend des cours de piano, se rend une fois par semaine à un cours de théorie, va même de plus en plus souvent à l'opéra et chante – avec l'autorisation de son professeur de chant – dans un choeur d'un bon niveau. Elle fait même des exercices et sa voix fait des progrès correspondants. Mais il y a un problème: la jeune dame a 28 ans, et elle ferait mieux de ne pas s'attendre à une carrière de scène. Cependant, ce cas montre bien à quoi nous avons à faire, au quotidien, dans les écoles de musique: à des gens qui cherchent, par le chant, par la musique, à enrichir leur vie. C'est chose difficile, il est vrai, pour les professeurs de chant travaillant dans les écoles de musique, de ramener sur terre les gens qui se sont fixé des objectifs trop élevés, et de les aider malgré tout à un enrichissement par le chant. Mais, s'ils réussissent, c'est la plus belle des tâches que je puisse m'imaginer.   *rt.*

Folk, Jazz, Rock and some Relatives

Folklore, Jazz, Rock und einige Verwandte

Trad, jazz, rock, quelques cousins

Let us say, in short, that the music which is taught today at music schools and music colleges is, for the main part, serious music – and above all, that serious «classical» music written since the beginning of the 18th Century. If one thinks of the 20th Century repertoire, neo-classical scores play a far larger role than truly contemporary or avant-garde works. There are kinds of music which until only a few years ago could still be described as «suspended». Traditional folk music, jazz, cabaret and rock music were heard far less often in schools and music schools than in clubs and private groups – that is, in their own «scene».

Traditional (folk) music is closely linked to the place of its origin and the occasions on which it is played. «Teaching» folk music can hardly be separated from simply passing on the tradition, i.e. playing. There is the anecdote about a master of the Breton bagpipes to whom someone came asking for lessons. His answer was: «That's very convenient: we've got a wedding next Saturday – come along then.» Often it is on just such occasions that the «teaching», or rather the apprenticeship, takes place. At a village fête, at a public meeting, at a competition or festival the «apprentices» listen, analyse, learn to understand and practise the music. A strong sense of community life forms the basis for passing on these traditions, some of which have been passed on without interruption, while others have been rediscovered.

Jazz musicians often mourn the good old days of pubs and clubs where one could while the night away sitting near the stage, listening to the great musicians, noting down their «standards» and learning them by heart. In the last 20 years these night spots have disappeared, so new venues and new ways have to be found for jazz traditions to be passed on. There exist private jazz schools, some of them very prestigious and in much demand, which have taken over the role of the old clubs to some extent. But people are still looking for better forms of jazz teaching, especially since jazz, for all its

Sagen wir, um es kurz zu machen, daß die Musik, die heute in Musikschulen und Konservatorien unterrichtet wird, in der Hauptsache ernste Musik ist – und zwar vor allem die «klassische» ernste Musik, die seit Beginn des 18. Jahrhunderts geschrieben wurde. Denkt man an das Repertoire des 20. Jahrhunderts, so spielen die neo-klassizistischen Partituren eine weitaus größere Rolle als die wahrhaft zeitgenössischen oder avantgardistischen Werke. Es gibt Musikarten, die man bis vor wenigen Jahren noch als «ausgeschlossene» Musik bezeichnen konnte. Sie wurde weit weniger in Schulen oder Musikschulen weitergegeben als in Vereinen und privaten Kreisen bzw. in einer eigenen Szene: die traditionsgebundene Musik, also Volksmusik, Folklore oder Folk, der Jazz, die Musik des Variété (der Kleinkunstszene), die Rockmusik.

Traditionelle Musik (Folklore) ist eng an ihren Ursprungsort und an die Anlässe gebunden, zu denen sie erklingt. «Ausbildung» und «Verbreitung», also Unterricht und Praxis, sind kaum voneinander zu trennen. Da gibt es die Anekdote von einem Meister des bretonischen Dudelsacks, zu dem jemand kam, um ihn um Unterrichtsstunden zu bitten. Seine Antwort war: «Das trifft sich gut, nächsten Samstag haben wir eine Hochzeit – kommen Sie hin.» Oft sind es eben solche Gelegenheiten, bei denen der Unterricht oder eigentlich die Lehrzeit stattfindet. Bei einem Dorffest, bei einem Treffen, auf einem Wettbewerb oder Festival hören die «Lehrlinge» zu, analysieren, verstehen und üben die Musik. Ein lebendiges Vereinsleben bildet die Grundlage zur Weitergabe dieser manchmal ungebrochenen, manchmal wiederentdeckten Traditionen.

Die Jazzmusiker trauern oft der guten alten Zeit der Kneipen und Clubs nach, wo man die Nächte durchmachte, neben der Bühne saß, um den Großen zuzuhören, ihre «Standards» aufzuschreiben und auswendig zu lernen. Diese nächtlichen Orte sind seit 20 Jahren verschwunden, und so müssen für eine Weitergabe der Jazzmusik neue Orte und Strukturen gefunden werden. Es gibt zwar private Schulen mit großer Nachfrage und Ausstrahlung, die manchmal die Rolle der alten Clubs übernehmen. Aber der Jazz-Unterricht ist immer noch auf der Suche nach Lösungen, zumal der Jazz, eigentlich eine sprudelnde und unmittel-

Disons, pour faire court, que la musique enseignée aujourd'hui dans les conservatoires et les écoles de musique est majoritairement la musique savante et même la musique savante «classique», écrite depuis le début du XVIIIᵉ siècle, prenant plus en compte, dans le répertoire du XXᵉ siècle, les partitions néoclassiques que les oeuvres résolument contemporaines ou d'avant-garde. Il est des musiques qu'on appelait il y a quelques années les musiques «exclues» dont l'enseignement se fait moins dans les écoles que dans le milieu associatif et privé: les musiques traditionnelles, le jazz, la musique de variété, le rock.

La musique traditionnelle est liée à son milieu d'origine. Dans son cas formation est indissociable de diffusion. Souvenons-nous de ce maître sonneur breton auprès de qui quelqu'un sollicitait des leçons. Sa réponse fut exemplaire: «Ça tombe bien, samedi prochain, j'ai une noce: venez!» C'est souvent en situation que se fait l'enseignement ou, pour mieux dire, l'apprentissage. C'est lors de la fête du village, lors d'un rassemblement, d'un concours, que les apprentis musiciens écoutent, analysent, comprennent et s'exercent. Le milieu associatif est très vivant et constitue la base de la transmission de cette tradition parfois ininterrompue, parfois redécouverte. Toutes les régions de France ne sont pas également pourvues de ces sortes d'enseignements.

Les musiciens de jazz regrettent souvent la bonne époque des boîtes, des clubs, où l'on venait passer la nuit, assis près de la scène, à écouter, noter, mémoriser les chorus des grands. Ces établissements nocturnes ont, pour beaucoup, disparu depuis vingt ans et l'apprentissage doit trouver de nouveaux lieux, de nouvelles structures. Il est des écoles privées dont l'intérêt et le rayonnement sont grands: elles sont également des lieux de diffusion et jouent quelquefois le rôle tenu naguère par les clubs. Il n'empêche que l'enseignement du jazz cherche encore ses solutions, d'autant plus que le jazz qui fut musique jaillissante et immédiate devient peu-à-peu répertoire. Il y a là matière à penser et à agir.

La musique de variété s'apprenait «sur le tas». On faisait ses humanités au bal où se réunissaient musiciens professionnels (de la variété), «semi-

sparkle and immediacy, is gradually starting to occupy a place in mainstream repertoire. This is reason enough to start thinking and take action.

Variety music (Chansons, cabaret and the better kind of light entertainment music) was generally learnt «sur le tas» – on the job. Musicians would learn their art at a Ball, where professional Variety artists, semi-professionals and classical musicians looking for new inspiration, and «traditional» (folk) musicians would all meet. A musician was a jack of all trades: instrumentalist, arranger, entertainer, singer, improvizer and general dogsbody. Dance music of this kind has largely disappeared; even in France, it has gone from the bars and the juke boxes. So there are now only a few places (such as the «Studio des Variétés») where Variety music can be picked up. It is still a meeting point for musicians of very different persuasions (classical, jazz, folk, etc.) – but things are not as they used to be, and the circle of musicians is getting smaller.

Rock music – can it be taught? People have been producing rock music since the 60s, but not much teaching has been associated with it. The rock musician learns by himself, or perhaps within the group – his own group. In rock music people exchange musical tips, use each other's guitar fingerings, chords, texts, amplifiers, software etc. The rock musician is someone who tries things out, a practising artist, an experimenter. But where are the schools of rock music? They are in garages, cellars, record shops and weekend gigs.

Today, at least, all these kinds of music enjoy their «civil rights» at many music schools, too. This new openness to other musical genres in music schools prompts two observations:

■ A music school must be aware of the quality of its links with the society which surrounds it and which is the source of its vitality; that is, it must react to the needs of that society. Many children do not ask to learn music because they want to study Bach or Debussy, but because they want to learn about Miles Davis, or to play a specific folk instrument, or to use a synthesizer. How are these relatively new teaching areas to be covered properly? How are all these things to be included on what is sometimes a very rigid curriculum? How are we to find appropriate

bare Musik, dabei ist, allmählich zum «Repertoire» zu werden. Grund genug, sich Gedanken zu machen und zu handeln.

Die Variété-Musik (Chansons, Kleinkunst- und gehobene Unterhaltungsmusik) lernte man «sur le tas» (im Gewühl). Man trieb seine Studien bei einem Ball, wo sich professionelle Variété-Musiker, Halbprofis und «klassische» Musiker, die auf der Suche nach neuen Reizen waren, und «traditionelle» (Folklore-)Musiker zusammenfanden. Man war Musiker für alles: Instrumentalist, Arrangeur, Animateur, Sänger, Improvisateur, Handlanger. Solche Bälle sind weitgehend verschwunden und sind auch in Frankreich den Kneipen und der Konserven-Musik gewichen. So gibt es nur noch wenige Orte (z.B. das «Studio des variétés»), wo Variété-Musik erlernt werden kann. Sie ist immer noch Drehscheibe für Musiker der verschiedensten Richtungen (Klassik, Jazz, Folklore usw.) – aber die Sache ist nicht mehr dieselbe wie vorher, und der Kreis der Musiker wird kleiner.

Rockmusik – kann man die unterrichten? Seit den 60er Jahren wird Rockmusik produziert, aber kaum vermittelt. Der Rockmusiker lernt alleine, allenfalls in der Gruppe – in seiner Gruppe. In der Rockmusik hilft man sich gegenseitig: Man borgt sich Fingersätze für die Gitarre, Akkorde, Texte, Verstärkeranlagen, Software usw. Der Rockmusiker ist jemand, der ausprobiert, ein Praktiker, ein Entdecker. Wo aber sind die Rockmusik-Schulen? In der Garage, im Keller, im Plattenladen und bei den Konzerten am Wochenende.

Jedenfalls genießen alle diese Musikarten heute ein «Bürgerrecht» auch in vielen Musikschulen. Diese Öffnung der Musikschulen für andere musikalische Genres veranlaßt zu zwei Überlegungen:

■ Die Musikschule muß auf die Beschaffenheit der Verbindungen zu der Gesellschaft achten, die sie umgibt und aus der sie ihre Lebendigkeit bezieht, das heißt, sie muß auf die gesellschaftlichen Bedürfnisse reagieren. Viele Kinder melden sich nicht an, um Bach oder Debussy zu studieren, sondern um Miles Davis kennenzulernen oder um ein sehr spezielles Folklore-Musikinstrument oder auch Synthesizer zu spielen. Wie kann diesen relativ neuen Unterrichtssparten Rechnung getragen werden? Wie kann man

professionnels», musiciens «classiques» en quête de frissons, voire musiciens «traditionnels». On était musicien à tout faire: instrumentiste, arrangeur, animateur, chanteur, improvisateur, déménageur... Le bal a largement disparu de nos communes pour faire place aux boîtes et à la musique enregistrée. La musique de variété n'a aujourd'hui que peu de lieux où elle puisse s'enseigner (comme par exemple le studio de variétés). Elle est toujours un carrefour entre musiciens issus de milieux différents (classique, jazz, trad...), mais le métier n'est plus ce qu'il était et le cercle des musiciens se réduit.

Le rock s'enseigne-t-il? Depuis les années soixante, le rock s'invente et se transmet peu. Le rocker apprend seul, ou plutôt en groupe – dans son groupe. Le rock est une musique où l'on s'entraide; où l'on se prête des doigtés de guitare, des accords, des paroles, des sonos, des logiciels... Le rocker est un expérimentateur, un pratiquant, un découvreur. Où sont les écoles du rock? Dans les garages, les sous-sols, dans les rayons de la Fnac et dans les concerts de fin de semaine.

Cependant, toutes ces musiques ont aujourd'hui droit de cité dans les écoles. Cette ouverture des écoles à «d'autres musiques» nous inspire deux réflexions:

- L'école doit mesurer attentivement la qualité des liens qu'elle tisse avec la société qui l'entoure et qui la fait vivre et il convient qu'elle puisse répondre à la demande sociale. Beaucoup d'enfants s'inscrivent non pour étudier Bach et Debussy, mais pour s'initier à Miles Davis, à la sardane ou au synthétiseur. Comment prendre en compte ces enseignements relativement nouveaux? Comment intégrer ces apprentissages dans des cursus parfois figés? Comment trouver des méthodes qui soient appropriées et performantes? Les réponses sont nombreuses, pas toujours adéquates. C'est un bon sujet de travail sur les objectifs et les contenus des enseignements qui s'impose dans toutes les écoles qui ont fait ce pari de l'ouverture.

- Quels que soient les échecs et les tâtonnements, l'entrée des musiques différentes de celles

and effective methods for teaching them? The answers and solutions are not simple and not always convincing. It is an urgent task for all music schools who take this bold step towards greater openness to work on the goals and content of their teaching programme.

■ In spite of failures and defeats, gains are to be achieved by extending the range of courses to include various different musical styles. Musicians – be they amateurs, professionals, schoolchildren or students – need to re-establish those links with tradition which have been lost for more than one and a half centuries: they need to find a new freedom of expression, the freedom to have new ideas. Since the Romantics, musicians have become for the most part mere performers, devoted and obedient servants of the score. Now there are those who dream again of ornamenting, adapting, «composing», improvizing just like their ancestors a good 200 years ago. «Traditional» (folk) music, jazz, light entertainment music and rock will bring in a breath of fresh air if they are taught at music schools. In company like this, conventional music teaching should find plenty of material to renew and extend its means of expression. That is, unless certain attitudes have become so fossilized that they are no longer capable of drawing on contact and communication with others for their own development, but merely encrust everything they touch with their own prejudices.

But let us look forward boldly and confidently to a process of mutual discovery – as a step towards increased understanding between human beings.

chj.

diese Inhalte in die manchmal recht unbeweglichen Ausbildungswege einbinden? Wie findet man angemessene und erfolgversprechende Methoden zu ihrer Vermittlung? Die Antworten und Lösungen sind vielfältig und nicht immer überzeugend. Für alle Musikschulen, die den Schritt zu einer solchen Öffnung wagen, ist es eine vordringliche Aufgabe, an den Zielen und Inhalten eines solchen Unterrichts zu arbeiten.

Trotz aller Fehlversuche und Niederlagen: Das Erweitern des Unterrichtsangebots durch verschiedenartige Musikstile bringt Gewinn. Ob Amateur, Berufsmusiker, Schüler oder Student – der Musiker muß den Anschluß an Traditionen wiederherstellen, die seit über anderthalb Jahrhunderten verlorengegangen sind: Er muß eine neue Freiheit des Ausdrucks finden, eine neue Freiheit zur spontanen Erfindung. Seit der Romantik ist er zumeist ein Ausführender geworden, ein eifriger und gehorsamer Diener der Partitur. Nun träumt er wieder davon, zu ornamentieren, zu bearbeiten, zu «komponieren», zu improvisieren – ganz wie seine Vorfahren vor gut 200 Jahren. Die «traditionelle» (Folklore-)Musik, der Jazz, die Unterhaltungskunst, der Rock werden, wenn sie in den Musikschulen unterrichtet werden, frischen Wind in die Sache bringen. In solcher Nachbarschaft wird auch der herkömmliche Unterricht Stoff genug zur Erneuerung und Erweiterung seiner Möglichkeiten finden. Es sei denn, daß bestimmte verknöcherte Haltungen nicht mehr fähig wären, sich im Kontakt und in der Auseinandersetzung mit anderen zu entwickeln, sondern alles, was sich ihnen nähert, überkrusten.

Wir wollen aber mutig und zuversichtlich auf eine beiderseitige Entdeckung setzen – als Schritt auch der zwischenmenschlichen Verständigung.

chj.

qu'on enseignait jusqu'alors est bénéfique. Le musicien, amateur, professionnel ou apprenti a besoin de renouer avec des traditions perdues depuis plus d'un siècle et demi. Il a besoin de retrouver une liberté d'expression, d'invention. Il était devenu, souvent, depuis le Romantisme, un exécutant, un serviteur de la partition zélé et obéissant. Il rêve maintenant d'orner, d'arranger, de «composer», d'improviser comme le faisaient ses ancêtres, il y a encore deux cents ans. La musique traditionnelle, le jazz, la variété, le rock, lorsqu'ils sont enseignés au sein de l'école sont de nouveaux poumons, de nouveaux lieux où l'air est plus frais. L'enseignement devrait trouver dans ces cousinages matière à rénovation, à libération. A moins que certains systèmes rouillés ne soient plus en état d'évoluer au contact d'autres systèmes et corrodent tout ce qui les approche!

C'est encore possible, mais comme beaucoup de mes collègues en France, nous ferons hardiment et joyeusement le pari de la découverte mutuelle (qui est le premier pas vers l'amour!). *chj.*

Keyboards, Synthesizers and Computers – Electronic Music in Music Schools

Keyboards, Synthesizer und Computer – elektronische Musik in der Musikschule

Claviers électroniques, synthétiseurs et ordinateurs – la musique électronique à l'école de musique

The first synthesizer was built almost 100 years ago. And as early as 1932, Aldous Huxley described electronic music in his book «Brave New World» – as a means of influence on the future society's daily life. Today this is long since reality, and electronic music has a firmly established place in our lives. Music in the media and in commercial entertainment consists largely of electronic or electronically imitated sounds that seem as authentic as those produced on traditional musical instruments. The traditional musician is becoming dispensable – the smaller the number of musicians, the lower the production costs. The role of the composer and arranger, on the other hand, is expanding. Pieces of music can easily be assessed for effectiveness in various versions and then altered. This is also, however, an efficient means of finding out where and how music can be used most effectively to specific ends, such as in advertising and to influence people's spending habits. Media studies experts talk of manipulation through music.

In such a situation it is important to know as much as possible about music. This is what musical education aims at, and it is particularly important where electronic instruments are involved. Here, too, the student should broaden his horizons with new sounds, harmonies, rhythms, structures and so on, not limit or reduce his potential for development. The «4/4 time C major society» is easily influenced by music. Anyone who has made experimental music himself (even on a modest scale) hears «light music» with new and more sensitive ears.

Is a synthesizer the same thing as an electronic keyboard? Electronic keyboards are instruments generally designed for a particular adaption – that is, for making as «much» music as possible with the smallest possible amount of effort and skill. Here we find certain functions such as built-in rhythm programmes, automatic accompaniments, «one finger technology» and pre-defined sounds (presets). Many keyboards offer hundreds of sounds, the individual quality of which, however, can hardly be varied. If one is looking for a particular sound, the choice is limited to the available options – and anyone who finds that testing and sorting just make life difficult is quick to say «OK» to a sound, even if it is not exactly that he was actually searching.

Der erste «Synthesizer» wurde vor fast 100 Jahren gebaut! Und schon 1932 beschrieb Aldous Huxley elektronische Musik in seinem Buch «Schöne neue Welt» – als Beeinflussungsfaktor im täglichen Leben der Zukunftsgesellschaft. Heute ist es längst soweit: Die elektronische Musik hat einen fest etablierten Platz in unserem Leben. Die Musik in den Medien und im kommerziellen Unterhaltungsbereich besteht größtenteils aus elektronischen bzw. aus elektronisch nachgeahmten Klängen, die so echt klingen wie von herkömmlichen Instrumenten. Der traditionelle Musiker wird verzichtbar – je weniger Musiker, desto billiger die Produktion. Die Rolle des Komponisten und Arrangeurs dagegen nimmt zu. Und Musikstücke können leicht in unterschiedlichen Fassungen auf ihre Wirkung hin erprobt und verändert werden. Somit kann aber auch effizient herausgefunden werden, wo und wie eine Beeinflussung durch Musik zu bestimmten Zwecken, etwa der Werbung und des Kaufverhaltens, erreicht werden kann. Medienpädagogen reden von Manipulation durch Musik.

Da gilt es, möglichst viel von Musik zu verstehen. Hier liegt die Aufgabe der Musikerziehung, und in besonderem Maß eben im Umgang mit elektronischen Instrumenten. Auch hier soll der Schüler seinen Horizont erweitern (neue Klänge, Harmonien, Rhythmen, Anwendungen usw.) und nicht eine Begrenzung oder gar Reduzierung seiner Entwicklungsmöglichkeiten erfahren. Die «4/4-Takt – C-Dur – Gesellschaft» ist leicht durch Musik zu beeinflussen. Wer experimentelle Musik selbst gemacht hat (auch in bescheidenem Maßstab), erlebt die «Unterhaltungsmusik» mit anderen und qualifizierteren Ohren.

Ist ein Synthesizer ein Keyboard? Keyboards sind Tasteninstrumente, die in der Regel auf eine bestimmte Anwendung ausgerichtet sind, nämlich mit möglichst wenig Aufwand und Spielfertigkeit möglichst «viel» Musik machen zu können. Hier finden wir bestimmte Ausstattungen wie eingebaute Rhythmusgeräte, Begleitautomatik, «Ein-Finger-Technik» und vorprogrammierte Klänge (Presets). Manche Keyboards bieten Hunderte von Klängen, die jedoch für sich kaum veränderbar sind. Sucht man hier einen bestimmten Klang, so ist die Klangvorstellung auf die vorhandenen Möglichkeiten eingegrenzt. Und wem schon das Aus-

Le premier «synthétiseur» fut construit voilà près de 100 ans! Et, en 1932 déjà, Aldous Huxley décrivit la musique électronique dans «Le meilleur des mondes» – à titre de facteur d'influence dans la vie quotidienne de la société de l'avenir. Aujourd'hui, il y a longtemps que nous en sommes arrivés à ce point: la musique électronique a sa place bien établie dans notre vie. La musique véhiculée par les médias et le domaine du divertissement commercial est constituée pour la plus grande part par des sons électroniques ou imités électroniquement qui ont une résonance tout aussi authentique que des instruments traditionnels. Le musicien traditionnel devient superflu – moins on a de musiciens, moins la production sera chère. Le rôle du compositeur et de l'arrangeur, par contre, grandit. Et il est possible d'essayer des morceaux dans différentes versions afin d'en contrôler l'effet et de les modifier. Ceci permet également de déterminer de manière efficace à quel moment et de quelle façon il est possible d'obtenir une influence par la musique dans des buts définis, par exemple dans le domaine de la publicité et du comportement d'achat. Les pédagogues des médias parlent de manipulation par la musique.

Il s'agit donc d'avoir de bonnes connaissances musicales. C'est en ceci que réside le rôle de l'éducation musicale, et en particulier, justement, dans le cadre de l'utilisation d'instruments électroniques. Ici aussi, l'élève doit élargir son horizon musical (sons, harmonies, rythmes, utilisations nouvelles, etc...) et non être confronté à une limitation ou même à une réduction de ses possibilités de développement. Il est facile d'influencer la «société-à-quatre-temps-en-ut-majeur» par la musique. Qui a fait lui même de la musique expérimentale (ne serait-ce que dans des proportions modestes), vit la «musique légère» avec d'autres oreilles, plus qualifiées.

Un synthétiseur est-il un clavier électronique? Les claviers électroniques sont des instruments à touches, orientés en règle générale en fonction d'une utilisation précise, c'est-à-dire pouvoir faire «le plus» de musique possible avec le moins de moyens et de savoir-faire possible. On trouvera ici certains équipements tels que des appareils à rythme, un dispositif d'accompagnement automatique, la «technique à un doigt» et des sons pré-pro-

Synthesizers, on the other hand, primarily have the function of making it possible to generate sounds. A good machine admits of innumerable possible variations. This is important, for if I am to «build» a sound, I must first «have» it in my imagination – something which challenges aural inventiveness and imaginative powers. Merely analysing a familiar sound (e.g. that of a traditional instrument) and trying to produce it by electronic means trains the ability to listen for detail and broadens our understanding of what makes up a particular sound.

Keyboard lessons are thus not the same thing as working with a synthesizer. Keyboard lessons serve mainly to transmit skills in playing – if the teaching is any good – just like violin, flute and drum lessons. Good training in using a synthesizer means investigating the qualities of sound. Experiments with sounds – a creative approach. Most electronically produced sounds aim at imitation of a traditional instrument. The real strength of the synthesizer, however, is precisely in producing sounds previously unknown – the more far-out, the better. Many sounds to which we have now become accustomed were invented without a previous model.

In working with students we divide electronic sounds into 1) sounds that can be used for melodic purposes, 2) sounds that are to be used for percussive effects and 3) experimental sounds. It is these experimental sounds that offer a playground for the imagination. Even sound panoramas, long chords that gradually change, can be created.

Students often find their first encounters with experimental music problematic – «Where's the message?». Here, film music offers a good way in: abstract music to abstract pictures. Setting music to go with a collage of photographs is also a good starting point: looking for the right photographs, distinguishing between abstract and concrete images, looking for themes and devising music to go with them is an absorbing task. Another approach is the expression of «moods» through music. What starts out as being made up of strong feelings of «happy» or «sad» can develop, through experimenting with different effects, to include more distinguished moods such as reflectiveness, a sense of release, loneliness or confusion.

testen und Sortieren das Leben schwer macht, der sagt schnell zu einem Klang «o.k.», auch wenn er nicht ganz so genau paßt.

Synthesizer dagegen haben primär die Aufgabe, Klanggestaltung zu ermöglichen. Ein gutes Gerät erlaubt zahllose Variationsmöglichkeiten der Klangveränderung. Das ist wichtig. Denn wenn ich gehalten bin, einen Klang zu «bauen», muß ich ihn erst in meiner Imagination «haben» – eine Herausforderung an die Klangphantasie und Klangvorstellung. Allein die Analyse eines vorhandenen Klangs (z.B. eines herkömmlichen Instruments) und der Versuch, ihn elektronisch zu erzeugen, schult das Vermögen differenzierten Hörens und vertieft die Kenntnisse über die Zusammensetzung eines bestimmten Klanges.

Keyboard-Unterricht ist also nicht identisch mit der Arbeit an einem Synthesizer. Der Keyboard-Unterricht dient hauptsächlich der Vermittlung von Spielfähigkeiten – wenn er gut ist, genau wie der Geigen-, Flöten- und Schlagzeugunterricht. Ein guter Unterricht am Synthesizer bedeutet ein Erforschen von Klängen. Experimente mit Klängen – ein kreativer Ansatz. Die meisten der elektronisch produzierten Klänge haben den Zweck, ein herkömmliches Instrument nachzuahmen. Die eigentliche Stärke des Synthesizers ist es aber gerade, Klänge zu erzeugen, die vorher nicht vorhanden waren – je ausgefallener, desto besser. Viele Sounds, an die man sich inzwischen gewöhnt hat, sind ohne Vorbild erfunden worden.

In der Arbeit mit Schülern teilen wir die elektronischen Klänge in drei Gruppen ein: 1) Klänge, die für melodische Zwecke verwendbar sind, 2) perkussiv einzusetzende Klänge und 3) experimentelle Klänge. Gerade die experimentellen Klänge bieten

grammés (presets). De nombreux claviers électroniques offrent des centaines de sons, mais qui ne peuvent à peine être modifiés en soi. Si l'on est à la recherche d'un son précis, l'imagination sonore est alors limitée par les possibilités existantes. Et si l'on trouve le fait d'essayer et de classer trop compliqué, on aura tôt fait de dire «OK» à un son, même si ce n'est pas exactement celui que l'on cherchait.

Le rôle primaire des synthétiseurs, par contre, est de permettre de créer un son. Un appareil de bonne qualité offre des possibilités de variations illimitées. C'est important. Car si je suis forcé de «construire» un son, il me faudra «l'avoir» tout d'abord dans mon imagination – un défi à l'imagination sonore et à la faculté de se représenter les sons. Seules l'analyse d'un son existant (par exemple, d'un instrument traditionnel) et la tentative de le reproduire électroniquement forment l'aptitude à une écoute nuancée et permettent d'approfondir les connaissances de la composition d'un son particulier.

Les cours de claviers électroniques ne sont donc pas identiques au travail avec un synthétiseur. Les cours de claviers électroniques servent principalement à la transmission d'une aptitude à jouer – s'ils sont bons, tout aussi bien que des cours de violon, de flûte ou de batterie. Un bon cours au synthétiseur signifie une recherche et une découverte de sons. Expérimenter avec des sons – c'est là un point de départ créatif. La plupart des sons produits électroniquement ont pour but d'imiter un instrument traditionnel. Le véritable point fort du synthétiseur, par contre, c'est de produire des sons qui n'ont pas existé jusque là – plus ils sont originaux, mieux c'est. Beaucoup de sounds auxquels on s'est habitué entre-temps, ont été inventés sans modèle.

Au cours du travail avec les élèves, nous divisons les sons électroniques en trois groupes: 1) les sons utilisables dans des buts mélodiques, 2) les sons à utiliser comme percussions et 3) les sons expérimentaux. Ce sont justement ces sons expérimentaux qui offrent un terrain de jeu pour l'imagination. Il est également possible de créer des images sonores, c'est-à-dire des sons prolongés qui se modifient au cours du temps.

«Ohne Musik wäre das Leben ein Irrtum.»

Friedrich Nietzsche

Players of traditional instruments can work with electronic music, too. By means of electro-acoustic distortion, the notes produced on the instrument can be changed and, according to the type and degree of such manipulation and the musical use that is made of this technique, some quite good piece of abstract or experimental music can be the result. The distortion of sound is achieved through the use of microphones and special effects equipment, which should also permit manifold permutations of sound parameters. The resulting sounds are emitted through an amplifier. As with a synthesizer, the putting together of sounds and effects is linked to an experimental process and involves a similarly intensive focussing on sound qualities, with a broadening of the awareness of sound.

Techniques of sound montage are another playground of electronic music: an existing recording is cut up and reassembled differently, thus producing new sound material. From a few seconds of recorded sound, whole pieces can be made. Previously, this could only be achieved through the use of tape recording equipment and cutting, and some things can be done with a cassette recorder. More

eine Spielwiese für die Phantasie. Auch Klangbilder, also länger andauernde Klänge, die sich im Zeitverlauf ändern, können kreiert werden.

Häufig haben Schüler Berührungsschwierigkeiten mit experimenteller Musik – «Wo ist die Message?». Hierbei ist die Filmmusik ein dankbarer Einstieg: abstrakte Musik zu abstrakten Bildern. Auch Musik zu einer Fotocollage eignet sich als Ausgangspunkt: entsprechende Fotos aussuchen, zwischen abstrakten und konkreten Bildern unterscheiden, die Suche nach Themen und das Erfinden passender Musik dazu, dies ist eine spannende Aufgabe. Ein weiterer Ansatz ist, «Stimmungen» musikalisch zum Ausdruck zu bringen. Was bei plakativen Gefühlsmomenten wie «happy» oder «traurig» beginnt, kann im Experimentieren meistens bei differenzierten Ergebnissen der Darstellung zum Beispiel von Nachdenklichkeit, Erlösung, Einsamkeit oder Verwirrung führen.

Auch Spieler herkömmlicher Instrumente können sich mit elektronischer Musik auseinandersetzen!? Mittels elektro-akustischer Verfremdung werden die vom Instrument erzeugten Klänge verändert, und je nach Art und Grad dieser Manipulation und des musikalischen Einsatzes dieser Technik kann ein qualitätvolles Ergebnis abstrakter/experimenteller Musik dabei entstehen. Die Verfremdung findet über Mikrophone und Effektgeräte statt, die ebenfalls über vielfältige Veränderungsmöglichkeiten der Klangparameter verfügen sollten. Das klangliche Ergebnis ertönt aus einer Verstärkeranlage. Wie beim Synthesizer ist das Basteln der Klänge und Effekte mit Experimentieren verbunden und bedeutet eine ähnlich intensive Auseinandersetzung mit dem Klang und Erweiterung der Klangvorstellung.

In den Bereich der elektronischen Musik gehört auch die Tonmontage-Technik. Eine vorhandene Musikaufnahme wird zerschnitten und neu zusammengestellt. So entsteht neues Tonmaterial. Aus einigen Sekunden Klangmaterial können ganze Stücke entwickelt werden. Früher hat man dies nur mit Tonbandgeräten und Schnittarbeit (Cutting) bewerkstelligen können, einiges geht auch mit einem Cassettenrecorder. Fortschrittliche Tontechnik wird jedoch mit einem Soundsampler gemacht. Auch bei dieser Arbeitstechnik geht es nicht um ein

Les élèves ont souvent des difficultés pour entrer en contact avec la musique expérimentale – «où est le message?». La musique de film est, ici, un point de départ pratique: aux images abstraites, musique abstraite. La musique correspondant à un collage de photos est également un bon point de départ: sélectionner des photos correspondantes, faire la différence entre les images abstraites et concrètes, rechercher par thèmes et inventer la musique adaptée, est un travail fascinant. Une autre introduction possible est l'expression musicale d'«atmosphères». Ce qui commence par des moments de sentiments évidents tels que «happy» ou «triste», peut conduire la plupart du temps, par l'expérimentation, à des résultats de présentation nuancée, par exemple de la réflexion, de la délivrance, de la solitude ou de la confusion.

Ceux qui jouent d'un instrument traditionnel peuvent aussi se confronter à la musique électronique!? A l'aide d'un système de dénaturation électro-acoustique, les sons produits par l'instrument sont modifiés, et, selon le type et le degré de cette manipulation et de l'utilisation musicale de cette technique, il est possible d'obtenir un résultat de musique abstraite/expérimentale de bonne qualité. Cette dénaturation s'effectue par l'intermédiaire de microphones et d'appareils à effets spéciaux qui doivent également disposer d'une foule de possibilités de modification des paramètres sonores. Le résultat sonore se fait entendre par l'intermédiaire d'une installation d'amplificateurs. Comme au niveau du synthétiseur, le bricolage de sons et d'effets est lié à l'expérimentation et implique une réflexion tout aussi intense sur le son et l'élargissement de sa représentation imaginaire.

Fait également partie du domaine de la musique électronique la technique du montage sonore. Un enregistrement musical existant est coupé en morceaux et reconstitué dans un ordre différent. Un matériel sonore nouveau est ainsi créé. Quelques secondes de matériel sonore peuvent permettre de donner naissance à des morceaux entiers. Ceci n'était possible autrefois qu'à l'aide de bandes magnétiques et d'un travail de coupe (Cutting), on peut également réaliser un certain nombre de choses avec un magnétophone à cassettes. La technique tonale avancée, cependant, utilise un soundsampler. Il ne s'agit pas non plus, dans cette tech-

advanced sound technology makes use of a sound sampler, though. With this kind of technology it is still not a matter of random patching together of scraps of sound, but a careful composition of notes, resonance and form.

Dealing with electronic music and working with experimental sounds can signify a leap into modern music. What can otherwise be difficult to discover can be experienced in practice with the help of electronic equipment and instruments. In music education the aim is to provide enough experience and knowledge for students to be able to encounter electronically produced music with more sensitive ears; to teach people to explore the creative potential of technology; to develop the aural imagination through analysis and experiment, and to put students in a position to realize their ideas by using the available technology.   *gas.*

Music School Courses Preparing for Professional Studies

Studienvorbereitende Ausbildung

Une formation de préparation aux études supérieures

Some thoughts on the training provided at music schools for entry to music college are to be put forward here in the rhetorical form of a «defence». Why? – Because this specialized form of teaching is often identified as elitism and questioned on all possible grounds by sceptics: therefore we shall examine those very questions. The «defence» thereby amounts to «praise».

Is it on the whole the job of music schools to train and encourage highly gifted individuals and a few more who show special talent? It is – for music schools see it as their role and indeed have an educational and cultural responsibility to look after the interests of the gifted, as well as working in the broader field of general musical education. It would certainly be irresponsible if they were not to do this and if it were not expected of them. Since nowadays, in almost all the countries of Europe, all practical musical education is undertaken in music schools, they are the natural place for musical gifts to be discovered – and this in itself turns out to be a valuable stimulus to those who are so identified. With the efforts they make to provide early musical training and to offer generally high levels of educa-

willkürliches Zusammenflicken von Tonfetzen, sondern um eine gezielte Gestaltung von Ton, Klang und Form.

Der Umgang mit elektronischer Musik und die Beschäftigung mit experimentellen Klängen kann den Sprung in die Moderne Musik bedeuten. Was sonst nur schwer erfahrbar ist, kann mithilfe der elektronischen Geräte und Instrumente praktisch erlebt werden. Ziel der musikerzieherischen Arbeit ist es, so viel an Erfahrung und Kenntnissen zu vermitteln, daß man die elektronisch erzeugte Musik «mit wachen Ohren» hören lernt; daß man lernt, der Technik eine kreative Seite abzugewinnen; daß in Analyse und Experiment die Klangimagination entwickelt wird und die Schüler in die Lage versetzt werden, ihre Vorstellungen durch den Einsatz der technischen Mittel zu realisieren.   *gas.*

La pratique de la musique électronique et l'intérêt pour les sonorités expérimentales peuvent être synonymes du pas en avant vers la Musique Moderne. Ce dont on ne peut faire l'expérience que difficilement, dans d'autres conditions, peut être vécu dans la pratique à l'aide des appareils et des instruments électroniques. Le but du travail de l'éducation musicale est de transmettre suffisamment d'expériences et de connaissances pour permettre d'écouter la musique produite électroniquement avec des «oreilles réveillées», d'apprendre à apprécier le côté créatif de la technique, de développer une imagination sonore par l'analyse et l'expérimentation, et de rendre les élèves capables de réaliser leurs propres conceptions en utilisant les moyens offerts par la technique.   *gas.*

Die Gedanken zur studienvorbereitenden Ausbildung an Musikschulen sollen hier in der rhetorischen Form einer «Verteidigung» entwickelt werden. Warum? – Weil dieses spezielle Unterrichtsangebot als ausgesprochene Spitzenförderung womöglich skeptischen Fragen ausgesetzt ist, die hier auch gestellt werden sollen. Und die «Verteidigung» gerät dabei zum «Lob».

Ist es überhaupt die Aufgabe von Musikschulen, einzelne Hochbegabte und ein wenig mehr besonders Begabte intensiv zu fördern? Ja – denn die Musikschulen haben das Selbstverständnis und auch den kultur- und bildungspolitischen Auftrag, sich neben der musikalischen Breitenarbeit auch den Begabten zuzuwenden. Es wäre ja geradezu verantwortungslos, wenn sie dies nicht täten und wenn man dies nicht von ihnen erwarten würde. Da heutzutage in fast allen Ländern Europas nahezu die gesamte praktisch-musikalische Ausbildung durch die Musikschulen wahrgenommen wird, sind sie der natürliche Ort, wo musikalische Begabungen ausfindig gemacht werden können – allein dies ist für die Betreffenden eine wertvolle Förderung! Mit den Bemühungen um die musikali-

Ces réflexions sur la formation de préparation aux études supérieures dans les écoles de musique seront développées ici sous la forme rhétorique d'un plaidoyer de «défense». Pourquoi? Parce que ces cours, de type particulier, sont exposés, à titre de promotion expresse d'un niveau performant de pointe, à des questions peut-être sceptiques, qui devront également être posées ici. Et le plaidoyer de «défense» se transformera alors en «louange».

Est-ce vraiment la tâche des écoles de musique d'encourager et de soutenir de manière intensive quelques surdoués isolés ou quelques élèves doués de plus? Oui. Car il réside dans la conception propre et dans la mission culturelle et éducative des écoles de musique de se consacrer également, parallèlement au travail de masse, aux élèves doués. Il serait irresponsable de leur part de ne pas le faire, et il serait irresponsable de ne pas l'attendre d'elles. L'ensemble de la formation musicale pratique étant assurée presque totalement, aujourd'hui, dans pratiquement tous les pays d'Europe, par les écoles de musique, elles sont le lieu naturel de la révélation et de la découverte de talents musicaux – ce qui constitue déjà, pour les élèves concernés, un

«Ein musizierendes
Kind nimmt keine Knarre
in die Hand...
Für mich ist Musik das
größte Heilmittel gegen
Gewalt, Intoleranz und
Dummheit!»

Hans Werner Henze

tion to all students, music schools are a fertile soil where the seeds of such gifts may germinate and grow.

Very good, but isn't that part of the regular work of a music school, not part of the training for admission to music college? – That is true, but it is evident that good teaching from the very beginning is an important prerequisite for students who may later wish to embark as professionals on a musical career. Of course, the seeds of talent will not all grow to the same height, and not everyone will wish or be able to study at music college; but for those who once may wish to turn to advanced studies, music schools do always have to «prepare» this step in a wider sense, i.e. by a teaching that generally renders it «possible» to take up a professional training.

All the same, aren't we concerned here with training in the narrower sense, the question of intensive coaching to enable students to meet the demands of the examination for admission to a music college? Certainly, this is a definite goal. But the aims of such preparation are broader: such specialist education does not merely provide technical drilling geared towards a brilliant examination performance, not artificial cultivation of individually excellent performances, but a broad general musical education of high quality with the highest artistic standards. The curriculum is therefore correspondingly varied and students are obliged to meet the following requirements:

- For the First Study, lessons with a highly qualified teacher; in some cases, two lessons a week;
- A Second Study instrument, balanced with the choice of First Study so that every student

sche Früherziehung und um ein insgesamt hohes Niveau der Ausbildung für alle Schüler sind die Musikschulen der ideale «Nährboden», auf dem Begabungen keimen und auch entsprechend wachsen können.

Gut, aber das ist dann Teil der normalen Musikschularbeit und noch nicht die eigentliche studienvorbereitende Ausbildung? – Das stimmt, aber es ist doch einsichtig, daß der qualitätvolle Unterricht von früh an eine wesentliche Voraussetzung dafür ist, daß Schüler später auch eine musikalische Berufslaufbahn einschlagen können. Sicher, es wachsen die «Pflänzchen» der Begabung individuell verschieden hoch, und es wird nicht jeder Musik studieren wollen oder können – aber für die Geeigneten sollte Musikschule von Beginn an und permanent «studienvorbereitend» im weiteren Sinne, also «studienermöglichend» arbeiten.

Trotzdem: Es geht doch hier um Studienvorbereitung im engeren Sinn, also um eine gezielte Intensivausbildung mit dem Ziel, daß deren Absolventen den konkreten Anforderungen für die Aufnahmeprüfung an einer Musikhochschule gewachsen sind? Ja – das ist das sichtbare Ziel. Aber es geht um mehr: Nicht der technische Drill zur glanzvollen Präsentation des Prüfungsprogramms, nicht das künstliche Hochzüchten von Spitzenleistungen ist Inhalt dieser besonderen Ausbildung, sondern eine gediegene, breit angelegte allgemein-musikalische Bildung mit hohem künstlerischen Anspruch. Dahor ist das Unterrichtsprogramm entsprechend vielseitig und verpflichtet die teilnehmenden Schüler auch zur Erfüllung dieses Pensums:

- im künstlerischen Hauptfach Unterricht bei einer besonders qualifizierten Lehrkraft, gegebenenfalls mit einer zusätzlichen zweiten Stunde in der Woche;
- ein instrumentales Nebenfach, das eine ergänzende Kombination zum Hauptfach darstellt, so daß jeder Teilnehmer ein Melodie- und ein Harmonieinstrument beherrscht;
- Besuch von Kursen zur Gehörbildung, Harmonielehre, allgemeiner Musiklehre und Musikgeschichte;
- Teilnahme in verschiedenen Formen des kammermusikalischen Zusammenspiels, für Pianisten auch Begleitpraxis, Mitwirkung in Orchestern sowie unbedingt auch in einem Chor.

précieux soutien! De par leurs efforts orientés au sens de l'éducation musicale précoce, et grâce à un niveau de formation élevé, dans l'ensemble, pour tous les élèves, les écoles de musique constituent le «terreau» idéal sur lequel peuvent germer et croître les dons particuliers.

Bien, mais ceci est une partie du travail normal des écoles de musique et non une formation de préparation aux études supérieures proprement dite? C'est vrai, mais l'on comprendra qu'un cours de qualité dès le départ est une condition essentielle pour que l'élève puisse, plus tard, embrasser une carrière musicale. Bien sûr, les «boutures» du talent croissent à des hauteurs différentes selon les individus, et tous ne voudront pas ou ne pourront pas étudier la musique – mais, pour ceux qui en sont capables, l'école de musique se doit, dès le départ et de manière permanente, de «préparer aux études supérieures» au sens large, c'est-à-dire de «rendre possible des études supérieures».

Tout de même: il s'agit ici d'une préparation aux études supérieures au sens restreint, c'est-à-dire d'une formation intensive visant à ce que les élèves soient en état de satisfaire aux exigences concrètes de l'examen d'entrée à une école supérieure de musique? Oui, c'est là l'objectif visible. Mais l'enjeu est plus important: le contenu de cette formation particulière n'est pas l'entraînement technique sévère en vue d'une présentation prestigieuse du programme d'examen, ni la culture élitaire artificielle de performances de haut niveau, mais une formation musicale générale solide et de spectre large, alliée à une volonté artistique élevée. C'est pourquoi les cours proposés sont d'une variété correspondante et que les participants sont tenus de suivre le programme suivant:

- dans la matière artistique principale, un cours auprès d'un professeur particulièrement qualifié, avec, le cas échéant, une deuxième heure supplémentaire par semaine;
- une matière secondaire d'apprentissage d'un instrument complémentaire de la matière principale, de sorte que l'élève possède un instrument mélodique et un instrument harmonique;
- fréquentation de cours d'éducation de l'ouïe, d'harmonie, de théorie musicale générale et d'histoire de la musique;

learns to play a melodic instrument and an instrument apt to play chords on.

- Attendance at classes in aural training, harmony, general music and music history;
- Participation in various chamber ensembles, experience as an accompanist for pianists, membership of orchestras and certainly of a choir.

This combination provides for a comprehensive basic education not solely aimed at passing entrance examinations, but at giving a strong foundation of knowledge and skills to be used as the basis for further study, so that students will be successful in their subsequent professional training.

But surely not every music school can offer this kind of education? No – it is mainly a job for larger institutions with a large pool of students and the right kind of teachers, numerous ensembles and ample teaching facilities. It is also desirable that there should be coordination of this kind of training and that the students involved should be grouped together, perhaps in their own department. However, no gifted student should be denied the opportunity of this kind of education simply because he may happen to live in the country. Smaller music schools could join forces here, as in other areas – for instance, to form a larger orchestra. Arrangements should also be made with general schools to allow for the enormous demands on the time and energy of students made by preparation for entrance to music college.

Might it not happen that the normal teaching functions of a music school suffer when such intensive tuition is provided for just a few pupils? No – for there are only ever a few pupils, probably less than 5%, for whom this kind of preparation can be considered. This group is hardly likely to disturb the balance of activities in a music school. On the contrary: it generally provides strong motivation both for the «ordinary» pupils and for the teaching staff when there

Diese Kombination ermöglicht jene umfassende und grundlegende Ausbildung, die nicht allein auf die Aufnahmeprüfung abzielt, sondern ein erhöhtes Grundniveau von Kenntnissen und Fähigkeiten zu Beginn des Studiums bereitstellt, so daß die eigentliche Berufsausbildung erfolgreich verlaufen kann.

Eine solche Ausbildung kann doch nicht jede Musikschule bieten? Nein – vorwiegend eignen und interessieren sich dafür große Institute mit einem großen Potential an Schülern und geeigneten Lehrkräften, zahlreichen Ensembles und Unterrichtskapazitäten. Auch ist eine Koordination dieser Ausbildung und der an ihr Beteiligten wünschenswert, etwa als eigene Abteilung. Jedoch sollte kein begabter Schüler von der Chance dieser Ausbildung ausgeschlossen sein, nur weil er vielleicht auf dem Lande wohnt. Kleinere Musikschulen könnten – wie auch in anderen Bereichen, etwa um ein größeres Orchester zusammenzubekommen – zu einer Zusammenarbeit finden. Auch mit den allgemeinen Schulen sollte eine Abstimmung wegen der enormen zeitlichen und kräftemäßigen Beanspruchung der Schüler der studienvorbereitenden Ausbildung erfolgen.

Kann es nicht passieren, daß der «normale» Unterrichtsbetrieb einer Musikschule darunter leidet, wenn für einige wenige eine solche intensive Förderung erfolgt? Nein – denn es sind ja immer nur einige wenige, wahrscheinlich unter 5% der Schüler, für die eine studienvorbereitende Ausbildung infrage kommt. Kaum fällt diese Gruppe in einer Musikschule störend oder belastend ins Gewicht. Im Gegenteil: Es ist sowohl für die «normalen» Schüler als auch für die Lehrkräfte meist sehr motivierend, wenn im Leistungsbild der eigenen Musikschule auch die besonders Begabten zu finden sind. Sowohl in ihren solistischen Leistungen wie in ihrer Mitwirkung in den diversen Ensembles setzen sie positive Akzente.

Eigentlich nimmt doch die Musikschule mit der Ausbildung junger Musiker im beruflichen Vorfeld wenigstens teilweise eine staatliche Funktion wahr. Ist das ihre Aufgabe? Das kommt darauf an: In manchen Ländern gibt es zwischen den Musikschulen und der Berufsausbildung noch die Konservatorien als institutionelle Zwischenebene der

participation à diverses formes d'ensembles de musique de chambre, avec pratique de l'accompagnement pour les pianistes, participation à des orchestres ainsi que, obligatoirement, à une chorale.

Cette combinaison permet une formation musicale complète et fondamentale dont l'objectif n'est pas seulement l'examen d'entrée, mais un niveau de base des connaissances et du savoir-faire élevé au début des études, de sorte que la formation professionnelle proprement dite puisse se dérouler avec succès.

Mais toutes les écoles musique ne peuvent pas offrir une formation de ce type? Non. Ce sont principalement des institutions importantes avec un grand potentiel d'élèves et des enseignants qualifiés, de nombreux ensembles et des capacités de cours correspondantes qui y sont adaptées et s'y intéressent. Une coordination de cette formation et des participants est également souhaitable, par exemple sous forme d'un département particulier. Cependant, aucun enfant doué ne devrait être exclu de cette formation sous prétexte, par exemple, qu'il habite à la campagne. Des écoles de musique de dimensions plus réduites pourraient mettre en place une collaboration – même dans d'autres domaines, comme, par exemple, pour réunir un orchestre important. Il faudrait également procéder à une coordination en raison de la sollicitation énorme de temps et d'énergie à laquelle doivent faire face les élèves suivant une formation de préparation aux études supérieures.

Ne peut-il pas arriver que le déroulement «normal» des cours à l'école de musique souffre de ce qu'un soutien aussi massif soit apporté à quelques-uns? Non. Car ce n'est jamais qu'une minorité d'élèves, vraisemblablement moins de 5%, qui sont concernés par une formation de préparation aux études supérieures. Ce groupe n'a pratiquement pas de poids et ne dérange donc pas le fonctionnement de l'école de musique. Au contraire: il est la plupart du temps très motivant, tant pour les élèves «normaux» que pour les enseignants, si l'on rencontre, dans le profil de sa propre école de musique, des élèves particulièrement doués. Ils apportent des accents positifs, tant par leurs performances de solistes que par leur participation à divers ensembles.

are some exceptionally gifted musicians among the students at their own music school. Both in their achievements as soloists and as members of various ensembles they have a positive influence.

By training young musicians on their way to becoming professionals, music schools fulfil at least part of one of the functions of governmental resonsibility. Should this be their task? That depends: in some countries there are Conservatoires, institutions designed to provide an intermediate stage of tuition between music school and professional studies. But where this is not the case, music schools are best equipped to give such tuition – it is too much to expect of the music colleges. In any case, there should be co-operation between the two. It is important for music schools to be familiar with the content and standards of entrance examinations and that teaching for those wishing to go on to music college should cater for the needs of the diverse courses of studies (as soloist, orchestral musician, specialist music teacher, church organist and choirmaster, school music teacher, band leader, sound engineer, etc). A further responsibility in teaching future professionals is to give students proper advice about working conditions, opportunities and employment prospects in the music business. Taking on these areas of general responsibility should have implications for funding, too: the students' contribution should not exceed the cost of financing the First Study; the remaining costs should be met by public funds.

If public funds are being spent on this kind of specialist training, surely something can be expected in return? Certainly – first, students are selected on grounds of suitability, by means of an assessment test; then the students' progress and levels of attainment are regularly assessed; finally, they have to demonstrate their ability in public performances. Here, at the latest, when they take this step into a public role in local musical life, it may be judged «what the good of all this is». This kind of intensive musical training ensures the competence of another generation of professional musicians – and in music teaching, too. For among the young music students who have been fortunate enough to pass college entrance examinations thanks to the preparation provided at music school, there are the specialist music teachers for the next generation.

Studienvorbereitung. Wo diese aber nicht vorhanden ist, da ist die Musikschule der beste Ort – die Hochschulen wären damit überlastet. Allerdings sollten die Musikschulen mit den Musikhochschulen kooperieren. Es ist wichtig, daß sie die Inhalte und Standards der Aufnahmeprüfungen kennen und daß sie beim studienvorbereitenden Unterricht die unterschiedlichen musikalischen Studienrichtungen (Solisten, Orchestermusiker, Musikschullehrer, Kirchenmusiker, Musiklehrer, Kapellmeister, Tonmeister usw.) im Blick haben. Eine weitere Aufgabe der studienvorbereitenden Ausbildung ist es, die Schüler über musikalische Berufsbilder und -felder, Chancen und Perspektiven kompetent zu beraten. Diese Wahrnehmung staatlicher Aufgaben sollte auch Konsequenzen für die Finanzierung haben: Der Anteil der Teilnehmer sollte den Beitrag für den einfachen Hauptfachunterricht nicht übersteigen und die öffentliche Hand sollte die übrigen Kosten tragen.

Wenn für eine solche Spezialausbildung schon öffentliche Mittel ausgegeben werden, dann muß man doch auch einiges dafür verlangen können? Richtig – zunächst findet ja eine Auswahl der geeigneten Schüler statt, etwa durch eine Eignungsprüfung; dann wird die Entwicklung und Leistung der Teilnehmer regelmäßig überprüft; schließlich sollen sie ihr Können in öffentlichen Auftritten vorstellen. Spätestens hier, bei dem Schritt ins lokale öffentliche Musikleben, ist zu sehen, «was man davon hat». Diese intensivierte Musikausbildung sichert den Nachwuchs in den Musikberufen – und zwar auch in den musikpädagogischen Berufen. Denn unter den jungen Musikstudenten, die dank ihrer Förderung in der Musikschule die Aufnahmeprüfung glücklich bestanden haben, befinden sich auch wieder die zukünftigen Musikschullehrer.

En fait, l'école de musique, en se chargeant de la formation des jeunes musiciens dans un contexte pré-professionnel, assume au moins en partie l'un des devoirs de l'Etat. Est-ce là son rôle? Cela dépend: dans certains pays, il existe, entre les écoles de musique et la formation professionnelle, des conservatoires, intermédiaires institutionnels de la préparation aux études supérieures. S'ils n'existent pas, l'école de musique en est vraiment le lieu idéal, la sollicitation des établissements d'enseignement supérieur serait, sinon, trop importante. Mais les écoles de musique devraient coopérer avec les écoles supérieures de musique. Il est important qu'elles connaissent les contenus et les standards des examens d'entrée et qu'elles ne perdent pas de vue, au niveau des cours de préparation à des études supérieures, les différentes directions des études musicales (solistes, musiciens d'orchestre, professeurs d'école de musique, interprètes de musique religieuse, chefs d'orchestre, ingénieurs du son). Autre tâche de la formation de préparation aux études supérieures est de conseiller les élèves de manière compétente sur les profils et les domaines des métiers de la musique. Cette prise en charge des devoirs de l'Etat devrait également avoir des conséquences sur le financement: la participation financière des élèves ne devrait pas dépasser les droits correspondant aux cours de la matière principale simples, et les pouvoirs publics devraient prendre en charge la part restante.

Si des subventions publiques sont accordées à une formation aussi spécialisée, on doit pouvoir attendre une contrepartie correspondante? C'est vrai. On effectue tout d'abord une sélection des élèves adaptés, par exemple par des tests d'aptitude; ensuite, l'évolution et les performances des participants sont contrôlés régulièrement; enfin, ils doivent faire preuve de leur talent au cours de représentations publiques. C'est au plus tard à ce niveau, par le passage à une vie musicale publique locale, que l'on verra «ce qu'on en tire». Cette formation musicale intensifiée assure la relève dans les professions musicales – et ce également dans les professions de la pédagogie musicale. Car, parmi les jeunes étudiants en musique ayant passé avec succès, grâce à l'encouragement et au soutien apportés par l'école de musique, l'examen d'entrée, il s'en trouvera également de futurs professeurs d'école de musique.

And what if a student in whom the state has «invested» so much does not finish in becoming a professional musician? Then he will still have become a good musician – a good amateur musician, who with his commitment and ability will influence musical life outside the profession and help to build a lively musical culture such as one justly expects to find in Europe.   *uw.*

Competitions as Part of an Educational Programme

Wettbewerbe als pädagogische Aktion

Les concours en tant qu'action pédagogique

Music competitions have a special part to play in the process of training children and young people to play an instrument or to develop their singing voice, for the demands and performance standards of a competition can and should include a concern with educational values. To put it plainly: participation in a competition is not in conflict with the aims of musical education as long as preparation for a competition does not become an end in itself, but is properly incorporated in the teaching programme, without the pupil being forced or drilled. With the proper approach, preparation for a competiton can stimulate artistic and technical development, offering an important boost to a young person's enthusiasm, determination and stamina.

A teaching programme becomes more effective where the teacher, too, focuses on the educational value of such an undertaking. The best thing is for pupil and teacher to agree on participation in a competition as a teaching goal. Thus both pupil and teacher adopt this as a target for lessons and take an equal responsibility for progress. This kind of teaching goal concentrates a teacher's attention, as well as it encourages the pupil to practise – something which can be of value at every level of attainment, from beginners through to top-ranking artists.

It is part of the responsibility of the teacher to reach an accurate assessment of his pupil's capabilities, so that these are not exceeded. Works which are musically and technically too difficult for the pupil's level of attainment and maturity should

Und wenn nun ein Schüler, in den der Staat solchermaßen «investiert» hat, schließlich doch kein Berufsmusiker wird? Dann ist er trotzdem ein guter Musiker geworden – ein qualifizierter Laienmusiker, der mit seinem Engagement und Können das nichtprofessionelle Musikleben prägen und eine lebendige Musikkultur mitgestalten kann, wie man sie im Kulturraum Europa zu Recht erwartet.

uw.

Et si un élève dans lequel l'Etat a «investi» de cette manière ne devient pas musicien de métier? Il sera devenu tout de même un bon musicien – un amateur qualifié, qui, par son engagement et son talent, empreindra la vie musicale non professionnelle et pourra contribuer à une culture musicale vivante, telle qu'on est en droit de l'attendre dans l'espace culturel européen.

uw.

Musikwettbewerbe für Kinder und Jugendliche haben bei der Ausbildung auf einem Instrument oder im Fach Gesang einen besonderen Stellenwert. Denn mit Leistungsforderungen und Leistungserwartungen eines Wettbewerbs können und sollen sich pädagogische Aspekte mischen. Kurz gesagt: Die musikalische Ausbildung und die Beteiligung an einem Wettbewerb vertragen sich dann, wenn die Wettbewerbsvorbereitung nicht zum Selbstzweck wird, sondern ohne Zwang und Drill in das Unterrichtsgeschehen eingebettet ist. Dann kann die beabsichtigte Teilnahme an einem Wettbewerb die künstlerische und technische Leistung anspornen, Bereitschaft, Wille und Durchhaltevermögen gerade eines jungen Menschen entscheidend stärken.

Es intensiviert den Ausbildungsprozeß, wenn sich auch der Lehrer auf diesen pädagogischen Vorgang einstellt. Optimal ist die Lösung, daß Schüler und Lehrer die Wettbewerbsbeteiligung als klares Unterrichtsziel verabreden. Damit stellen sich beide, Schüler und Lehrer, im Unterricht auf diese Vorgabe ein und stehen beide in gemeinsamer Verantwortung. Ein solches Unterrichtsziel optimiert den pädagogischen Einsatz ebenso wie das Üben des Schülers – ein Prozeß, der für jede Ausbildungsstufe von der Unterstufe bis zur künstlerischen Spitze Gültigkeit haben kann.

In der Verantwortung des Lehrers liegt es, das Leistungsvermögen seines Schülers richtig einzuschätzen, so daß es zu keiner Überforderung kommt. Musikalisch und technisch für den Ausbildungs- und Reifestand des Schülers zu schwierige

Les concours musicaux pour les enfants et les adolescents occupent une place toute particulière dans l'apprentissage d'un instrument ou une formation de chant. Car des aspects pédagogiques peuvent et doivent se mêler aux exigences et aux attentes de performances liées à un concours. En résumé: la formation musicale et la participation à un concours sont compatibles dans la mesure où un concours n'est pas un but en soi, mais qu'il est inclus sans contrainte et sans entraînement sévère dans le déroulement du cours. La participation prévue à un concours peut alors stimuler la performance artistique et technique, et renforcer de manière décisive la volonté et la ténacité, en particulier chez l'individu jeune.

Si le professeur se prépare intérieurement à ce phénomène pédagogique, le processus d'apprentissage s'en trouvera intensifié. La solution optimale serait que l'élève et le professeur se mettent d'accord en commun sur la participation à un concours comme objectif précis des cours. Ainsi, professeur et élève se préparent tous deux intérieurement à un cours correspondant à ce but fixé et leur responsabilité est commune. Un tel objectif optimalise la mise en jeu pédagogique ainsi que l'exercice de l'élève – un processus valable à tous les niveaux de la formation, du niveau inférieur à la performance artistique de pointe.

L'appréciation correcte des facultés de l'élève, de sorte qu'il ne se produise pas de sollicitation exagérée, revient à la responsabilité de l'enseignant. Sur le plan musical et technique, il convient d'éviter des oeuvres trop difficiles pour le niveau et la maturité

be avoided. It is up to the teacher to obtain an accurate idea of the requirements and organization details of a competition. Disappointments for candidates, their parents and teachers can be avoided by not attempting to prepare unrealistically difficult, over-ambitious pieces.

The pupil's mental attitude also has an important role here. If entering a competition ought to be a positive and useful experience, then no false hopes should be aroused in preparing for it. Of course, both pupils and teachers hope to win recognition and praise in the competition. Already in preparing for a competition there are positive gains to be had, such as the impetus to a higher level of attainment, increased confidence in playing to a critical audience and overcoming nerves and anxiety. Playing in front of other students can serve as preparation for this. Neither the prize itself nor the awarding of the prize should be identified as ends in themselves; the envisaged gain should be in intensive work on the chosen pieces, contact with other musicians and the opportunity to compare one's performance with that of others of the same age. Listening and learning – through sharing experiences and talking to each other and to members of the jury – should be seen as the chief benefit in all this. Whether young competitors are able to take this attitude depends largely on the approach adopted by responsible adults, that is, parents and teachers. They have achieved the most important objective if they succeed in cultivating this kind of constructive approach in the young performers and in themselves.

Werke gilt es zu vermeiden. Aufgabe des Lehrers ist es, sich ein genaues Bild über Ansprüche und Gepflogenheiten eines Wettbewerbs zu machen. Enttäuschungen für Wettbewerbskandidaten, Eltern und Lehrer lassen sich vermeiden, wenn auf überzogene, allzu ehrgeizige Vorspielprogramme von vornherein verzichtet wird.

Eine wichtige Rolle spielt auch die psychologische Begleitung des Schülers. Soll eine Wettbewerbsbeteiligung positiv und als Gewinn erlebt werden, so darf schon im Vorfeld keine falsche Erwartungshaltung erzeugt werden. Natürlich erhoffen sich Schüler und Lehrer durch den Wettbewerb Bestätigung und Anerkennung. Schon in der Vorbereitung zum Wettbewerb ist Positives zu sehen, z. B. der erreichte Leistungsschub, die gewonnene Spielsicherheit vor kritischem Publikum und das Überwinden von Aufregung und Angst. Dies kann bereits vorweg in Schülervorspielen trainiert werden. Nicht Preis und Prämierung sollen als Ziel deklariert werden, sondern die intensive Erarbeitung des gewählten Programms, die Begegnung mit anderen, der in Aussicht stehende Leistungsvergleich mit Gleichaltrigen. Zuhören und Lernen – im Erfahrungsaustausch untereinander und mit den Juroren – sollten als der entscheidende Gewinn im Vordergrund stehen. Ob die jugendlichen Wettbewerbsteilnehmer diese Einstellung finden können, liegt vor allem an der pädagogischen Verantwortung der Erwachsenen, also der Eltern und Lehrer. Sie haben das Entscheidende erreicht, wenn es ihnen gelingt, bei dem jugendlichen Teilnehmer und bei sich selbst ein solches konstruktives Verhältnis zu dem Wettbewerb zu entwickeln.

Es ist wichtig, sich zu vergegenwärtigen, daß Juryentscheidungen – trotz einiger weniger objektiv feststellbarer Kriterien wie Technik, Tonbildung, Texttreue – im Hinblick auf die musikalisch-künstlerische Beurteilung letztlich nur subjektiv sein können. Jedes Jurymitglied hat eigene Maßstäbe, persönliche Geschmacksvorstellungen und Vorlieben, die vorwiegend aus der eigenen Ausbildungstradition herrühren. Zu den Spielregeln eines Wettbewerbs gehört, daß alle Beteiligten – der Wettbewerbskandidat genauso wie sein Lehrer, die Mitglieder der Jury genauso wie der Veranstalter – die Teilnahmebedingungen akzeptieren. Das bedeutet auch die vorbehaltlose Anerkennung der Be-

de l'élève. La tâche du professeur est de se faire une idée précise des exigences et des habitudes du concours. Les déceptions pour les candidats, les parents et les enseignants peuvent être évitées si l'on renonce dès le départ à des programmes de représentation exagérés, trop ambitieux.

L'encadrement psychologique de l'élève joue également un rôle important. Si l'on veut parvenir à une expérience positive du concours, considérée comme un enrichissement, il ne faut pas, dans la période préliminaire, donner naissance à une attitude d'attente erronée. Bien évidemment, élèves et enseignants attendent du concours une approbation et une reconnaissance. La préparation du concours même a des côtés positifs, par exemple la progression de la performance, l'acquisition d'une certaine assurance du jeu devant un public critique et la capacité à surmonter sa nervosité et sa peur. Ceci peut faire l'objet d'un entraînement préparatoire en jouant devant les autres élèves. Le but déclaré du concours ne doit pas être le prix ou la distinction, mais le travail intense du programme choisi, la rencontre avec les autres, la comparaison avec les enfants du même âge. Le fait d'écouter et d'apprendre – et d'échanger ses expériences avec les autres et avec le jury – devrait constituer le gain décisif à placer au premier plan. C'est la responsabilité pédagogique des adultes, c'est-à-dire des parents et des enseignants qui décideront de ce que les jeunes participants au concours parviennent à cet état d'esprit. Ils auront apporté leur contribution décisive s'ils parviennent à développer, chez le jeune participant et pour eux-mêmes, une relation constructive de ce type vis-à-vis du concours.

Il est important de réaliser que les décisions du jury – malgré quelques critères objectifs contrôlables peu nombreux, tels que la technique, la formation du ton, la fidélité au texte – ne peuvent qu'être subjectifs dans leur jugement musical artistique. Chaque membre du jury a ses critères propres, son goût et ses préférences personnels, provenant la plupart du temps de sa propre tradition d'apprentissage. Le fait que tous les participants – le candi-

It is important to remember that decisions reached by a panel of judges – notwithstanding a few criteria which may be assessed with a degree of objectivity, such as technique, quality of tone, accuracy – must remain subjective with regard to musical and artistic assessment. Every judge has his or her own standards, personal tastes and preferences, which generally stem from their own background and training. It is one of the rules of the game that all participants in a competition – the candidates entering the competition as well as their teachers, judges and organizers – accept the conditions of participation. This includes unquestioning acceptance of the judges' decision, whatever it may be and whether or not others agree with it. It is not unknown for candidates, their parents or teachers to challenge the judges' decision, because their impressions of a competition performance are mixed with what they know of the candidate's playing through long acquaintance and previous experience, where a pupil may have given better or more impressive performances in the past. In a competition, however, it is just the one performance that has to be evaluated, with whatever happens to be shown or heard in that single performance, rather than judging a candidate's broader potential.

This does not mean, however, that talent may not be discovered through performance in competitions: here, teachers and those responsible for music schools have to begin considering ways of helping to develop the gifts thus discovered. Panels of judges who make themselves available to give advice after the competition make what may be the most useful educational contribution of the whole event. Music schools, too, might invite people to follow-up discussions with the judges, where the competition results, problems in presentation, selecting appropriate pieces, interpretation and preparation could be talked through. In this way, evaluation of competition results could be a useful training procedure for teachers and serve at the same time as preparation for the next competition they enter.

urteilung durch die eingesetzte Jury, ganz gleich wie sie ausfällt und ob andere damit konform gehen oder nicht. Es kommt vor, daß Teilnehmer, Eltern oder Lehrer Juryentscheidungen beanstanden, weil sich die Wettbewerbseindrücke mit Kenntnissen und Erfahrungen aus einer langen Beobachtungszeit vermischen, wo dem Schüler andere Vorspiele besser oder eindrucksvoller gelungen sein mögen. Im Wettbewerb aber geht es allein um die Bewertung der im Vorspiel ad hoc gezeigten und gehörten Leistung und nicht um die Beurteilung einer latenten Begabung.

Dies schließt wiederum nicht aus, daß in Wettbewerben sehr wohl Begabungen erkannt werden. Hier haben nun die Pädagogen und die Musikschule mit Überlegungen einzusetzen, wie die erkannten Begabungen weiter zu fördern sind. Jurygremien, die nach dem Wettbewerb für beratende Gespräche zur Verfügung stehen, erfüllen damit die vielleicht wichtigste pädagogische Funktion des Wettbewerbs. Auch die Musikschule könnte zu einem nachbereitenden Gespräch mit den Juroren einladen, in dem die Ergebnisse des Wettbewerbs, Probleme der Präsentation, des Programms, der Interpretation und der Einstudierung offen erörtert werden. Damit würde die Wettbewerbsauswertung zur konstruktiven Lehrerfortbildung und diente gleichzeitig der Vorbereitung zur nächsten Wettbewerbsbeteiligung.

Wichtig erscheint die Einsicht, daß die Weiterförderung entdeckter musikalischer Talente nicht im, sondern nach dem Wettbewerb einsetzen muß. So sollte dem Wettbewerb selbst ein Förderprogramm für dessen Preisträger, möglicherweise für alle Teilnehmer nachfolgen. Neben anschließenden Konzerten mit den Preisträgern können dies vor allem Angebote für Beratungsgespräche mit den Juroren sein, aber auch spezielle Workshops, Seminare und Kurse mit ausgesuchten Fachleuten. Für Solisten und deren Begleitpartner sollten Initiativen für kammermusikalische Betätigung unter fachkundiger Betreuung geschaffen werden. Regionale, nationale und internationale Jugendorchester stützen sich bei ihrer Zusammensetzung gerne auf junge Musiker, die sich vorher in Wettbewerben qualifiziert haben. Preisträger von Wettbewerben sind dankbare Teilnehmer bei Musik-Camps und anderen internationalen Begegnungsprogrammen. Die

dat aussi bien que son professeur, les membres du jury et les organisateurs – acceptent les conditions de participation fait partie des règles du jeu. Ceci implique la reconnaissance sans réserve du jugement du jury, quel qu'il soit, et que d'autres soient d'accord avec lui ou non. Il arrive que des participants, des parents ou des enseignants remettent en cause les décisions du jury, parce que les impressions de concours se mêlent avec des connaissances et des expériences résultant d'une période d'observation prolongée au cours de laquelle l'élève a interprété des morceaux avec plus de réussite ou d'expressivité à d'autres occasions. Mais, lors du concours, il s'agit seulement de l'évaluation de la performance montrée et écoutée ad hoc, et non du jugement d'un talent latent.

Ceci n'exclut cependant pas, d'autre part, le fait que les concours puissent contribuer à la découverte de talents. C'est là que doivent s'amorcer les réflexions des pédagogues et de l'école de musique sur la manière de soutenir et d'encourager les talents découverts. Des conseils composés des membres du jury, qui se tiennent à disposition pour des rendez-vous conseils après le concours, remplissent la fonction pédagogique la plus importante du concours. L'école de musique pourrait également inviter à une discussion avec les membres du jury, discussion reprenant et expliquant ouvertement les résultats du concours, les problèmes de la présentation, du programme, de l'interprétation et de l'étude. Ainsi, l'évaluation du concours se transformerait en une formation continue constructive des professeurs et servirait en même temps de préparation à la prochaine participation.

Il est important de comprendre que le soutien et l'encouragement des talents musicaux découverts ne doit pas avoir lieu pendant, mais après le concours. Un programme de soutien et d'encouragement devrait faire suite au concours même pour le gagnant, dans la mesure du possible pour l'ensemble des participants. Outre des concerts donnés par les participants ayant obtenu un prix, il pourrait s'agir principalement de conversations conseils avec les membres du jury, mais également d'ateliers de travail spéciaux, de séminaires, de cours avec des spécialistes sélectionnés. Pour les solistes et leur partenaires d'accompagnement, il pourrait être créé des initiatives en vue d'une acti-

It seems important to emphasize that further measures in developing those musical talents that are discovered should begin after, rather than during, the competition. A competition should thus be followed up with a programme of support for prize-winners – maybe even for all the candidates. As well as having prize-winners perform in concerts following the awards, this might well take the form of offering consultations with the panel of judges, but there could also be workshops, seminars and courses with visiting specialists. For soloists and their accompanists, opportunities should be created for playing chamber music with coaching by experts. Regional, national and international youth orchestras are always glad to draw in young musicians who have already demonstrated their worth in competitions, and competition prizewinners go on to enjoy participation at music camps and other international events. Practical support through state funding or sponsorship is an important consideration here.

It is the responsibility of music schools to support and encourage the exceptionally gifted, as well as contributing to general musicianship. Therefore it is right for them to be closely involved in music competitions and their organization. This can include providing opportunities for participants who are not regular pupils at music schools. There are many ways in which music schools can support the idea of educationally oriented competitions:

- providing consultations before and after a competition for candidates and their parents and teachers;
- providing information on music colleges and careers advice for young people who hope to become professional musicians;
- providing various opportunities for ensemble playing, particularly for young «soloists» looking for groups to play in;
- providing opportunities for competition candidates to perform in music school concerts, even when they are not pupils at the school, and inviting them to music weekends and special courses.

It remains one of the tasks of music schools to work towards a goal formulated thus in 1975 by Siegfried Borris, President of the German Music

materielle Förderung durch staatliche Mittel oder durch Sponsoren ist dabei ein wichtiger Gesichtspunkt.

Musikschulen haben die Aufgabe, neben der Breitenarbeit auch Spitzenförderung zu leisten. Darum ist es richtig, wenn sie mit den Musikwettbewerben und ihren Organisationen intensiv zusammenarbeiten. Dies kann auch Angebote für solche Teilnehmer einschließen, die nicht als Musikschüler unmittelbar von ihrer Musikschule betreut werden. Es gibt eine Reihe von Möglichkeiten, wie Musikschulen die Idee pädagogisch orientierter Wettbewerbe unterstützen können:

- beratende Gespräche vor und nach dem Wettbewerb für Teilnehmer sowie deren Eltern und Lehrer;
- studien- und berufsberatende Information für Jugendliche, die einen Musikberuf anstreben;
- vielfache Angebote des Ensemblespiels, gerade auch für junge «Solisten», die Spielpartner suchen;
- Angebote, Wettbewerbsteilnehmer in Konzerten der Musikschule auftreten zu lassen, auch wenn sie nicht Schüler sind und sie zu Musizierwochenden und -freizeiten mit einzuladen.

Es bleibt eine der Aufgaben der Musikschulen, einem Ziel nachzustreben, das Siegfried Borris 1975 als Präsident des Deutschen Musikrats so formulierte: «Sicher aber ist, daß die Musikschulen in Zukunft wesentliche Verantwortung dafür tragen könnten, daß dieses kostbare Kapital an Musizierwillen und Begabung jugendlicher Spieler später

vité dans le domaine de la musique de chambre, avec un encadrement spécialisé. Les orchestres de jeunes régionaux, nationaux et internationaux s'appuient volontiers sur de jeunes musiciens qui ont fait preuve de leur qualification auparavant dans des concours. Les candidats ayant obtenus un prix sont des participants tout trouvés pour les camps de musique et autres programmes de rencontre internationaux. Le soutien matériel apporté par l'intermédiaire de subventions de l'Etat ou par des sponsors constitue ici un aspect important.

Les écoles de musique ont la tâche, parallèlement au travail de masse, de contribuer à l'encouragement et au soutien des élèves doués. C'est pourquoi il est important qu'elles travaillent en étroite collaboration avec les concours et leurs organisateurs. Ceci peut impliquer une série de possibilités offertes aux participants qui ne sont pas directement élèves de l'école de musique et ne sont pas encadrés directement par celle-ci. Les écoles de musique peuvent apporter leur soutien à l'idée de concours à orientation pédagogique de maintes manières:

- par des conversations-conseils avant et après le concours pour les participants ainsi que leurs parents et leurs professeurs;
- une information concernant les études et les professions pour les jeunes désirant exercer un métier musical;
- des possibilités de jouer dans un ensemble, surtout pour de jeunes «solistes», la recherche de partenaires;
- des possibilités de donner des concerts à l'école de musique pour les participants au concours, même s'ils ne sont pas élèves, et de les inviter à des week-ends et loisirs musicaux.

L'aspiration au but formulé comme suit par Siegfried Borris en 1975, en sa qualité de président du Conseil allemand de la musique reste une des tâches de l'école de musique: «Mais il est certain que les écoles de musique pourraient contribuer de manière essentielle, à l'avenir, à ce que le précieux capital de la volonté de faire de la musique et des dons des jeunes interprètes puisse profiter vraiment un jour à la vie musicale. Ceci implique que les écoles de musique devraient s'occuper de cette foule d'enfants doués qui n'ont pas réussi à faire le

«It is more important to learn to play an instrument than learning to use a typewriter.»

Bertel Haarder
former minister
for education in Denmark

Council: «What is certain is that music schools will in future have to bear a considerable responsibility that this valuable stock of musical enthusiasm and talent among young players will later be making a real contribution to public musical life. This means that music schools should also attend to the needs of that large group of talented people who do not manage the difficult leap into the sunshine and the limelight so far reserved for the first prize winners. But resources must be found for the development and encouragement of that other large group for whom no authority previously felt responsible.»

er.

Further Training for Music School Teachers

Fortbildung für Musikschullehrer

La formation continue des professeurs d'école de musique

If music schools are to provide pupils with an up-to-date curriculum and teaching methods which answer their technical and artistic needs, then it is vital to provide for the further training and professional development of their teaching staff. Interest in programmes of this kind is evident from the great voluntary demand for opportunities to extend professional competence and add to qualifications (only in Upper Austria is there a contractual obligation to involvement in staff development programmes). There is clearly a call for courses, seminars and workshops for music school teachers; such courses are already available in many places, but need to be extended continually. It is important that this high level of commitment should not be wasted through financial shortsightedness on the part of those responsible for music schools and for the allocation of public funds.

In-service training for music school teachers can have two distinct principal aims:

- Firstly, it helps teachers to maintain and extend knowledge and skills which they may already have acquired in their years of training, and to adapt these to the needs of a changing profession.
- Secondly, «further education» can lead to the attainment of additional professional qualifications: training in teaching methods, a teaching qualification in another subject, or improved qualifications to support the advancement of a teaching career.

auch wirklich einmal dem Musikleben zugute kommen wird. Das beinhaltet, daß sich die Musikschulen auch um jene große Gruppen von Begabten zu kümmern hätten, denen nicht der Sprung auf den schmalen Streifen der Sonnenseite und des Rampenlichts geglückt ist, das sich bisher nur auf die 1. Preisträger richtete. Aber gerade für die vielen anderen, mit denen sich bisher keine Instanz zu beschäftigen verpflichtet fühlte, sollten Wege zur Entfaltung und Förderung gesucht werden.»   *er.*

saut du côté ensoleillé mais étroit des feux de la rampe, qui ne se tournent jusqu'à présent que vers le premier prix. Mais c'est justement pour les autres, nombreux, dont aucune instance ne se sent moralement obligée de s'occuper, qu'il faudrait rechercher des possibilités d'épanouissement, et d'encouragement et de soutien.

er.

Damit Musikschulen ihren Schülern einen Unterricht erteilen können, der den aktuellen pädagogischen und inhaltlichen Erkenntnissen folgt und fachlich und künstlerisch überzeugt, ist die qualitätvolle Fortbildung der Lehrkräfte unverzichtbar. Ihr prinzipiell freiwilliges Engagement dazu (nur im österreichischen Bundesland Oberösterreich gibt es eine vertragliche Fortbildungspflicht) äußert sich in der ausgesprochen starken Nachfrage nach Möglichkeiten zur Erweiterung der beruflichen Kompetenz und Qualifikation. Dieses offensichtlich vorhandene Bedürfnis der Musikschullehrer sucht ein Angebot von Kursen, Seminaren, Workshops und dergleichen, das vielerorts auch vorhanden ist, aber kaum breit genug sein kann. Schließlich darf sich dieses erfreuliche Engagement nicht durch finanzielle Kurzsichtigkeit von Musikschulträgern und anderen Zuschußgebern der öffentlichen Hand gebremst sehen.

Fortbildung für Musikschullehrer kann grundsätzlich zwei verschiedene Ziele haben:

- Zum einen dient sie dem Erhalt und der Vertiefung von bereits vorhandenen, in der Berufsausbildung erworbenen Kenntnissen und Fertigkeiten sowie zur Anpassung an ein sich veränderndes Berufsbild.
- Zum andern führt sie als «Weiterbildung» zum Erwerb zusätzlicher beruflicher Qualifikationen: einer pädagogischen Ausbildung, einer Lehrbefähigung in einem weiteren Fach oder zur Absicherung eines beruflichen Aufstiegs.

Afin que les écoles de musique puissent donner à leurs élèves des cours correspondant aux connaissances pédagogiques et spécialisées actuelles et convaincants sur le plan artistique et des contenus, une formation continue de qualité est indispensable pour les enseignants. Leur engagement volontaire de principe dans ce domaine (il n'existe une obligation de se soumettre à la formation continue réglée par contrat que dans le Land autrichien de la Haute-Autriche) se traduit par une demande extrêmement forte de possibilités d'élargissement de la compétence et de la qualification professionnelles. Ce besoin manifeste des professeurs d'école de musique appelle une offre de cours, de séminaires, d'ateliers de travail et autres, existant déjà dans beaucoup d'endroits, mais qui ne saurait être suffisante. Enfin, cet engagement réjouissant ne doit pas être freiné par la myopie financière des responsables des écoles de musique et autres donneurs de subventions des pouvoirs publics.

La formation continue des professeurs travaillant dans les écoles de musique, peut, par principe, avoir deux objectifs différents:

- D'une part, elle sert au maintien et à l'approfondissement des connaissances et du savoir-faire existants, acquis au cours de la formation professionnelle, ainsi qu'à l'adaptation d'un profil professionnel qui se modifie.
- D'autre part, elle conduit, à titre de «formation complémentaire», à l'acquisition de qualifica-

The need for in-service training to maintain, develop and extend existing professional skills is illustrated simply by a glance at the increasingly large publishers' catalogues: the wealth of printed matter even extends to the methodology of music teaching. Music written for tuition purposes, studies, pieces designed to develop students' playing skills, ensemble repertoire, and then books and papers on the theory and methodology of teaching in music schools, too – all this is expected to be noted and studied by the teacher. In addition, a music school teacher has to devote considerable time to maintaining his or her own instrumental skills through practice. Music practice requires and develops patience, concentration and discipline, and here the teacher is a role model for his or her pupils. Every teacher of music has to set aside considerable time and energy for all these aspects of «further training», being regular activities, in the course of the normal teaching duties.

Then there are specific in-service training courses, seminars and conferences. These are vital to the work of the music teacher, for routine establishes habits and patterns of behaviour which are not otherwise questioned. People become set in their ways and start to reason that «It has stood the test of time, because that's the way we've always done it.» In-service training sessions can encourage people to be self-critical and to examine their own behaviour. Training events can introduce new teaching materials, new approaches, new and old ideas for lesson plans and for dealing with problems, far more effectively than individual private study; they provide an opportunity to examine issues, join in discussions and exchange experiences with interested colleagues. Even one's own playing as a musician needs new input – extending and developing technique, or new approaches to interpretation – which can best be supplied through direct contact with properly qualified colleagues.

The knowledge, skills and abilities acquired in a few years' training are not sufficient reserves for a

Die Wichtigkeit einer «Fortbildung» mit dem Ziel des Erhalts, der Vertiefung und Weiterentwicklung des bereits vorhandenen beruflichen Rüstzeugs zeigt allein schon ein Blick in die an Umfang zunehmenden Verlagskataloge: Die Menge an Gedrucktem betrifft auch die Fachdidaktik des Musikschullehrers. Unterrichtswerke, Etüden, pädagogische Spielstücke, Ensemble-Literatur, aber auch Bücher und Zeitschriften zur Didaktik und Methodik des Musikschulunterrichts – das alles will vom Lehrer zur Kenntnis genommen und studiert werden. Es kommt hinzu, daß sich der Musikschullehrer ständig um den Erhalt seiner eigenen instrumentalen Fertigkeiten bemühen, also üben muß. Üben trainiert auch Geduld, Konzentration und Disziplin, und das Üben des Lehrers ist Vorbild für seine Schüler. Dies sind alles regelmäßige Fortbildungsaktivitäten im Rahmen der normalen Unterrichtsverpflichtung, für die jeder Musikpädagoge Zeit und Energie in beträchtlichem Ausmaß reservieren muß.

Hinzu kommt die spezielle Fortbildung in Lehrgängen, Seminaren und Tagungen. Sie ist für den Alltag des Musikschullehrers jedoch von großer Bedeutung: Der Beruf bildet Gewohnheiten und Verhaltensweisen aus, die nicht mehr hinterfragt werden. Diese erstarren zu Schematismen, die mit der Begründung beibehalten werden: «Das hat sich bewährt, denn wir haben das schon immer so gemacht.» Der Besuch von Fortbildungsveranstaltungen kann Selbstkritik auslösen und zur Überprüfung des eigenen Verhaltens anregen. Fortbildungen bringen neues Unterrichtsmaterial, neue methodische Ansätze, neue und alte Inhalte und Probleme viel intensiver nahe als das Selbststudium; sie bieten Gelegenheit, gemeinsam mit engagierten Fachkollegen zu hinterfragen, zu diskutieren, und Erfahrungen auszutauschen. Auch der eigenen Musizierpraxis können praktisch nur im direkten Kontakt mit Dozenten neue Impulse – Vertiefung und Erweiterung von Techniken oder Anregungen zur Interpretation – zuwachsen.

Das während der Ausbildung erworbene Wissen, die Kenntnisse und Fähigkeiten reichen als Vorrat nicht für ein ganzes Berufsleben aus. Wertvorstellungen verändern sich und prägen Hörgewohnheiten und Interessen der jungen Generation. Entsprechend verschieben sich die Schwerpunkte zeit-

tions professionnelles supplémentaires: formation pédagogique, certificat d'aptitude à l'enseignement dans une autre matière ou garantie d'un avancement professionnel.

Un coup d'oeil dans les catalogues – de plus en plus volumineux – des maisons d'édition suffit à montrer l'importance d'une «formation continue» ayant pour but le maintien, l'approfondissement et le développement d'un outillage professionnel déjà existant: la masse des publications concerne également la didactique du professeur à l'école de musique. Les ouvrages scolaires, les études, les morceaux pédagogiques, la littérature d'ensemble, mais aussi les livres et revues de didactique et de méthodologie du cours de musique – le professeur doit en prendre connaissance et étudier tout cela. S'y ajoute le fait que le professeur de musique doit travailler constamment au maintien de son propre savoir-faire instrumental, c'est-à-dire qu'il doit s'exercer. S'exercer est aussi un entraînement à la patience, à la concentration et à la discipline, et le professeur qui s'exerce est un modèle pour ses élèves. Ce sont là des activités de formation continue régulières, dans le cadre des devoirs liés au cours normal, pour lesquelles tout enseignant doit réserver du temps et de l'énergie dans une proportion non moindre.

S'y ajoute la formation continue particulière au cours de cycles de formation, séminaires et sessions. Elle est cependant d'une grande importance pour la vie quotidienne du professeur enseignant à l'école de musique: le métier conditionne des habitudes et des comportements sur lesquels on ne réfléchit plus par la suite. Ils se fixent en schématismes qui sont conservés avec l'argumentation suivante: «Cela a fait ses preuves, car on a toujours fait ça comme ça.» La participation à des manifestations de formation continue peut déclencher un phénomène d'autocritique et inciter à examiner de plus près son propre comportement. Les mesures de formation continue apportent un matériel d'enseignement nouveau, des points de départ méthodologiques nouveaux, et permettent d'être confronté de manière plus intensive avec les contenus et les problèmes anciens et nouveaux qu'on ne peut le faire soi-même en autodidacte; elles offrent la possibilité de réfléchir ensemble avec des collègues engagés, de discuter et d'échanger des expérien-

«Si la musique nous est si chère, c'est qu'elle est la parole la plus profonde de l'âme.

Cette maxime du Prix Nobel de la littérature Romain Rolland traduit à merveille le sens et la valeur de la musique qui, sous toutes ses formes, est le plus noble instrument de communication. C'est un moyen d'expression universel, une véritable médiatrice culturelle, qui balaye toute barrière linguistique et toute frontière étatique.

La connaissance du solfège n'est certes pas une condition sine qua non pour apprécier la musique, mais les programmes scolaires devraient néanmoins tenir compte dans une plus large mesure de l'éducation musicale, partie intégrante d'une bonne culture générale.

L'objectif d'une formation musicale élémentaire des enfants et adolescents à l'école n'est pas d'en faire à tout prix des musiciens professionnels ou même des virtuoses. L'enseignement musical doit plutôt servir à familiariser davantage les jeunes avec les différentes civilisations à travers cet art sublime qu'est la musique.

life-long professional career. Values change and influence the listening habits and interests of the younger generation. To keep pace with this, the focus of contemporary work at music schools has shifted to include popular music and its instruments. The teacher should be familiar with music that young people can relate to, and should use it in lessons. He will have difficulty in stimulating lasting interest in young people if he confines himself to ideas formed in his own youth and moulded by his own years of study. A further example of this is found in group tuition, a mode of teaching that has its own dynamic and which calls for teaching methods very different from those still favoured by many teachers schooled in individual tuition. Training courses which demonstrate convincing methodology can be very effective in overcoming such prejudice and providing practical support for classroom teaching.

All the European associations of music schools see the continuing professional development of teachers as one of their principal tasks. Even those societies recently formed for the sake of promoting particular instruments – often with European umbrella organizations such as the «European String Teachers Association» (ESTA), the «European Piano Teachers Association» (EPTA), the «European Guitar Teachers Association» (EGTA) and others – all organize their own seminars and conferences. The music school teacher looking for further training opportunities will, however, find others in the calendar of events of societies whose membership is not specifically geared towards music school teachers, such as the «International Society for Development in Music Education» or the «International Music Association».

Further professional training with the aim of acquiring additional qualifications, as a second focus of interest, has some appeal for numerous groups within the profession. There are those, on the one hand, who are not fully qualified as music teachers, lacking either instrumental diplomas or teaching certificates. In-service training can enable them to «catch up» on these qualifications; educationalists, music teachers at general schools or musicologists can pursue artistic development as instrumentalists; church musicians, players in military bands and orchestral musicians, all highly skilled in play-

gemäßer Musikschularbeit bis in den Bereich der Popularmusik und ihres Instrumentariums. Der Lehrer sollte Musik kennen, die dem Lebensgefühl der Jugend entspricht, und in seinen Unterricht einbeziehen. Es wird ihm nur schwer gelingen, Jugendliche dauerhaft zu motivieren, wenn er sich ausschließlich auf seine in der eigenen Jugend gebildeten und im Studium geprägten Wertvorstellungen beschränkt. Ein anderes Beispiel ist der Gruppenunterricht, eine Unterrichtsform mit eigener Didaktik, der noch bei vielen Lehrern das im eigenen Studium erworbene Credo für den Einzelunterricht entgegensteht. Fortbildungen mit überzeugenden didaktischen Modellen können dieses Vorurteil durchaus korrigieren und gleichzeitig praktische Unterrichtshilfen für die Lehrkräfte zur Verfügung stellen.

Alle europäischen Musikschulverbände sehen in der Lehrerfortbildung eine ihrer Kernaufgaben. Auch die in jüngerer Zeit gebildeten Vereinigungen zur Förderung und Pflege bestimmter Instrumente – oft mit europäischen Dachverbänden wie die «European String Teachers Association» (ESTA), die «European Piano Teachers Association» (EPTA), die «European Guitar Teachers Association» (EGTA) und andere – führen Seminare und Kongresse durch. Der fortbildungswillige Musikschullehrer findet aber auch Angebote in den Veranstaltungskalendern solcher Gesellschaften, zu deren Zielgruppen nicht spezifisch die Musikschullehrer zählen, etwa die der «Internationalen Gesellschaft für musikpädagogische Fortbildung» (IGMF) oder des «Internationalen Arbeitskreises für Musik» (IAM).

Die «Weiterbildung» mit dem Ziel des Erwerbs zusätzlicher Berufsqualifikationen als zweiter

ces. Et c'est seulement le contact direct avec des enseignants qui peut permettre de donner des impulsions nouvelles à sa propre pratique musicale – approfondissement et élargissement de techniques ou d'incitations à l'interprétation.

Le savoir acquis pendant la formation, les connaissances et le savoir-faire ne suffisent pas à remplir toute une vie professionnelle. La conception des valeurs change et détermine les habitudes auditives et les intérêts de la jeune génération. Les points forts du travail actuel des écoles de musique se décalent de manière correspondante jusque dans les domaines de la musique populaire et des instruments en relevant. Le professeur devrait connaître de la musique répondant au sentiment vital de la jeunesse et l'inclure à son cours. Il lui sera difficile de motiver les jeunes de manière durable s'il se limite exclusivement aux valeurs conçues dans sa propre jeunesse et empreintes par ses études. Un autre exemple est le travail de groupe, une forme de cours à la didactique propre, qui, pour beaucoup d'enseignants, s'oppose encore au credo du cours particulier. Des formations continues avec des modèles didactiques convaincants peuvent corriger ce préjugé et mettre à la disposition des enseignants des auxiliaires d'enseignement précieux.

Toutes les associations internationales d'écoles de musique considèrent la formation continue des professeurs comme l'une de leurs tâches centrales. Les associations d'encouragement et de soutien d'instruments particuliers fondées plus récemment – souvent avec des organismes de tutelle européens tels que la «European String Teachers Association» (ESTA), la «European Piano Teachers Association» (EPTA), la «European Guitar Association» (EGTA) et autres – organisent des séminaires et des congrès. Mais les professeurs d'école de musique désirant se soumettre à une formation continue trouvent également des possibilités de le faire dans des calendriers de manifestations de sociétés dont les groupes-cibles ne sont pas spécifiquement les professeurs d'école de musique. C'est le cas, par exemple, de la «Société Internationale de Formation Continue Pédagogico-musicale» ou du «Cercle International de Travail pour la Musique».

*Les écoles de musique vien-
nent heureusement combler
les lacunes qui existent trop
souvent au sein des dif-
férents systèmes d'en-
seignement. Leur mission
doit consister non seulement
à fournir de solides connaissances de base aux plus
doués afin de leur permettre
de développer et de mettre
en valeur leur talent, mais il
leur incombe aussi d'assurer une instruction plus
intensive des jeunes instrumentistes et choristes. Ces
écoles doivent être accessibles à tous ceux qui désirent
s'initier à la musique et c'est
justement pour cette raison
que leur implantation régionale revêt une importance
indéniable.*

*A un moment où l'Union
européenne ne cesse de
s'agrandir et où l'entente
entre les peuples devient
plus nécessaire que jamais,
puisque l'Europe ne devra
pas se limiter à une
immense communauté
d'intérêts économiques,
l'Union Européenne des
Ecoles de Musique aura à
jouer un rôle primordial
d'organisation et de coordination. Si nous voulons que
l'Europe se fasse à l'échelle
humaine, il sera indispensable de privilégier, à l'avenir plus que par le passé,
les activités culturelles, dont
la musique est une compo-
sante essentielle.»*

Erna Hennicot-Schoepges
Présidente de la Chambre des
Députés

ing their instruments, learn educational theory as a new dimension. These courses also include training in teaching methodology geared towards music schools.

Other courses can help towards the acquisition of an additional teaching qualification. The majority of music school teachers originally trained to teach «just» one First Study instrument. Their career opportunities increase, however, if they are able to teach more than one subject. At music schools, the combination of teaching an instrument as well as a core subject (pre-school or elementary music) is highly desirable. It is also a good idea to combine an instrumental specialization with ensemble directing or orchestral conducting. Piano teachers, too – who continue to train in numbers exceeding requirements in schools – may teach an instrument currently in great demand, once they have completed an appropriate training course: the electronic organ or keyboard. More and more pupils are asking for lessons on these new keyboard instruments, while there are not enough suitable teachers to cater for them.

In-service courses offering training in aspects of management should also be mentioned: directing and managing a music school requires, among other things, knowledge of personnel organization,

Schwerpunkt steht im Interesse zahlreicher Berufs-
gruppen. Da sind zum einen jene, denen die volle
Qualifikation als Musikschullehrer fehlt, entweder
am Instrument oder in der Fachdidaktik und
Pädagogik. Berufsbegleitende Lehrgänge können
solche «Defizite» ausgleichen: Pädagogen, Musiklehrer an allgemeinbildenden Schulen oder Musikwissenschaftler erhalten eine künstlerisch-instru-
mentale Ausbildung; Kirchenmusiker, Militärmusi-
ker und Orchestermusiker, die ihr Instrument auf
hohem Niveau beherrschen, lernen Pädagogik als
neue Dimension. Diese Ausbildungen beinhalten
auch ein musikschulbezogenes Unterrichtstraining.

Andere Lehrgänge dienen dem Erwerb einer zusätzlichen Unterrichtsqualifikation. Der überwie-
gende Teil der Musikschullehrer hat im Studium
die Lehrbefähigung für «nur» ein Hauptfach erworben. Ihre beruflichen Chancen erhöhen sich jedoch, wenn sie mehrere Fächer unterrichten können. Für Musikschulen ist besonders die Kombination eines Instrumentalfachs mit einem Grundfach
(Früherziehung oder Grundausbildung) wünschenswert. Zweckmäßig ist auch die Verbindung
von Instrumentalfach und Ensemble- oder Orche-
sterleitung. Auch die Klavierlehrer, von denen nach
wic vor mehr ausgebildet als benötigt werden, können nach einer entsprechenden Weiterbildung ein
sehr gesuchtes Fach unterrichten: Elektronenorgel
oder Keyboard. Immer mehr Schüler fragen Unterricht auf diesen neuen Tasteninstrumenten nach,
für die es jedoch zuwenig geeignete Lehrer gibt.

Auch berufsbegleitende Lehrgänge zur Weiterbildung für Leitungsaufgaben sind zu nennen:
Führung und Leitung einer Musikschule erfordern
unter anderem Kenntnisse im Bereich des Perso-
nalwesens, des Haushalts- und Arbeitsrechts sowie
in Marketing und Management.

Die durch solche Lehrgänge der Weiterbildung
erworbenen Qualifikationen sind vergleichbar mit
Zusatzfächern in den Studiengängen der Musikhochschulen; die Anforderungen der abzulegenden
Prüfungen liegen aber im Umfang und in ihrer Viel-
seitigkeit teilweise darüber. Eine Beteiligung der
Hochschulen an solchen Lehrgängen bringt fachliche Kompetenz ein und wertet das erworbene Ab-
schluß-Zertifikat auf. Die Mitwirkung der Musikschulverbände sorgt für die musikschulspezifische

La «formation complémentaire» dans le but d'acquérir une qualification professionnelle supplémentaire est le second point fort de l'intérêt de
nombreux groupes professionnels. Il s'agit pour
une part de ceux à qui il manque une qualification
de professeur d'école de musique complète, soit au
niveau d'un instrument, soit au niveau de la didactique et de la pédagogie. Les cycles de formation
suivis parallèlement à l'exercice de la profession
peuvent compenser des «déficits» de ce type: les
pédagogues, les professeurs de musique dans des
institutions d'enseignement général ou les musicologues reçoivent une formation instrumentale artistique; les interprètes de musique religieuse, mili-
taire et les musiciens d'orchestre qui maîtrisent
leur instrument à un haut niveau apprennent des
dimensions nouvelles de la pédagogie. Ces formations comportent un entraînement à l'enseignement rapporté à l'école de musique.

D'autres cycles de formation ont pour but l'acquisition d'une qualification à l'enseignement supplémentaire. La plupart des professeurs de musique
enseignant dans des écoles de musique n'ont obtenu un certificat d'aptitude à l'enseignement
«que» dans leur matière principale. Mais leurs
chances professionnelles augmentent s'ils sont capables de donner des cours dans plusieurs matières. Pour les écoles de musique, la combinaison
d'une matière instrumentale et d'une matière de
base (éducation précoce ou formation élémentaire)
est particulièrement souhaitable. La relation matière instrumentale et direction d'un ensemble ou
d'un orchestre est également opportune. Les professeurs de piano, dont on continue de former plus
qu'il n'en est besoin, peuvent également, avec une
formation complémentaire correspondante, don-

budgeting and wages or labour regulations, as well as marketing and management skills.

The qualifications obtained through further education courses of this kind are on a par with subsidiary subjects taken on a degree course at music college, while the examinations that have to be passed are in some respects more demanding in scope and breadth of content. Collaboration by music colleges on courses like these brings in expertise and raises the status of the examination certificate. The involvement of Associations of Music Schools ensures the appropriate orientation of syllabus and course content. In Germany a type of course has emerged where a central Institute of Further Education, such as that in Trossingen, is responsible for assuring the high quality of course planning and delivery.

As a rule, music teachers set aside weekends and time in the school holidays to attend training courses. Where weekdays in termtime are affected by such courses, efforts should be made to win the understanding of parents and pupils. The best argument for accepting a small loss of lesson time should always be the teacher's performance: lively and imaginative lessons and increased motivation more than make up for the few hours lost.

hwb.

Ausrichtung der Inhalte. In Deutschland hat sich ein Modell von Lehrgängen bewährt, bei denen zudem eine zentrale Fortbildungsakademie, wie sie in Trossingen besteht, für ein hohes Niveau der Lehrgangskonzeption und -durchführung sorgt.

In der Regel setzen Musikschullehrer für den Besuch von Fort- und Weiterbildungen Wochenenden und Zeiten in den Schulferien ein. Sofern auch Wochenarbeitstage betroffen werden, sollte bei den Eltern und Schülern um Verständnis geworben werden. Das beste Argument für die Akzeptanz eines geringfügigen Unterrichtsausfalls dürfte immer die Arbeit des Lehrers sein: Ein attraktiver und einfallsreicher Unterricht und eine erhöhte Motivation machen die verlorene Stunde hundertfach wieder wett.

hwb.

ner des cours dans des matières très recherchées comme l'orgue et le clavier électroniques. De plus en plus d'élèves demandent des cours sur ces nouveaux instruments à touches pour lesquels il y a encore trop peu d'enseignants qualifiés.

Il faut mentionner également les cycles de formation complémentaire parallèles à l'exercice de la profession visant à des tâches de direction: la direction d'une école de musique exige des connaissances dans le domaine du personnel, du droit financier et social, ainsi que dans le domaine du marketing et du management.

Les qualifications acquises au cours de cycles de formation de ce type sont comparables avec des matières supplémentaires dans le cours des études dans les écoles supérieures de musique; mais les exigences des examens à passer sont en partie supérieures de part leur ampleur et leur variété. Une participation des écoles supérieures à des cycles de formation de ce type constitue un apport de compétence spécialisée et valorise le certificat final. La participation des associations musicales assure une orientation spécifique des écoles de musique sur le plan du contenu. En Allemagne, le modèle de cycles de formation pour lesquels une académie de formation continue centrale, telle qu'elle existe à Trossingen, assure un niveau élevé de conception et de réalisation a fait ses preuves.

En règle générale, les professeurs enseignant dans une école de musique profitent des week-ends et des vacances scolaires pour fréquenter des cours de formation continue et de formation complémentaire. Dans la mesure où des jours ouvrables s'en trouveraient concernés, il faudra faire appel à la compréhension des parents et des élèves. Le travail du professeur sera le meilleur argument pour faire accepter que les cours n'ont pas lieu pour une durée limitée: un enseignement attrayant et imaginatif, et une motivation accrue rattrapent cent fois l'heure perdue.   *hwb.*

«*Music educators deserve special recognition for the valuable service they perform for our children.*»

Ronald Reagan

Snapshots of European Encounters

Momentaufnahmen Europäischer Begegnungen

Instantanés de rencontres européennes

Youth Festivals of Music

The park around the Olympic stadium in Munich is already full of activity, although it is only 9 o'clock in the morning: countless young people with musical instruments are covering this extensive area. In the midst of a crowd of people outside the main entrance to the Olympic arena a youth choir from Maribor is singing Slovenian folksongs and dance melodies. The applause of the young listeners emboldens the choir to move on to ever livelier dances, and soon thousands of young people are dancing and clapping to the strange tunes.

Fragments of orchestral pieces are buzzing together all over the place. Individual players and groups are dotted about in the open air, preparing for performances in various parts of Munich. In the middle of the park a trombone quartet from Holland is warming up, while just a few paces away the 1st clarinettist of the Youth Symphony Orchestra from Vasteras (Sweden) rapidly practises a few difficult slurs and the accordion orchestra from Volos (Greece) shows the astonished members of the Helsinki Chamber Orchestra how simple and effortless a dance in 7/8 rhythm can be. An Orchestre des Jeunes from France has set up under the broad canopy of a plane tree and is rehearsing the march from Carmen. The conductor indicates to the members of other orchestras standing around listening that they are to fetch their instruments and join in. Within a few minutes a gigantic French-Austrian-German-Danish-Swiss orchestra has been formed, with several players on every wind part and four violinists at every desk of 1st and 2nd violins. Precision and intonation are no longer the most important thing, with joy in spontaneous music-making together outweighing everything else.

At the final concert in the Olympic Stadium, 9,000 young singers and musicians from 23 countries stand up, visibly moved and filled with enthusiasm, to sing the European Anthem, Beethoven's Hymn of Joy: «Freude schöner Götterfunken». My eyes fill with tears of joy and delight.

The babble of more than 3,000 young voices fills one of the vast exhibition halls of the «Foire» in Strasbourg. For the 2nd European Youth Festival of Music it has been transformed into the largest res-

Musikfeste der Jugend

Im Park rund um das Olympia-Stadion in München herrscht bereits reges Treiben, obwohl es erst 9 Uhr vormittags ist. Unzählige junge Menschen mit Musikinstrumenten bevölkern das weite Areal. Mitten in der Menschenmenge vor dem Haupteingang zur Olympia-Halle singt ein Jugendchor aus Maribor slowenische Volks- und Tanzlieder. Der Applaus der jungen Zuhörer treibt den Chor zu immer schwungvolleren Tanzweisen, und bald tanzen und klatschen tausend Jugendliche nach den fremden Melodien.

Bruchstücke von Orchesterpartien schwirren überall durcheinander. Unter freiem Himmel bereiten sich überall einzelne Spieler und Gruppen auf ihre Auftritte in den Stadtteilen der Stadt München vor. Mitten auf der Wiese bläst sich ein Posaunenquartett aus Holland ein, während ein paar Schritte nebenan der 1. Klarinettist des Jugendsinfonie-Orchesters aus Västeras (Schweden) noch schnell ein paar schwierige Läufe übt und das Akkordeonorchester aus Volos (Griechenland) den erstaunten Mitgliedern des Helsinki-Kammerorchesters demonstriert, wie leicht und selbstverständlich ein Tanz im 7/8-Takt sein kann. Ein Orchestre des Jeunes aus Frankreich hat sich unter einer weitausladenden Platane aufgestellt und probt den Carmen-Marsch. Der Dirigent bedeutet den umstehenden Mitgliedern anderer Orchester, sie sollen ihre Instrumente holen und mitspielen. In wenigen Minuten ist ein französisch-österreichisch-deutsch-dänisch-schweizerisches Riesenorchester entstanden, in dem jede Bläserstimme mehrfach besetzt ist und von jedem Notenblatt der 1. und 2. Violinen vier Geiger spielen. Die Präzision und Intonation ist nicht mehr das Wichtigste, die Freude am spontanen Zusammenspielen überwiegt alles.

Abschlußkonzert in der Olympia-Halle. 9 000 junge Sängerinnen und Sänger, Musikerinnen und Musiker aus 23 Ländern erheben sich sichtlich bewegt und begeistert zur Europa-Hymne, Beethovens «Freude schöner Götterfunken». Mir kommen die Tränen in die Augen – vor Freude und Begeisterung.

Das Stimmengewirr von mehr als 3 000 jungen Menschen füllt eine der riesigen Messehallen des «Foire» in Straßburg. Für das 2. Europäische Mu-

Les Festivals Musicaux Européens de la Jeunesse

Une vive agitation règne déjà dans le parc qui entoure le stade olympique de Munich, bien qu'il ne soit que 9 heures du matin. Une foule de jeunes gens portant des instruments occupent la vaste surface. Au milieu de la foule, devant l'entrée principale du hall olympique, une chorale de jeunes de Maribor chante des chansons populaires et des danses slovènes. L'applaudissement des jeunes spectateurs entraîne la chorale à des danses de plus en en plus vives, et, bientôt, ce sont des milliers de jeunes qui dansent et frappent dans leurs mains au son de mélodies étrangères.

Des bribes de partitions d'orchestre volent de toutes parts. Partout, des musiciens isolés et des groupes se préparent, en plein air, à leurs représentations, dans les divers quartiers de la ville de Munich. Au beau milieu de la prairie, un quatuor de trombones venu de Hollande s'échauffe, tandis que, à quelques pas de là, le premier clarinettiste de l'orchestre symphonique des jeunes de Västeras (Suède) s'exerce encore à quelques passages rapides difficiles et que l'orchestre d'accordéon de Volos (Grèce) démontre aux membres étonnés de l'orchestre de musique de chambre d'Helsinki comme il peut être facile et naturel de jouer une danse en 7/8. Un Orchestre de Jeunes, venu de France, s'est formé derrière un large platane et répéte la marche de Carmen. Le chef d'orchestre fait signe aux membres des autres orchestres alentours d'aller chercher leurs instruments et de jouer avec eux. Quelques minutes plus tard est né un orchestre géant franco-austro-germano-dano-suisse dans lequel chaque partie des cuivres est occupée plusieurs fois et où quatre violons jouent à partir de chaque partition des premiers et seconds violons. Ce ne sont plus la précision et l'intonation qui sont importants, la joie éprouvée à jouer ensemble de manière spontanée est prédominante.

Concert de clôture dans le hall olympique. 9.000 jeunes chanteuses et chanteurs, musiciens et musiciennes venant de 23 pays se lèvent, visiblement émus et enthousiasmés par l'hymne européen, l'Hymne à la Joie de Beethoven. Les larmes me viennent aux yeux – des larmes de joies et d'enthousiasme.

taurant in France. The participants are standing in long queues waiting for food and drink. None of them finds the wait tedious, for here all nations and languages come together. «Where do you come from?» – «What's your name?» – «What instrument do you play?» – «When is your orchestra performing?» – «What works are you performing?» – «Will you give me your address, so that I can write to you?»

Outside the hall two guitarists from Spain are playing and a girl is clicking castanets and dancing along with them. People coming out of the hall are drawn into the dance, and in a trice we have a Spanish folk festival. When it comes to the Seguidilla, a Dutch girl feels inspired to be Carmen and a young Swede is the Toreador. What does it take to unite a crowd of young musicians from so many different countries in a dance? Two guitars and a pair of castanets. After this Spanish Intermezzo they all go off into the different exhibition halls where rehearsals for the various Euro-Orchestras and for the Euro-Choir of 600 voices are taking place.

In the Philips Stadium of PSV Eindhoven in Holland a cloudburst pours down over the final celebrations of the 3rd European Youth Festival of Music, almost drowning the loudspeaker through which the EMU president is congratulating the thousands of young musicians from all over Europe on this wonderful festival of joy, new encounters, shared music-making and communication across all national borders. However, he also mentions the war in the former Yugoslavia, one of the countries that helped to found the EMU and which sent various youth ensembles to previous festivals. He appeals for peace. In a wordless demonstration, the young festival participants join hands and form a chain of people throughout the stadium, a chain which seems in spirit to link the whole of Europe, even the whole world.

School Exchange Visits

The local music school from Erding in Bavaria has invited the Liechtenstein music school on a visit. The 60 pupils from the tiny principality stay

sikfest der Jugend ist sie zum größten Restaurant Frankreichs umfunktioniert worden. In langen Schlangen stehen die Teilnehmerinnen und Teilnehmer um Speis' und Trank an. Keinem wird dabei die Zeit zu lang, denn hier trifft man alle Nationen und Sprachen. «Wo kommst Du her?» – «Wie heißt Du?» – «Welches Instrument spielst Du?» – «Wann trittst Du mit Deinem Orchester auf?» – «Welche Werke spielt ihr?» – «Gibst Du mir Deine Adresse, damit ich Dir schreiben kann?»

Vor der Halle spielen zwei Gitarristen aus Spanien, ein Mädchen schlägt die Kastagnetten und tanzt dazu. Die aus der Halle Kommenden werden in den Tanz hineingezogen, und im Handumdrehen entsteht ein spanisches Volksfest. Bei der Seguidilla fühlt sich die Holländerin als Carmen und der Schwede als Torero. Wieviel braucht es, um eine Schar junger Musiker aus vielen unterschiedlichen Ländern in einem Tanz zu einen? Zwei Gitarren und ein Paar Kastagnetten. Nach diesem spanischen Intermezzo verteilen sich alle auf die verschiedenen Messehallen, in denen die Proben für die unterschiedlichen Euro-Orchester und den 600 Personen zählenden Euro-Chor stattfinden.

Im Philipps-Stadion des PSV Eindhoven in Holland prasselt ein gewaltiger Wolkenbruch über die Abschlußfeier des 3. Europäischen Musikfestes der Jugend 1991 nieder und übertönt fast den Lautsprecher, durch den der EMU-Präsident die Tausende von jungen Musikerinnen und Musikern aus ganz Europa zu diesem wunderbaren Fest der Freude, der Begegnung, des gemeinsamen Musizierens und der Verständigung über alle Grenzen hinweg beglückwünscht. Er erwähnt aber auch den Krieg im ehemaligen Jugoslawien, in einem Land, das die EMU mitgegründet hat und aus dem verschiedene Jugend-Ensembles noch an den vergangenen Musikfesten teilgenommen hatten. Er ruft zum Frieden auf. In einer stummen Demonstration reichen sich die jugendlichen Festivalteilnehmer die Hände und bilden eine Menschenkette durch alle Ränge des Stadions, die in ihrer Absicht jedoch ganz Europa, die ganze Welt umfassen möchte.

Schüleraustausch

Die Kreismusikschule Erding/Bayern hat die Liechtensteinische Musikschule zu einem Besuch

Les voix mêlées de plus de 3.000 jeunes remplissent l'un des halls gigantesques de la Foire de Strasbourg, devenu le plus grand restaurant de France à l'occasion de la deuxième Festival Musical Européen de la Jeunesse. Les participants et participantes font la queue pour recevoir leur repas. Personne ne trouve le temps long, car on rencontre ici toutes les nationalités et toutes les langues. «Tu viens d'où?» – «Comment tu t'appelles?» – «Tu joues de quel instrument?» – «Ton orchestre joue quand?» – «Vous jouez quoi?» – «Tu me donnes ton adresse pour que je puisse t'écrire?»

Devant le hall, deux guitaristes venus d'Espagne jouent, une jeune fille joue des castagnettes et danse. Ceux qui sortent du hall sont entraînés dans la danse, et, en un tournemain, naît une fête populaire espagnole. En dansant la séguedille, la Hollandaise se prend pour Carmen et le Suédois pour un torero. De quoi a-t-on besoin pour réunir en une danse un groupe de jeunes musiciens provenant de pays différents? De deux guitares et d'une paire de castagnettes. Après cet intermède espagnol, tous se répartissent dans les divers halls d'exposition où ont lieu les répétitions des divers orchestres européens et de la chorale européenne, forte de 600 personnes.

Dans le stade Philips du PSV Eindhoven, en Hollande, une averse tombe avec fracas sur la cérémonie de clôture de la troisième Festival Musical Européen de la Jeunesse, en 1991, et couvre presque la baffle par laquelle le président de l'EMU félicite les milliers de jeunes musiciens et musiciennes venus de toute l'Europe à cette merveilleuse fête de la joie, de la rencontre, de l'exercice commun de la musique et de l'entente au-delà de toutes les frontières. Mais il mentionne aussi la guerre dans l'ancienne Yougoslavie, pays co-fondateur de l'EMU qui a participé par l'envoi de divers ensembles de jeunes aux Festivals des années passées. Dans une démonstration muette, les jeunes participants au festival se donnent la main et forment une chaîne humaine tout le long des gradins du stade. Mais cette chaîne, c'est l'Europe entière, le monde entier qu'elle veut embrasser.

Echange d'élèves

L'école de musique de la circonscription de Erding, en Bavière, a invité l'école de musique du

with host families and become acquainted with the Bavarian way of life. Their attempts at spoken communication provoke plenty of laughter, for the Bavarian and Liechtenstein forms of German sound very different, and High German is only used when all else fails. After all, they want to get to know each other. They spend three days rehearsing and making music together. Friendships are formed which have lasted to this day. After the final concert there is folk dancing, an unexpected and totally new experience for those from Liechtenstein. They have great fun learning the Bavarian polka, the Seven Step and the Landler and laugh at everyone who stumbles over the Two Step. «Why should we always have disco dancing?», they all say afterwards, «folk dancing is fun, too, sometimes.»

At the «Antal Molnar Music School» in the 7th district of Budapest the school's youth orchestra is rehearsing together with the «Youth Sinfonietta» from Vaduz. None of the guests speak Hungarian, but this does nothing to spoil the intensity of their music-making. The conductor's gestures are clear, the required articulation, bowing or dynamics are demonstrated by singing or playing, the Italian terms are international in any case and written

eingeladen. Die 60 Schülerinnen und Schüler aus dem kleinen Fürstentum sind bei Gastfamilien untergebracht und lernen die bayerische Lebensart kennen. Die sprachliche Verständigung verursacht viel Lachen, denn das bayerische und das liechtensteinische Deutsch klingen doch sehr verschieden, und Hochdeutsch wird nur angewendet, wenn's nicht mehr anders geht. Man will sich ja schließlich kennenlernen.

Drei Tage wird miteinander geprobt und musiziert. Freundschaften werden geschlossen, die bis heute Bestand haben. Nach dem Abschlußkonzert gibt es Volkstanz. Ein unerwartetes und völlig neues Erlebnis für die Liechtensteiner. Sie lernen mit viel Spaß die bayerische Polka, den Siebenschritt und den Landler und lachen über jeden Stolperer beim Zwiefachen. «Warum immer Disko?», ist danach die allgemeine Meinung, «es kann ja auch mal Volkstanz sein.»

In der «Antal Molnar Musikschule» im 7. Bezirk von Budapest probt das Jugendorchester dieser Schule zusammen mit der «Jugendsinfonietta» aus Vaduz. Ungarisch, nein, das spricht niemand von den Gästen. Das tut der Intensität der musikali-

Liechtenstein. Les 60 élèves, garçons et filles, de la petite principauté sont logés dans des familles et apprennent à connaître la façon de vivre bavaroise. La communication provoque bien des rires, car l'allemand du Liechtenstein et celui de la Bavière sont fort différents, et l'on ne parle haut allemand que si l'on ne peut faire autrement: on veut faire connaissance.

Trois jours durant, on répète et joue ensemble. On lie des amitiés qui persistent jusqu'à aujourd'hui. Après le concert de clôture, la danse populaire est à l'ordre du jour. Un événement inattendu et totalement nouveau pour les jeunes du Liechtenstein. Ils apprennent avec grand plaisir la polka bavaroise, le Siebenschritt et le Landler, et rient de chaque faux pas au Zwiefachen. «Pourquoi aller toujours en boîte? On peut danser de temps en temps des danses populaires». C'est là l'opinion générale peu après.

Dans l'école de musique «Antal Molnar», dans le 7ème district de Budapest, l'orchestre de jeunes de cette école répète avec la «Jugendsinfonietta» de Vaduz. Aucun des hôtes ne parle le hongrois. Cela ne porte aucunement atteinte à l'intensité du travail musical. Les gestes du chef d'orchestre sont clairs, l'articulation exigée, les coups d'archets ou la dynamique sont chantés ou joués, les termes italiens sont, de toute manière, internationaux, et la notation est une langue universelle que connaît chacun des élèves. Tant que l'on joue, on n'a pas de mal à se comprendre et à se faire comprendre.

Pendant les pauses, les repas et si l'on entreprend quelque chose ensemble, on invente un mélange de communication à partir de quelques mots d'allemand, d'anglais et de français, ainsi qu'à l'aide d'une riche mimique et d'un langage corporel plein d'imagination, mélange qui déclenche beaucoup d'hilarité et remplit tout à fait sa fonction.

Les élèves de Vaduz sont pour la première fois dans un pays qui se trouvait autrefois «derrière le rideau de fer». Ils sont surpris que beaucoup de choses soient les mêmes ou semblables à celles qu'ils connaissent chez eux. Mais ils voient aussi que d'autres habitudes de vie, d'autres conditions de travail, d'autres systèmes scolaires etc... ont également un sens et des avantages. Ils entendent

«Je suis d'abord soucieux – je dirais, chronologiquement – que l'enseignement musical, et d'abord la sensibilisation à la musique, existe de la maternelle jusqu'au secondaire, dans le cadre donc de l'éducation publique et privée. Vous savez que le Ministère de la Culture s'y emploie, en relation bien évidemment avec les Ministères compétents en matière d'éducation et de jeunesse.

Je suis ensuite et surtout, es-qualité, soucieux d'optimiser la facon dont l'enseignement spécialisé, du stade des écoles musicales jusqu'aux CNSM, délivre à plus d'un million d'enfants et adolescents, les clés de la pratique musicale, pouvant aller jusqu'à l'accession au rang de musicien professionnel.

J'ai fait de cette réflexion, qui va être suivie de propositions concrètes, l'une des priorités de mon Ministère, en matière de musique.»

Jacques Toubon
Ministre de la Culture et de la Francophonie

«Wenn die musikalische Ausbildung nicht nur pädagogisch-didaktisch erfolgt, sondern phantasie-reich-sinnlich, dann ist musikalische Ausbildung der Grundstein für Bildung. Wir müssen alles daran setzen, daß in unserer über-bilderreichen Zeit diese Bildung uns nicht verloren-geht.»

Prof. August Everding

music is a language learned by music students all over the world. While they are playing, there are no communication problems.

During the breaks, at meals and in group activities a pidgin language is put together consisting of a few German, English and French words, plenty of facial expressions and imaginative use of gestures, causing much hilarity and quite fulfilling its purpose.

The schoolchildren from Vaduz are all on their first visit to a country that was formerly «behind the Iron Curtain». They are surprised at how much is the same or similar to what they know at home. They also see, however, that different customs, working conditions, school systems etc. fulfil a function and have their advantages. They hear with astonishment of Hungary's enormous struggle to improve its economy, and the names of the great composers and performers produced by this nation are spoken with the greatest respect.

When it is time to say goodbye there is much exchanging of souvenirs and embraces. «Thank you so much for everything you have given us. Now we know a little more about you and your country. It was all wonderful, and so friendly. Come to visit us soon on a return visit so that we can show our country to you!»   *jf.*

schen Arbeit keinen Abbruch. Die Gesten des Dirigenten sind klar, die verlangte Artikulation, Strichweise oder Dynamik werden vorgesungen oder -gespielt, die italienischen Bezeichnungen sind ohnehin international, und die Notenschrift ist eine Weltsprache, die jeder Musikschüler lernt. Während des Musizierens gibt es keine Verständigungsprobleme.

In den Pausen, beim Essen und bei den gemeinsamen Unternehmungen wird aus einigen deutschen, englischen und französischen Worten sowie einer reichen Mimik und phantasiereichen Körpersprache ein Verständigungsmix erfunden, der viel Heiterkeit verursacht und durchaus seinen Dienst erfüllt.

Die Schülerinnen und Schüler aus Vaduz sind alle zum erstenmal in einem Land, das ehemals «hinter dem eisernen Vorhang» war. Sie sind überrascht über die vielen Dinge, die gleich oder ähnlich wie in der Heimat sind. Sie sehen aber auch, daß andere Lebensgewohnheiten, Arbeitsbedingungen, Schulsysteme etc. ihren Sinn und ihre Vorzüge haben. Sie hören mit Staunen von den enormen Anstrengungen Ungarns um den wirtschaftlichen Aufschwung und wiederholen mit größter Hochachtung die Namen der großen Komponisten und Solisten, die das Land hervorgebracht hat.

Beim Abschied gibt es viele Erinnerungsgeschenke und Umarmungen. «Tausend Dank für alles, was Ihr uns geboten habt. Jetzt kennen wir Euch und Euer Land schon etwas besser. Es war alles so schön, so herzlich. Kommt bald zu uns zu einem Gegenbesuch, damit wir Euch unser Land zeigen können!» *jf.*

parler avec étonnement des efforts énormes de la Hongrie sur la voie d'un redressement économique et répètent avec un profond respect les noms des grands compositeurs et solistes nés dans ce pays.

On prend congé les uns des autres en échangeant des cadeaux en souvenir et en s'embrassant. «Mille fois merci pour tout ce que vous nous avez donné. Maintenant, nous vous connaissons un peu mieux, vous et votre pays. C'était si beau, si cordial. Venez nous rendre visite à votre tour, pour que nous puissions vous montrer notre pays!» *jf.*

THE NEW EMONTS

Fritz Emonts
The European Piano Method

3 volumes, four-colour printing
illustrations by Andrea Hoyer

In 3 languages (Ger. / Engl. / Fr.)
with many assets:

- Songs from many European countries
- Easy beginning without music
- Playing with black keys
- Ear training and creation of an inner tonal concept
- Systematic structure with learning steps easy to comprehend
- Technical training and music interpretation
- Many pieces for piano duet

Each volume contains „yellow pages" with proposals for improvi-sation, e.g. simple song accompaniment, basic concepts of harmony, invention of melodies and modern dances such as blues, tango, boogie-woogie etc.

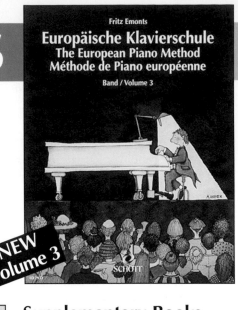

Volume 1
Order No. ED 7931

Volume 2
Order No. ED 7932

Volume 3
Order No. ED 7933

You will find further informations in the coloured leaflet „The European Piano Method". For the leaflet please contact:
Schott Music Publisher, POB 3640, D-55026, Mainz

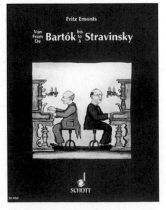

Supplementary Books

TO VOLUME 1
Playing with Five notes
Order No. ED 5285

Let's play Duets
Order No. ED 4793

TO VOLUME 2
Easy Baroque Piano Music
Order No. ED 5096

Easy Piano Pieces from Bach's Sons to Beethoven
Order No. ED 4747

From Bartók to Stravinsky
Order No. ED 4769

Traditional Festive Dances
for piano duet
Order No. ED 5176

Easy Romantic Piano Music I
Order No. ED 4748

TO VOLUME 3
Easy Romantik Piano Music II
Order No. ED 8277

Contrapuntal Piano-Playing
2 Books, Order No. ED 5451/52

SCHOTT

musiklabor & compudaktik

Frese-Fischer GbR • Kleine Str. 8 • 38116 Braunschweig

Die Firmen **musiklabor** und **compudaktik** haben ab Januar 1995 ein gemeinsames Dach. Mit dem neuen Hauptsitz in Braunschweig setzen wir auf folgende Schwerpunkte :

- **Hardware**   Tastaturen, Soundmodule/Soundkarten, Interfaces, Gesamtpakete ...
- **Software**   Notation, Sequenzer, Composer, Kandinsky (KMP), Gehörbildung ...
- **Literatur**   midi - pädagogische schriftenreihe (mps)

Neuer Katalog im Februar für unsere Stammkunden und auf Anfrage von Interessenten.

Ihre Ansprechpartner (Beratung, Bestellung) sind :
- Zentrale, Beratung Kandinsky: **Volker Frese**, Braunschweig   Tel/Fax: 0531 - 57 78 43
- Beratung PC, Interfaces, Cubase: **Gene Strasbaugh**, Berlin   Tel/Fax: 030 - 745 31 75
- Beratung Atari, Tastaturen, Expander, SPP: **Ekkehard Arnold**, Berlin   Tel/Fax: 030 - 323 66 16

 # Die Querflötenfibel

von Alexander Hanselmann

Diese neue Querflötenschule vermittelt in 53 thematisch abgeschlossenen Kapiteln einen gründlichen Einstieg in das Querflötenspiel. Kurze Übungen und Spielstücke verschiedenster Herkunft und Stile sind unauffällig in den didaktisch durchdachten Aufbau des Stoffplanes eingebettet. Das Unterrichtswerk besteht aus folgenden vier Bänden:

Die Fundgrube	Lernhilfen, Theorieteil, Tabellen und Register,	DM 36.-*
	sie ist **Voraussetzung** für den sinnvollen Unterricht mit:	
Die ersten Schritte	(Band 1) Behandelt den Grundlehrstoff,	DM 30.-*
Tanzen und Springen	(Band 2) Differenziertere Rhythmik, Chromatik,	DM 30.-*
Gratwanderungen	(Band 3) 3. Oktave und moderne Spieltechniken,	DM 36.-*

Die Bände 2 und 3 können parallel erarbeitet werden.
* sFr. 25.-/30.-; ÖS 210.-/250.-, Preisänderungen vorbehalten.

Verlagsadresse: Gitarren Forum Wintorthur, Christian Bissig,
Lustgartenstr. 9, CH-9000 **St.Gallen**
Tel. (D: 0041 71) (A: 0 50 71) (CH: 071) 27 99 93

The aim to offer the best is our challenge to create it.

STUDIO 49
MUSIKINSTRUMENTENBAU
D-82153 Gräfelfing · Postfach 11 68
Fax: 089/ 854 54 12

NEU BEI BOSWORT

Mit Spielheften von BOSWORTH kommt SCHWUNG in die Musikschule!

Hans-Günter Heumann
CHILDRENS BOOGIE PIANO
Echt coole und fetzige Boogies
in leichter Fassung für Klavier/
Keyboard

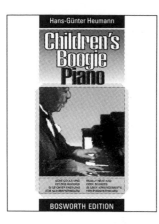

In the Mood/Mountain Bike
Boogie/Michael, Row the Boat
Ashore
u.a.

BoE 4161   **DM 16,50**

Johann Pachelbel
KANON UND GIGUE
Das berühmte Barockwerk in
Bearbeitung für Blockflöten-
quartett oder -gruppe mit
Klavier (Gitarre ad lib.) von
Albrecht Rosenstengel
BoE 4157   kpl. DM 24,00
Einzelst.   je DM 3,00

Wesley Schaum
RHYTHM & BLUES
Aus den bekannten Klavier-
heften, bearbeitet für Klari-
netten-/Saxophon-Trio von
Jürgen J. Schmidt
Bd.1: BoE 4162   DM 28,50
Bd.2: BoE 4164   DM 28,50
je kpl. (Part. + 6 Sti.)

Wesley Schaum
RHYTHM & BLUES
Aus den bekannten Klavier-
heften, bearbeitet für
2 Sopranblockflöten (Klavier/
Gitarre ad lib.) von
Günter Kaluza
BoE 4164   **DM 9,00**

Hans-Günter Heumann
OLDIE PIANO

Die Super-Oldies in leichten
Arrangements für
Klavier/Keyboard
Down Town/Ruby Tuesday/
No Milk Today/Monday,
Monday/Lola/Rock My Soul/
Red River Rock/I Got You Babe
u.a.

BoE 4167   **DM 17,50**

BOSWORTH EDITION KÖLN - WIEN - LONDON

Für den modernen Klavierunterricht   *The modern way of teaching piano*

Erika und Christa Holzweißig
Klavierschule
EP 9480

EDITION PETERS

Erika and Christa Holzweissig
Piano Method
EP 9480

Leichte Spielstücke für Klavier zu vier Händen
Ergänzungsband zur Klavierschule
EP 9481 DM 24,50

Diese Klavierschule ist in
erster Linie für Kinder ohne
musikalische Vorkenntnisse
eingerichtet. Jedes Kapitel
enhält genügend Spiel-
literatur in unterschiedlichen
Schwierigkeitsgraden, die
dem Lehrer eine individuelle Auswahl ermöglichen.
Teil I führt mit vielen Beispie-
len in die Musiktheorie ein,
Noten, Rhythmus, Tonarten
und Vortragszeichen werden
dem Anfänger erläutert.
Teil II enthält darauf aufbau-
end Übungen, Lieder und Spielstücke. Dieser Band schafft
eine hervorragende Grundlage zum praktischen Verständnis
der Klaviertechnik und der Musiktheorie.

Easy Pieces for Piano Four-Hands
Supplementary volume to the Piano Method
EP 9481 DM 24,50

This piano method is pri-
marily designed for children
who have no previous
knowledge of music. Each
chapter contains a sufficient
amount of teaching material
at various levels of difficulty
to enable the teacher to
make an individual selection.
Part 1 introduces the pupil
to music theory, explaining
notes, rhythm, keys and
expression marks for the
benefit of novices. Building
an this, Part 2 contains exer-
cises, songs and pieces for performance. This volume creates
a solid foundation for a practical grasp of piano technique
and music theory.

C. F. PETERS · FRANKFURT
Leipzig · London · New York

LEHRBÜCHER & LERNVIDEOS

Blasmusik-Dirigent

von Militärkapellmeister
Oberst Prof. Hans Eibl

vom Anfänger
bis zum
Orchesterleiter

| Bestell-Nr.: Lehrbuch | 022 046 | DM 56,-- |
| Lernvideo | 500 046 | DM 59,-- |

Das Schlagzeug in der Blasmusik

von Laszlo Demeter

für Anfänger
und ausübende
Schlagzeuger

| Bestell-Nr.: Lehrbuch | 022 051 | DM 39,-- |
| Lernvideo | 500 051 | DM 49,-- |

Die Gitarre in der Alpenl. Volksmusik

von Martin Kern

für Anfänger

| Bestell-Nr.: Lehrbuch | 022 047 | DM 56,-- |
| Lernvideo | 500 047 | DM 59,-- |

Trompete

von Erich Rinner

für Anfänger
und leicht
Fortgeschrittene

| Bestell-Nr.: Lehrbuch | 022 049 | DM 56,-- |
| Lernvideo | 500 049 | DM 59,-- |

Das Schlagzeug-Set in der Blasmusik und Tanzmusik

von Laszlo Demeter

auch für
Anfänger

| Bestell-Nr.: Lehrbuch | 022 050 | DM 36,-- |
| Lernvideo | 500 050 | DM 49,-- |

Zither

von Heinz Gamper

für Anfänger
und
Fortgeschrittene

| Bestell-Nr.: Lehrbuch | 022 048 | DM 56,-- |
| Lernvideo | 500 048 | DM 59,-- |

KOCH International GmbH
Hermann-Schmid-Straße 10, D-80336 München
Tel 089 746135 49 - Fax 089 7254759

KOCH MUSIKVERLAG

Die einzigartige neue Reihe bei Peermusic

◆ dynamisch ◆ phantasievoll ◆ vierfarbig illustriert

Musik macht Freude

◆ Eine Keyboardschule für Kinder	Best.-Nr. 4000
◆ Eine Blockflötenschule für Kinder	Best.-Nr. 4002
◆ Leichte Klavierstücke für Kinder	Best.-Nr. 4001

je DM 22,50 / ÖS 196,– / sFr 27,–

peermusic
Postfach 602129 - 22231 Hamburg
Mühlenkamp 43 - 22303 Hamburg

Statistics

Statistiken

Statistiques

Total Expenses for Music Schools

Country	Local Currency	
A	ÖSH	2 mia.
B	BFR	3,2 mia.
BG	BGL	-
CR	HRD	-
DK	DKR	300 mill.
FIN	FIM	370 mill.
F	FFR	2,5 mia.
D	DM	814 mill.
GR	GRD	-
H	HUF	1 695 mill.
IS	ISK	700 mill.
I	ITL	-
FL	CHF	4,7 mill.
L	LUF	72 mill.
NL	NLG	320 mill.
N	NKR	280 mill.
SL	SIT	1,7 mia
E	ESB	-
S	SKR	1 mia.
CH	CHF	180 mill.

Divisions of costs (%)

Country	Public	Pupils
A	85	15
B	95	5
BG	100	0
CR	85	15
DK	67	33
FIN	87	13
F	85	15
D	58	42
GR	27	73
H	99	1
IS	80	20
I	63	37
FL	75	25
L	98	2
NL	63	37
N	78	22
SL	82	18
E	30	70
S	92	8
CH	62	38

Number of Schools, Teachers and Pupils

Country	Population (mill.)	Music Schools	Teachers	Activity Pupils
A	7,5	641	6 376	170 000
B	9,6	205	5 000	249 000
BG	9	9	500	4 500
CR	4,7	62	563	27 700
DK	5	225	3 675	110 000
FIN	5	103	4 097	81 000
F	57	960	18 000	640 000
D	80	978	35 100	759 000
GR	10,5	325	3 000	79 000
H	11	228	4 508	82 000
IS	0,3	67	677	10 000
I	56	50	1 900	21 000
FL	0,03	1	90	3 000
L	0,4	12	609	15 000
NL	15,1	180	6 150	346 000
N	4,5	310	3 398	76 000
SL	2	53	1 200	19 177
E	36,5	148	1 762	41 370
S	8,6	283	5 986	316 000
CH	7,0	352	12 400	220 000
Total	329,73	5 192	114 991	3 269 747

Dispersion of Age (Person – Pupils)

	Children age	%	Young Persons age	%	Adults age	%
A	0–	60	–	30	–100	10
B	8–12	50	13–18	32	19–100	18
BG	–	–	–	–	–	–
CR	–	–	–	–	–	–
DK	0–6	7	7–25	82	26–100	11
FIN	0–15	83	16–21	11	22–100	6
F	0–15	55	13–18	35	19–100	10
D	0–9	41	10–25	55	26–100	4
GR	–	–	–	–	–	–
H	0–14	84	15–18	13	19–100	3
IS	0–6	8	7–15	71	16–100	21
I	0–10	30	11–18	65	19–100	5
FL	6–8	29	9–20	47	21–100	24
L	0–7	12	8–18	73	19–100	15
NL	0–21	79	22–65	20	66–100	1
N	–	–	–	–	–	–
SL	–	–	–	–	–	–
E	–	–	–	–	–	–
S	–	–	–	–	–	–
CH	–	–	4–20	95	21–100	5

Do you have any kind of competitions for music school pupils?

A	EMCY (Jugend musiziert)
B	EMCY (Concours national belge de musique)
BG	EMCY (Concours Svetaslov Obretenov)
CR	-
DK	Steinway-competition – Berlingske Tidenes Music Competition
FIN	Yes
F	By FNUCMU and EMCY (Royaume de la musique)
D	EMCY (Jugend musiziert)
GR	-
H	EMCY
IS	No
I	No
FL	Landeswettbewerbe
L	EMCY (Union grand duc Adolphe)
NL	EMCY (Stichting jong muziektalent)
N	EMCY (Norske musiklæreres landsforbund)
SL	-
E	EMCY (Concurso permanente de jóvences intérpretes)
S	No
CH	EMCY (Schweizerischer Jugendmusikwettbewerb + lokal competitions)
T	-

Do you have a law for music schools or something like that in your country?

A	Yes
B	Yes
BG	Yes
CR	-
DK	Yes
FIN	Yes
F	Yes, concerning organization of cursus and studies and teachers status
D	No
GR	No
H	Yes
IS	Yes
I	No
FL	Yes
L	No
NL	No
N	No
SL	-
E	No
S	No
CH	Yes
T	No

Percentage of Pupils in Relation to Population

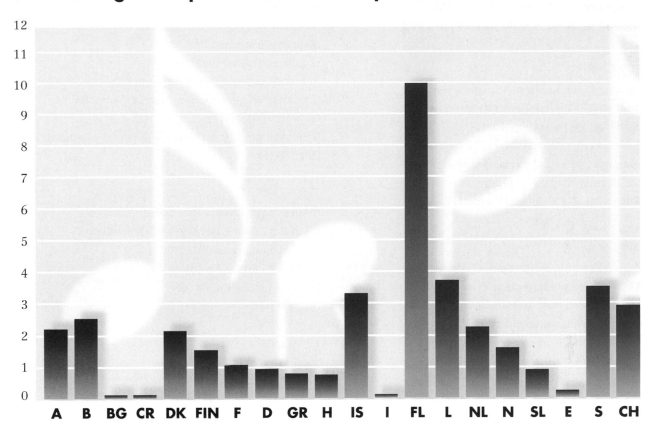

Part of Finances from the Pupils (%)

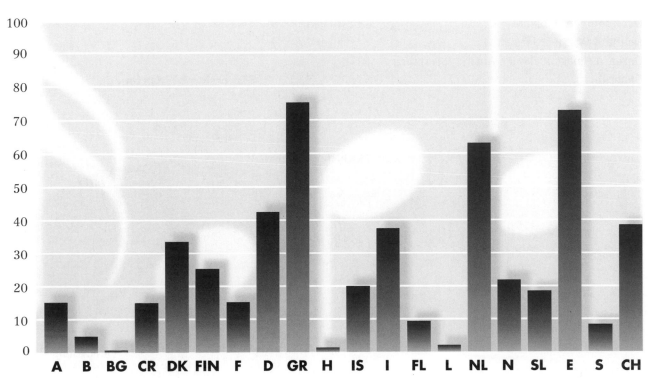

Members of Presidency 1973-1995
Präsidiumsmitglieder 1973-1995
Membres de la Présidence 1973-1995

1973-1977

Diethard Wucher, Germany (President)

Maurice Gevaudan, France (Vice-President)

Slobodan Petrovic, Yugoslavia

Edwin Ruegg, Switzerland (1973-1975)

Armin Brenner, Switzerland (1975-1977)

Dr. Herman Waage, Netherlands

Rainer Mehlig, Germany (Secretary General)

1977-1980

Armin Brenner, Switzerland (President)

Maurice Gevaudan, France (Vice-President)

Slobodan Petrovic, Yugoslavia

Diethard Wucher, Germany

Olli Ruottinen, Finland

Franz Constant, Belgium

Martin Seeger, Switzerland (Secretary General)

1980-1983

Heinz Preiss, Austria (President)

Armin Brenner, Switzerland (Vice-President)

Maurice Gevaudan, France

Slobodan Petrovic, Yugoslavia

Camille Swinnen, Belgium

Olli Ruottinen, Finland

Diethard Wucher, Germany

Gerhard Heiligenbrunner, Austria (Secretary General)

1983-1987

Heinz Preiss, Austria (President)

Diethard Wucher, Germany (Vice-President)

Maurice Gevaudan, France

Camille Swinnen, Belgium

Ib Planch Larsen, Denmark

Gerhard Heiligenbrunner, Austria (Secretary General, till 1985)

Helgard Edda Dorner, Austria (Secretary General, from 1985)

1987-1991

Heinz Preiss, Austria (President)

Diethard Wucher, Germany (Vice-President)

Josef Frommelt, Liechtenstein

Ib Planch Larsen, Denmark

Maurice Gevaudan, France

Helgard Edda Dorner, Austria (Secretary General)

1991-1995

Josef Frommelt, Liechtenstein (President)

Heinz Preiss, Austria (Vice-President)

Ib Planch Larsen, Denmark

Maurice Gevaudan, France (till 1994)

Hans Heimans, Netherlands (1991 - 1992)

Timo Veijola, Finland

Reinhart von Gutzeit, Germany

Louis Vogt, Liechtenstein (Secretary General)

Dispersion of Instruments

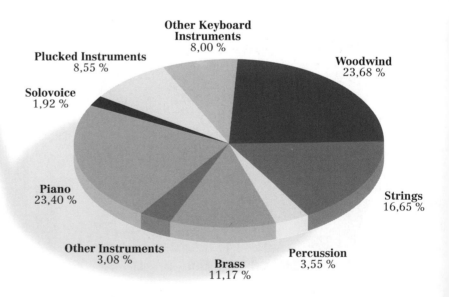

Other Keyboard Instruments 8,00 %

Plucked Instruments 8,55 %

Solovoice 1,92 %

Woodwind 23,68 %

Strings 16,65 %

Piano 23,40 %

Other Instruments 3,08 %

Brass 11,17 %

Percussion 3,55 %

Number of Pupils in Groups

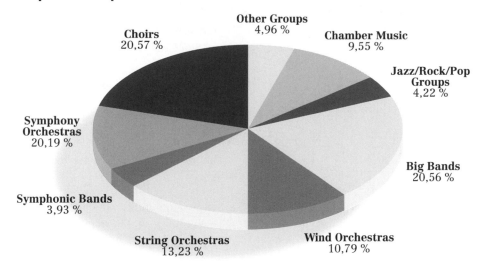

Other Groups
4,96 %

Choirs
20,57 %

Chamber Music
9,55 %

Jazz/Rock/Pop
Groups
4,22 %

Symphony
Orchestras
20,19 %

Big Bands
20,56 %

Symphonic Bands
3,93 %

String Orchestras
13,23 %

Wind Orchestras
10,79 %

General Assemblies/Congresses of EMU
Generalversammlungen/Kongresse der EMU
Assemblées Générales de l'EMU

1973 – Saarbrücken/Germany
1974 – Paris-Surenes/France
1975 – Tampere/Finland
1976 – Liestal/Switzerland
1977 – Spa/Belgium
1978 – St.Pölten/Austria
1979 – Lysebu/Norway
1980 – Latina/Italy
1981 – Sigtuna/Sweden
1982 – Eisenstadt/Austria
1983 – Amersfoort/Netherlands
1985 – Marktoberdorf/Germany
1986 – Vaduz/Liechtenstein
1987 – Holstebro/Denmark
1988 – Florenz/Italy
1990 – Schloss Weinberg/Austria
1991 – Rovaniemi/Finland
1992 – Ried/Austria
1993 – Arvika/Sweden
1994 – Tours/France
1995 – Budapest/Hungary

European Youth Festivals of Music
Europäische Musikfeste der Jugend
Fêtes Européennes de la Musique de la Jeunesse

1985 – München/Germany
1989 – Strasbourg/France
1992 – Eindhoven/Netherlands
1995 – Budapest/Hungary

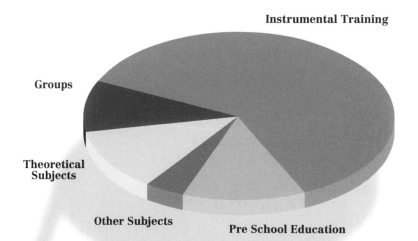

Instrumental Training

Groups

Theoretical
Subjects

Other Subjects

Pre School Education

Statutes

Satzung

Statut

Article I – Name, Address, Business Year

1. The European Union of Music Schools is an Association under Swiss Civil Law (Art. 60 ff ZGB = Civil Code) headquartered in Liestal, Switzerland.

2. Its business year coincides with the calendar year.

Article II – Objectives

The Union of Music Schools has the following objectives:

a) to promote music education and music practice

b) to cooperate by exchanging information on all questions concerning music schools

c) to promote exchanges of student delegations, teachers, pupils, orchestras, choirs, other music groups and the like,

d) to raise the interest of the competent authorities and the public on questions of music education in general and to encourage amateur music and music studies

e) to help creating and developing nation-wide federations of music schools

f) to keep up systematic contacts with interested international Institutions such as the United Nations Educational, Scientific and Cultural Organization (UNESCO), the International Music Council (IMC) and its international organizations.

Article III – Purpose

The Association does not pursue any economic objective; its purpose is exclusively of direct public interest. All funds received by the Association shall be used to implement the aims and tasks set out in these Statutes and no funds shall be paid back to members, even in the event of their withdrawal from the organization.

Disproportionally high subsidies to individuals or to institutions shall not be permitted.

Article IV – Membership

1. Federations of Music Schools from all European countries or their national representatives may be ordinary members of the Music School Union: Only one organization per country may be member.

Artikel I – Name, Sitz, Geschäftsjahr

1. Die Europäische Musikschul-Union ist ein privatrechtlicher Verein nach schweizerischem Recht (Art. 60 FF.ZGB) mit Sitz in Liestal, Schweiz.
2. Das Geschäftsjahr ist das Kalenderjahr.

Artikel II – Aufgabe

Die Musikschul-Union hat folgende Aufgabe:

a) Förderung der Musikerziehung und der musikalischen Praxis.
b) Zusammenarbeit durch Informationsaustausch in allen die Musikschule betreffenden Fragen.
c) Förderung des Austausches von Studiendelegationen, Lehrern, Schülern, Orchestern, Chören, anderen Musiziergruppen und ähnlichem.
d) Wecken des Interesses der zuständigen Behörden und der Öffentlichkeit an Fragen der Musikerziehung allgemein, der Hinführung zum Laienmusizieren und zum Musikstudium.
e) Mithilfe bei der Gründung und beim Aufbau nationaler Zusammenschlüsse von Musikschulen.
f) Systematische Kontakte zu den interessierten supranationalen Institutionen, etwa zur United Nations Educational, Scientific and Cultural Organization (UNESCO), zum Internationalen Musikrat (IMC) und seinen internationalen Organisationen.

Artikel III – Zweck

Der Verein verfolgt keine wirtschaftlichen Ziele, sondern ausschließlich und unmittelbar gemeinnützige Zwecke. Alle dem Verein zufließenden Mittel sind zur Erfüllung der in dieser Satzung angegebenen Ziele und Aufgaben zu verwenden und dürfen auch bei Ausscheiden von Mitgliedern nicht an diese zurückgewährt werden.

Unverhältnismäßig hohe Zuwendungen an einzelne Personen oder Einrichtungen sind nicht gestattet.

Artikel IV – Mitgliedschaft

1. Ordentliche Mitglieder der Musikschul-Union können Zusammenschlüsse von Musikschulen in einem europäischen Staat oder deren nationale Vertretungen sein. Pro Land kann nur eine Organisation Mitglied sein.

Article 1 – Dénomination, siège, exercice

1. L'Union Européenne des Ecoles de Musique (EMU) est une association de droit privé suisse (Art. 60 ff.ZGB) avec siège à Liestal, Suisse.
2. L'exercice correspond à l'année civile.

Article II – Objet

L'Union Européenne des Ecoles de Musique a pour objet:

a) d'encourager l'éducation musicale et la pratique de la musique,
b) de collaborer, grâce à des échanges d'information, dans tous les secteurs qui intéressent les écoles de musique,
c) de développer les échanges entre délégations d'études, professeurs, élèves, orchestres, choeurs, autres groupements de musique et similaires,
d) de susciter l'intérêt des autorités compétentes et du grand public pour les questions touchant à l'éducation musicale en général ainsi qu'à la promotion de la pratique musicale amateur et de l'étude de la musique,
e) d'apporter son soutien à la création et au développement d'associations nationales d'écoles de musique,
f) d'assurer des contacts réguliers avec les institutions internationales intéressées, tels l'Organisation des Nations Unies pour l'Education, la Science et la Culture (UNESCO), le Conseil International de la Musique (CIM) et ses organisations nationales.

Article III – Objectifs

L'Association ne poursuit aucun but économique: ses objectifs sont exclusivement d'utilité publique immédiate. La totalité des fonds versées à l'Association sera utilisée pour la réalisation de l'objet et des objectifs de l'Association tels qu'établis dans les présents Statuts et ne sera en aucun cas réstituée aux membres de l'Association, ni même en cas de leur démission.

Le versement de subventions disproportionnées à des particuliers ou à des établissements est illicite.

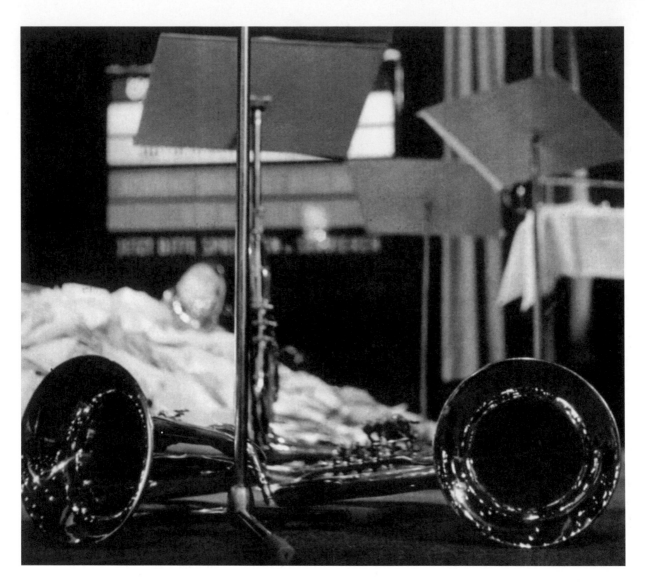

2. Each ordinary member shall notify his designated delegate or deputy to the Music School Union.

3. The General Assembly shall decide on the admission of new members.

4. Membership ends by resignation notified in writing to the Bureau three months before the end of the business year.

5. National music school associations or federations in the process of being formed and/or their representatives may be invited to EMU events, as well as institutions from non-member countries.

6. Firms and private persons may be admitted as supporting members if they support EMU with a minimum annual contribution. Supporting members shall not have the right to vote. The duration of their membership shall not be limited in time.

2. Jedes ordentliche Mitglied benennt der Musikschul-Union seinen Delegierten und dessen Stellvertreter.

3. Über die Aufnahme neuer Mitglieder entscheidet die Generalversammlung.

4. Die Mitgliedschaft endet durch den Austritt, der dem Präsidium mit einer Frist von drei Monaten zum Ende des Geschäftsjahres schriftlich mitzuteilen ist.

5. In Entstehung begriffene nationale Verbände oder Zusammenschlüsse von Musikschulen bzw. deren Vertreter sowie Institutionen von Nichtmitgliedländern können zu Veranstaltungen der EMU eingeladen werden.

6. Firmen und Privatpersonen können als Fördermitglieder aufgenommen werden, wenn sie die EMU mit einem jährlichen Mindestbeitrag unterstützen. Fördermitglieder haben kein Stimmrecht. Die Dauer der Mitgliedschaft ist zeitlich nicht begrenzt.

7. Die Generalversammlung ist berechtigt, Personen zu Ehrenmitgliedern zu ernennen. Ehrenmitglieder sind berechtigt, an Generalversammlungen und anderen öffentlichen EMU-Veranstaltungen teilzunehmen. Das Präsidium kann Ehrenmitgliedern bestimmte Aufgaben übertragen. Ehrenmitglieder haben kein Stimmrecht. Die Dauer der Mitgliedschaft ist zeitlich nicht begrenzt.

Artikel V – Organe

Organe der Musikschul-Union sind
1. die Generalversammlung
2. das Präsidium

Artikel VI – Generalversammlung

1. Die Generalversammlung besteht aus den Delegierten der Mitglieder und ihren Stellvertretern sowie den Mitgliedern des Präsidiums.

2. Die Aufgaben der Generalversammlung sind:
   a) Wahl der Präsidiumsmitglieder auf die Dauer von vier Jahren
   b) Genehmigung des Tätigkeits- und des Geschäftsberichtes des Präsidiums
   c) Entlastung des Präsidiums
   d) Wahl zweier Rechnungsprüfer auf die Dauer von vier Jahren
   e) Beschluß über das Arbeitsprogramm auf der Grundlage der Aufgaben nach Artikel II

Article IV – Composition

1. Toute association ou représentation nationale des écoles de musique d'un Etat européen peut devenir membre actif de l'Union Européenne des Ecoles de Musique. Un pays n'est représenté que par une seule organisation.

2. Tout membre actif communique à l'EMU les noms de son délégué et de son suppléant.

3. L'admission de nouveaux membres est prononcée par l'Assemblée Générale.

4. La qualité de membre prend fin par déclaration de démission notifiée par écrit au Bureau au moins trois mois avant la fin de l'exercice.

5. Les associations ou groupements d'écoles de musique en cours de formation et/ou leurs représentants ainsi que les institutions de pays non membres peuvent être invitées à participer à des manifestations de l'EMU.

6. Les compagnies et particuliers peuvent être admis à titre de membres bienfaiteurs sur la base d'une contribution annuelle minimale. Les membres bienfaiteurs n'ont pas le droit de vote. La durée du statut de membre bienfaiteur n'est pas limité dans le temps.

7. L'Assemblée Générale peut nommer des membres honoraires. Les membres honoraires ont le droit de siéger aux assemblées générales et aux autres manifestations publiques de l'EMU. Le Bureau peut confier certaines tâches déterminées aux membres honoraires. Les membres honoraires n'ont pas le droit de vote. La durée de leur statut n'est pas limitée dans le temps.

Article V – Organes

Les organes de l'EMU sont:
1. l'Assemblée Générale
2. le Bureau.

Article VI – L'assemblée generale

1. L'Assemblée Générale est composée des délégués et suppléants nommés par les membres actifs ainsi que des membres du Bureau.

2. L'Assemblée Générale
   a) élit les membres du Bureau pour une durée de quatre ans,
   b) approuve les rapports moraux et financiers du Bureau,
   c) donne quitus au Bureau,

7. The General Assembly may nominate Honorary Members. Honorary Members may participate in General Assemblies and other public EMU events. The Bureau may entrust Honorary Members with specific tasks. Honorary Members shall not have the right to vote. The duration of their membership shall not be limited in time.

Article V – Organs

The Organs of the Music School Union are:
1. The General Assembly
2. The Bureau

Article VI – The General Assembly

1. The General Assembly consists of the delegates of the members, their deputies and the members of the Bureau.
2. The General Assembly has the following duties:
   a) to elect the members of the Bureau for a term of four years,
   b) to approve the progress report and business report of the Bureau,
   c) to give final discharge to the Bureau
   d) to elect two auditors for a term of four years,
   e) to adopt a resolution on the working programme on the basis of the tasks set out under Art. II,
   f) to admit new members,
   g) to fix the membership fees,
   h) to modify the Statutes,
   i) to designate Honorary Members
   j) to dissolve the Association.

f) Aufnahme neuer Mitglieder
g) Festsetzung der Mitgliedsbeiträge
h) Änderung der Statuten
i) Ernennung von Ehrenmitgliedern
j) Auflösung des Vereines

3. Die Generalversammlung wird vom Präsidenten jährlich, mindestens alle zwei Jahre, durch schriftliche Einladung mit einer Frist von zwei Monaten unter Mitteilung der Tagesordnung zu einer ordentlichen Sitzung einberufen. Beantragt mindestens ein Fünftel der Mitglieder die Einberufung oder beschließt das Präsidium eine außerordentliche Sitzung der Generalversammlung, so ist diese vom Präsidenten spätestens einen Monat vor der Sitzung einzuberufen.
4. Jede ordnungsgemäß einberufene Generalversammlung ist beschlußfähig.
5. In der Sitzung führt der Präsident den Vorsitz, im Falle seiner Verhinderung der Vize-Präsident.
6. Jedes ordentliche Mitglied hat eine Stimme, sofern der Mitgliedsbeitrag termingerecht eingegangen ist (siehe Artikel VIII, 2). Die Beschlüsse der Generalversammlung werden mit einfacher Stimmenmehrheit gefaßt. Für die Satzungsänderung, die Festsetzung der Mitgliedsbeiträge und die Auflösung des Vereines ist die Dreiviertelmehrheit aller erschienenen Stimmberechtigten erforderlich. Stimmübertragungen sind nicht möglich.
7. Über die Beschlüsse der Generalversammlung wird eine Niederschrift gefertigt, die vom Leiter der Sitzung und dem Protokollführer zu unterzeichnen ist.
8. Die Generalversammlung kann sich eine Geschäftsordnung geben.

Artikel VII – Präsidium

1. Das Präsidium besteht aus dem Präsidenten, dem Vizepräsidenten und drei bis fünf weiteren Präsidiumsmitgliedern.
2. Die Präsidiumsmitglieder werden von der Generalversammlung für die Dauer von vier Jahren gewählt. Wiederwahl ist zulässig.
3. Das Präsidium ist verantwortlich für die Verwirklichung der Aufgaben der Musikschul-Union im Sinne der Beschlüsse der Generalversammlung.

d) élit deux commissaires aux comptes pour une durée de quatre ans,

e) adopte le programme de travail sur la base de l'objet énoncé à l'Article II,

f) décide de l'admission de nouveaux membre

g) fixe le montant des cotisations

h) est habilitée à modifier les statuts

i) nomme les membres honoraires

j) est qualifiée pour dissoudre l'Association.

3. L'Assemblée Générale est convoquée en session ordinaire une fois par an et au moins tous les deux ans par le Président par invitation écrite envoyée aux membres au moins deux mois à l'avance et accompagnée de l'ordre du jour. A la demande de 1/5 au moins des membres ou sur décision du Bureau, le Président convoque l'Assemblée générale en session extraordinaire, avec notification au moins un mois à l'avance.

4. Toute Assemblée Générale convoquée en bonne et due forme est qualifiée pour délibérer et statuer valablement.

5. La présidence de séance est assurée par le Président et, s'il est empêché, par le Vice-Président.

6. Tout membre actif, à jour de sa cotisation, dispose d'une voix (v. Article VIII, 2). Les décisions de l'Assemblée Générale sont prises à la majorité simple. Une majorité de 3/4 des membres présents ayant droit de vote est requise pour la modification des statuts, pour la fixation des cotisations et pour la dissolution de l'Association. Le report des voix n'est pas admis.

7. Il est tenu procès-verbal des délibérations de l'Assemblée Générale. Le procès-verbal est signé par le président de séance et par le secrétaire.

8. L'Assemblée Générale pourra se doter d'un règlement intérieur.

Article VII – Le Bureau

1. Le Bureau comprend le Président, le Vice-Président et trois à max. cinq autres membres.

2. Le Bureau est élu par l'Assemblée Générale pour une durée de quatre ans. Il est rééligible.

3. Le Bureau est responsable de la mise en oeuvre de l'objet de l'Union Européeene des Ecoles de Musique sur la base des délibérations prises par l'Assemblée Générale.

3. Once a year, and not less than every second year, the President shall convene the General Assembly to an ordinary session, by means of a written convocation including the order of business and sent out two months in advance. Upon request of not less than a fifth of the members or upon decision of the Bureau, the President shall convene the General Assembly for an extraordinary session, not less than one month in advance.

4. Any General Assembly duly convened forms a quorum.

5. The session shall be chaired by the President, or in his/her absence, by the Vice-President.

6. Each ordinary member has the right to vote, on condition his/her membership fee has been paid in time (see Art. VIII,2). The General Assembly shall take its decisions by simple majority. A three quarters majority of all voting members present is required to modify the Statutes, to fix the membership fees or to dissolve the association. Voting by proxy is prohibited.

7. The resolutions of the General Assembly shall be put on record and signed by the chairman of the session and by the recording clark.

8. The General Assembly may fix its rules of procedure.

Article VII – The Bureau

1. The Bureau consists of the President, the Vice-President and three to five additional members of the Bureau.

2. The members of the Bureau shall be elected by the General Assembly for a term of four years. They may be reelected.

3. The Bureau is responsible for the implementation of the duties of the Music School Union in conformity with the resolutions taken by the General Assembly.

4. Each member of the Bureau shall be given specific tasks.

5. The Bureau may appoint a Secretary General, entrusted with the current busines on behalf of the Board. He/she takes part in the meetings of the Bureau with advisory functions.

6. The Bureau shall meet at least once a year.

7. The President or Vice-President may sign individually with legally binding effect and represent the Association to the outside.

4. Jedem Präsidiumsmitglied werden bestimmte Aufgaben zugeordnet.

5. Das Präsidium kann einen Generalsekretär bestellen, der in seinem Auftrag die laufenden Geschäfte ausführt. Er nimmt an den Sitzungen des Präsidiums mit beratender Stimme teil.

6. Das Präsidium tritt mindestens einmal jährlich zusammen.

7. Der Präsident oder der Vize-Präsident können einzeln rechtskräftig zeichnen und den Verein nach außen vertreten.

Artikel VIII – Beiträge

1. Der Jahresbeitrag der Mitglieder setzt sich zusammen aus
   – einem Grundbeitrag
   – plus einem Beitrag pro angeschlossene Schule

4. Chaque membre du Bureau se voit confier des tâches précises.

5. Le Bureau peut désigner un Secrétaire Général qui gère les affaires courantes par délégation. Il participe aux réunions du Bureau avec voix consultative.

6. Le Bureau se réunit au moins une fois par an.

7. Le Président ou le Vice-Président ont, individuellement, pouvoir de signer valablement. Ils représentent l'Association vers l'extérieur.

Article VIII – Cotisations

1. La cotisation annuelle des membres comprend:
   – un montant de base
   – majoré d'un montant par école affiliée

2. La cotisation est due au premier semestre de l'année civile.

Article VIII – Membership Fees

1. The annual fee for members shall consist of
   - a basic fee
   - plus an additionnal fee for each associated school
2. The membership fee shall be paid during the first six months of each calendar year.
3. The annual minimum contribution to be paid by supporting members shall be fixed by the General Assembly. Honorary members shall not pay any contribution.
4. In case the EMU has no proper funds available, members shall give persons from their own association interested in taking part in commun EMU activities the opportunity to do so by granting them financial support.
5. Only the property of the association shall be liable for commitments; any personal liability of the members is excluded.

Article IX – Legally Binding Text Version

In case of uncertainties arising in relation with the interpretation of provisions contained in these statutes, the German version shall apply as the authentic version.

Article X – Dissolution

1. The dissolution of the Association requires the presence of three quarters of the voting members. If the General Assembly does not have the quorum for a dissolution, it may convene a further meeting which will in any case be a quorate meeting.
2. The resignation of members or the dissolution of the association shall not entail the refunding of contributions made to the association nor the distribution of the association's property to the members.
3. The dissolving General Assembly shall decide on the use of the existing property, which may only be used for non-profit-making purposes in the interest of music schools.

Article X – Entry into Force

This revised version of the Statutes shall enter into force on 1st October 1992.

2. Der Mitgliedsbeitrag ist jeweils im 1. Kalenderhalbjahr zu überweisen.

3. Der jährliche Mindestbeitrag für Fördermitglieder wird durch die Generalversammlung festgelegt. Ehrenmitglieder zahlen keinen Beitrag.

4. Sofern die EMU nicht über eigene finanzielle Möglichkeiten verfügt, sind die Mitglieder gehalten, Interessenten aus ihren Reihen die Teilnahme an gemeinsamen Aktivitäten der EMU durch finanzielle Unterstützung zu ermöglichen.

5. Für die Verbindlichkeit haftet ausschließlich das Vermögen des Vereines; die persönliche Haftbarkeit der Mitglieder ist ausgeschlossen.

Artikel IX – Verbindliche Textfassung

In Zweifelsfragen bei der Textauslegung von Bestimmungen dieser Satzung ist die deutsche Fassung maßgebend.

Artikel X – Auflösung

1. Für die Auflösung des Vereines ist die Anwesenheit von dreiviertel der stimmberechtigten Mitglieder erforderlich. Ist eine Mitgliederversammlung für eine Auflösung nicht beschlußfähig, kann eine weitere Sitzung einberufen werden, die in jedem Fall beschlußfähig ist.

2. Im Falle des Ausscheidens von Mitgliedern sowie bei Auflösung des Vereines finden etwaige Zuwendungen an den Verein sowie eine Verteilung von Vereinsvermögen an die Mitglieder nicht statt.

3. Die auflösende Generalversammlung beschließt über die Verwendung des vorhandenen Vermögens, die nur für gemeinnützige Zwecke des Musikschulwesens erfolgen darf.

Artikel XI – Inkrafttreten

Die Satzung tritt in dieser Neufassung am 1. Oktober 1992 in Kraft.

3. La cotisation annuelle minimale pour membres bienfaiteurs est fixée par l'Assemblée Générale. Les membres honoraires ne payent pas de cotisation.

4. Dans la mesure où l'EMU ne disposerait pas de moyens financiers adéquats propres, les membres devront faciliter, par des subventions financières, la participation de personnes issues de leurs rangs à des activités communes de l'EMU.

5. Le patrimoine de l'Association est seul garant des obligations de l'Association. Toute responsabilité personnelle des membres est exclue.

Article IX – Version linguistique authentique

En cas d'interprétation divergente des dispositions des présents statuts, seule la version allemande fera foi.

Article X – Dissolution

1. La dissolution de l'Association requiert la présence des 3/4 des membres ayant droit de vote. Si cette proportion n'est pas atteinte, l'Assemblée est convoquée à nouveau: elle peut alors statuer quel que soit le nombre des membres présents.

2. En cas de démission de membres ou de dissolution de l'Association, il n'y aura ni restitution d'éventuelles subventions versées à l'Association ni répartition des biens de l'Association entre les membres.

3. L'Assemblée Générale réunie en vue de sa dissolution, décide de la liquidation des biens qui seront exclusivement utilisés dans l'intérêt commun des écoles de musique.

Article XI – Entrée en vigueur

Les statuts entrent en vigueur, dans la présente version, le 1er octobre 1992

Addresses

Adressen

Adresses

Presidency/Präsidium/Présidence

- **Josef Frommelt**
  President/Präsident/Président
  Liechtensteinische Musikschule
  St. Florinsgasse 1
  FL-9490 Vaduz
  Tel. (+41) 75 232 46 20
  Fax (+41) 75 232 46 42

- **Heinz Preiss**
  Vice-President/Vizepräsident/Vice-Président
  Amt der O.ö. Landesregierung
  O.ö. Landesmusikdirektion
  Waltherstrasse 15
  A-4020 Linz
  Tel. (+43) 732 7720-0
  Fax (+43) 732 7720-5669

- **Ib Planch Larsen**
  Musikskole Holstebro
  Bisgardmark 16
  DK-7500 Holstebro
  Tel. (+45) 97 42 46 00
  Fax (+45) 97 41 47 13

- **Reinhart von Gutzeit**
  Musikschule Bochum
  Westring 32
  D-44777 Bochum
  Tel. (+49) 234 68 11 11
  Fax (+49) 234 18 254

- **Timo Veijola**
  Espoo Institute of Music
  Kulttuuriaukio
  FIN-02100 Espoo
  Tel. (+358) 0 4307 270
  Fax (+358) 0 4307 261

Secretariat General
Generalsekretariat
Secrétariat Général

- **Louis Vogt**
  Secretary General/Generalsekretär/
  Secrétaire Général
  Liechtensteinische Musikschule
  St. Florinsgasse 1
  FL-9490 Vaduz
  Tel. (+41) 75 232 46 20
  Fax (+41) 75 232 46 42

International Music Organisations
Internationale Musikorganisationen
Organisations de Musique Internationales

- Association for the Good of European Choirs (AGEC)
  Arbeitsgemeinschaft Europäischer Chorverbände
  Bernhardstrasse 166, D-50968 Köln

- Europäische Vereinigung von Liebhaberorchestern (EVL)
  Association Européenne des Orchestres d'Amateurs
  European Association of Amateur Orchestras
  c/o René Pignolo, Mätteli 103, CH-3323 Bariswil

- European Alliance for School Music
  Europäische Arbeitsgemeinschaft Schulmusik (EAS)
  Bundesgeschäftsstelle Verband Deutscher Schulmusiker
  Weihergarten 5, D-55116 Mainz

- European Piano Teachers Association (EPTA)
  Secretary General: Frau Göke
  Rosensteinstrasse 29, D-72461 Albstadt

- European Voice Teachers Association (EVTA)
  Secretary General: Maria Rondel
  Neckerweg, NL-1463 LA Noordbeemster

- European Guitar Teachers Association (EGTA)
  President: Frank Hill
  Pasteurstrasse 29, D-10407 Berlin

- Union Nationale des Compositeurs de Musique
  Président: Pierre Ancelin
  Château de Ville d'Avray, 10 rue de Marnes, F-92410 Ville d'Avray

- European Association of Music Festivals (EAMF)
  Association Européenne des Festivals de Musique (EAMF)
  122 rue de Lausanne, CH-1202 Geneve

- European Federation of Young Choires (EFYC)
  Fédération Européenne des Jeunes Chorales
  Grosser Hillen 38, D-30559 Hannover

- European Union of Music Competition for Youth (EMCY)
  Union Européenne des Concours de Musique pour la Jeunesse
  Europäische Union der nationalen Musikwettbewerbe für die Jugend
  c/o Dr. Eckart Rohlfs, Bundesgeschäftsstelle «Jugend musiziert»,
  Herzog-Johann-Strasse 10, D-81245 München

- European Conference of Promotors of New Music Union
  Conférence Européenne des Organisateurs de Musique Nouvelle
  Europäische Konferenz der Veranstalter Neuer Musik
  c/o Gaudeamus Foundation
  Swammersdamstraat 38, NL-1091 RV Amsterdam

- Association Européenne des Conservatoires, Académies de Musique et Musikhochschulen
  Secretary General: M. Richard Lowry
  Conservatoire National de Région
  26, rue Monaigne, F-49100 Angers

- Fédération Internationale des Jeunesses Musicales
  Secrétaire général: Emil Subirana
  10 rue royale, B-1000 Bruxelles

- International Music Council U.N.E.S.C.O. (IMC)
  Secretary General: Guy Huot
  1, rue Miollis, F-75732 Paris Cedex 15

- Europäischer Musikrat
  European Music Council
  Conseil Européen de la Musique
  Secretary General: Ursula Bally-Fehr
  Bahnhofstrasse 78, CH-5000 Aarau

- International Society for Music Education
  Secretary General: Jacques Haldenwang
  104 rue de Carouge, CH-1205 Geneve

- International Viola Society (IVS)
  Secretary General: Günter Ojstersek
  Im Nonnengarten 1, D-67127 Rodersheim-Gronau

Members of EMU

Mitglieder der EMU

Membres de l'EMU

Austria/Österreich/Autriche
Konferenz der österreichischen
Musikschulwerke
Amt der O.ö. Landesregierung
O.ö. Landesmusikdirektion
Waltherstrasse 15
A-4020 Linz
Tel. (+43) 732 7720-0, Fax (+43) 732 7720 5669

Belgium/Belgien/Belgique
Association de l'Enseignement
Musical subventionné (A.E.M.S.)
Place de la Wallonie 131
B-5100 Jambes
Tel. (+32) 81 30 49 35, Fax (+32) 61 21 59 00

Bulgaria/Bulgarien/Bulgarie
Akademie für Musik und Tanz
Str. Samodumov 2
BG-4025 Plovdiv
Tel. (+359) 32 44 01 23, Fax (+359) 32 23 16 68

Croatia/Kroatien/Croatie
Odjel Pedagoga Gl. i.Pl. Skola
Gl. Skola Franje Kuhaca
Prof. Buric
TRG sv. Trojstva 1
CR-54000 Osijek
Tel. (+385) 31 31422, Fax (+385) 31 31064

Denmark/Dänemark/Danemark
Sammenslutningen af Danske
Musikskoler
Ole Helby Petersen
Nørrebrogade 45 3 tv
DK-2200 København N.
Tel. (+45) 31 35 63 33, Fax. (+45) 31 35 06 98

Finland/Finnland/Finlande
Suomen musiikkioppilaitosten liitto,
Finlands musikläroinrättningarnas förbund
Association of Finnish Music Schools
FIN-00100 Helsinki
Tel. (+358) 0 694 3394, Fax (+358) 0 694 3394

France/Frankreich/France
Fédération Nationale des Unions des Ecoles et
Conservatoires Municipaux de Musique, de Dance
et d'Art Dramatique (FNUCMU)
5, rue Edouard Nieuport
F-92150 Suresnes
Tel. (+33) 1 41 38 94 10, Fax (+33) 1 41 38 08 16

Germany/Deutschland/Allemagne
Verband deutscher Musikschulen e.V. (VdM)
Plittersdorfer Strasse 93,
D-53173 Bonn 2
Tel. (+49) 228 95706-0, Fax (+49) 228 95706-33

Greece/Griechenland/Gréce
New Conservatory of Thessaloniki
58, Tsimiski str.
GR-546 23 Thessaloniki
Tel. (+30) 31-277 251, Fax (+30) 31-276 406

Hungarie/Ungarn/Hongrie
Hungarian Association of
Music Schools
Rottenbiller U 16-22
H-1075 Budapest
Tel. (+36) 1-122 14 88, Fax (+36) 1-227-2674

Iceland/Island/Islande
Association of Icelandic
Music School Directors
P.O.Box 44
IS-300 Akranes
Tel. (+354) 3 12 109

Italy/Italien/Italie
AISM Associazione Italiana
Scuole di Musica
Via delle Fontanelle 26
I-50016 S. Domenico di Fiesole
Tel. (+39) 55/59 95 65, Fax (+39) 55/59 88 09

Luxembourg/Luxemburg/Luxembourg
Association des Ecoles de
Musique du Grand-Duché de
Luxembourg, 14 Kuelegruecht
L-6231 Bech
Tel. (+352) 79 330

Liechtenstein
Liechtensteinische Musikschule
St. Florinsgasse 1
FL-9490 Vaduz
Tel. (+41) 75 232 46 20, Fax (+41) 75 232 46 42

Netherlands/Niederlande/Pays-Bas
Vereniging voor Kunstzinnige
Vorming (VKV)
Lucasbolwerk 11
NL-3512 EH Utrecht
Tel. (+31) 30-313424, Fax (+31) 30-322950

Norway/Norwegen/Norvège
Norsk Musikskoleråd
Olavskvartalet
Olav Tryggvasonsgt. 2
N-7011 Trondheim
Tel. (+47) 73 51 10 90, Fax (+47) 73 52 85 10

Slovenia/Slowenien/Slovénie
Musikschulgemeinschaft
Republik Slowenien
Emonska 20
SL-61000 Ljubljana
Tel. (+386) 61 222 474, Fax (+386) 61 1251 121

Spain/Spanien/Espagne
ACEM
Associació Catalana d'Escoles de Música
c/. Puig i Cadafalch, s/n «Granja Soldevilla»
E-08130 Santa Pèrpetua de Mogoda
Tel. (+34) 3 560 01 03, Fax (+34) 3 560 76 56

Sweden/Schweden/Suède
Svenska Kommunförbundet
Hornsgatan 15
S-118 82 Stockholm
Tel. (+46) - 8 772 41 00, Fax (+46) - 8 41 15 35

Switzerland/Schweiz/Suisse
Verband Musikschulen Schweiz (VMS)
Postfach 49
CH-4410 Liestal
Tel. (+41) 61 922 13 00, Fax (+41) 61 922 13 02

Turkey/Türkei/Turquie
Minar Sinan Universitesi
Devlet Konservatuvari
Dolmabahce Caddesi
TR-80080 Istanbul-Beriktas
Tel. (+90) 212 1050, Fax (+90) 261 0041

Ab sofort auch einzeln lieferbar

Aktualisierter Ergänzungsband A-Z

Der aktualisierte Ergänzungsband erweitert die 7000 Stich-
wörter der Taschenbuchausgabe um 1700 Artikel (1550 Per-
sonen- und 150 Sachartikel) und bietet somit auf 350 Seiten
Zugriff zu aktuellsten Informationen.

Best.-Nr. SP 8359 (ISBN 3-7957-8359-3)
DM 29,90 / öS 233,– / sFr 29,90

Das nach wissenschaftlichen Kriterien erarbeitete Grundla-
genmaterial wurde mit der Erfahrung beider Verlage in der
Lexikonarbeit für eine breite Leserschaft neu gefaßt, ergänzt
und für diese Taschenbuch-Ausgabe mit einem zusätzlich
aktualisierenden Ergänzungsband versehen.
Das Brockhaus Riemann Musiklexikon bringt alles Wissens-
werte über: Komponisten/Komponistinnen · Interpreten ·
Musik in Geschichte und Gegenwart bis zur Elektronischen
und Computermusik · Musikalische Gattungen und Instru-
mentenkunde · Hinweise auf weiterführende Literatur und
Notenausgaben · Musikverlage u. v. a.

Das Standardwerk als Taschenbuch-Ausgabe

Brockhaus Riemann
Musiklexikon

Herausgegeben von Carl Dahlhaus
und Hans-Heinrich Eggebrecht

4 Bände A-Z
mit über 7000 Stichwörtern (Personen- und Sachartikel), zahlreichen Abbildungen und Notenbeispielen auf 1447 Seiten

und

1 aktualisierter Ergänzungsband A-Z
mit 1700 Stichwörtern (1550 Personen- und 150 Sachartikel)
auf 350 Seiten

Fünfbändige Taschenbuch-Ausgabe
in Kassette
Best.-Nr. SP 8400
(ISBN 3-7957-8400-X)
DM 128,– / öS 999,– / sFr 128,–

Allein,
zu zweit,
zu dritt,
zu viert!

1 2 3 Klavier

- ist speziell für den Gruppenunterricht mit 6–10jährigen Kindern entwickelt und hat sich auch im Einzelunterricht bewährt
- verbindet die Lehrziele des Klavierunterrichts mit der Didaktik und Methodik der Elementaren Musikerziehung
- schließt nahtlos an die Musikalische Früherziehung an

Das **Spielheft** enthält

- abwechslungsreiche und stets gut singbare Lieder und Spielstücke, die aus leicht erfaßbaren musikalischen Strukturen bestehen und von Beginn an mit Melodie und (Bordun-)Begleitung gespielt werden
- zahlreiche improvisatorische Aufgaben
- kindgerechte Spielanweisungen
- farbenfrohe Illustrationen

Der **Lehrerkommentar**

- führt in die Konzeption des Lehrwerks ein
- betrachtet den „Gruppenunterricht am Klavier" aus pädagogischer, organisatorischer und methodischer Sicht
- gibt mit Themenbildern zu den einzelnen Stücken detaillierte methodische Anregungen für eine spielerische Vermittlung im Gruppenunterricht

Breitkopf 🐻 Härtel

Claudia Ehrenpreis
Ulrike Wohlwender
1 2 3 Klavier
Klavierschule für 2–8 Hände
illustriert von Julia Ginsbach
2 Hefte

Heft 1
EB 8619   DM 21,–
Lehrerkommentar zu Heft 1
BV 298   i. V.
erscheint im Mai 1995

"In der Musikerziehung geht es ums Ganze: Sie ist eine der wenigen verbliebenen Positionen, wo ganzheitliche Wahrnehmung und intuitives Verstehen von Gesamtzusammenhängen geübt wird."
(Norbert Geldner)

Bei uns finden Sie das Material dazu:
- Pädagogische Werke
- Didaktische Musikspiele
- Schriften zur Musikpädagogik
- Zeitgenössische Musik.

In Ihrem Musikfachgeschäft.

Musikedition
Nepomuk

KINDER-
FAGOTT
VON MOOSMANN

Bernd Moosmann hat die Tradition des Fagottinos als idealen Einstieg für Kinder ab ca. 7 Jahren wieder aufleben lassen.
Bitte fordern Sie ausführliches Informationsmaterial, auch über die anderen hochwertigen Holzblasinstrumente, an:

Anton-Schmidt-Str. 19
71332 Waiblingen
Tel. 0 71 51/90 56 33
Fax 0 71 51/90 56 50

N E U

**BERND
MOOSMANN**
Meisterwerkstätte für
Holzblasinstrumente
GmbH

Impressum

Publishers/Herausgeber/Editeurs
Josef Frommelt, Heinz Preiss, Reinhart von Gutzeit,
Louis Vogt für die Europäische Musikschul-Union

Editor/Redaktion/Rédacteur
Dr. Ulrich Wüster

Articles/Beiträge/Articles
National reports by EMU Member organizations.
We thank the following authors for their contribution to
the background articles (alphabetic order of initials):

Länderberichte der nationalen Musikschulverbände.
(Sprachliche Koordinierung: Renée Gautron)
Für ihre Mitarbeit am Sachteil wird folgenden Autoren
gedankt (in alphabetischer Folge der im Text verwendeten
Kürzel):

Rapports nationaux des associations membres de l'EMU.
Nous remercions les auteurs des articles de fond
(présentés ci-après par ordre alphabétique des sigles
utilisés dans le texte):

chj.	Claude-Henry Joubert
dw.	Diethard Wucher
er.	Eckart Rohlfs
gas.	George A. Speckert
hwb.	Hans-Walter Berg
jf.	Josef Frommelt
mg.	Manfred Grunenberg
rt.	Rainer Templin
ub.	Ursula Brandstätter
um.	Ulrich Mahlert
uw.	Ulrich Wüster
wp.	Werner Probst

Translation/Übersetzung/Traduction
Martine Paulauskas, Julia Rushworth

Statistics/Statistik/Statistiques
Ib Planch Larsen

Photos
Archives of EMU member organizations

Archive der EMU-Mitgliedsländer

Archives des associations membres de l'EMU

Layout
Gassner & Seger AG, Vaduz

ED 8402
© 1995 Schott Musik International, Mainz
Printed in Germany · BSS 48 410
ISBN 2-7957-0291-7

Notes

Notizen

Notes

Notes

Notizen

Notes

Notes

Notizen

Notes

Notes

Notizen

Notes